A Faint ⠀

"*The title suggests that Michael knows himself pretty well. Always a controversial figure, you may disagree with him but he is never dull and you are never bored with him. A fascinating and stimulating read.*"
Frank Williams, actor and sometime member of the Crown Appointments Commission.

"*Michael Saward has packed a catalogue of unusual experiences into his life. Anyone who has been a neighbour to De Gaulle, survived the indignities of a brutal attack in his home and who plays such a strategic role in British evangelicalism is worth knowing more about.*"
Revd Joel Edwards, General Director, Evangelical Alliance.

"*Michael Saward's story in unrepeatable. Michael is one of God's one-offs. His opinions are rarely moderate, his sufferings undiluted, and this book is not one for the small-minded. Agree or disagree with Michael, either way he will provoke what Poirot succinctly calls, 'the little grey cells.' I'm grateful to Michael for the way he has always encouraged me – and made me think through issues that otherwise I might ignore. For those who enjoy a spontaneous character seeking to learn from God, then this promises to be a great read, but for the complacent, Michael Saward is a dangerous man.*"
Revd Clive Calver, President of World Relief Corporation, USA.

"*I recall Michael Saward's energy and enthusiasm raising £300,000 to help restore St Mary's in my constituency where he was Vicar. That energy and enthusiasm runs through his book. Michael's wide range of interests, linked with his ability to write with humour and perception, makes this a book that deserves a wide audience.*"
Sir George Young, Bt, MP, formerly Cabinet Minister and Comptroller of Her Majesty's Household.

A Faint Streak of Humility

Michael Saward

paternoster press

First published in 1999 by Paternoster Press

05 04 03 02 01 00 99   7 6 5 4 3 2 1

Paternoster Press is an imprint of Paternoster Publishing,
PO Box 300, Carlisle, Cumbria, CA3 0QS, UK
http://www.paternoster-publishing.com

British Library Cataloguing in Publication Data
A catalogue record for this book is available from the British Library

ISBN 0-85364-965-0

Front cover photograph copyright © Jackie Saward

Cover Design by Mainstream, Lancaster
Typeset by WestKey Ltd, Falmouth, Cornwall
Printed in Great Britain by
Cox & Wyman Ltd, Reading, Berkshire

Autobiography, a form of writing in which both honesty and humility are famous for their absence.

Susan Howatch

A man's worth is no greater than the worth of his ambitions.

Marcus Aurelius

You know, I think I once detected a faint streak of humility in him.

John Hughes, sometime Bishop of Croydon, talking about Michael Saward to Derek Osborne, an Anglican clergyman – all three have remained friends for forty years

For Jackie, who has tried, mostly
unsuccessfully, to keep me humble, for
more than forty years; for Cathie Trillo,
who, in typing this, has learnt far more
than is good for any secretary to know
about her boss; and in memory of Eric
Evans, Dean of St Paul's, who died
within hours of this book's completion.
With grateful thanks to them all.

Contents

Preface

I have no time for astrology. I think it largely bogus and a means of seducing the gullible. One day, in a bookshop, I saw a volume called *The Secret Language of Birthdays* and, with a high degree of sceptical amusement, I opened it at 14 May, my birthday. This is what I read:

> May 14th people are not at all shy about making a break with traditional methods in their field of endeavour. They push themselves on, seeking perfection, but their need to eliminate all faults from what they do can be extreme. Their capacity for moderation bears most strongly on their success.
>
> They may be misunderstood and even scorned at the beginning of their career. They demand respect, however, and, sooner or later, others begin to appreciate the value of their work. Basically, it just takes people a bit of time to catch up with them.
>
> Moderation is the key to their success: They cultivate calm. May 14th is the day of the modern irrepressible.

As I said, I have no time for astrology. I think it largely bogus and a means of seducing the gullible. However, I should be less than honest if I did not admit that on this occasion I am duly seduced by the amazing accuracy of the prediction for those born on 14 May. It's like looking at oneself in a mirror.

'Everybody', says Mordecai Richler, 'writes a book too many.' OK, so that's the risk you take when you decide yet again to put pen to paper. But I've been doing it for thirty-five years and the ideas still keep flooding into my mind.

This one is, of course, different. To write about your convictions is one thing. To write about yourself is something else. Isn't it inevitably mere egocentricity? As someone I know well said, 'Who wants to know?'

That's a tough question. 'Does anyone really want to know what you've been up to all these years and, anyway, are you going to tell them the truth, the whole truth, and nothing but the truth? According to Jerome K. Jerome, 'No man will ever write the true story of himself . . . we dare not reveal ourselves for fear of wounding our dear ones . . . it would be too painful.' I can only promise to tell almost all of it and to hold back, knowingly, very little of any consequence.

Maybe it just runs in the blood. My great-grandfather, William Saward, kept a diary for over twenty years. It was laconic but it still revealed a lot about him. My grandfather, Henry Kendall (who caught the murderer, Dr Crippen), published his autobiography when he was sixty-five. I read both with tremendous interest. I am immensely glad that they put pen to paper and told their readers about their lives. William did nothing of any special interest. Henry was in the public eye for much of his life. What made both volumes fascinating was that real people were revealing themselves as real people and real people are always interesting.

'The man who commits himself to paper', wrote General Sir Ian Hamilton long ago, 'is building a house for his reputation to inhabit – and, too often, when he has finished, he finds he has been at work upon a tomb'.

Well, that's the risk. So perhaps you should defer such self-exposure until you're eighty or more? If you do, a different factor emerges. Philip Ziegler warns us of Earl Mountbatten who 'was beginning to show one of the failings of old age: an inability to distinguish between what had happened and what he would like to have happened'.

The truth, then, while you can still recall it with some credible degree of accuracy. But what about humility? What is it? There was once a nauseating hymn with the line 'oh, to be nothing,

nothing'. That's not true humility. That's cant and it's sickening. Nobody wants to be nothing. Nor should they.

The Greeks had a good phrase *gnothi seauton*. It meant 'know yourself' and Charles Haddon Spurgeon, the great Victorian Baptist preacher, took it as a fair definition for humility, which is, he says, 'the proper estimate of oneself'.

By the time I was twenty-five I had reached a self-estimate which has been a not-wildly inaccurate guide ever since. I reckoned that I was never going to be really outstanding at anything, never the top man. But I also knew that across a wide range of areas I was going to be a lot better than average and that I wanted to extend that range and stretch myself to the utmost. Faced with that possibility, I learnt a real lesson from C.S. Lewis, who once said that 'If anyone would like to acquire humility, I can, I think, tell him the first step. The first step is to realise that one is proud. And a biggish step, too.'

I don't doubt that when Bishop John Hughes, forty years ago, mentioned the 'faint streak of humility' which he thought he had found in me, he was seriously expressing anxiety about my dubious nature. Alas, I didn't take it that way and I've had it lined up for the title of any autobiographical work that I might one day write. Which only goes to show that clergymen don't agree on these things. I happen to live a few yards away from the house in which my famous predecessor, Canon Sydney Smith, was required to reside when, a hundred and sixty years ago, he served on the St Paul's Cathedral Chapter. He too was gently rebuked by the Bishop of London (on that occasion) and, replying, wrote that 'you must not think me necessarily foolish because I am facetious, nor will I consider you necessarily wise because you are grave'.

To be serious is not necessarily to be solemn. I'm simply not made to be solemn. I see the ridiculous side of everything, myself included, and freeing oneself from pride is greatly assisted if you can do just that.

Centuries ago, Bianco da Siena wrote a hymn which has become very famous in its English translation. It includes the lines:

> Let holy charity my outward vesture be
> and lowliness become my inner clothing.

Bishop Lesslie Newbigin, who recently died, and one of the great Christians of the twentieth century, was renowned for his comment on those two lines. 'Humility', said Newbigin, 'is strictly underwear.'

You certainly won't find me wearing my pants on top of my trousers (or even my cassock). Whether they're on underneath, I leave you to decide.

This is an appropriate occasion on which to thank Richard and Moira Fordham, David and Jenny Francis, and John and Felicity Summers, for the use of their homes in which to write this book.

It is also provides me with an opportunity to thank Rita, Rosanne, Sue, Ann, Iris, Catherine, Pauline, Daphne, Cathie, Rosie, Emma and Anne, my faithful secretaries over almost thirty-five years, and Eldo Barkhuizen, whose editorial eagle eye on behalf of the publishers has saved me from the kinds of errors that every author fears.

Lastly, a warm word of gratitude to Jenny Chapman, my agent, without whose enthusiasm and know-how this book would never have been published.

Chapter One

When We Were Very Young

It was my parents' custom to go on their holidays each year in August. I do not know which watering hole they chose for 1931 but clearly they successfully launched me on my way during the course of the trip. My mother, being a somewhat superstitious woman, was not a little anxious when she went into labour on Friday 13 May 1932. She hung on grimly until midnight was past and I duly arrived at 7.20 on the Saturday morning, in the Vernon Shepherd Nursing Home in St John's Park, Blackheath. Little did I, or they, know that we were only a few yards from the Old Dover Road along which the Roman legions had marched, along which the mob had passed en route to London during the Peasants' Revolt, and along which King Henry V had returned after Agincourt. Indeed, so many events were related to men and women who had walked that way that you could say that I was propelled straight into the mainstream of English history.

On that same Saturday an appointment was announced which was to have a very significant impact on my life more than twenty years into the future. The Headmaster of Repton, Geoffrey Francis Fisher, was to be the new Bishop of Chester. From the relative obscurity of an East Midlands school he was launched into public life as a diocesan bishop. Later translated to London, he became, as the Second World War ended, Archbishop of Canterbury and Primate of All England. In that capacity, he ordained me priest.

Home in 1932 was the top-floor flat of my grandparents' house in Lee. We had our own front door to what was, in effect, an attic and there we lived contentedly for my first four years –

Dad, Mum, me and Kim, our white-and-black wire-haired terrier. I loved Kim dearly until, eight years later, he was savaged to death by a Petts Wood bull terrier. From that day on I have never felt any kind of affection for dogs.

My first conscious memory was of the day I discovered fear. My mother had put me on a china pot and informed me that I was not to move until I had completed the necessary ritual. A battle of wills ensued, leading to my having, as I thought, the last word on the subject. 'I am', I shouted at my mother, 'never going to do it again. It smells.' Lily's patience came to an end. 'You naughty, naughty, boy,' she snarled. 'I've had enough. I'm going and I'm never coming back!' Saying which, she marched out of the flat, down the stairs, the house front door slammed and the silence was terrifying. I waited and waited. Not a sound. Then I began to scream, and scream, and scream. Eventually, after an eternity, she reappeared. 'I'll never, never, never, be a naughty boy again,' I sobbed. She comforted me and in due course I calmed down. Years later she said, ruefully, 'I should never have done it. I just didn't realise what fear could strike at the heart of a two-and-a-half year old.' Over sixty years later the memory remains as vivid as ever.

A special treat for children in those days was to be taken on the 75 bus to Blackheath pond. I had a toy wooden yacht and bliss it was to sail it there. Dressed like Christopher Robin, I chatted politely to other children and their nannies and ran around the pond launching and retrieving my boat.

Talking of buses, we lived only a hundred yards from the 94 stop by the United Dairies depot. Milk carts and their horses came out from the depot, delivering milk to the district, and leaving a permanent aroma of horse dung. The two bus stops, on each side of Baring Road, offered exciting prospects in both directions. Going north meant a trip to Chiesmans, the big store in Lewisham. It had a toy department and to be taken there by Granny Kendall ('Minnie') was to be assured of some new plaything to bring home. I liked Chiesmans. Incidentally, in those days, long before the Second War, nobody queued at bus stops. Granny was only about five foot two and suffered badly from asthma. Even so, wherever we were when the bus arrived, Granny was first on, and I was dragged behind her, bumped and buffeted by corseted female thighs.

Going south, the 94, having passed Grove Park railway station, wound up at Bromley Market Square. Here there was a noisy fish shop, an old-fashioned butchers, but, best of all, it had Medhursts. Medhursts competed directly with Chiesmans. They were the only two department stores in that part of south-east London and Medhursts also had a toy department in the basement. In short, a trip on a 94 bus, whichever way it went, was a guarantee of yet another toy to add to the Saward collection.

But there was a price to pay, and it was more demanding at Medhursts. On the top floor was a restaurant, where Bromley's middle-class ladies went for afternoon tea. The chairs had seats and backs of interlaced rattan strips and waitresses in caps and aprons served the delicacies on double-decker silver-plated cake dishes. At one end of the room was a low platform on which, as if right out of Gilbert and Sullivan's *Patience*, sat three greenery-yallery females playing Viennese melodies. They were the ultimate caricature of gentility, a trio of gaunt maiden ladies, earnestly scraping at fiddle and cello, in approximate time with the pianist. I had never heard of purgatory in those days but I knew instinctively that this was it. Still, you did get to clutch a new toy on the way home so it was a swings-and-roundabouts experience and eminently unforgettable.

One day the three of us, Mum, Granny, and I, were out shopping in Bromley Market Square. We were on the inside of the square, the northern side, when I stepped briefly off the pavement. The traffic flows in a one-way direction around the square and the bicycle hit me a glancing blow and knocked me over into the gutter. No real damage was done beyond a bruise or two but I was submerged under a scrum of clucking women all anxious to pat me, to reassure me, to put me back on my feet. They were undoubtedly moved by the kindest of motives but I was far more anxious to get out of their clutches than I had been to avoid the bicycle, which, in any case, I had not seen till it struck me. I don't often find myself in Bromley Market Square these days but I know exactly the spot where I became the ball in the scrum of Bromley's matrons.

King George V and Queen Mary celebrated their Silver Jubilee on the throne with a great Thanksgiving Service at St Paul's Cathedral on 6 May 1935 at which the Dean and Chapter wore magnificent new red-and-gold copes. The splendour of the occasion was caught by the artist Frank Salisbury. As a three-year-old I could hardly imagine that one day I would possess a copy of his painting and, even more, would wear one of those Jubilee Copes at the fiftieth anniversary of VE Day on 7 May 1995. Then, sixty years and one day later, I should be greeting both the Queen and Queen Mother, all the Royal family, and over fifty Heads of State from around the world.

Living in the flat meant seeing much more of my Kendall grandparents than I did of George and Cissie Saward. Nevertheless Christmas 1935 stands out because we were all at a party and there, by the tree, was Father Christmas himself. It wasn't the first time I met him because he had certainly put in appearances at Chiesmans and Medhursts but this time he had something indefinably suspicious about him. The room was full. Grandpa Saward was there. So were Uncle Allen and Auntie Agnes. So, too, were Mum and Dad. Eyeing me with disdain, as she often seemed to, was Wendy, my six-year-old cousin. Finally, there was baby Janet, her year-old sister. And, of course, Father Christmas, in his red-and-white clothes and hat and his big white beard. But something was quite clearly not right and the penny suddenly dropped. 'That's not Father Christmas,' I announced to the family. 'Of course it is,' they cheerfully lied. 'No, it isn't,' I said with growing conviction, 'that's Granny Saward. I can see her shoes.' There's nothing like a cocky little know-all brat to spoil the fun.

Since I was his only grandchild, Grandad spoiled me, to the growing concern of my parents. He never gave me a moment's peace. Always some new toy, some sweets, or chocolates, and incessantly he bounced me up and down on his knee, threw me in the air, exhibiting unashamedly his grandfatherly pride. Every Sunday afternoon he piled us all into his capacious Morris Oxford saloon and drove us out to the Old Barn, a tea house near Hildenborough. There, amid cream teas and strawberries, he showed me off to the world, his latest achievement, the grandson of the famous Captain Kendall, who had caught Crippen. Everyone knew who he was and I was given the Exhibit A treatment.

Before I was four, my mother took me to see the doctor, Charlie Carey. She was worried, and so was he. 'Your father's turning him into a hyperactive bag of nerves,' he said. 'You must get him away and quickly.' Mum and Dad discussed it. There was no way that he could get away from the office so they decided that she would take me to Cornwall for as long as was necessary.

We took the *Cornish Riviera Express* to Teignmouth in South Devon and stopped there for the night, during which I was violently and comprehensively sick. The next day we went on to Bude and stayed in the cottage of a Mrs Mills for a couple of weeks. Every day we were on the beach or walking the lanes nearby. There were primroses everywhere and nowhere more than in Coombe Valley. To today's children, an eight-mile walk for a not-yet-four-year-old might seem unbelievable. Nevertheless we did it.

On the beach I made friends with a girl whose parents had arrived in their own small yacht. I still recall seeing them sail away out of my life. If my memory is not playing tricks, the popular song of the day was *Red Sails in the Sunset* and, though their sail wasn't red, it left its small mark on whichever side of the brain these things register. That same week, a local child was drowned and the whole of Bude seemed to be in black as the horse-drawn funeral cortège wended its way through the town.

Once or twice we went along the coast to the magnificent beach at Widemouth Bay. Just above Black Rock stood a white tea house and Mum asked if we could stay there. They declined, not being geared to residents. She pleaded and they agreed to let her have the one spare room for a few nights while she found somewhere else. It being the end of April, the beach was almost empty. We met and talked to a young German couple (Mum was later convinced that they were Nazi spies!) and became friends with two local men, Wilfred and Joe, who earned their living collecting seaweed from the beach with a horse and cart. Twenty years later, on my honeymoon, I called in at the tea house and mentioned my earlier visit. 'There were two men called Wilfred and Joe on the beach,' I added. The manageress pointed to the beach. 'Wilfred's still there,' she said, and sure enough he was, though the horse had long since been displaced by a tractor.

Mum's searching led us to a caravan in a field close to Widemouth Farm, half a mile away. Today the field has been turned into a 'Holiday Village' of the kind that disfigures so much of the Cornish coast. That spring it was ours and to my great delight Dad came down for a weekend and we celebrated my fourth birthday with a cake covered in orange icing. One more memory is very vivid. Mum and I climbed a field gate and set out across the grass. For no reason that I know, the field's only inhabitant, a cow, took off in our direction, snorting and bellowing like a bull at a bullfight. We ran for our lives, clambered over the gate, and reached safety just as the cow came crashing to a halt three feet away, staring at us with ill-concealed venom. To a four-year-old, a cow looks as big as an elephant and we clung to each other as we gave it the eyeball-to-eyeball treatment.

Meanwhile, back in London, Dad had acted quite decisively. He had bought a house in Petts Wood, five miles from Lee, and put down a deposit on a mortgage. Grandad would always be a welcome guest but I should be largely free from his well-meaning, but ill-judged, attentions. Nothing would ever be too expensive for his only grandson and he and Granny would come over in the car on most weekends, but the old overpowering interference, dominating our lives, was broken.

Even so, he did nothing by halves. Most of my friends had Hornby gauge 'O' model railways. A small circle of tin rails, a tin engine and two carriages, powered by clockwork. That wasn't good enough for Henry Kendall's grandson. So, he imported from America a Lionel train-set, complete with streamlined loco, two carriages, and an observation car, a large oval-track, and all powered by electricity. It was set up on a table in our old flat when we went over there on Christmas morning. Mum said, quite quietly, 'He's far too young for that,' and she was right. I knocked hell out of it, wrecking the whole thing within a few months, ripping the roofs off and bashing everything about until even the loco's wailing American siren refused to work. I never saw a Lionel train-set again until I discovered one in the railroad museum in Sacramento, California, in the summer of 1993. It was like greeting a long-lost friend.

Two days before my fifth birthday the new King, George VI, was crowned. My mother set off for London at the crack of dawn, intent on climbing lamp-posts wherever she could get a good view. Apparently she had gained considerable experience of lamp-post climbing at a succession of royal events in the 1920s. The day dragged on interminably for me as I sat on the window ledge of Mum and Dad's bedroom waiting, waiting, waiting, for her to come into sight.

Petts Wood was a brand-new suburb, full of trees, and the ideal place for a middle-class, respectable community to develop. It straddled the main Southern Railway line from Charing Cross to Dover and Hastings and was bounded to the north by the other Southern line from Victoria to Ramsgate, beyond which stood Tongs Farm and the Willett Memorial Woods, a National Trust area commemorating the founder of 'Daylight Saving.'

At Petts Wood's centre stood the railway station, and the appropriately named, mock-Tudor hostelry, the Daylight Inn. It was the only pub and eminently respectable. Across the railway line, to the west, were somewhat cheaper areas of semi-detached housing but, fortunately, few of the real Petts Wooders had to meet their inhabitants socially and, in any case, they sent their children to Crofton Lane Council School while most of us were hermetically sealed by attendance at various private schools. I was indoctrinated from the start with the instruction that I was not to play in the street and certainly to have nothing to do with the Council School kids who were 'rough'.

Only one road linked the two halves of Petts Wood and it was at the opposite end of the 'village', nearly a mile away from our home in Silverdale Road, which was on the way to nowhere, wedged between the two railway lines at the north-west end. Roads were wide. Houses were solid, generally semi-detached, and gardens were about eighty feet long and twenty-five feet wide. Oak and birch were the chief varieties of tree in the area and each garden was surrounded by slatted wooden fences nearly six feet high. Silverdale Road's men were mostly London commuters, enjoying an excellent and not-too-crowded electric train service to Cannon Street (for the City), Charing Cross (for the West End), and Victoria (for Knightsbridge and Westminster). Even journalists were catered for with special late-night services to Blackfriars and Holborn Viaduct, more than adequate for Fleet Street. In short, Petts Wood, and its neighbour, Orpington, had the best choice of rail services of anywhere in London's Kentish suburbs. Not surprisingly, Mum and Dad stayed there for thirty years until Don's retirement in the 1960s, when they finally decamped to rural North Devon.

Four months after the Coronation, I set off on my newly acquired tricycle (it had thick, inflated tyres, not like most children's solid rubber tyres, and guess who bought it), alongside my walking mother, not at all 'unwillingly to school' for the first time. Hesitant, and uncertain, but bursting to learn and already an avid reader of books. Indeed I had, by the age of seven, already read *The Wind in the Willows* seven times and many other of the obvious children's books of the day, not least the two volumes of A.A. Milne verse, which I had mostly learnt by heart. Strangely, I never did get hooked on the Pooh and Piglet volumes and I positively loathed Alice and all her tribe of loonies.

Anyway, Petts Wood Preparatory School it was to be. A 'dame school', housed in a large detached building, with its own hard tennis court, in Ladywood Avenue, about a mile away. Owned and run by a Miss Styles, it offered boys and girls (for a fee, paid by Grandad, naturally) the necessary grounding in the three Rs and sundry other accomplishments suitable to middle class offspring. It suggested that a uniform of 'mauve and amber' be worn whether as caps, blazers, or hatbands and its children were 'well-behaved'. What is more, they meant it. My best friend's brother was expelled within a few days for punching some child too obviously.

I returned home, collected, of course, by my mother, at the end of the first day and announced that, since two boys in the new class were called 'Michael', I was to be known as 'Mickie', for convenience. Next morning, my mother went straight in to see Miss Styles. When the day ended I informed my parents that there had been a mistake and the other little boy was to be 'Mickie'. My mother looked grimly satisfied. The subject was never again mentioned.

I soon teamed up with a boy called David Mitchell. He was somewhat taller and had a rather more robust attitude to life. His elder brother, Bill (later to be Head Boy of Dulwich College, an Oxford cricket blue, and a Lloyd's insurance broker), had been expelled, as already mentioned, and David was always a more rugged customer than his brother. At the first Christmas concert, three months later, he and I were two-thirds of Old King Cole's 'fiddlers three' and, at a suitable moment, we were to toss artificial rose petals gently into the audience of parents. David distinguished himself by breaking his tin fiddle and hurling handfuls of paper petals in the general direction of his mother.

Each morning began with an assembly of about fifty children in an arc round the largest (but not very large) room. We sang worthy but tedious hymns which, regrettably, I cannot forget, like 'Do no sinful action, speak no angry word', 'Fair waved the golden corn', 'Loving shepherd of thy sheep' and 'There's a friend for little children'. Those dear, well-meaning, Victorian ladies who first wrote, and then foisted, this stuff on unresisting children, have a lot to answer for. We dutifully warbled, folded our hands, and imbibed a form of the Christian religion which did not, I suppose, do us very much harm and did at least stick in the memory if not the gullet. Since my family never went near a church, or a Sunday school, it was, perhaps, better than nothing.

At the end of February we heard that Granny Saward was not at all well. George and Cissie had moved to Hythe on his retirement from the Royal Mint in the early 1930s and we rarely saw them. Less than a week passed of growing concern as her illness became pneumonia, which in those days was almost a sure ticket to the cemetery. She died on 3 March. Still a good-looking woman at sixty-four, she succumbed to what within five years would be curable with the new drugs. For her they came too late. She was buried in a small, peaceful cemetery, a mile from the sea, where she would eventually be joined by George.

Ten days later I was taken in to the Miller Hospital, on the Lewisham edge of Greenwich, in order that my tonsils and adenoids should be removed. Surgery in those days involved, first, being subjected to a mask over the nose and mouth on to which chloroform was dropped. It was an appalling experience for a child since it felt like forcible suffocation. When I came round, minus my appropriate organs, I was unpleasantly sick and distinctly frightened, a prisoner in a children's ward the size of a large barrack room. Two or three nights later I felt very ill and in great pain in my ears. I called and called for a nurse but none came. Next day I was taken home to Petts Wood, still whimpering with pain. The pain grew steadily more unbearable, our local doctor was called in, and off I went in Grandad's car, back to the Miller and a further operation for an abscess in the middle ear. Grandad arrived at the hospital in a foul temper and demanded an explanation. He had sent in a basket of fruit to his grandson last week and it had never reached the boy. Why? In vain the matron explained that most of the children came from poor homes and to give one such a present would be hard to justify. 'Damn and blast it,' said Grandad, 'I support this charity hospital with a regular and large subscription. I expect my grandson to get the best.' When I came round from the second operation I found myself in a private ward, full of men. I was the only child in the place and molly-coddled by all. This time I was in for over a month and the baskets of fruit never stopped!

On the day I entered the hospital for the second time, I remember so vividly the almond trees in bloom as we drove up Birchwood Road, Petts Wood's classiest part. It was St Patrick's Day, 17 March 1938.

That month in the Miller provided me with a new experience – jigsaws. I had never attempted a big jigsaw before and now I set out on a 1500-piece picture of the signing of the Magna Carta. I was never in danger from then on of forgetting what happened in 1215 at Runnymede when the barons met with King John. I can still see the picture vividly.

I never did come to like the Miller. The hospital was close to a brewery and the smell permeated everything. Even to this day that smell has one overpowering significance and it isn't beer. But they committed a worse crime than that. Until those weeks I had loved rice pudding. The Miller comprehensively destroyed that craving and I have never, to this day (and not even at school) been willing or able to eat the stuff. No, not once.

At last I was taken home, in April, and less than a week later Moira, my sister, was born. The family took me to the same Vernon Shepherd Nursing Home, where I also had emerged from the womb, and there was my mother and the new baby. I have nothing whatever against my only sister but I would be lying if I said that I had any recall whatever of her birth. One day she wasn't there and the next she was. She simply became part of the furniture, my little sister. We grew up quite normally, side by side, but the six-year gap seemed too much to overcome until we were adults. She had her friends. I had mine. They didn't overlap at all.

That summer Grandad decided to take us all to see the Empire Air Display at nearby Biggin Hill. From home it was a mere five miles but by the time we reached Leaves Green, two miles short of the airfield, the road was jammed solid with cars. Grandad was never a patient man and after a bout of vitriolic swearing at every driver in sight he turned the car for home. It wasn't till years later, and long after the Battle of Britain, that I saw that famous fighter station for the first time.

By way of consolation, I suspect, he decided to give me two special treats. As Marine Superintendent of the Surrey Docks, he took me on the Grand Tour. Canals, lockgates, warehouse, huge sheds stacked high with timber, and, above all, dozens of ships, all it seemed swarming with dockers in chokers and cloth caps who deferentially touched their foreheads to the man in the suit and Homburg hat with the small boy in tow. Today one of my closest friends, Bishop Michael Baughen, has a house on the edge of the great Greenland dock, on the very ground that I walked so many years ago.

The second treat was when we travelled to Gravesend, boarded a small cutter, and were taken out into midstream where a

Canadian Pacific liner, the *Montcalm*, was moored, waiting for the next tide to set out for Canada. Again, I received the full treatment, trailing all over the ship and ending up on the bridge with the Captain, one of Grandad's old friends.

One further excitement was in store. I discovered the cinema. It was called the New Gallery and it was in Regent Street, in the heart of London's West End. Disney's early cartoons were in town and the excitement of seeing the *Three Little Pigs and the Big Bad Wolf* was palpable. 'Who's afraid of the Big Bad Wolf?' chorused the Little Pigs from the safety of their house, while the Wolf roared from outside that 'I'll huff, and I'll puff, and I'll blow your house in!' Squeaks from the Pigs and scores of small moppets like me. Only a year or two later came *Snow White* and the absolute terror caused by the Queen turned Witch. I had nightmares about it for weeks afterwards. When next I saw it, in 1994, the children in the cinema laughed at the very scenes that had so paralysed me. Times change.

Meanwhile, back at school, the Munich crisis was the cause of the creation of an underground air-raid shelter beneath one end of the tennis court. There, by way of rehearsal, we sat in a dimly lit corridor lined with benches and dutifully used our little fingers in the work of dismantling cotton shirts into their constituent threads, 'to make bandages for the hospitals', or so we were told.

The Headmistress, Miss Styles, suddenly translated herself into Mrs Sidwell, and sold the establishment to two elderly spinsters, Miss Porter and Miss Worthington, who set up residence on the upstairs floor. Today they would be instantly described as two lesbians, visibly fulfilling the stereotype roles. Whether they were or not, I have no idea and not much interest. What I do know is that they were excellent teachers and I owe them a good deal. Not that I fulfilled their stereotype either. I enjoyed woodcarving, when we made mahogany bookends which I still possess, but they were greatly surprised when I opted for embroidery instead of boys' games on the tennis court playground. 'But, Michael, dear,' they cooed, 'boys don't do embroidery. That's only for girls.' 'Well, I want to,' I said and in due course turned out a cushion cover with a floral design that lasted for about thirty years.

At the end of the term, just before Christmas, we were required to undergo seven written examinations. I still have them. They weren't in 'joined-up writing' but I answered questions on: General Knowledge ('Who wrote *Alice in Wonderland*?' 'Who designed St Paul's Cathedral?'); History (ten questions about the Norman Conquest, for which I achieved 93 per cent); Composition (a 300-word essay about 'My Half-Term Holiday'); English Grammar (89 per cent); Geography; Scripture; and French (92 per cent, including 16 out of 20 for dictation). In 1998 my French is rather better than it was in 1938 but I've yet to meet a child today who is learning even rudimentary French at school at the age of six. In those days, of course, not many of the teachers were graduates but that 'Dame School' taught me to write legibly, to do arithmetic, to spell, to know some basic facts about history, geography, the Bible, and a foreign language. Children of that age today cannot do any of those things and many cannot begin to read coherently and with comprehension. Nor was I abnormal. Most of us achieved the same levels. Indeed, when I came to change schools at nine, I was a full year ahead of most of my form-mates from state schools.

1939 was the year in which I learnt to ride a bicycle. It had been lying, unused, in our garden shed for over a year since Grandad (inevitably) had bought it. Try as I might, I couldn't get the hang of cycling and I had more or less given up in despair. Then, one day, as Granny and Grandad were getting into their car to drive home to Lee, I dragged it out of the shed, stood at the top of our short drive – it was quite a slope – waved to them and the bike ran away with me. Down the slope I moved, grabbing the handle-bars with my fists, and the pedals with my feet, and successfully turning the front wheel as I met the road surface (only recently tarmacked), the bike gathered speed while I pedalled for dear life, until two hundred yards away, where Silverdale Road met Hazelmere Road at a T-junction, I failed to negotiate the right-angle and collided with the curb facing me. I ended up sprawling in the gutter, slightly shocked but wholly triumphant. When, seconds later, my parents and grandparents arrived, anxiety all over their faces, I announced, 'I did it, I can ride a bike,' and one more hurdle on life's way had been passed.

There was a sequel. Only a few days later, telling no-one, I set out to ride my bicycle to the top of Birchwood Road. The railway bridge just round the corner was the effective boundary of Petts Wood. On the nearside stood the largest house in the village, a two-winged mock-Tudor 'manor' with gardens far too small for its extrovert splendour. Opposite, on the other side of the railway's deep cutting, was a strange futuristic, art deco, flat-roofed, white villa, owned by one Arthur Lucan, better known as stage and radio's Old Mother Reilly.

Having got that far, the lure of the world beyond seduced me. I decided to ride the five miles to Lee to show Grandad and Granny how well my cycling skills had developed. I had no fear of getting lost since we had been backwards and forwards in Grandad's car many times. I negotiated the main road through the woods, crossed Chislehurst Common, sailed through Chislehurst Village, up and over White Horse Hill, past the farm (long-since gone), into Mottingham, round the memorial by the Porcupine, turned right at Grandpa's old house, where Dad had grown up, along Mottingham Lane, up the steep hill of Winn Road, where Charlie Carey had his home and surgery, and arrived, tired but triumphant, at St Mildred's Road.

The shock waves reverberated at once. Grandad was stunned, Granny was anxious. The telephone – one of those upright stalks with a hornlike mouthpiece – was grabbed and a voice roared 'Lily! Michael's here on his bicycle.' No-one at home had so far missed me. 'We're bringing him back in the car.' My Grandad didn't grumble at me. After all, he had careered down hills on a Penny-Farthing when he was a boy and both he and my dad had got into far worse scrapes than I ever achieved. Back we drove to Petts Wood, the small bicycle securely strapped on the car's boot, and it was, I think, on that trip, or another soon after, that passing Eltham College, at the end of Mottingham Lane, I informed them, 'That's the school I want to go to.' Two years later I got there.

The process of growing up continued. One evening Dad, Grandad and Uncle Harry (Mum's younger brother), took me to Crayford Stadium to see the greyhound racing. Grandad was an almost uncontrollable gambler on horses, dogs and football pools, and Harry followed in his footsteps. Indeed, the week before his marriage, later in 1939, Harry lost all his savings on the dogs and had to be bailed out financially by Grandad. Doris, Harry's wife-to-be, was a pleasant girl but she came from a council estate near Eltham and Grandad never forgave her or Harry for the marriage. At the wedding he refused to look at the photographer's camera and, scowling, wrecked every picture. He was never reconciled to them.

Anyway, there we were at Crayford. I don't recall a single race but I do most vividly remember demanding to be allowed to put sixpence on a dog that had caught my seven-year-old eye. All three firmly refused to assist me in my planned plunge into wickedness and I riposted that I would never bet on a dog again. I never have!

One evening Dad took me, for a treat, to the Lewisham Hippodrome, actually in Catford, to see Max Miller in the Music Hall. The audience were in hysterics at his jokes – he was undoubtedly the most popular blue comedian of his era and an absolute master of innuendo. Even a small boy had to be outstandingly virtuous – or ignorant – to resist joining in the universal belly laughs. I went through the whole performance utterly mystified, not understanding a single remark leeringly whispered by the maestro. 'What did it mean?' I enquired of my father as we left at the end. 'One day you'll understand,' said my smiling Dad and left it at that. It was a good many years before I did. I remained remarkably ignorant, until would-be virtue took over in my teens.

And why was that? Children at the Council school might acquire an early knowledge of what lay within small girls' knickers and some undoubtedly did, when I later met them, and was on one occasion permitted, at the exorbitant price of one penny, to peer, courtesy of a young rascal named Geoffrey, into his small sister's nether regions, in their back garden. Nice children, like those tutored by Miss Porter and Miss Worthington knew nothing of such mysteries or, if they did, never once hinted at such knowledge. With the hatches securely battened down in Reith's

BBC, how was a properly brought-up child to be made aware of sex. I don't ever remember hearing the word spoken in my presence, till Geoffrey whatever-his-name capitalised on his small sister's assets.

There was, of course, no television in our house. Almost nobody had one. Except, now I think of it, John Astley's parents. There it stood, a wooden pedestal, with a tiny translucent inverted bowllike screen and a strangely flickering picture. He allowed me to see it in their home in Priory Avenue, just once, not long before the War broke out.

Just round the corner from their house was the Dump. It was a piece of rough land, on which we boys mucked about in small groups. In later years it would be the site of the United Reformed church. It was bounded by a small stream, a tiny tributary of other streams which eventually flowed into the Thames at Deptford Creek. Sure enough, in one bout of infantile horseplay, I was deposited neck-and-crop into its messy embrace and had to run all the way home, coughing up (at least in my imagination) frogspawn, tadpoles and sticklebacks, while the water ran down, and inside, my sodden short trousers.

That summer we spent our holidays just outside Bognor Regis, in a rented house at Middleton-on-Sea. Someone (guess who) had bought me a small fishing rod and my dad and I walked out on Bognor pier to christen it. Far out, above the deep water, I hung my rod over the railings and lowered the baited hook into the sea. Beginner's luck! Almost at once it bobbed and, overcome with excitement, I hauled it up and inspected the minute silvery object wriggling at the end. Dad took one look, eased it off the hook and tossed it back into the water. 'It was too small,' he said. So I tried a second time. Lightning struck twice! Up came the fish, the identical twin for all I knew. Dad tossed it back and I informed the world that 'I'll never fish again.' And I never have. Indeed, I was so incensed by the whole matter that, had I known the word (and I didn't for years to come), I would have loudly echoed my late Sovereign's comment on that regal watering place and uttered the memorable phrase 'bugger Bognor'. I've only ever been there twice since, and one of those occasions was on a Sunday school outing with a coachload of impossible kids from Croydon. Curate or not, I felt just the same sentiments on that occasion.

With the world only hours from a declaration of war, Grandad drove Dad and me down to the safety of Grandpa's house at Hythe. We left at about 7.30 on that Sunday morning, 3 September 1939, and arrived to find Allen, Agnes, Wendy and Janet all there before us. The key, as all agreed, was to get out of London before the bombing started. It was decided that we, from Petts Wood, were in greater danger than the others from Sevenoaks, so Grandad and Dad turned straight round and drove back to collect Mum and the eighteen-month-old Moira. 'Your grandfather drove like a maniac,' recalled my dad in later years. 'I've never been so frightened in my life. He ranted and swore, at the top of his voice, at every car we passed. We did the journey in not much over an hour. Clearly the old man's experience as a ship's captain must have taught him to put the fear of God into those sailors. He certainly succeeded with me.'

While this drama was careering its potentially lethal way across Kent, Wendy, Janet and I were despatched to the beach, a mere hundred yards from St Hilda's Road where Grandpa had made his home. Thus it was that, at the fateful hour of 11.15, as the nation listened to Neville Chamberlain's thin tones proclaiming that 'This country is at war with Germany,' three small children, two girls and a boy, all less than ten years old, were standing on the shingle beach at Hythe, unaware that they were England's front line, the very first of the Home Guard to defend our island heritage. Not another soul was in sight. We alone stood between the British Empire and the Nazi hordes.

Moments later a gesticulating old trout appeared. We could hardly hear a word she said but the general drift seemed to be that 'We'll all be murdered in our beds,' and she grabbed us, hauled us off the beach, and told us to go home this very moment before the Heinkels and the Stukas and that fat Field Marshal Goering caught us in the open. No sooner had she spoken than (to use Prokofiev's words) 'a big grey wolf did come out of the forest' in the guise of a wailing air-raid siren, the first of many that would interfere with our young lives in the months ahead.

There followed some weeks of total inactivity, at the end of which we returned to Petts Wood. School continued and winter, a hard one, descended upon us. One morning, walking to school in the snow, I had reached Willett Way, just opposite to the Dump, when I heard the clanging bell of the local fire engine sweeping round the corner behind me. I stooped, made a snowball, and threw it at the fire engine as it came up to me. Then Nemesis struck. It screeched to a halt thirty yards ahead of me as I stood rooted to the pavement. An enormous fireman (when you're seven, they all look enormous) climbed out, clipping on his belt and adjusting his helmet until he towered over me. To my dying day, I shall never forget what happened next. 'How old are you, Sonny?' he hissed. 'Seven,' I gasped in a strangled voice. His reply ended the encounter as he turned to retrace his steps. 'Do you want to live to be eight?' I have never, I swear it, ever even considered throwing anything at a fire engine from that moment.

Winter dragged into spring but nothing seemed to happen. We all reassured ourselves that we were about to 'hang out the washing on the Siegfried Line', and we instructed any listening rabbits to run while we rolled out the barrel. Months earlier we had stuck our little Union Jacks along the so-called Western Front on the map on the wall at home but they hadn't moved an inch. April saw the fall of Denmark and Norway and on 10 May the dam burst. In quick succession Holland and Belgium both fell to the Nazi invaders and the little paper flags formed two tiny rings round Dunkirk and Calais. Ten days later it was all over and I stood at the level crossing over the Ramsgate-to-Victoria line and watched as train after train after train of seemingly dead soldiers rolled on to London. Only half-a-dozen or so stood looking out of the open windows, faces blackened, eyes just open, hardly managing a smile or a wave for the kid watching from the level-crossing gate. Churchill might roar the lion's defiance but the small boy had got a fleeting glimpse of what remained of the old British Expeditionary Force. He could see only too clearly that the BEF had been expeditiously bundled out of France by a far greater Force and that all that they had left was the set jaw of being British.

Within a few days of Dunkirk, the refugees came. Silverdale Road's residents did everything that they could for the new inhabitants, the Dutch settling in quickly and becoming model citizens throughout the war. The Belgians, however, were filthy. They urinated in the gutters and on the front garden walls, they sat out on the same walls till all hours making a terrible noise, and they kept their children up till midnight. Quiet, respectable Petts Wood was simply not willing to tolerate such behaviour, even from deprived refugees, and vocally complained to the appropriate authorities. The Belgians vanished one day to everyone's great relief. If anyone needed a lesson in the tensions created by cross-cultural intermingling, this was it. Our grandparents might have eulogised 'plucky little Belgium' in the First War but our parents in 1940 called them, with some justification, 'dirty little Belgians', and I grew up with that description ringing in my ears.

The next four months etched deep and lasting memories into Michael Saward. One morning, on the way to school, I cycled up Birchwood Road. A little way up on the right stood a staff car. Out from the house in which he was briefly staying strode a beanpole of a man with a little moustache, crowned by a circular hat (which I later learned to call a 'kepi'). Even I knew who he was. His face was in the papers. General de Gaulle. Here in Petts Wood. Whatever next?

It wasn't long before the Heinkels and the Dorniers arrived. Great squadrons of them, flying in perfect formation. In August we had watched the occasional dogfights overhead as the attacks had been pressed on the RAF's fighter airfields. Glorious summer weather and up there, mostly further out in Kent, the Battle of Britain had raged. One Sunday morning Dad and I watched a dogfight between a Messerschmidt 109 and either a Spitfire or a Hurricane. High in the western sky over Bromley they twisted and turned until one started to flutter like a leaf and fell. 'We got one, we got one!' I shouted to Dad. He didn't react. Then, quietly, he said, 'It's one of ours.' In those moments I grew up a lot. In the Saturday morning kids' cinema it was always the Injun or the baddy who bit the dust. Suddenly I realised, for the first time, that goodies got killed as well as baddies.

But, in early September, the Luftwaffe squadrons flew overhead. Today, 7 September, a Saturday afternoon, they were going for London itself. Not the City or the West End but the Docks. They were actually bombing my Grandad's Surrey Docks! True, he had retired in 1939 but to me they were still his Docks. And, as night began to fall, I looked out of my bedroom window, straight over Chislehurst's Camden Park ridge, and there in a great arc of orange and crimson was the evidence before my eyes. Eight miles away, with woods in between, but, even so, I could see the actual flames shooting up into the glowing night sky, hundreds of feet high. It was a most awesome sight, never to be forgotten.

They came again in the night, this time with high explosive bombs. They didn't need compasses or radio beams. From the French coast they must have seen their target and they simply flew straight for it. They came straight over the top of Petts Wood. Fortunately for us, they didn't need to press their 'bombs gone' buttons for eight more miles.

Then, eight days later, the crisis passed. On Sunday 15 September they suffered their heaviest daylight casualties and the Battle of Britain was over. It gave way to the Blitz as, night by night, they came, pounding London, with only the occasional bomb to remind Petts Wood that we were under the flight path.

Even so, the Luftwaffe helped to kill my Granny. They dropped a landmine by parachute which created a ninety-foot-long crater at the bottom of the back garden of 10 St Mildred's Road. The house was badly damaged and uninhabitable. Not so the terrace of 1930s houses in Linchmere Road behind. There the devastation was terrible and I walked over what looked like a battlefield a few days later. Grandad took his latest car, a much smaller Ford Popular, and drove Minnie out into Surrey to find rooms. She, only sixty-four, was frail and growing daily weaker. They found a willing landlady in Fetcham, just beyond Leatherhead, and settled down for the few months that were left.

One consequence of the Blitz was the need to find homes for those bombed out. The other half of our semi-detached house was empty and the Harrises arrived. Bill, his wife, Charlie his brother, and two small children moved in. They had been bombed in Woolwich (or was it Greenwich?) and, in fairness to them, they struggled manfully to adapt their street culture, with all its working-class virtues and vices, into that of quiet suburbia. They were salt-of-the-earth South-East Londoners and gradually, over twenty years, assimilated themselves into a respectable, middle-class, white-collar family. But, especially in the first year, it wasn't easy. They talked over the back garden fence, they didn't misbehave like the Belgians the year before, but they needed to keep up with their family and old friends and the time came for them to have a 'par'y'. Courteously they called round in advance to alert us, indeed to invite us, but Mum and Dad said, 'Thank you, but no,' in equally friendly manner and all seemed well. The party got going around nine o'clock and only by eleven did it dawn on my parents just how many crates of bottled beer had been delivered earlier in the day. The noise grew and grew until every sound was penetrating the walls – and they weren't thin either. By one o'clock, the rhythmic stamping of feet was getting intolerable and by two o'clock all the neighbouring families were in open rebellion. Dad finally called the police soon after two and the constabulary broke up the fun. Two cultures had once more come into collision, neither understanding the other, or seriously prepared to try. Relationships between numbers 27 and 29 Silverdale Road plummeted and did not warm up for months. I, not having got to sleep until four o'clock, was no more understanding than anyone else. Not until many years later, as a curate in a working-class community, did I begin to understand the other side of the equation. Fun, real family fun, meant noisy togetherness and Mother Brown really did get her knees up and show off her bloomers.

On the morning of 9 April 1941, the telephone rang. I sat on the hall box while Mum answered it three feet away. She began to cry quietly. 'Mother's dead,' she said to my dad who was in the kitchen. I hadn't known Granny Saward all that well so her death hadn't been too bad. But Granny, my own kind gentle Granny. That hurt. They didn't take me to her funeral at Chislehurst Cemetery. I wish they had.

Dad, meanwhile, had joined the Auxiliary Fire Service. He was thirty-six when the war began, far too old for an early call-up. Like most men of his age, going to town on the 8.47 and returning on the 5.26 didn't feel like a major contribution to the war effort. So, in the evenings he presented himself at the Dunstonian Garage, just off the Station Square and awaited the call to fight fires in the vicinity. Next day, in the City, he, in company with countless others, walked round, or over, hoses and debris from the previous night's raid, on the way to the office. One night his AFS group were sent off to Waterloo Station. Beneath it were bonded warehouses packed with whisky. 'We stayed there all night and most of the next day,' he recalled in later years. 'It was an inferno and very frightening.' They brought him home on the fire engine next evening, his face black with smoke, totally exhausted. I little thought then that fifty years later I should assist the Queen Mother in the dedication of London's monument to the firefighters.

The time was fast approaching for me to leave my 'Dame School' and move on. I duly sat the entrance examination for the Eltham College Junior School and passed. One more term to go before the big change to the big school.

One morning, during break, I decided to conduct an experiment. Coming up behind two small pupils, I grabbed them by their necks and banged their little heads together. Not surprisingly, they both started yelling loudly. Miss Worthington came rapidly on the scene. They pointed accusing fingers at me. 'Why did you do such an unkind thing, Michael?' she said gently. 'Well,' I said, 'I read about it in a school story and wanted to try it out.' You can see why I've never been persuaded by those TV and film producers who loudly deny the possibility that sex and violence on screen can produce copycat reactions.

It was a bit like that with Jean Findon. She lived in a large detached house behind ours and we were quite good friends. One day I asked her round for tea. She was nine or ten and she turned up on her bike which was a little bigger than mine. When it was time for her to go home, we were both straddling our respective bikes at the top of our drive in readiness for me to escort her back the six hundred yards to her house. Suddenly, without warning, I leant across and kissed her on the cheek. 'What was that for?' she exclaimed. 'You can't expect to come to tea for nothing,' I answered. Today it's called sexual harassment. I haven't the faintest idea what made me do it, or say it. Still it was the first time I ever kissed a girl and it was eleven years before I tried it again. The second one married me.

I wasn't exactly into the fooling-about-with-girls thing but I did perform one courageous feat calculated to save the life of two damsels in distress. Sheila Scudamore, and her younger sister, Judy, lived in one of the finest houses in the district. It was just across from the Willett Woods and I was gratified to be asked for tea. When tea was over, Mrs Scudamore cheerfully released us. 'Go and play hide-and-seek, children,' she said, and we dashed off to do so. I was deputed to find the other two and I searched the whole house for them. Finally, at a loss, I walked into the bathroom. I heard just the slightest sound from one end, saw that the airing-cupboard was not quite shut, bent down, opened the door and there they were. 'Caught you,' I said, crashing in and, without thinking, pulling the door shut behind me.

Unfortunately, I then realised, I had also closed the bathroom door. What a delightful prospect, you might think. There I was with two pretty little girls, hidden away from prying adult eyes and ears. What more could a boy want? Well, you would be quite mistaken. I wasn't that sort of a boy and, anyway, the boiler was on and the airing-cupboard was fast growing extremely over-heated and I began to fear that we might all suffocate. 'Let's shout,' we said. So we did. At the top of our voices, yelling 'Help!' for all we were worth. The sound had to travel through two doors, down a floor, and break into the consciousness of a mother doing the washing up. Fortunately, she heard it. Unfortunately, she thought we were having fun. 'Enjoy yourselves, darlings,' we dimly heard her call. We were in real trouble.

At that moment, Superman (not yet invented) Michael leapt to the rescue. 'We must break down the door,' I said to the girls. I was just a fraction taller than they were, which wasn't saying much, so I put my feet against the boiler and my back to the door and straightened my legs. Nothing happened. I tried again, and again. Suddenly, the doorcatch on the outside gave way and I was catapulted down two steps onto the bathroom floor. The three of us ran downstairs, explained, and I apologised for the broken doorcatch. I never got asked to tea there again. Still, it did teach me not to go playing hide-and-seek with girls. 'Don't never, never, trust a woman,' said the song, 'For she will make a monkey out of you.' Not twice, I thought.

But monkey I was made, and this time by the same Geoffrey who had earlier capitalised on his sister's charms. Half-a-dozen of us were playing in a small field close to one of the railway lines. A footbridge crossed a single-track branch-line and the mesh fence was badly rusted. We all climbed through. It was at that point that Geoffrey warned us about the witch who lived in a culvert which carried the stream under the railway. 'If we creep up quietly, she might not hear us and we can get a good look at her,' he suggested. So, step by step, we crept down the field until we were three or four feet from the culvert. We bent down to look and there was a terrible, cackling scream. 'Run!' yelled Geoffrey (whose scream it had been). 'She's after us!' Six pairs of legs took off in abject terror as we fled back up the field. Snow White's wicked stepmother has a lot to answer for. Nine-year-olds are, or certainly were, remarkably prone to superstition.

One of the biggest debts I shall ever owe to Petts Wood Preparatory School is my love of poetry and verse. We were made to learn it by the yard and to recite it in public. Come the final Parents' Day, and I reeled off, if my memory is right, a large chunk of 'Hiawatha's Childhood', together with 'How They Brought the Good News from Ghent to Aix', 'Sherwood in the Twilight, Is Robin Hood Awake?', and 'There's a Breathless Hush in the Close Tonight'. Do that to a small boy and there's a fair chance that you'll instil in him a love of spoken English for the rest of his life.

Miss Worthington certainly wasn't pleased at one of my last public utterances before term ended. My friend David Mitchell had been evacuated in 1939 to a school in Porthcawl, in South Wales. Coming back to Petts Wood for his Easter holidays in

1941, he had taught me some of the songs he and his school-friends knew. I wasn't entirely familiar with the meaning of some of the words but they fitted the tune well.

Imagine my surprise, then, when dear, fragile, ever-so-proper, grey-bunned Miss Worthington started to teach us the wrong words to a chirpy tune from America. 'Altogether, now, children,' she said, 'the Camptown ladies sing this song, doodah, doodah,' and so on. Our hero's hand shot up. 'Please, Miss Worthington,' he said helpfully, 'my friend David Mitchell knows the real words and he's taught them to me.' 'Well, I never,' said the prim Miss Worthington, 'what are they, Michael, dear?' My clear treble (and I could sing) pierced the classroom. 'Let's go down to the boozing shed, doodah, doodah, going to booze all night, going to booze all day . . .' Miss Worthington, I noticed, had turned puce. I hoped she was all right. She opened her mouth and at that moment I knew that the time had come for me to move on to Eltham College.

Chapter Two

Floreat Elthamia

Sporting my new cap, of golden yellow segments on a bright-blue background, my new grey suit with short trousers, and clutching my new leather satchel, I presented myself one mid-September morning at the door of Form One in the junior school extension to the facade of Eltham College.

The college occupied a site, roughly square, of three hundred yards in each direction. The main Grove Park Road cuts across one corner leaving an area of about sixteen acres. The buildings lie in the north-east corner, with the older building, once Fairy Hall, having a Georgian frontage, a tower and an inner quadrangle. At right-angles to this lie a large building, constructed in the 1930s, and a Free Church chapel, which lies closest to the road and the main drive. Behind was the gymnasium, since replaced. Between all these buildings stands a magnificent plane tree of enormous girth and considerable age. To the south and west are playing fields, partly screened by a row of forest trees which effectively divide the playing area into a front cricket field (for the Second Eleven) and various rugby and cricket pitches, topped on the north side by the main First Eleven cricket table. In those days the college had some four hundred pupils, all boys, and was proud of its relatively recent promotion to the Headmasters' Conference, which gave it public school status. Outshone (in its own estimation) only by Dulwich and Whitgift, both of which were six or more miles away, it felt itself some degrees better than its grammar school rivals in Bromley, Beckenham and Sidcup or its other independent competitors in Catford, Lee or Kidbrooke.

So the great day dawned and I began. Very soon I became aware that I was going over old ground and learning very little that was new to me in that first year. Our form mistress, Miss Joan Brown, still alive as I write over fifty years later, was to become a legend to Elthamians, in common with at least eight other members of staff who all served for over thirty years at the school. One eventually retired after forty-three years' service. They do not make teachers like that these days.

Joan Brown, universally known as Ma Brown, was a kind, firm woman with a sharp tongue who taught all subjects that nine-year-olds needed to know, excepting only what my school report called 'games, drill, and handiwork'. Drill was not a military exercise but merely involved strenuous exercises in the gymnasium.

I was, my report states (and I still have it), 'a very good Pharaoh in the Scripture play' and, under 'Music', became 'a keen member of the band'. Certainly I remember well learning to sing an English version of Offenbach's 'Judgement of Paris' song from *La Belle Helene*, which began 'Goddesses three to Ida came, immortal strife to settle there.' Long before I ever discovered anything else about Offenbach or the operetta, I knew the lilting sound of 'Evoe, wonderful ways, have those goddesses, now as then, for subduing the hearts of men.'

Clearly my first year at Eltham was the most successful that I spent there, since I carried off the top prize for General Proficiency and I am still faintly embarrassed to look at the marks, both for classwork and examination, that I achieved. Of seventeen marks in the report, there was one alpha plus, ten alphas, three alpha minuses, two beta pluses and a solitary beta. That beta was in Handiwork, with the inevitable 'could do better' comment, while both beta pluses were for Writing (classwork and examination) and the not unhopeful remark that 'he has made more effort to improve'. My nine-year-old's writing was hardly a thing of beauty but few children in the 1990s could match it. The one cerebral subject not to be given marks, as such, was Poetry at which, it seems, I was 'excellent'. Not much reason, then, for me to have acquired 'a faint streak of humility' by the time I was ten.

First in the form, not a 'detention' in sight, without doubt a sporty, swotty, cocky, little 'teacher's pet' who was 'very keen', 'showing real promise', 'an interesting reader, with very good diction'. Even the headmaster, Geoffrey Turberville, signed off the report with 'a very good record'. Humility, with that kind of year behind me? Pull the other one! Are you surprised that my mother kept the report and I still have it? Come to think of it, I still have the prize, a bound and embossed book about the court of King Arthur and his noble knights. Yes, you've guessed right. Not a line about any of the naughty bits. Following the prize-giving some senior boys performed Shakespeare's *Love's Labour's Lost* which bored me considerably.

School life was not, even for a day boy, all lessons. The junior school played soccer, at which I was enthusiastic if not outstanding, and cricket, in which my eye was certainly developing. I tried athletics without much success and my only claim to short-term fame was when, fooling about with some of my friends, I turned and ran, at a yard's range, full tilt into a very substantial tree. Almost knocked out, I was carried into a nearby upstairs room, which did duty for the school sanatorium, and had sal volatile administered to me, a substance of which I had never heard. In due course, I was released, increasingly becoming aware of a lump on my forehead the size of a small hen's egg. For weeks after, my fellows addressed me as Seaweed Lumpèd, the 'Seaweed' having been inevitable from the earliest days of my arrival at Eltham. The bump acquired a scaly surface and left me visibly scarred for some weeks.

In July 1942, as my first year at Eltham ended, Dad was called up into the army. At thirty-nine, he was near the end of the conscription age range, and was initially posted to a camp at Chichester, before being allocated to the Royal Corps of Signals in Catterick. Shortly before he left, he went to see the headmaster, Mr Turberville, to discuss my future. 'He didn't want to know me, he thought I was a madman, the scoundrel,' was Dad's later comment. 'I thought, I'm going to fight for you,' he added. It was an interesting reaction that bore out my own unease about his whole style and manner. He was one of the most dispassionately cold fish I ever met and, try as I might, I never once then or since could raise the faintest affection or respect for him. Even in my schooldays I thought he was a weak and colourless headmaster, running a school at an admittedly difficult time but allowing it to drift along, seemingly going nowhere, with minimal discipline or punishments. His thin-lipped, weak smile and dry voice made no positive impact on me at any time and it came as a great surprise to discover, years later, from other Old Boys, and chiefly from my most respected mentor, that they thought he was a quite outstanding head whom they loved and admired. 'He was', said my favourite teacher, 'a superb man to work with and the staff revered him greatly.' Well, you can't please everybody.

Dad, with a friend Ben Saville, moved on from Catterick, via Prestatyn, to Barnard Castle where 'A very nasty sergeant-major said, "Here's a couple of right ones, we'll post them where they don't want to go." So he posted us to the Airborne, thinking he was doing us a bad turn, but a finer lot of blokes you couldn't have wanted to be with.' That was very early in 1943 and Dad was in Bulford until, on 27 May, he went to Liverpool and, boarding the *Stirling Castle*, set out for Algeria with the First Airborne Division, as part of its Divisional Signals.

Meanwhile, I at Eltham, was beginning to find life a little less comfortable. My schoolwork was not so outstanding and I did not take to my new form mistress particularly well. Nevertheless, I persevered and eventually the day arrived when the all-important scholarship exam was to take place. I remember sitting in the largest classroom in the college as we started the papers. When I got home I told Mum that I had sat close to a boy with inky fingers, who had covered his papers with more ink. 'He certainly won't pass,' I said. But he did. He was a brilliant maverick, utterly undisciplined, always 'agin the government', but I think he got a First at university and, I suspect, later committed suicide.

Along came 9 June. It was to be a red-letter day for Mum and me. First, there was a letter from Dad. He was in North Africa but he couldn't say where. Since the German Afrika Korps had finally been thrown out at the end of May it was obvious that he must have been in either Algeria or Tunisia. Then, secondly, there was a letter with my exam results. I had passed the scholarship! That meant a free ride for the rest of my time at Eltham. Finally, to crown it all, the cat gave birth to two kittens.

What cat? Well, I blush to admit it, but early in 1943 I had been listening to *ITMA* (the famous Tommy Handley radio series *It's That Man Again*) on the wireless one evening when I heard a scream from the kitchen. I ran in, saw my mother standing on top of the kitchen stool. She was holding a broom and waving it ineffectually. 'Shut the door!' she yelled. So I did. 'It's a mouse!' she shouted. With alacrity I joined her on the stool and we waved the broom together! A hero I was not.

She wasn't keen on cats and nor was I but there was clearly no choice. We purchased a feline tabby from a neighbour and the mouse-supply ran out rapidly. But Tibs had been a naughty cat and got herself pregnant. Thus on 9 June we had not one, but three cats. One was a tabby like its mother, the other was a splendid male Persian. Its sire was often seen stalking the nearby roads. Our next-door neighbour was a wiry Greek and drowning a newborn kitten was child's play to him. I watched in sick horror as the creature was despatched. Tibs, the mother, did not long survive and we were left with a despotic, leonine, aristocratic cat who should have been marked out with some solemn, monarchic appellation but suffered the indignity of being called Fluff for the next twenty years, while, spayed, he sneered at all of us from his regal, eunuch splendour on the arm of our settee.

Enough of him. What really mattered was *that* scholarship and the extra pleasure of being told by the chairman of the school governors, an old family friend, that I had come out 'very high on the list'. I never knew whether he had seen the results or was merely being avuncular but it rocketed my morale no end!

To crown it all, in the last weeks of term I took part in two cricket matches which have forever stuck in my mind. The two junior school houses, Bentley and Gilmore, met in head-on collision. I rather think, I can't be sure, that I got six wickets for our house, though the others got a reasonable score, but it was what came next that was so memorable. We scored the outstanding total of one run (and the boy who scored it was the youngest in our side). I didn't trouble the scorers but then who else did? Incidentally, we lost the match.

Not so the other game. This was a Saturday morning form match and towards the end I collected four wickets with four successive balls. Not a lot of people know that. Once more humility was a non-starter as I ended my career in the junior school.

School, of course, was not everything. Close by were the Willett Woods, about a square mile of delightfully peaceful trees, with a pond and a stream. I loved going there alone, or with my friends, throughout my childhood. Most of my Saturday mornings were spent out in the woods with a gang of boys. We picked up sides and played English and Germans (not popular as no-one wanted to be a Jerry) or Cowboys and Indians (we'd all seen Buck Jones at the winter-time kids' cinema, shooting everything that moved). Each Saturday morning seemed an eternity as we stalked each other with home-made rifles and tommy-guns and taught ourselves to creep in silence through clumps of bracken. We were very good at it long before we joined the Scouts. The boys, I fear, were not always as unblemished and 'nice' as my mother would have preferred, but those summer mornings were really enjoyable and I can still walk silently through woods. It is a sad fact that to-day, in those same woods, no woman willingly walks alone and no mother would even contemplate letting children go there to play, alone or in groups.

Two earlier visits to the Cubs had failed to hold me but, at eleven, I was eligible to become a Boy Scout. I did not cover myself in glory. I had the hat and the shorts, and the proper shirt, the scarf and the woggle but it took me a full six months to earn my tenderfoot badge and two more years to secure a second-class one. In most Scout troops that might not have been despicable behaviour but the Second Petts Wood troop was no ordinary troop. In those days the ultimate award was, I think, a 'Bushman's Thong' and we had a patrol in which every Scout had one – the first troop in the world, in the history of Scouting, to have achieved such a distinction. Well, that's what they told us. Michael Saward, in that company, was an embarrassment, a Scouting disaster. I stayed three years but they got rid of me brutally in the event, as soon as they could. We played British Bulldog together, we camped together, we did our knots, and tried to cook strips of dough into something faintly edible, but when the chance came they struck with the venom of a cobra. I was in the *Mikado* at school, a stand-in for Yum-Yum no less, when the letter reached my parents, dismissing me for my 'bad behaviour'. This referred to my absences from the troop during rehearsals at school, which clashed, and I had given them courteous advance warning, all to no avail. In later life as a clergyman, I have occasionally been asked to preach at special Scout services. I get great delight by telling them that I was kicked out 'for teenage transvestite practices'. That usually creates a sudden silence and allows me to recall my appearance as a Japanese maiden, 'from scholastic trammels free'. I don't usually get invited twice, which evens the score with Baden Powell's offspring!

The new school year began with me, a scholarship boy, in the main school. Doubtless in some superior public schools there might have been some snobbery about it. Not at Eltham. Virtually no-one came from that sort of family background and a scholarship was a cause for pride and some status. Most of us, fee-paying or not, were from middle-class homes and the ones who weren't generally assimilated over the years.

For the first year of the main school we were divided into two parallel forms, by virtue of our surnames, while they decided who would go to the A stream, and who the B. That year, 1943–44, was the nadir of my school fortunes. As I saw it, my form master was a dullard, my English master a genial incompetent, my Geography master a pompous prig, my Maths master an unintelligible neurotic, my French master a superior snob, my Art master a sarcastic boor, my Physics master was incomprehensible, my Scripture master the dreariest of bores, which only left History (which was my best subject), with the most sympathetic of teachers.

Anyway no small boy can afford to have so low a view of his teachers and hope to do well. I slid slowly down the form until it was inevitable that I should find myself in the B form in the following year. It does no good to say with the hindsight of half a century that I still stand by my assessment of those teachers.

That's how I found them, but, in fairness, they succeeded well enough with many of my contemporaries, so they can't have been all bad.

My mother, however, was seriously worried. She went to the school authorities and together they decided that my father's absence had affected me adversely. They would, they said, try to keep a sympathetic and open mind about my performance. Perhaps they did but when September came it was 3B and not 3A. That damaged my pride very badly but it made me angry and disgruntled, not humble.

Life at home continued fairly smoothly. Moira was now six, a small, auburn-haired, rotund package, sporting either a fringe or a huge bow, and closely wedded to a large doll. I don't suppose she was any better or worse than most small sisters are, or were, to any boy schooled on the *William* books of Richmal Crompton to whom they are inevitably carbon copies of Violet Elizabeth Bott. It isn't, of course, fair on small sisters but then being six years younger than your only brother is bound to be somewhat overwhelming and Moira, by her own admission, was thoroughly overwhelmed by this misfortune. Adulthood eventually enabled her to overcome the disability but parents ought perhaps to think twice before creating a six-year gap between two children. Among her friends was the daughter of our Greek next-door neighbour, Lanti, short for Atalanta, Mondinos. They played the games that small girls do while Mr Mondinos, who came from the island of Chios, regaled me with stories of diving for sponges and, most exciting of all, of his encounter with a large octopus. Fortunately, he had carried a knife in the belt of his swimming trunks and he had killed the beast as it was wrapping its tentacles round him. With such neighbours, who needs the cinema?

But we did. Regularly. Good, stiff-upper-lipped war films plus cartoons like Max Fleischmann's *Hoppity Goes to Town* and, memorably, *Dumbo*. Reluctantly, I agreed to take Moira to see it and the inevitable happened. As the dewy-eyed baby elephant was separated unwillingly from his mother the cinema audience was assailed by a howling, screaming, tearstained, auburn-haired brat yelling incoherent cries about taking babies away from mummies.

Furious at this unmannered intrusion, I dragged the caterwauling irritant out of the cinema and seriously contemplated tying her hands and feet to the railway line next to the Embassy Cinema. Alas, she was too short to stretch the four feet eight-and-a-quarter inches, so, like the heroines of earlier films, she survived. I often returned to the Embassy, but never again, I think, with my sisterly encumbrance.

By this stage in the War, food was not easy to come by and most essential items were rationed into minute portions. My mother kept well-in with the local butcher and, in addition to our proper allocation managed to acquire (quite legally) rabbits and all kinds of offal. I grew up loving, and I still do love, hearts, kidneys, liver, sweetbreads and brains. I drew the line at tripe (which was endorsed when I later saw a Lancashire relation eating it raw, covered in pepper). Fish in those days was still plentiful and we ate halibut, turbot and other, by now expensive, fish quite frequently. Eggs were a rarity (we had ghastly packets of dried eggs) so we kept our own chicken run at the end of the garden and consumed the produce. Mostly the birds were docile Rhode Island Reds but one memorable and violent specimen was a Plymouth Rock cockerel named Joe. He came at you like a tank and got his inevitable come-uppance one Christmas Day. Sentimental we were not.

Grandad, meanwhile, had returned to his second house in Lee, 114 Burnt Ash Hill, and lived in one of its flats. Every Sunday he arrived by about twelve o'clock and settled into one of the armchairs by the fireplace – a coal fire, of course – where he smoked his pipe or, occasionally, a cigar (he never smoked cigarettes), while avidly perusing, in order, the *Sunday Express*, *Reynold's News* and the *News of the World*. By extracting the finished pages, I managed to widen my education (and my eyes) with the serialisation of *Forever Amber*. I didn't really understand what that woman was doing with all those dashing men but they seemed to be enjoying it, especially when sentences ended with a series of dots. That completed, we sat down to eat our Sunday lunch, after which he gave me my week's pocket money, half a crown, which had, presumably, come from his success with the dogs, horses or football pools.

Dad had returned from Tunisia and, on leave, regaled us with stories of a journey across Algeria and eventually to Sousse, on the Mediterranean coast. The heat had taken its toll and Dad had found himself in an American army field hospital. Having only known British Army catering, he was delighted to have ice cream, fruit juice, and an array of delicacies not seen for years. He had suffered bad dehydration but rapidly recovered in response to such treatment and came home on 10 December on a Cunard liner. The Airborne Signals were posted to Caythorpe, in Lincolnshire, where he contracted double pneumonia and was sent to Lincoln Hospital in conditions hugely contrasting with his American experience. It was significant that his illness was far worse than that which killed his mother six years earlier but, with the first generation of antibiotics available, he survived.

Throughout 1944 he came home on regular weekend passes and tried to reassert some paternal authority. It didn't work and he and I ended most of his visits with a row. I was glad to see him go and, with the abandon of youth, frequently told him so. I was only twelve but already, a year earlier, Mum had, on holiday in a lodge at Lulworth Castle, tried to administer corporal punishment but had failed lamentably while I laughed at her. It wasn't that I was physically large – I was still one of the smallest in the form at school – it was just that I was beginning to assert myself well before adolescence set in.

By this time I had already taken one initiative, some months earlier, which was quite out of keeping with the family's life-style. Throughout the whole of my childhood and well beyond, the Saward family virtually never went into a church except for weddings and baptisms. I only recall going twice, on both occasions to St Nicholas on Chislehurst Common, for Moira's baptism (which they naturally called her 'christening') and to Uncle Harry's wedding to Doris Marmion in 1939 (when Grandad never smiled, as earlier mentioned). Of course, if asked, the Sawards would have pronounced themselves 'Christians' but that meant no more than a vague belief in Someone, Somewhere, and feeling that one should pray privately, as my dad unwittingly put it, 'to myself'. Mum went annually to the local Good Friday Three-Hour service, returning in suitably chastened mood to commence another year of vaguely masochistic convent-rooted nothingness.

At Eltham we did, of course, have a daily morning assembly in the school chapel. Although the school had been founded in 1842 to educate the sons of Baptist and Congregationalist missionaries (none of whom were there during the War years), the assemblies were a model of dull, liberal non-conformist practice with not a shred of any spiritual vitality that I could ever detect. The hymns were typical of the period and tradition, teaching an almost pantheistic universalism coupled with a bit of worthy, do-gooding, idealistic humanism. As Adrian Hastings puts it so devastatingly in his *A History of English Christianity 1920–1985*, they had reduced the gospel 'to a vague ethical concern, to a liberal watering down of incarnation and atonement, of Church and sacrament'. Their inner religious life consisted, he adds, 'of little more than institutionalised emotionalism and moralising'. Remove the emotionalism, of which there was none, and you have Eltham College religion in the 1940s exactly described. Recent headmasters and chaplains have tried hard to improve things but (and I say this as one who has preached in many public school chapels), having preached there three times since I left the college, I can only report that it remains the least inspiring building and worship that I have found in any public school that I have ever visited. I don't enjoy saying that but it's true.

So it was, to everyone's surprise, including my own, that I applied to join the choir at St Francis, Petts Wood's parish church. I had never once been to a Sunday school (I once poked my head round a door and fled) so I was literally entering a totally new world. Being wartime, the choir consisted of a few elderly men and a dozen or so trebles, conducted by a spinster schoolmistress, Miss Winnie Cowling. The vicar was a Kelham-trained celibate, and the worship was conducted in the austere, but Anglo-Catholic tradition for which Kelham (a monastic theological college near Newark) was famed. The building was brick, 1930s mock-Gothic, and there were no concessions made to anyone unfamiliar with the tradition. The vicar, as the years went by, grew increasingly ill-kempt and the whole combination of astringent worship and scruffy priesthood created in Petts Wood an open challenge to every Free Church. By the 1960s, Free Church ministers of varying hues had made national reputations from the strong congregations which they had created out of the large numbers of Anglicans who were quite unwilling to stomach the parish church and its prickly vicar but were willing to join almost any other body of local Christians. Into such a situation, innocent of all such matters, I unwittingly pitched myself at the age of eleven. I stayed for over three years.

I wasn't a good choirboy because my attendance was very erratic. We were paid a penny a service and my quarterly takings hardly amounted to a shilling. Since it was wartime, standards were deplorably low and there was very little competition. I had a good voice so they could hardly afford to sack me and I enjoyed it. The one long-term benefit was that I learnt how to sing Merbecke's setting for Communion, which is ironical since I have never needed to do so. I recall nothing else of lasting value which I acquired at St Francis and in over three years there was only one sermon, by a returned overseas missionary, that captured my attention, even briefly.

In the outside world, hope was growing. Everywhere the War was fast swinging in favour of the Allies and, as the Russians advanced westwards towards the Polish border, the British held the Japanese at Kohima and Imphal, the Americans moved inexorably forward in the south-west Pacific and, on 6 June, Operation Overlord was unleashed against the German forces in Normandy. Not surprisingly, we were all excited, but exactly a week later the first German V-1 flying bomb landed and within a few days we were inundated by the horrible brutes. Like many of my contemporaries, my normal name for them was 'doodlebugs' and we soon got used to their approaching snarl, cough, silence, and shattering explosion. In our part of Petts Wood we rapidly recognised that they came over on one of three routes. Those travelling to our west and those to our east could be detected a couple of miles away and provided no cause for anxiety. The third, central, route was another matter. While all three routes headed north-west, in parallel tracks, the central route came right over the top of us and to hear a doodlebug approaching on that track meant that you looked for shelter and held your breath, hoping that its engine would not cut out before it reached you.

A few nights later, *en route* from the Scouts, I was cycling home in the darkness. The local anti-aircraft guns were blazing away at a flying bomb when I heard a clang on the road alongside me. Next morning on the way to school I passed the spot and saw a jagged piece of shrapnel about six inches long. It must have missed me by less than a yard. The thought of what it could have done just three feet to the left was not calculated to brighten the day.

The most terrifying experience of the War came soon after. Mum, Moira and I had returned once more to the solid overground brick air-raid shelter in our back garden. It gave us a false sense of security to shut ourselves in there each night, sleeping on narrow bunks in a darkness lit only by the tiniest of electric bulbs. On the night in question, probably in late July, soon after midnight, we heard one coming on the central route. Moira was fast asleep but Mum and I were tense, waiting to see if it would pass safely overhead. Nearer and nearer it came and then, at the most critical point of all, the engine cut. We heard a swishing sound and, suddenly, the engine restarted for perhaps ten seconds, a light flickered through the grill of our airbrick, flashing a pale yellow image on the facing wall. The noise cut a second time and twenty seconds later a distant roar announced its landing.

The sequel to this nerve-wracking half-minute came next morning. A nearby neighbour accosted Mum with the news that he had been in his front porch, a hundred yards up the road, and had witnessed everything. 'It came in sight over the trees and houses facing you, flames still spurting from its jet. Suddenly they vanished, it dropped its nose directly at your house and I thought, "That's the end of the Sawards," when, to my amazement, it fired again, lifted, passed over you on its way, cut out, and vanished in the direction of the farm. I heard the explosion from half a mile away.'

Later that morning the news came that it had landed in a field close to the farm, killed two cows, and done no further damage beyond digging a large crater of mud beside the stream.

Christians are very prone to claim divine intervention about such things, forgetting the death and damage suffered by others. Yet, even allowing for that, the temptation to feel, like John Wesley, that one is 'a brand plucked from the burning' is strong. He, you remember, was saved from his father's burning rectory at Epworth, when he was a boy. The only comment I will allow myself is to say that I have never heard of any other doodlebug whose engine, once stopped, restarted before crashing.

Following hard on the heels of the doodlebugs came the V-2 rockets. One landed in Petts Wood, almost opposite Crofton Lane Council School. I went to see it. The devastation was total but the shock was even greater. At least with the flying bombs you heard them coming. The rocket simply arrived, soundless until it exploded. For the first time since the War began I experienced fear, real fear. These horrible weapons, the V-1 and the V-2, got to me in the way that nothing else did. By September, Mum decided to send me out of range for ten days and I was put on a train at Euston heading for Manchester. There I was met by Auntie Alice and entered a world unlike anything I had ever known. Alice was related to me in the most obscure way. Her mother was my grandad, Henry Kendall's, sister. To complicate matters, her paternal grandfather's second wife, the sister of his dead first wife, was my granny, Minnie's, mother. Strictly, then, Alice was my mother's cousin while being also Mum's grandmother's step-grand-daughter!

Alice had married a swarthy little Lancastrian named Jack Tighe and lived in a typical working-class terraced house in Eccles, just outside Manchester. They had lost one child tragically and Jack suffered from infected lungs from his working environment. Their pride and joy was Glynn, aged nineteen, home on leave from the Navy where he had been serving in the Far East. Also living under their crowded roof was Alice's father, Uncle Dick, the son of my maternal great-grandfather. He was seventy-seven and was the man who ate tripe raw, covered in pepper.

Here, then, was this twelve-year-old southerner, a scrubbed public schoolboy from one of London's prettier suburbs, sharing a double bed with a nineteen-year-old sailor in a dark and gloomy terraced house with an outside lavatory in deepest, urban, working-class Lancashire. Talk about culture shock!

Alice was nine years older than my mother but they had always been friends and wrote regularly to each other throughout their lives. She did everything she could to make me feel at home, took me to the church and let me loose on a nearby railway bridge to collect London, Midland and Scottish Railway train numbers as they approached the nearby Patricroft engine sheds. This was a welcome extension to my train-spotting hobby which had previously been confined to the Southern Railway. I still possess my carefully underlined ABC of Southern locomotives, published by Ian Allan (with whom, years later, I was to serve on a committee!), price 2s.

The days passed quickly, my only real memory being that of waking early on my first morning and kicking the much larger bulk of Glynn out of the bed on to the floor while he was still asleep. Considering that it was his first night home on leave after months afloat I think I was lucky to survive. We stayed friends, even if distantly, for the rest of his life.

It was while I was in Eccles that the news broke that First Airborne had been sent to Arnhem, in Holland, and that the battle was not going as planned. But was Dad with them, and, if so, at forty-one, wasn't he a little long in the tooth for such mayhem?

'I watched them go,' said Dad, years later. 'A lot of the young ones, the glider pilots, I knew well. They were towed out from Caythorpe.' Nearly two thousand of them were killed, including almost all the friends of a young, tough, soldier called Ginger Railton. Ginger was a Geordie and drove Dad home on leave in a lorry once or twice. He was in a military prison for some skulduggery, which saved his life, since, as he told us, 'I'd have been with them.' Dad, being in the Signals quartermaster's stores, would have been shipped out if the landing had succeeded.

Back in London, at school and in the church choir, it seems strange that I have no recollection of the sudden, and very unexpected death, of William Temple, Archbishop of Canterbury throughout the latter part of the War. Churchill, when appointing him in 1942, had described him as 'the only six-penny article in a penny bazaar' and his death opened the way for Geoffrey Fisher, the Bishop of London, to become Archbishop. Churchill, who 'knew and cared nothing about the church' and was 'an agnostic with a touch of pantheism' was utterly unwilling to consider the other contender, George Bell, who had criticised his war policy on various occasions, so it was Fisher for Canterbury. One element of my own future was falling into place.

School, that academic year, meant the B form and it had come as a surprise and a blow to my pride. In reality, I should have seen it coming, but for a term I couldn't be bothered until I began to realise that it offered me the challenge to get to the top of the form.

As the European war drew to its close so my marks began to show signs of improvement. At much the same time I finally learnt to swim. Eltham had a fairly small indoor swimming bath behind the tuck shop and we often went there. The practice was nude bathing for the whole school which seemed to be a matter of total indifference to almost everyone, its only interest being the visible signs of puberty as adolescence developed. I never was, or have been, a strong swimmer but it was another milestone. It did have one consequence for me which was to save me in the future from a repeat performance of the day in the crowded open-air public baths at Bromley, on which I almost drowned in the midst of scores of people. Nobody had noticed as I yelled for help, just out of my depth. The only other effect of the school bathing custom was to leave me with a lifelong dislike of having to swim in any sort of clothing. Even well into my clerical days I have been known, on holiday, to get into the sea, remove my trunks, and wrap them into a ball in one hand until the time comes to return to land, suitably reclothed for the beach. Needless to say, tabloid journalists would find it totally impossible to believe that such behaviour could have any motive other than a sexual one. Obviously they went to the wrong schools!

Summer 1945 was the year I began to keep my batting averages and I haven't failed to record any innings since then. Our part of the War was over, the General Election had returned a Labour government and we were on holiday in Mortehoe when the results were declared, weeks after the election itself. I hung my head out of the window of the *Atlantic Coast Express* all the way from Waterloo to Exeter (well, it seemed like that) and eventually verified one fact passed on by that unpleasant Geography teacher. As we, the nine o'clock from Waterloo, drew into Exeter St David's, there, coming in the opposite direction, was the 10.30 *Cornish Riviera Express* from Paddington. The Great Western Railway was, evidently, much faster than the Southern on the Exeter run.

On my return, I was just about to go to a Scout camp when, one evening, there was a knock at the front door. Dad was on leave (he wasn't demobbed until 1946) and he and Mum invited in a young man by the name of Douglas Quadling. They talked in our back room and eventually invited me to join them. It was to be, though I little knew it, a life-changing fifteen minutes. 'This young man', said Dad, 'has come to invite you to go to a Crusader camp.' I knew a boy who attended Crusaders and I didn't like him, though fortunately he belonged to a different Crusader class. 'Do you want to go?' asked Dad. 'Don't know,' I answered, with the certainty of youth. Douglas Quadling, who seemed a pleasant if somewhat owlish young man, then explained that, with the War virtually over, the Orpington Crusaders were planning to grow and that 'your headmaster, Mr Turberville, has given us your name as a boy in the district who might be interested, especially in camping'. He added that he was also approaching Richard Greenhalgh another local boy in my form, so I shouldn't be lonely. Camping, not Crusaders, was, of course, the bait and I thought it sounded interesting. 'I'll discuss it with Richard,' I said, 'and we'll let you know.'

The idea, in the 1990s, that a headmaster would give out names to a religious organisation seems incomprehensible but Turberville had done it and, if I owe him little else, I am certainly indebted to him for that one act. By so doing, he set me on a path which has been the chief way in which my life has gone from that day.

'Richard,' I said, a day or so later, 'what shall we do about the Crusader thing?' 'It can't do much harm,' he said. 'Let's go to the camp, turn up for a couple of Sundays after that, just to be polite, then we can forget it.' That sounded eminently sensible so we clinched the deal, and, a week after Hiroshima and Nagasaki vanished under the atom bomb, we set out for Ide Hill, ten miles away, for the Orpington Crusader class camp. The War finally ended that very week.

The camp was fun, quite different from a Scout camp. We played two strange new games – 'halo', a kind of quoits with a rubber ring, and 'podex', variously spelt, a cross between cricket, rounders and tip'n run, played with a baseball bat and a soft white leather ball – and I discovered I was good at both. We played 'wide games' around the countryside and the only snag was the camp 'epilogue' when we were the victims of some fairly solid Bible-bashing, from a visiting speaker, a man called John Inchley. The class leader was a somewhat eccentric bachelor, with the unfortunate name of Jack Belcher, but he seemed fairly harmless. Inchley helped spare my blushes when I got overtaken by a sudden attack of diarrhoea and I repaid him by falling asleep during his epilogue in a manner which I couldn't conceal. One afternoon some Bromley Crusaders visited us to play podex and I was very struck by a boy with hair all over the place, who was a very good player and who went by the name of Peter Dawes. It would have been inconceivable to think that we should, years later, be fellow ordinands, fellow Church Commissioners, fellow members of General Synod and that he would become Bishop of Derby. Our paths did not cross again for seven years.

My year in 4B was utterly different from the two previous miserable years. Chief architect of this was, without doubt, my form master, Sammy Duchesne. If one man put his mark on my schooldays it was Mr Duchesne. The school Latin master, he was also in charge of cricket, and a disciplinarian who threw chalk with unerring aim at miscreants. No-one ever even considered disrupting his classes (as we did to lesser mortals and, most of all, the English lessons of the luckless Mr Parkinson). 'Parky' was incapable of discipline.

With Duchesne as my guardian angel and idol-worshipped mentor, life acquired a completely new quality. True, I was never any good at Physics and even worse at Chemistry (a disagreement with a flagon of sulphuric acid which ruined a sports jacket and, nearly, my face, hadn't helped) but all the non-scientific subjects were going well and I was, I had no doubt, heading for both History and Geography prizes. It was, however, my misfortune to be taught both by a young man, recently appointed, named W.H.O. Chambers. 'Wocky' did not like being asked questions (he often didn't know the answers) and I was an inveterate questioner. Occasionally, to make it worse, I knew answers which he didn't (or, worse still, got wrong) and war was nearly declared between us. To this day, I believe his spite robbed me of both prizes but time has long since healed any hurt, though I did feel hurt.

The first six months of 1946 witnessed one major change. The headmaster was taken seriously ill and had two terms' leave of absence. He was temporarily succeeded by the second master F.W. ('Bill') Scott. Scott was a hangover from Victorian times, at least in style, and he was renowned for putting the fear of God, and his cane, into everybody under the age of sixteen. He wore a flowing black graduate grown which billowed out behind as he stalked into the daily assembly in chapel. He also sported a stiff white winged collar and a drooping black bow tie and his white hair was long at the back spilling out from a high bald dome at the front. To top it all he was a Quaker and a pacifist who saw nothing odd about coupling these characteristics with the capacity to beat anyone who even remotely crossed his path. He probably beat more boys in his six months' rule than Geoffrey Turberville did in nearly thirty years. The result was a tremendous rise in morale, a huge improvement in discipline, both inside and outside the school, and a respect for 'Bill' which was almost universal. On one occasion, as was his daily custom, he announced the names of boys who were to 'come to my study after chapel' and 'Saward' was among them. Expecting this, following a small contretemps in a classroom the day before in which I was a relatively innocent victim, I padded up with thick woollen trunks under my trousers and presented myself. He totally dismissed my plea of innocence, swiftly beat me and sent me on my way. Being a philosophical animal, I came to the conclusion that although I genuinely was wronged on that occasion I had probably deserved it at other times, when not discovered, and honour was satisfied all round.

Scott was everything the modern educational establishment deplores and I have no doubt that he was one of the two or three finest masters in the school. When Turberville returned in the autumn, everything rapidly drifted back to the *status quo ante*. Doubtless the Ministry of Education's inspectorate sighed with relief that the flogger was back on the shelf. Even so, it was the best six months of my five-and-a-quarter years in the main school. We had a pride, and an *esprit de corps* that was never present before or after. It left me with the conviction, which has never shifted, that moderately applied corporal punishment for boys is an excellent element in disciplining a community. Scott beat many boys but he never overdid it in quantity and very few resented it. No-one could have accused him of brutality and he didn't draw blood.

When the 1946 cricket season arrived I was in the school Colts Eleven, batting usually at number four and also playing for Carey, our house. Carey was named, not after our doctor but William Carey, the famous 'consecrated cobbler' who launched Baptist missionary work in India at Serampore at the beginning of the nineteenth century. The boarders had finally returned from Taunton and one of my friends was a tall, curly-haired boy named Arthur Wyatt, one of three brothers, sons of Harry Wyatt, a Baptist missionary, murdered by brigands in China in 1938. It was in that same year, 1945–46, that we heard the sad news of the death in an internment camp of Eric Liddell, the school's most famous athlete, Olympic champion and Scottish rugby International, later to be recalled in the film *Chariots of Fire*. Liddell had been a missionary in China and was a model of all that the school ostensibly stood for.

Whenever I could that year, I went to Lord's to watch the superb one-day matches played between Service teams, which featured most of the famous names of post-war cricket: Len Hutton, Walter Hammond, Dennis Compton, Keith Miller, Learie Constantine – the list was endless. Doug Wright bowled quick leg-breaks, Alf Gover, the really fast stuff, and Godfrey Evans kept wicket with a speed that deceived the eye. I copied them all shamelessly.

Two catches stand out. Leslie Compton, Dennis's brother, caught Learie Constantine, one handed, with his left hand, over the back of his head, while leaning against the pavilion rails, with the ball over the boundary. Quite rightly it was legal and Constantine was out. Uproar and cheers everywhere. Then, in the so-called Victory Tests, the young Trevor Bailey caught the Australian opener, Keith Carmody, at backward square leg off a glance that left the whole crowd looking at the boundary. Bailey ended up star-shaped on his face with the ball in his outstretched right hand. I've never seen better catches than those two and the quality of that one-day cricket far surpassed any of today's artificially limited-over matches.

There was a slight price to pay on one Saturday. Coming back, to Charing Cross on the Bakerloo line (as it was then) from St John's Wood, I got talking to a kind and friendly elderly man who invited me home. I politely declined so he said he would see me on to my train for safety. Ignoring the lift, we walked up the spiral stairs where he attempted to grope me. I fled up the remaining stairs, terrified that I had been drugged and was about to be 'white slaved', and sat in the train home quivering with shock. It didn't stop my going to Lord's but it was a distinctly unpleasant experience and warned me off would-be pederasts (even if I'd never heard the name) for good.

School speech day that summer introduced a new item – a school song. Written by Parky the English master, and composed by his 'Music' counterpart, the owl-like Mr Connolly, it began 'Sing we the men whose steps have trod the stones of Blackheath and the Eltham fields,' and ended, with a slight parody of a more famous institution, *'Floreat Elthamia*, stand and flourish ever.' We, in the school choir, stood and flourished as we gave it a world première. As school songs go, it's not unworthy.

Throughout the school year I had spent my Sundays in ways quite different from those of the rest of my family. While Mum, Moira and Grandad continued in the accustomed manner, occasionally joined by Dad on a 48–hour pass, I cycled off to St Francis in the morning and a private school in Orpington in the afternoon where the Crusaders had their Bible class at three o'clock. Richard Greenhalgh had kept to his plan and soon vanished but I quite enjoyed the new choruses and hymns and listened with varying interest to the talks from Jack Belcher and others. Some of the boys were archetypal 'wets' and few were sporting types but the whole thing was geared to boys in a way which neither the school chapel nor St Francis either could, or did, attempt to match. Looked at with hindsight it is easy to dismiss it as a predictable 'hymn-sandwich' formula, without much imagination, but it was passable and to my taste during the weeks that I 'earned' my Crusader badge (ten consecutive weeks) and, far harder, the fifty consecutive Sundays in order to acquire my embossed Crusader Bible. I got both, though the latter created collisions of loyalty with my family who did not much appreciate having a son who declined to go anywhere with them for a whole year while he slogged on to win his Bible. One other task was to learn the names of all sixty-six books of the Bible in consecutive order. Genesis, Exodus, Leviticus, Numbers, and so on, came quite easily but all sixty-six was a tall order, though probably a lot simpler for a child than an adult. Once learnt, incidentally, and they're never forgotten.

Orpington Crusaders, I discovered, was just one class in a national union and each week we saw the full attendance lists and vowed to overtake the competition. About that time I discovered that there were national 'Union' camps and I booked in to 'Studland I', to be held near Swanage, in Dorset, for a couple of weeks in August.

The main party met at Waterloo station on 5 August, travelled to Swanage, where our luggage was taken by road to Studland while we walked nearly three miles up and over Ballard Down. Eventually about 150 of us settled in, 8 to a bell tent, and the camp began. We played all the same Crusader games as before, at which I did well, with our tent winning the inter-tent podex. We went on outings to the naval dockyard at Portland and Corfe Castle. What has made Studland 1946 stand out for me was, however, something quite different. Every Crusader camp had its chaplain. They varied from one another not only in personality and style but also in denomination. Studland's chaplain on that occasion was a Baptist minister from Leigh-on-Sea in Essex, the Reverend John Pritchard. In later years he was to be pastor of the Auckland Baptist Tabernacle in New Zealand and later still principal of the New Zealand Bible Training Institute before his sudden death in the late 1970s.

Apart from those few days in Dorset, I was hardly ever again to meet John Pritchard but it was probably the most crucial encounter I ever had with anyone. Night by night we teenage boys sat on hard and narrow backless benches, for what seemed ages, in a large marquee lit by smoky hurricane lamps. I have no idea what he said on any night except one. A friend who was there has just told me that it was 11 August and that we sang the hymn 'Give Me a Sight, O Saviour.' It has taken over fifty years for me to learn that.

Suddenly, as dusk was beginning to close in, and the boring preacher continued to grind on, his voice broke through the crust of my adolescent indifference. What he said was, as I later came to realise, no more than the timeless core of the Christian gospel. No doubt I had heard it many times before but, as one of my daughters was to say years later of another preacher, 'I didn't listen, I only heard him.' Tonight it was different, I heard him and I listened hard because, despite all those 150 boys round me, it was to me he was speaking. He told me of a man who had died for me; of a man who had been weighed down on a cross by my sin, my pride, my disobedience; of a man who had suffered its consequences, felt its guilt, had agonised through it; because that man, who had done it, was the one guiltless, perfect human being, to whom its very presence was exquisite torture spiritually. That man had done it all for me, was offering me forgiveness, cleansing, a new heart, and peace with God and how was I going to respond? With gratitude or with indifference, with the open hands that receive an undeserved gift, or the clenched fists of rejection?

The epilogue ended. We could, he concluded, come to his tent if we wanted to pursue the matter. And that was that. But it wasn't. I walked, in the near darkness, around the edge of that field for about fifteen minutes, wrestling, wrestling. Fourteen is no great age but it's old enough to know the core of your needs, your failings, and your loyalties. Unsure of myself, I walked to his tent. I don't know what I expected to find. Perhaps a man sitting alone on a camp stool smiling at me? I lifted the flap, and crept into a corner among maybe twenty or thirty boys. To this day I only know who one of them was. There, in the deep gloom, I made the most serious decision of my life. I, as solemnly as I knew how, invited that man, Jesus of Nazareth, to take me on. The proper phrase was 'Saviour and Lord'. In later months and years I came to fill those words with solid, theological content. That night I just took them at face value.

Ought a preacher to ask so much of an adolescent in the fraught years surrounding puberty? I've always been desperately cautious when faced, as a preacher myself, with that question. Can a boy really know what is involved? Should an adult, any adult, ask him to make such a choice? I can only report what I know to have been true that night. I was conscious, fully conscious, that I was facing the first great adult decision of my life and I made it, not, of course, perceiving all its ramifications and consequences, not grasping all the theological nuances and subtleties, but with a mind ice-cold clear that this was the biggest step that I would ever take.

Never, not for one single moment in the fifty years that have come and gone since, have I ever regretted that night's Damascus Road. Not once have I ever had cause to doubt its meaning or consequence. Oh yes, of course, I have puzzled over scores of questions about God, about the incarnation, about sin, about the cross, the resurrection, the meaning of life, of suffering, the whole gamut of perfectly proper queries that every thoughtful human being must face. I have looked at myself in the mirror and enquired, 'Am I deluded, conned, misled, a victim of this, that, or the other mental or psychological fantasy?' Still the reality, as I know it, stares back. Take your choice. Gamble. Stake your life on it. And I have. That's what faith is. Not an absolute mathematical certainty but, as Kierkegaard once said, swimming with all those fathoms underneath you, held up.

'Damn,' I said the next morning, about some trivial irritant. 'Did you hear that?' said two priggish youngsters. 'That kid swore.' It hit me. A new life meant a new guard on my tongue. The battle had begun.

I came home to some tremendous and totally unexpected news. Eltham was changing its policy. From now onwards, the top five in 4B would go up to Lower 5A and the bottom five in 4A would move on into Lower 5B. The miracle had happened. I was going into the A form. What was even more unexpected was the news that Sammy Duchesne was to become Lower 5A's form master. There was a God in heaven. If I had worked hard in the previous year I now set my nose to the grindstone in a totally new way.

Crusaders became a weekly delight. I started a daily 'Quiet Time' of prayer and Bible reading. I joined the cast of the *Mikado*, giggling as I was transformed into a simpering Japanese maiden. I didn't get the solo spot as Yum-Yum but I was understudy. What a magnificent term it was! The cast included both staff and pupils. It was particular fun getting to know Pooh-Bah, Lord High Every-thing-Else, because he, Mr Slader, was my new Geography teacher and a great improvement on his two predecessors. 'Name a "gap" town on the River Stour in Kent,' he demanded in class one day. My hand shot up. 'Saward?' 'Wye, Sir,' I replied. 'Don't try that cheek on me,' he answered. 'But it is Wye, Sir.' The penny dropped. 'You're right,' he said, 'but I was thinking of Canter-bury.' One up to me but one up to him, too, for the smile in his eye as he changed tack so quickly. And that story is true. I didn't get it from an old black-and-white Will Hay film. This Pooh-Bah certainly wasn't born sneering.

The dress rehearsal arrived, attended by thick fog, a classic London pea-souper. All went well until, towards the end of Act One, Katisha (Mr Slader's wife) sang dolefully, 'The hour of glad-ness is dead and gone, in silent sadness I live alone, the hope I cher-ished all lifeless lies, and all has perished . . .' At which moment all the lights fused. Frustrated we set off home in the fog (all except those who made use of the opportunity for a little slap and tickle with some of the damsels from a local grammar school, specially invited for the occasion). It took me over two hours to travel the five miles and I never once saw a damsel.

Christmas 1946 saw Dad home from the army and back at

work in the Commercial Union in the City. We celebrated as a family with a large turkey. Turkeys in those days were once a year specialities and had hardly been seen in wartime. Dad looked at me and said, 'This Christmas you can have as many helpings as you can eat.' I got through six. At fourteen, with years of austerity and rationing not yet ended, no boy would pass up such a challenge. Dad brought home a German Schmeisser submachine-gun and a paratrooper's dagger. He left them in the loft where they stayed until he handed them in during a government amnesty. Both were superb, if lethal, weapons.

The spring of 1947 was the worst in living memory. Snow and ice set in for nearly three months. Daily travel to and from school was long, cold and wearisome. On one awful occasion I fought my way into a six-a-side railway compartment at Grove Park and stood on the ball of one foot for almost half an hour before we reached Petts Wood. There were, I swear it, thirty-one people in that compartment, nineteen of them standing. *Guinness Book of Records*, are you listening?

In May, just before my fifteenth birthday, Mum and I met Frank Haslam, my godfather, and, while sitting in a taxi in the forecourt of Charing Cross station, he gave me my birthday present. It was an Irish Sweepstake ticket. The earnest young Christian declined to accept it. 'I won't gamble,' I said firmly. Embarrassment all round. Frank had been a bookmaker in his time (unsuccessfully) and Mum had been a great friend and neither could begin to understand. The irony of a godfather who encouraged his spiritual charge to gamble was quite lost on them. I stood firm. We stayed friends but it was a tricky moment. I'm glad I had the courage to say no, but teenagers can rarely convince their elders in these matters.

My second Union summer camp with Crusaders was at Atherfield on the south-western coast of the Isle of Wight. One lunchtime the camp quartermaster, faced with 150 hungry teenagers (though no-one called us that in those days), provided roast sheep's hearts. It was one of my favourites but obviously lots of campers had never eaten offal and refused to try it. What a lunch that turned out to be! By the time I finished, I had put away nine hearts. A day or two later we were given stewed prunes for pudding. Not my favourite. This time another boy worked his way through seventy-two prunes (I actually counted the stones) and, then, he suddenly let out a despairing yell and was last seen running at top speed down the field towards the camp latrines. Hearts were clearly not trumps. Prunes were.

Those two years working for School Certificate, with Matriculation exemption, were hard but satisfying. I had virtually no social life. I left the church choir, to Father Hampson's open disgust. I played cricket for the school Second Eleven. I was an enthusiastic train-spotter. I read the *Hotspur* and *Wizard* which, while not great literature, had good stories for a boy. I collected stamps in growing collaboration with Dad, now back in the City, and I never once looked at a girl. Girls just bored me. They did nothing but simper, giggle and blush. You couldn't get a decent conversation with any of the ones I knew. In contrast, I really enjoyed the Yukon verse of Robert Service about a man's world where 'a bunch of the boys were whooping it up in the Malamute saloon'.

I was fortunate in being able to get into the second day of the 1948 Lord's Test against Bradman's Australians. I left home in the dark at 4 a.m. and was in the queue by 5.15. Already it was 250 yards long, stretching from the Wellington Place gates almost to St John's Wood church. I recall watching, fascinated, as a street entertainer bent an iron bar round his neck. Let into the ground soon after 9 a.m., we still had to wait until 11.30 before England took the field, with Australia at 253 for 7. Their last three wickets put on about a hundred runs and despite Hutton, Washbrook, Edrich and Compton, England were facing an uphill struggle. Twice that summer I went to see Don Bradman, and on both occasions he was fielding.

Early one morning I cycled twenty-five miles to meet and pace the Olympic torch between Westerham and Godstone, on its final stage to Wembley for the first Games since 1936. I was home before breakfast.

Then, one day in August 1948, the post revealed a scruffy slip of paper, completed by Sammy Duchesne, who, even more miraculously, had stayed my form master for the third consecutive year.

As I look at it today it merely says, in blue, 'Congratulations!' and sets out my Matriculation results. One distinction (History), one 'good' (whatever that meant) in French Oral, five credits, one pass (in Latin, Duchesne's own subject!) and the totally predictable failure in Physics. I had managed, after much parental pleading, to persuade Turberville earlier in the term to permit me to omit Chemistry since I had never achieved twenty per cent in any exam in the four years I had suffered from it. 'Bill' Scott summed it up. 'I thought we might get some History distinctions,' he said with a twinkle, 'but I never thought you'd get one.' I was pleased, but not overpleased. The form had amassed seventy-one distinctions, one boy doing so in all nine subjects. In later years we, but not me, collected seven First Class Honours degrees. Pleasure? Yes, but coupled with a faint streak of humility. Alongside those distinctions what else do you expect?

That autumn I began the sixth-form course for Higher Certificate. One term of that and I had had enough. The History and Geography were enjoyable but the French literature was wearisome and as for the Economics, I was no Chancellor of the Exchequer in the making. I duly sang bass as a sailor in *HMS Pinafore* and said farewell to Eltham College a week before Christmas. It didn't really dawn on me during my childhood that my parents, good, steady, kind, not very imaginative, middle-class suburbanites, didn't own a dictionary, an encyclopaedia, any books worth mentioning, any pictures, or records, or musical instruments – indeed nothing beyond a wireless set. Mum read lightweight novels from the local lending library and Dad never read anything. In reality, I doubt if he read twenty books in the whole of his adult life. The range and richness of English culture simply passed us by. We never went to theatres, to museums, to art galleries, to concerts, and no-one ever mentioned the word 'opera'. Of course, for much of the time there was a war on but even so these things simply passed us by. The cinema and the wireless were our culture, and they were very potent. I probably knew every popular song between 1938 and 1950 and I can still remember a great many of them and, moreover, can be moved emotionally by the associations they conjure up. It may be that, by deliberately soaking myself in books and classical music throughout my adult life, I have been somehow compensating for an aesthetically bleak childhood. That said, it certainly wasn't an unhappy childhood. Actually, we did go to the theatre in London a couple of times. Once was to a pantomime, the other time it was *A Midsummer Night's Dream*. I'm not sure which bored me the more. I've never really been a theatre man, perhaps as a consequence, though the most recent ones I've attended have all been brilliant – light years away from the dullness of the 1940s.

Eltham had given me much, for which I remain grateful. It had almost inoculated me against the Christian faith but Crusaders had filled that gap. It wasn't in those years, dogged by wartime, a very impressive school though it had a handful of superb masters and one mistress who gave it high quality in their departments. I was glad to leave but even more glad to see the huge improvements which have raised it academically in the intervening years and turned it into one of Greater London's top dozen independent schools in the past decade.

So, I left. And that same week, having started in September to worship regularly at Christ Church, Orpington, I was confirmed within the Church of England. I was sixteen-and-a-half and the adult world was beckoning.

Chapter Three

From City to White Man's Grave

'If you've had enough of school', said Dad, 'I'll talk to Allen. He knows everyone at Lloyds. You'd better come up to the City.' I had indeed had enough of school though I had no idea what I wanted to do with my life. Advanced education had never been a part of the life of the Sawards or the Kendalls. Not one had ever been to university or even considered such an eventuality. So, Dad and Allen talked to a man who knew a man, the normal way things happened in the world of insurance, and a couple of weeks later I was on the 8.25 from Petts Wood to Cannon Street, bound for Bland, Welch and Co. Ltd., in their offices in Sackville House, 143 Fenchurch Street, London EC3. Mr Chandler, one of the firm's directors, informed me that they were starting me right at the top with a big salary as junior office boy and run-around at £3 a week. Riches beyond the dreams of avarice! By the time I had given Mum her proper cut, paid my season ticket, and provided myself with a daily lunch I was left with about 15s a week for my every other need. To a young man used to half a crown's pocket money that seemed eminently satisfactory.

To start me off in style, a few days earlier Mum and I went into the Fifty Shilling Tailors in Victoria Street and she provided me with a navy suit, discreetly striped, the very model of what the not-so-well-dressed office boy was wont to wear. The moment I entered Bland, Welch, I knew it wasn't right for the ambitious would-be insurance broker. It said 'clurk' in Essex tones not 'broker' in the accents of Surrey or the Chilterns. Double-breasted was the fashion. My sad little suit was single-breasted. Charcoal-grey was for winners. Navy blue was for also-rans. I hated it from then on but it was all I had.

There were three juniors, glorified messenger-boys – Hugh Spratt, from St Mary Cray; John Pearmain, a Scot living in Caterham; and me. We were kept in line by a comic-opera figure in the uniform of the Corps of Commissionaires. 'Bomber' Gilbert, a huge part-Maltese ex-sergeant, with a fist full of suspiciously heavy rings, gold teeth, a flashing leer of a smile that would have done credit to a Barbary pirate and an aptitude with the xylophone which assured him of an extra moonlit income from clubs all over London, was our immediate boss. Bomber was unlike any other Commissionaire I ever met and Bland, Welch were obviously pleased to have such a character lording it over the front counter. He fawned over the directors and senior brokers, joked with the office staff, and licked his lips lecherously and obviously at, and especially behind the backs of, the typists. To a well-behaved, innocently ignorant, Christian teenager like me, he was Disney's Big Bad Wolf incarnate.

My job was chiefly made up of two elements. Twice a day I was sent off round a string of local insurance offices to deliver and collect whatever was in the out-trays. Before, between and after these forays, I was installed as chief operator of the state-of-the-art electric Gestetner with instructions to produce from the skins, which constantly appeared, perfect copies on foolscap duplicating paper, and ultra-perfect copies, with interleaved blotting paper, on Bland, Welch letterheads. Anything due for signature by Reg Cheesman, the Managing Director, or Messrs Martin and Chandler, his fellow directors, was to be spotless. I learnt the lesson well. On paper, quality production was everything and it's a lesson I've applied throughout the whole of the rest of my life. I dare not think of the hundreds of reams of paper I then, and since, have discarded in waste-paper baskets in the achievement of that goal but before I was seventeen the concept of excellence was very effectively drummed into me. 'Your reputation rests on your presentation.' That can never, of course, be the whole story. Integrity and quality must lie behind it or the whole thing is no more than a glossy sham.

Outside the office, I walked the streets and alleyways of the old City (or what was left of it after the Luftwaffe had left their calling cards in 1940 and 1941). Bomb sites were still everywhere in 1949, though there were far less in that part of the City than there were around and to the north of St Paul's Cathedral. The offices on my daily beat were almost all within the eastern half of the old Roman walls (none of which were visible), bounded on the west by the Mansion House and Cannon Street station. I soon got to know it intimately and worked out half a dozen routes to vary the monotony. I poked my nose into almost all the churches as I passed, mostly Wren's post-Fire masterpieces, and got acquainted, superficially at least, with over twelve of them. I saw, but didn't enter, the old pubs and chop-houses, the former because I was teetotal, and the latter because I couldn't afford them. I vowed that one day I would lunch at the George and Vulture but, inexplicably, I never have.

Hugh and John and the junior typists generally went to the cellar cafes and cheap restaurants for lunch but I much preferred to go early, at noon, into Allmans, a high-quality sandwich bar in Cullum Street, and, perched on a barstool in the non-alcoholic (and quieter) section, ate sandwiches and listened to the conversation of my elders. Women never went there but the brokers did and, going early, I watched Mr Bowman, a fat, thick-lipped, middle-European entrepreneur, consuming rollmops, smoked salmon, frankfurters and other delicacies unknown to me while I settled for ham, beef, pork and sausages. Among other interests, he was into stamp-dealing and I still possess a *tête-bêche* first-day airmail cover from Switzerland, addressed to him. Mesmerised by his reptilian consumption, I experienced my first seduction and have never regretted losing my culinary virginity to a rollmop and a frankfurter in quick succession. Harry, the little Cockney behind the bar, cut and stuffed (and I mean stuffed) superb fish, meat, fowl and cheese into the sandwiches, talking throughout, taking the money and tips and exuding the kind of not-quite-servile presence that City businessmen (and one wide-eyed office boy) affect to enjoy.

My first week's work ended, I set off on the Friday, straight from the office, in my 'clurk's' suit and burning with blisters from a too-new pair of shoes, to a girls' school in Bromley. Everything about me felt wrong for a sixth form social but the invitation had come from a big, dumb, bovine blond, who was the daughter of one of my mother's friends. I had been virtually dragooned into accepting, for solely diplomatic reasons, and only did so after an explicit assurance that there would be 'hardly any dancing' and that office clothes would be absolutely satisfactory. I couldn't dance and, as a Crusader, was forewarned that it wasn't a proper leisure activity for a Christian. Having obtained the necessary guarantees from Miss Dumbelle, I presented myself, prepared to be a courteous escort. To my consternation, I, alone, wore a suit and the evening was filled with non-stop dancing. My feet were agony and I 'sat out' most of it, indulging in desultory conversation and urging the lady to enjoy herself with someone else. I lacked, to my shame, any capacity for smooth or titillating small talk and we departed promptly at the end. We travelled from Bromley South to Petts Wood where good manners demanded that I walk her home. She lived three-quarters of a mile from the station, all of which I stumbled with burning blisters. It wasn't exactly the romantic, or passionate, encounter of her dreams and there wasn't the remotest chance of my providing the kisses she was evidently expecting. We said good night in the most minimal manner and I faced a final, mile-long, walk home.

'Hello, dear, did you enjoy yourself?' enquired my mother, clearly anxious for material for a gossipy phone-call to her friend next morning. History has not recorded my reply, but, to my considerable relief, Miss Blondie didn't come near me for the next six months. Soon after, my mother got a good gossip with all her other friends when Dumbelle's older sister was spied, coming out of a West End hotel at breakfast time, with a very well-set-up older married man. A divorce followed the affair, which kept the Petts Wood telephones in business for weeks.

The day's work in an insurance brokers' office is not calculated to provide much variety or excitement. Brokers may spend a good deal of time in the Room at Lloyds, chatting up syndicate underwriters and persuading them to initial 'slips' for their percentage of the risk or repeating the performance in the underwriting rooms of the big insurance companies. Allen, my uncle, did it all his working life, while Dad, from a clerk's desk in the Commercial Union across the road in Lime Street, watched it happening day by day. It gave Allen a very comfortable life-style and a beautiful house on the north Downs with panoramic views, while Dad's end of the process provided just enough for an adequate semi but no car. It was soon clear to me that, unless I was given an early taste of the broker's life, before I left to do my National Service, a suburban clerk's existence was stretching out before me. Bland, Welch encouraged, and paid for, its juniors to do courses in readiness for the Associate and Fellowship exams of the Insurance Institute but I found the material uninspiring and produced only a moderate result at the end of the first year. Despite an early promise that I would get 'Room' experience, it never came.

The company, as do most of its kind, provided its staff with a number of social activities throughout the year. I joined the firm's cricket team and did quite well but it was obviously not well received when, in both 1949 and 1950, I politely declined the big annual match and party at Reg Cheesman's country estate, near East Horsley, on the grounds that I didn't play Sunday cricket and wouldn't miss either church or Crusaders because of regular commitments there. Such an attitude was, it was hinted, no way to get on in the world of insurance and certainly not in Bland, Welch and Co. Ltd. I put in an appearance at the annual dinner and dance, a splendid affair, at the Great Eastern Hotel, but since I didn't dance and (like most of the plebs) didn't wear a dinner jacket, it didn't add much to my sagging credit rating. I hadn't tasted roast goose before – it was a Christmas party – and enjoyed it very much, together with Bomber Gilbert's highly exhibitionist xylophone-playing but, yet again, the dancing bit left me out in the cold.

During my lunch hours, after sandwiches at Allmans, I went, for some weeks, to the weekly open-air meeting on Tower Hill conducted by Donald, later Lord, Soper. That ebullient and swashbuckling Methodist minister was a past master at the art of quick-fire repartee, a pacifist and Socialist who wielded a rapier, skewering opponent after opponent. His liberal theology was wedded to his militant Socialism and the City's mix of Conservative gents and atheist lightermen, plus a sprinkling of heckling layabouts, provided a fast-moving entertainment in the Hyde Park Corner manner. I admired his skill, rejected his theology and politics, and seriously questioned whether wounding opponents, and winning arguments with devastating one-liners, would ever actually commend the gospel of Jesus Christ. Did men become disciples by being made to look fools, I wondered? The last time I heard Soper, in a 1980s debate in the House of Lords, he was still totally confrontational, aggressively dogmatising about facts (yes, facts, not ideas) which I knew to be demonstrably erroneous. I wasn't impressed.

On other occasions I would walk over to London Bridge and watch the ships unloading in the pool of London. One day I climbed the Monument in Fish Street Hill, recalling the site of the baker's shop in which the Great Fire of 1666 started. In 1949 it was still, by City standards, a tall building. Now it's a mere matchstick.

My most regular occupation was to sit in Foster's stamp shop in Cullum Street and talk with Foster, or his customers, about philately. He was a wild-looking eccentric, with white hair, not unlike Michael Foot to look at. He taught me an immense amount about stamps and encouraged me in building up both a good general collection and, my pride and joy, an extensive Swiss album. When, later, I got married, he bought all but the Swiss off me to help me pay for the nuptials. I couldn't bring myself to sell him the 800 stamps from Switzerland, including the very valuable post-war Pax Hominibus set, and, nearly fifty years later, I still have them.

Dad, also, in those years, took a real interest in my stamps and together we worked hard to build them up. We joined the local stamp club in Orpington and regularly attended its meetings in Green Street Green. It was our joint interest in stamps that slowly restored our relationship, largely fractured by his wartime absence in the army. I deeply appreciated the time and trouble he spent, patiently rebuilding the link between father and son. I never forgot it and we soon put the troubled years behind us.

Cricket remained a major interest and I decided to pay the not inconsiderable fee to enable me to attend the Sandham, Strudwick, and Gover cricket school in East Hill, Wandsworth. Andy Sandham who, in his day, had made the highest score, 325, by a batsman in test cricket was now quite elderly, a little man of few words. He took me into the indoor nets at Wandsworth and in five minutes, or less, corrected a fundamental flaw in my batting technique which no-one at Eltham had ever thought to mention. He then showed me how to drive more effectively than I had ever done before, but, try as he might, he couldn't get me to time a late cut! The short-term result of the changes was two of the worst seasons I ever had. By the third year, everything was falling into place and the runs started to come.

While Sandham coached the batsmen, Alf Gover, Surrey and England fast bowler, whom I had seen at Lords earlier, was putting young bowlers through their paces. The best of these, whose bowling I faced a few times, was Alan Moss, a young Middlesex colt who eventually opened the bowling for England. He was one of seven young men against whom I played in those years who were to gain England caps, or, in the case of the seventh, become a test umpire. The very first, Mickie Stewart, was, a few years ago, the England manager. I also enjoyed the experience of watching the Kent versus Surrey match at Blackheath, sitting in a deckchair next to Alec and Eric Bedser the redoubtable Surrey twins. To be in touching range of Alec, who had collected, quite often, the unique scalp of Don Bradman, was awesome!

To ensure that I was adequately equipped for all this activity, Dad and I had been to Slazengers, a famous City sports firm, and purchased a fine cricket bag, a 'Don Bradman' cricket bat, and a protective box for my person, of a size and padding that I never saw matched, before or since. My prospects of ultimately siring a future England cricketer were safe from then onwards. With lads like Alan Moss around in the nets such caution was absolutely justified. My Don Bradman bat will re-enter this story, half a lifetime on, in a context where not even a well-padded box could have saved the day.

That same summer, my old childhood friend David Mitchell, long a pupil at Dulwich College, was in his last year and found himself keeping wicket for the school. One day we were talking and he bubbled over with excitement. 'Yesterday', he said, 'we were playing Tonbridge and I kept wicket behind some kid in short trousers who took a hundred off us. I reckon he could one day play for England.' The small boy's name was, as you might have guessed, Colin Cowdrey.

Out of office hours and at weekends, my life was frenetically busy. Four evenings in every week I cycled a round trip of seven miles, up and down hill, to Christ Church, Orpington, right on the edge of the so-called Green Belt. On Wednesdays and Fridays, I got back from town, gulped down supper in half an hour and set off, come wind, come rain. Wednesday was the church Bible study and prayer meeting and Friday was the choir practice. Now a bass, I sang with various members of a family called Baughen, including the youngest, Michael, who has remained a close and lifelong friend and who became Bishop of Chester. A younger treble, Michael Blackley, was in due course to be a Vicar Choral at St Paul's Cathedral, retiring just before I became a canon there in 1991.

On Saturday I was an enthusiastic member of the young people's fellowship, and served on its committee, returning home at a very late hour, having paused at the road junctions to have ongoing theological discussions with two YPF girls as, one by one, our paths diverged. And by theological discussions, I mean just that! They were the first eighteen-year-old girls with whom I had intellectually stimulating friendships, so it could be done. Finally, on Sundays, there was the 6.30 evening service and sermon, with a repeat performance with the same girls on the road home.

More important than the girls, Jean Stafford and Jean Oswald, were four men whose combined influence inspired and shaped me for the crucial years between 1947 and 1951. The youngest, aged twenty-one, was Jean Stafford's older brother. Roy Stafford, a muscular rugby three-quarter and quarter miler was to spend most of his life in Kenya as an Anglican missionary, translating the Bible. A big, laughing, stimulating man, he was unknowingly a role model for me as a Christian. Then there was the quieter, fair-haired, twenty-four-year-old, theological student, Bob Beak, who had come out of the RAF where he had served in Burma at the end of the war. He had a moustache, a motorbike, and a very relaxed sense of humour. He too, was equally important, but quite different in style. He seemed to know a lot about theology and I listened intently. The third man, a good deal older, probably in his late thirties, was Guy Gowing-Scopes. Unmarried, he was one of the Crusader leaders, warm, always gently smiling, the kind of bachelor boys instinctively liked and with whom they felt safe. Bob was also a Crusader leader and Roy assisted them when he was home from college. Together with the amusing but eccentric Jack Belcher, they were my heroes, the kind of Christians I admired and aspired to emulate.

Fourth, and altogether a different character, was the vicar of Christ Church, Herbert Taylor. A delightful, big, but gentle bachelor, very much 'Mr' Taylor in those days, he looked like a large St Bernard dog with deep jowls and a formal manner that successfully concealed a twinkle in his eye. Never a man who could easily relax with the boys, he walked into church with a solemn dignity, conducted services with rarely a smile, and preached fairly predictable devotional sermons usually structured with three-point alliteration in the time-honoured manner of Anglican Evangelical clergymen of that and earlier eras. Herbert was undoubtedly an Evangelical of truest blue but he was a very proper Anglican and a model exemplar of a canon, which in due course he became.

These four, Roy, Bob, Guy and Herbert, gave me the initial framework within which both my life and my Christian convictions were to take root. Their teaching was plain, unexciting, and far from profound, but biblical in origin and persuasive in influence. There was very little speculative theology, hardly anything about church, ministry or sacraments, but more than enough for a teenager to apply to himself in terms of faith and behaviour. As regards the latter, their teaching and practice was, common among

Evangelicals in those days, firmly Puritan and mostly negative. I was imbued with a long list of things that Christians didn't do, high among which were dancing, drinking, smoking, the cinema and the theatre. Sex was rarely mentioned and, since all four were bachelors at the time, not obviously a matter engaging their attention, though Bob did succumb to an engagement which, painfully, didn't last.

Saturday nights at the Christ Church YPF were not exactly exciting affairs. Apart from a half-hour religious epilogue, it was mostly table tennis. Still they provided me with an atmosphere where it was possible to mix with boys and girls of my own age and, after years of hard brainwork at a single-sex school, that was a real plus factor.

Most of it was pleasant, innocent fun and, had it not been for Goggle-eyes, there would have been no tensions of any kind. Goggle-eyes was nearly eighteen, an athletic girl with protruding eyes and glasses, who had obviously decided that I was Catch of the Year. She didn't bother to tell me of this fact but, instead, decided to invite me to her coming birthday party. 'All the YPF will be there,' she cooed, 'so it should be fun.' Suspecting nothing, I accepted. As week followed week, a number of them, it seemed, were not after all going to be free and, finally, on the Saturday afternoon in question, I arrived at her house to be greeted at the door by her mother, hatted and coated, saying, 'Enjoy yourselves, I've got to go out.' The fly had landed in the spider's web and Goggle-eyes apologised that, sadly, no-one else had been able to come. 'What shall we do?' she enquired, in wide-eyed innocence. I leapt at the only safe option, seeing two table-tennis bats and a ball on the nearby dining room table, with 'How about ping-pong?' 'Oh, all right,' she said and we played game after game after game. At least we were eight feet apart. Finally, she claimed, it was time to eat. She dragged out all the fizz, cake and ice cream and sat me down in an armchair. Then, seated on the floor propped against my legs, she plied me with food and fond stares. I solidly munched and swallowed till bursting point, when she played her ace. '*Now*, what shall we do?' she enquired with sofa-eyes (no half-respectable girl in those days could risk bedroom-eyes), sure that my options had finally been reduced to one. 'Hey,' I said, 'the YPF are having a tennis evening at Locksbottom. Why don't we go?' So we did. Not one word did Goggle-eyes say to me throughout the remaining year prior to my call-up into the army. 'Well,' I thought, 'no girl's going to try that kind of thing on me.' No-one else did.

A month or so before the Mata Hari incident, I faced up to a challenge which I would have done almost anything to avoid. The vicar and church council had planned a mission to the parish which involved an attempt to visit every house. The whole congregation was invited to join the team of visitors and the offer was open to everyone of seventeen and over. The mission started on a Monday and my seventeenth birthday was on the Sunday! I longed to duck it but the pressure was inescapable. In retrospect I think it was very foolish of the church to send out such striplings, on their own, to visit house-to-house but that was the requirement. The fateful Monday came and off I set to win the world for Christ. Then disaster struck. At the first house, I rang the bell. The door opened. A dog leapt out, tore a hole in my trousers and crouched snarling ferociously. The owner politely enquired as to my business, hardly bothering to apologise for the damage to my clothing, let alone my morale. The gospel of Christ didn't get much of a look in and I retreated in considerable shock. I never was to be much good at doorknocking, even as a vicar, and I know, to this day, exactly why!

I continued to attend Crusaders, though its venue moved at least twice. The first move was to a vast semi-derelict Victorian house in Tower Road, Orpington. It was anything but an ideal venue and I, unwittingly, caused our next move, when, one Sunday afternoon, unable to get in, I forced a window. Considering the state of the place I was hardly doing much harm, but the owners rejected the plea and kicked us out. We moved to a much more congenial site, a prep school in Petts Wood. I was rewarded for my burglarious entry by being placed in charge of sales of the *Crusader* magazine. I kept methodical paperwork, another consequence of the Bland, Welch 'quality control' expectations, and added a second dimension to my *modus operandi* which was to stand me in good stead thereafter. My one embarrassing failure was in the Crusaders' Union national athletics finals at Motspur Park. Orpington were in the lead at the end of the four by a hundred yards relay's third leg and the baton reached me for the final anchor leg. I came second. I still have the little medallion but it wasn't the one we wanted. One up to humility and it was all my fault.

One night that winter, I was returning home in a thick fog (they didn't really stop until the late 1950s) and turned into the top end of Silverdale Road. A female voice rang out, evidently needing help. A young woman appeared through the fog and enquired in some incoherent and foreign tongue for something. What, I couldn't tell but one phrase was being constantly repeated. I struggled with it and finally disentangled some English syllables. 'Birchwood Road?' I enquired hesitantly. 'Si, si,' said the girl. Even I knew that had to be Italian. She was obviously hopelessly lost, half a mile away from Birchwood Road, and the thought of trying to explain how she could get there in a 'pea-souper' was quite beyond my abilities. 'Parlez-vous français?' I volunteered (well, I had got 'Good' in my French Oral, hadn't I?) and she at once replied, 'Un mot, peut-être, deux mots.' It wasn't a lot to go on, since I only knew one Italian word, 'si', and we'd tried that already. 'Sprechen sie Deutsch?' she added. 'No, er, *nein*,' I replied. 'Venez avec moi,' I suggested tentatively and turned for home, two hundred yards away.

I left her at the front gate with a peremptory 'Attendez-vous ici,' and wandered in through the kitchen door. 'I'm taking an Italian girl to Birchwood Road,' I said, leaving my parents with open-mouthed amazement as I disappeared. It wasn't all that long since we'd been at war with Italy and I had studiously avoided any fraternising with Italian prisoners of war who had worked on a nearby farm in the immediate post-war years. Mum and Dad were, as they say, gobsmacked at this unpredictable son's behaviour.

It was only a ten-minute walk, even in thick fog. She talked in French, German and Italian with the very occasional word of English. Her French was as fractured as mine was so we ignored all the nuances of grammar and syntax. In those brief moments we discovered each others' names, those of our families, her age and mine, her home town (Milano), and what she was doing in Petts Wood. She was an au pair. When I deposited her at the Birchwood Road house (ironically, almost next door to De Gaulle's brief staging-point all those years before), we gabbled our good-byes and she walked out of my life. But I had been taught a powerful lesson. If you don't share a language, at least try anything, and use your hands – not on the girl but on the ideas. It has always stood me in good stead since that night.

The year progressed and National Service loomed ahead. I knew nothing about the services and was, like most of my generation, not overpleased about the need to put on uniform. Dad had, like all old soldiers, passed on horror stories about barrack rooms and drill sergeants, and the prospect was far from rosy. Still, it was only going to be eighteen months. That was manageable. True, relationships between our lot and the Russians were frigid. The Berlin airlift wasn't long over and now, with only a few weeks to go, Korea was plunged into war. The Labour government immediately jacked up the eighteen months to two years.

Bland, Welch wished me well, and Bomber assured me that the Army would soon knock all the Christian rubbish out of me. 'Don't miss out on the women,' he leered, and I walked out of the office absolutely sure of one thing. I knew I wasn't going back to marine insurance in any capacity. Where my future lay, I had no idea, but, Don Camillo-like, I told the Lord that he had two years in which to make up his mind and I assumed that by the end he would have communicated this decision to me. With that settled, I thought no more about it. My posting arrived. 'Report to 67th Selection Regiment, Royal Artillery, Park Hall Camp, Oswestry, by 5 p.m. on Thursday, 7th September, 1950.'

The Day of Reckoning arrived. Mum came up to see me off from Paddington Station. I produced my travel warrant and was directed to the appropriate platform for the express for Birkenhead, via Shrewsbury. 'Change at Gobowen,' said the ticket collector. Mum and I wandered a little disconsolately down the platform. I, on the advice of my Christian friends, was wearing my Crusader badge in my lapel. It was an excellent idea. A rather good-looking well-scrubbed, obviously public school youth, was standing near an open carriage door, eyeing me speculatively. He had a Scripture Union badge (gold lamp on a green background) in his lapel. 'Are you going to Oswestry? So am I. Shall we travel together?' Mum looked relieved. She waved as the train pulled out and I got on with the business of introductions. His name was David Maybury. He had just left Sherborne School. He had often been to 'Iwerne'. (What on earth was that? I didn't even know how to spell it.) We decided that we were clearly fellow-Christians and that, metaphorically, we had better cling together in the coming storm. In due course, years later, he was an usher at my wedding and was ordained a year after me.

At Gobowen, we, and scores of other young men, descended from the train, climbed into army lorries and arrived at the camp, where we were, quite politely, told to form three ranks and await instructions. A sergeant arrived. 'Who plays rugby football?' he bellowed. Dad had firmly instructed me never to volunteer for anything. I hesitated, but decided, in common with about twenty-five others, that I did (not very well, mind you, but I did, didn't I?). So we all stepped out and were marched off to a barrack room. Then the penny dropped. This was the army's diabolical, secret plan to sort out the public school boys from the rest!

That night, three of us, David, me and an owlish bespectacled youth named Sefton Elsdale, quietly knelt by our beds, in the manner urged upon us by our Evangelical mentors, and awaited a volley of boots, obscenities and jeers. No-one offered the slightest response and, relieved, we climbed in and went to sleep. We had, at least, nailed our colours to the mast.

Each squad was, at intervals, detailed to perform 'fatigues' which included not only 'spud-bashing' with a machine but also, and far worse, washing up the pans and dixies which had been used in the cookhouse for food preparation. These were covered in thick, congealed and filthy fat and the washing-up water was, at best, tepid. After that, I never again in my time as an 'other rank' ate a single breakfast. The army regarded such asceticism as a chargeable offence but I was never caught. As to the 'ablutions', as the wash-house and its adjacent lavatories were described, they were probably no worse than those to be found in any institution of the time but the latter encouraged a cavalier attitude towards self-inflicted constipation.

Those of us chosen to attend a WOSB (War Office Selection Board) were sent off to Barton Stacey, near Andover, in Hampshire, where our capacity to lead men was put to the test. We tried our skill at bridging unbridgeable ponds with short poles and rope; we were interviewed as to which person in the squad should get the only decent accommodation when fighting a war (the officer of course!) though I did allow my Christian convictions to assert themselves by saying, 'Unless there is a desperately wounded man needing shelter and warmth.' That answer produced a slightly embarrassed grunt of seeming disapproval from the major conducting the interview but it wasn't enough to fail me on the spot. Finally, came the question and answer which, I suspect, assured me of my entry into the Officer Cadet school. 'What are you hoping to do in the army', asked the major, 'if you aren't selected for a commission?' 'That', I said, with my humility straining at the leash, 'is not a possibility I have ever even considered.' Well, regimental pride and all that. Humility is a word the army simply can't spell. 'You've passed,' they told me.

One month later, awaiting our white 'gorget' patches on our collars, I and the subalterns-to-be set off for Mons Officer Cadet School in Aldershot. Towering over that establishment was Regimental Sergeant-Major Brittain, the army's most famous parade-ground voice. It was said that you could hear him a mile away. Six foot five and weighing about twenty stone he was a fearsomely imposing figure, the epitome of the Guards' sergeant-major. I don't even faintly remember the face or name of the Commandant but Brittain is etched into the memory for life. Our own squad was drilled by a staff sergeant from the Rifle Brigade, one of those light infantry characters who made you march at about 140 paces to the minute. If we thought the 'drill-and-bull' at Oswestry was exhausting we were soon shown what real, crack, infantry behaviour was all about in those first weeks at Mons. And infantry it was. Although we were all gunners or cavalrymen, it was required for us, soldiers who were 'right of the line', that we could outmarch and outdrill the 'poor bloody infantry' who did their cadet training at Eaton Hall, outside Chester, far away from Aldershot.

It certainly had the right effect on me. The Guards' standards we were taught produced tremendous *esprit de corps* and for a few weeks I seriously considered applying for a transfer to Sandhurst and a regular commission. In the event, I decided to wait until I had actually been an officer for a bit and it was a very wise decision. A year later and I wouldn't have given the idea two consecutive thoughts.

Moreover, there was an unexpected setback ahead. We spent a damp night trailing around the woods and gorse to the west of Aldershot, a 'night exercise'. None of us got much sleep but we did get our first weekend leave and I went home via the Royal Albert Hall, where Tom Rees, Britain's best-known evangelist was conducting a large meeting. The place was packed, I was up 'in the gods', and I promptly fell asleep. I've never met anyone else who fell asleep in such a meeting (a bit like a Billy Graham crusade) but before the weekend was over I was home in bed with heavy flu. The family doctor wouldn't let me return for about five days and when I did, instead of sympathy, I was marched in front of the Commandant, torn off a massive strip, and threatened with RTU (return to unit), the most terrifying prospect for any officer cadet. Eventually, after leaving me in a state of shock, and anger, at such insensitive treatment, I was 'relegated' which meant a repeat performance of the exhausting first six weeks. Humiliation, if not humility.

I joined the new squad as an 'old-sweat', who knew the ropes, and was put in charge. In due course, two others became 'Under Officers', but I was always in the top five and that was to have considerable consequences. In E Troop we discovered the secrets of Bofors 40 mm. light anti-aircraft guns and moved on to 3.7 'heavies', the guns which had defended London during the Blitz ten years earlier. Not being at all technically or mechanically minded I had a hard struggle to understand how these pieces of machinery worked but, determined not to fall at the last fence, I reduced it all to a written logical sequence, learned that, and passed the necessary exams.

Our battery commander was a Major John Singleton. I didn't see him after Mons until, on the fiftieth anniversary of VE Day, 7 May 1995, I recognised him in St Paul's Cathedral. Not bad after 44 years!

In the bed next to me at this time was a pleasant, slightly cynical young man, by the name of Barry Ingham. We never met again but he became an actor and appeared regularly, via television, in our home in one of the BBC's series on the Caesars. He played Sejanus, who was not the most pleasing of men. I also, at well past midnight on a dark night's guard duty in Tournai barracks (next to Mons), met a cavalry cadet whose name was John Lang. He later became the BBC's Head of Religious Broadcasting and Dean of Lichfield. It's not often you can say, 'We met in the guardroom at Aldershot.'

Halfway between Mons and Tournai was a small hill with a tree-lined road and an isolated, ugly, army brick 'cottage'. One day, while marching past, between lectures, a glimpse to our right showed what looked like a stranded barrage-balloon in the garden. In a voluminous pair of army trousers and braces was the rear-end of RSM Brittain (whose house it was), bending over gardening, while a tiny woman stood beside him laying down the law with great vehemence. Our staff sergeant was a shrewd man. 'Squad,' he bellowed, 'double march! Leff, ri, lef, ri, lef, ri, lef,' and the squad, convulsed with laughter, rocketed up the hill and out of the danger zone.

The night before our pass-out parade we all jammed into the upstairs room of a pub in Aldershot town centre for a farewell dinner. Most of us would never meet again and those going to Korea might never see England again. It dragged on into a very alcoholic event and as the only non-drinker there I began to worry about what state the squad would be in for the parade. Eventually the party broke up and sixteen of us got into, or onto, our troop commander's open tourer. I was hanging half over the back, two layers down, with one leg in danger of amputation. Major Shearme drove us back to Mons in relative safety until the turn-off into the long straight approach road by the sports stadium. His sense of direction wavered a little and the car's progress became serpentine. We were doing about thirty-five m.p.h. when there was a cry of 'man overboard'. Shearme clearly didn't hear until we reached the camp buildings, three hundred yards ahead. Sobered slightly, we unloaded ourselves, anxious to learn of the fate of the depth charge we had fired. Then, out of the darkness, staggered the victim, a Scotsman, shaking his head ruefully and groaning, 'What happened?' No bones were broken. He would survive.

Next morning we were duly commissioned in a ceremony attempting to copy the Sandhurst ritual of slow marching in threes up the steps. The inspecting officer was, in fact, the Sandhurst commandant, Major General Kit Dawnay, one of Montgomery's blue-eyed-boys, and following the normal pattern he stopped occasionally to ask some luckless cadet a question. He paused when he reached me (and I have a photo to prove it) and enquired in a high-pitched drawl, 'Whar you gaying?' 'West Africa, Sir,' I replied. 'You'll like that,' he responded, and passed on. Would I? The White Man's Grave? Well, I had only myself to blame if I didn't.

Our squad were offered the widest range of jobs of any from Mons in the previous two years. Malta, Gibraltar, the Canal Zone, East Africa, West Africa, Hong Kong, Northern Ireland (a quiet backwater in those days) and Germany, plus all the dreary military towns in England. When the list came though I looked at it and did some quick calculations. Peter and John, the Under Officers, both wanted Malta, the so-called plum posting. I was likely to be fourth or fifth in seniority so provided I avoided these I should get my choice quite easily. If the King, in the year 1951, was willing to pay me to travel, travel I would. We all had three choices, of which one must be in the UK. I picked up my pen. East Africa; West Africa; Northern Ireland. In due course East Africa was withdrawn (thus safely protecting me from the Mau Mau uprising) and I was told to prepare for a heavy anti-aircraft battery in Sierra Leone. 'You'll need tropical kit, there's an allowance, and you'll get a thirty per cent bonus for West Africa.' They didn't call it danger-money but disease had been rife there for centuries. 'You've got to report to Woolwich after you're commissioned.

Then you'll get twenty-one days embarkation leave after which you return to Woolwich and when there's a plane seat free you'll fly.'

I see from the *London Gazette* that my commission was to date from 26 May 1951 and that I hereby relinquished 22407340 in favour of 416679. No-one ever forgets his army number and I still recall both of mine.

While on leave I managed to get half-a-dozen games of cricket and averaged over forty including my then highest score of sixty-five. On my return to Woolwich there was no sign of a flying date. I was allocated an upper room on the east side of the south face of the great Georgian facade and told to appear at breakfast and dinner. I only performed one duty in the three weeks. That was when I was deputed to take a totally unknown soldier to the magistrates' court in Kingston and, as the adjutant put it, 'give him a good character'. The magistrates were far from pleased when I said that I had been sent to do just this but that I had never seen him before that morning and was merely a messenger boy. One huffed and puffed at me about it. 'Don't blame me,' I said, 'I'm merely obeying orders.'

With nothing else to do, I borrowed Gerry's Surrey member-ship card and went to the Oval to see all three days of Surrey ver-sus Gloucestershire, the only time in my life when I've watched the whole of a county cricket match from start to finish. I can't re-member who won but I do vividly recall Tom Graveney and George Emmett scoring 140 runs in little over an hour on the final day with a superb display of class batting. None of your slog 'em for six stuff. It was wrists and subtlety all the way.

I also used the opportunity to spend an afternoon at the Festi-val of Britain on the South Bank close to Waterloo station. The only remaining building is the Royal Festival Hall but, at the time, the most visible symbol was the vertical Skylon, a hanging needlelike object which dominated the exhibition area. The Festi-val was intended to assure the weary British that despite a terrible war and its austere aftermath a new science-and-technology-dominated-and-enriched society was just round the corner.

Twice during my brief stay at Woolwich I was present at a

dinner night in the superbly Victorian red plush splendour of the magnificent Officers' Mess. The silver displayed on the tables was breathtaking, the 'yard-and-a-halfer' playing the *Posthorn Gallop* was a bravura display, and everything formed an awe-inspiring introduction, for a young man from an ordinary suburban home, to the gloss and glitter of the old army. Even the morning breakfasts with dozens of men in uniform sitting eating toast and marmalade at a host of solitary tables, silent behind their copies of *The Times*, was no caricature, but the actual reality. Woe betide a subaltern who opened his mouth at that sacred gathering.

At last, in the first week of July 1951, my embarkation date was settled. Not, to be sure the old ritual of travel by ship. Most civilians, especially colonial service types, were still using Elder Dempster's *Accra* and *Apapa*, from England to Takoradi. Not us. We were to go on a two-engined Viking from the military airstrip at Bovingdon, near Watford, at 180 m.p.h., with two overnight stops, en route to Accra, our destination in the Gold Coast. Yes, at the last minute my posting had been changed. Not Freetown, in Sierra Leone, but Accra, capital city of what would one day be Ghana. Not 3.7 heavy ack-ack but 40 mm. Bofors guns. The Eighth Independent Light Anti-Aircraft Troop of six guns, the only unit of its size in the whole British army. It was attached to the Second Light Battery of 3.7 Howitzers, the old Kipling 'screwguns' (modernised) from North-West Frontier days. Ours were not loaded on mules (or even on soldiers' heads, as they once were) but towed behind jeeps.

One morning I decided that I ought to pay my last respects to Bland, Welch before setting off for darkest Africa. I spent an unmemorable hour in the office before finally seeking out Bomber. 'So, Michael,' he said, 'you've learnt the truth about life at last? Drinking, smoking, women?' 'No, Bomber,' I answered quietly. 'You mean you're still not drinking and smoking?' 'No, Bomber.' 'You haven't taken any women to bed?' 'No, Bomber.' 'Well, I can see you're not lying, boy.' 'No, Bomber.' Puzzled, the great boozer, wencher and fighter, looked hard at me. 'Michael boy, I take off my hat to you. You've got guts.' My humility quotient plunged yet again. 'Good-bye, Bomber. I don't think we'll meet again.' We never have.

I collected my tropical kit from Humphreys and Crookes, military tailors of Suffolk Street, Pall Mall (and appropriately expensive they were, too) and set off with Mum and Dad on my last walk round Piccadilly and Green Park. An idea had crossed my mind. Being in battledress, with Sam Browne belt and service dress cap, I was unmistakably an officer. Slowly we drew nearer and nearer, crossed the road at the foot of Constitution Hill and turned right, ready to walk over the road to the great Queen Victoria statue facing Buckingham Palace. In those days the guard was mounted by their sentry boxes, outside the Palace railings. Suddenly, I heard the expected sound. It was a rifle butt and boot crashing into the pavement in readiness for the next two movements. 'What was that?' said Mum in her innocence. 'Oh,' I said dismissively, 'it's just the sentries saluting me.' Dad grinned, I waved an appropriately casual salute, and we proceeded on our way down the Mall. Humility's all well and good, but you don't miss that chance when you're nineteen and Second Lieutenant Saward. It would never happen again.

We said our fond farewells and at the crack of dawn our unpressurised Viking flew off on the first leg of its journey. At a speed of 180 m.p.h. a journey of 4000 miles takes forever. We touched down for an hour at Bordeaux, then set off again, over the Pyrenees, heading for Gibraltar. Flying low over the mountains was extremely unpleasant and we bumped about forcing many of us, me included, to put the heavy duty brown paper bags to good service. The descent produced earache and flying across the bay of Algeciras at fifty feet above the sea into Gibraltar's frightening airstrip (miss the sea and you hit the base of the rock) was enough to spoil the evening. We were staying at the Rock hotel, much the classiest in those days, but reveille was scheduled for 2 a.m. so I collapsed into bed.

Early next morning we climbed over the Sahara Atlas mountains and flew on to the first oasis of El Aoulef. There in the middle of nowhere, the 'airport' was a mudbrick hut with a petrol pump. It took an hour to refuel (hand-pumping!) and when we climbed back in we had a quick glimpse of what a crematorium oven must feel like to a coffin. We took off down a sand-and-grit runway – just flat desert – and the temperature slowly descended as we went up. At about four thousand feet we crossed the Sahara all the way to Kano in Nigeria, watching out for anything that moved below. Not a lot did.

The Kano airport hotel was all bungalow and we were treated to the most stupendous tropical storm. It was the most memorable welcome Africa could have offered and we had no doubt left that we were well and truly in the tropics.

Next day, after two short stops at Kaduna and Lagos, we reached Accra where I was met by a Land-Rover, taken to the camp two miles away, right below the flight path, and settled into my *giddah*, which, I was told, was Hausa for a mud hut, which is exactly what it was. Circular, one-roomed, painted black at the base and white above, it had a wooden-slatted roof (no ceiling), two windows (no glass, but diamond-gridded iron shutters), and a wooden door. The furniture was an iron bedstead, a table, a wooden-chair, a wash bowl, a mirror and a rush mat to cover the baked-earth floor. The bed had one mattress, two sheets, and a boot-shaped hanging mosquito net. It was to be my home for the next year. A young black soldier in battered khaki trousers and a jungle hat stood by the door, naked from the waist upwards. 'This is Gunner Doe, your "boy",' I was told, and the 'boy' smiled politely. He had short black, crinkly hair, a very dark complexion, and a small moustache which hardly showed against his skin. I was left with him, to agree his duties, which seemed obvious, and minimal enough. 'Tell me a bit about yourself,' I said. 'Doe, sah, Emmanuel Doe. I am an Ewe (he pronounced it 'ehway', I noticed) and I come from Mafi Kpedzeglo. I am Presbyterian. My number is GC84091, sah.' I duly discovered that he was married and had a small son aged four but that he was still in single quarters, his family being at his home village near the border with Togoland, close to the River Volta. Emmanuel and I were to become good friends and the barrier of rank and race hardly existed from then on. We might be officer and gunner, European and African, master and servant, but, above all, we were brother

Christians and in colonial Africa in 1951 that was a rare relationship for white and black soldiers to enjoy. He and his little son were to go on writing to me on and off for almost twenty years from then on so there was nothing transient about it.

I walked out of my hut door, through the minimal ground-level veranda and surveyed the scene. The officers' compound was a slightly sloping piece of volcanic ground. There was little visible earth for the surface was laterite, a red, porous rocklike substance. Fall on that and you rip your flesh with wicked grazes. Lower down the slope was a tennis court, a bath-house, and a couple of officers' huts similar to my own. To my left were three more and, to my right, one in a corner. Seven huts in all. A hundred yards to the left a mud cookhouse and a small officers' mess building. Some of my fellow officers (all single men) had attempted to create small gardens by piling earth six inches high on top of the laterite and marking out borders with whitewashed rocks. Some plants grew but the chief vegetation was created by twelve-foot high border hedges, banana palms and pineapples. The one blaze of colour came from red flame-of-the-forest trees which relieved the overall tedium of laterite and scrawny bush grass.

Throughout the year the daytime temperature remained constant at around 80 °F and rain was largely confined to torrential downpours in May and June. This much the books had already told me. What they couldn't convey was the appalling humidity of the evening hours, when the slightest effort was to leave me soaked through with sweat. Still, the first glance that morning seemed promising enough.

Army life began with a parade at 6.30 a.m., work until 8, then an hour for breakfast, more work till 1 p.m. and the rest of the day free. The temperature was, naturally, very hot with over 90 per cent humidity, especially after dark, but we all wore sensible clothes, or lack of them, and life was very pleasant, certainly for the British officers and sergeants. The first black officers had just come from Sandhurst but, although I knew three, none was in our small battery.

The first week brought real anxieties, not to be later repeated. With three hundred black soldiers, one hundred of them in my ack-ack troop, I was faced with a sea of black faces, under green jungle hats, topping glistening black torsos, above denims, and, quite often, bare feet. How on earth would I distinguish any of them? I need not have worried. In a few weeks I knew almost all of them at sight.

A few days after my arrival an army padre turned up. He was Irish (aren't most army chaplains?), a Captain Paddy Rennison, and I enquired about a place of worship. 'Do you want to go to one or do you want to help in one?' was his unexpected reply. I assumed that the latter meant assist in a Sunday school class or something of the kind. 'I don't mind helping,' I said. 'Right,' he replied, 'you've got one. You can start on Sunday at Teshi. We need someone to take services there. The last chap's just gone home to England.' In less than three minutes I had acquired a wooden church building, a congregation of black soldiers and their families, a black sergeant-major who played the harmonium and translated into four dialects, and a lorry to get us the seven miles. I had also acquired the obligation to preach there each Sunday for the next twelve months. I was only two months past my nineteenth birthday. God help them – and me! 'Can you do it?' asked Rennison. 'Yes,' I replied, without hesitation, 'I can do it.' Bang goes that humility. But I could. And I did. And I've still got most of the sermons to prove that I did. And they weren't too bad for a beginner, all things considered.

The third anxiety concerned Kwame Nkrumah. That very week he was to be let out of prison, the country's most famous political dissident eventually to become its first president. Accra was alight with excitement and serious rioting was a distinct possibility. Both our battery and the neighbouring battalion of the Gold Coast Regiment, the front-line fighting troops of the Royal West African Frontier Force in Accra, were put on a two-hour security alert for my first Saturday. Every vehicle and gun was lined up, every soldier dressed and ready, waiting on the parade ground. The sun got higher, the temperature rose, emotions were keyed up, and sweat started trickling down our backs. I stood, at ease, with my fellow-officers, in front of our soldiers. And then it began. My head began to swim, my eyes started to glaze, the black-and-white horizontal line on the buildings looked like the Himalayas and I felt ready to keel over and collapse. You've probably seen it happen occasionally at the Trooping the Colour on television. A Guardsman? Perhaps. But never a Guards' officer. Now I might only be a Gunner officer, and a National Service one, but I had been trained by Guards' drill sergeant-majors and come what may I was staying vertical. To go down on my first Saturday parade, and in such circumstances, was utterly out of the question. I reeled, but I stuck it out, and ten minutes later, the Battery Commander called us to attention and fell us out. The emergency was over. I walked over to the Battery Captain, Harry Gibbings. 'Permission to fall out, Sir?' 'OK,' he said, then looked twice. 'Are you all right?' 'No,' I said, ran to my hut and collapsed. It never happened again and I realised the value of discipline and grit. I was learning.

I was going to need it. My two immediate seniors were Ken, a captain, and Ian, a lieutenant. Ken had been badly hurt by Israeli terrorists in Jerusalem, two years earlier and was not just hitting the bottle, he was demolishing the bar. He drank gin and whisky like water and was disintegrating before our eyes. Ian, on the other hand, was a raffish Errol Flynnlike young regular with a sports car and a libido geared to the more compliant of the young air hostesses arriving at the nearby airport. Even he overstepped the mark one morning when he appeared at breakfast brandishing a wisp of female underwear and announcing that he could not recall where, or from whom, he had acquired it last night. Harry Gibbings was the kind of decent English 'county' type for whom this was intolerably tasteless. 'Get out,' he roared, 'and don't come back till you have learned to behave like a gentleman!' Ian vanished. To Ken and Ian I was shackled, come what may.

A few weeks later we took the whole unit, field and ack-ack, out into the bush to a practice camp at Nungwa, twenty miles east of Accra. Right alongside the sea, we lived in tents for about a fortnight. Food was in short supply and one morning I watched as seven or eight gunners dropped everything, grabbed spades, and set off in howling pursuit of something scuttling through the rough grass. A spade flashed, a scream of delight followed, and one soldier emerged holding a nearly decapitated iguana. The creature was about three feet long and, I was assured, was delicious food. 'You de go cook him, Sah, and he be foine, foine chop.' Grinning from ear to ear, the gunner and his friends returned to their work, dumping the fly-covered lizard on the ground.

English officers, however hungry, did not go much on lizard so that evening three of us set out with shotguns to seek any large edible birds. One, the size of a pheasant, flew up from under my feet and I gave it both barrels at about ten feet range. I had never shot anything before but it dropped like a stone. Quite excited, I and my colleagues went to collect it. It wasn't there. We searched and searched in increasing circles but we never found it. Wherever it was, presumably it was condemned to a lingering death. That finished shooting as far as I was concerned. Fishing, I had dropped at the age of seven. Hunting, I was unlikely to start. There didn't seem to be much future for an army officer who didn't hunt, shoot or fish and, any way, having seen the British army shorn of its glossy Guards' traditions, I no longer had the slightest intention of becoming a regular.

Practice camp did, however, offer us artillery practice and we were permitted to train 'sub-calibre'. Since we had no available Bofors 40 mm. shells, we tied Bren guns to our Bofors gun barrels and fired that way at aerial targets. We were merrily blazing away when, to my horror, I saw the daily BOAC airliner fly straight into the line of fire. 'Stand fast!' I screamed, giving the most urgent command known to the Royal Artillery. No-one, it seemed, had contacted the Accra airport authorities to warn them of our firing hours and no-one had thought to tell me that the plane was on its way from Lagos. To my immense relief, the guns stopped instantly and since no-one on the plane seemed any the wiser we quietly forgot the incident. 'Canon-to-be shoots down airliner' would not have looked too good in the world's Press.

We returned to our camp in Accra and, before long, Ken went round the bend and we had to keep guard on him, in the military hospital without his knowing. This was both difficult and unpleasant. I hadn't joined the army to be a policeman or a spy and we each had to combine those roles until he was sent back to England. Ian, in due course, was posted elsewhere and suddenly I found myself for some months in sole charge of the troop. After a lot of argument with the Battery Commander, a moustachioed Hooray-Henry, I finally received Captain's pay. Since I had been doing a Captain's job, it only seemed fair.

Health was undoubtedly a problem for Europeans. Every member of our Mess was ill at least once, except for me. I suspect the reason, in my case, was sheer fear. I took my anti-malarial tablets religiously, I never drank doubtful water, I visited the wooden hut containing the celebrated 'thunder box' absolutely every day (a big life-style change, that), I avoided sun-bathing, I never walked anywhere, not even on the beach, without sandals and in thirteen months never went into the nearby sea once! It all seems neurotic today, but it certainly worked. My only problem was caused by prickly heat which caused a stinging rash in the groin. Finally I went to see the nearby army doctor. There was virtually no privacy and when I dragged up one leg of my Bermuda-type army shorts to show him the rash, a murmur went round all the African soldiers in the nearby waiting room. 'Der lieutenant, him der get der Mammy-palaver.' Since venereal disease seemed to be endemic there was little I could do to persuade these knowing primitive tribesmen (and most of our soldiers were just that, having walked eight hundred miles or more from the French territories near Timbuctoo, as it was, to join the British army). 'Nudge, nudge, wink, wink, know what I mean,' was transmitted in Hausa, Fulani, and a dozen northern Gold Coast dialects. I shrugged my shoulders at the Scottish medical officer, also a fellow Christian. 'Don't worry,' he said, 'first of all, it isn't, and secondly, not one of them would believe me, or you, if we told them the truth.'

Soon after I was put to the test in no uncertain manner. My neighbouring subaltern, a field gunner called Peter Duggan, employed a local child to do some rudimentary gardening. Since we all lived on top of volcanic laterite, gardening was chiefly what you put on top of it, since it was far too hard to dig. One afternoon, there was a knock on my door. 'Sah,' said a boy's voice. I opened the door and, before I could open my mouth, was informed by the small gardener, 'Sah, my sister she verra, verra, nice girl. She go like English officer, Sah. You go come to dis house I take you, she go give you plenty, plenty, nice time, Sah.' Pimping, especially by a nine-year-old, was totally outside my experience and I slammed the door in his face and shouted that he was never to show it again at my front door. At the time I felt thoroughly righteous, and shocked at the implication that anyone locally might think otherwise. With what wisdom the years have since brought, I now reckon I was unable to cope with the very idea of sex and that my outburst was much more to do with the affront to my self-righteousness than because of any immoral doings that were on offer, even with a child as a go-between.

Contact with black women in the culture of the 1950s was virtually non-existent as far as I was concerned. I saw them in the Accra market, sitting surrounded by great trays of fruit and vegetables, wonderfully colourful in gaudy cloth and headdresses, smiling, chatting and, as they reached their thirties, becoming vast lumps of matronly flesh. They offered a vivid contrast to the deformed beggars with outstretched hands lying by the smelly roadside gutters.

One afternoon, one of these vast ladies was sitting on the curb by the main road selling bananas. I told my Land-Rover driver to stop, bought a bunch, paid, and was thoroughly embarrassed when she rolled her eyes, and in a husky voice said, 'You come be my husband.' 'Step on it,' I said to Daniel Dokey, my driver, and we fled from the scene of would-be passion. What an adolescent I was!

Funnily enough, I wasn't at all embarrassed when, a few days later, watching a hockey match in our lines, a weird young woman, slim and angular, came up to me and proceeded to strip off. She was almost naked when an angry group of women came racing up, grabbed her, beat her, and shouting noisily, hustled her away. 'She mad, Sah,' they apologised. To my surprise, I felt quite detached, a young man seeing a virtually naked black woman for the first time in his life. Call it anthropological study, if you like, but she neither shocked nor excited me. I felt sorry for her but, inevitably the picture is still vivid, more than forty years later.

Living in an army camp, the temptation to spend all one's time within the military ghetto was very strong and most English officers, especially the single ones, did just that. I hardly ever saw any in the other worlds I inhabited. First, I joined the British Council and sang in their choir on Radio Gold Coast. Then we did *The Pirates of Penzance*, probably the most deliciously improbable vehicle for a mixed-race cast. Major-General Stanley was a milky-coffee-coloured tenor. His daughters were the full range from English rose to darkest mahogany Ashanti. We pirates and policemen were an equally ill-assorted crew, reasonable enough for pirates but I would be willing to bet that not one late-Victorian Cornish policeman ever looked remotely as negroid as half our lot. It was outrageously ridiculous and Accra's social cream, both black and white, immensely enjoyed the joke.

On Sunday evenings I joined the Ridge church, an Anglican church of 'central churchmanship' style, to which many of the British community, including the governor-general, went. A few black Africans also came but it was very much a 'white' church. It was also radically different from the rest of the Accra diocese which offered the most extreme brand of old-fashioned Anglo-Catholicism that I had ever seen. Among the key couples in the Ridge church were Tony and Eve Wilmot. He was one of those classic Cambridge expatriate Evangelical Christians who rode lightly to denominations but threw his weight wherever he went into the best church he could find. Eve was a daughter of famous missionary parents, linked to what was then Ruanda, and they kept open house to anyone looking for a free Sunday supper and Christian fellowship. After church each week they were like surrogate parents to me and their home was the one oasis in a domestic wilderness.

Now it so happened that I was deputed to go to brigade headquarters, a mile away, on the morning of Wednesday 6 February 1952. I got out of the Land-Rover, walked on to the veranda by the main office and came face to face with one of the staff officers whom I knew by sight. He was white, and not just European white. 'Good God,' he said, 'the King's dead!' I heard just the basic facts and then turned tail to the Land-Rover. 'Fast as you can back,' I said to the driver and we tore down Switchback Road. I shot into the new battery commander's office. 'The King's dead,' I blurted out. I knew what would come next. Every man in sight was sent to the guns and the vehicles. Best clothing was drawn from the stores. By 4 p.m. every gun, every vehicle, was gleaming, cleaned by dozens of hands. Every gun crew looked fit for a Buckingham Palace guard-mounting. We set off for Accra's legislative building, came into line on the facing football ground, and the guns, Kipling's little toy popguns, fired a 53–gun salute, one for each year of the old King's life. I wasn't a field gunner so I stood and watched. I'd done my day's duty by getting the news back to the battery before most people in England even knew and there we were, ready, the British Empire still in control, at least in Africa. It was a sobering day.

Running a troop of a hundred men, almost all of whom were pagans from tribal villages far away, though some had a thin Muslim veneer covering a great deal of superstition, meant that very few of those for whom I had direct responsibility were likely to turn up on Sundays at the little wooden church hut in Teshi. Once, however, a young clerk from one of the southern tribes, who were somewhat more sophisticated and westernised, found himself on parade in front of me for the evening's guard-mounting. I was orderly officer and immediately noticed that he, among all the pagans, was wearing scruffy kit and dirty boots. None of them had uniforms or boots capable of a high standard of presentation but his were appalling. I tore him off a strip, saying what a disgrace he was to the unit, and his eyes got bigger and bigger. Finally, he could contain himself no longer and blurted out, 'Sah. Sah. I be Christian man, Sah.' 'That's another reason why you're a disgrace,' I said angrily. 'You're not only a mess, you're trying to hide behind your churchgoing. Sa'rnt Kenny, put this man on a charge!'

Sergeant Kenny, the epitome of the not-too-bright but utterly loyal and well-disciplined Irish soldier, sprang to attention and did his duty. 'Yus, sor, sor. Done sor!' said Kenny, smartly saluting. 'Never throy dat koind of ting on de offisorr, yez stupid eejot,' said Kenny, marching the offending soldier off parade.

Kenny, a good Catholic boy, was not prepared to have any soldier try to take advantage of a subaltern, even a Protestant English one.

Living and working with such a diverse group of men, English, Scots, Irish, Welsh, Nigerians, Gas, Fantis, Ewes, Ashantis, Moshi, Dogombas, Fulanis, and a host more, was both colourful and culturally fascinating. One of the most delightful was our battery's police chief. A stocky pagan, with a wicked grin, a heavily scarred face covered in tribal markings, teeth filed to sharp points and the unforgettable name of Bombardier Number One Grumah, he could and did run the legs off any recalcitrant soldier who had been placed in detention. Grumah would stand on the corner of the battery parade ground while the luckless gunner would be forced to run round the perimeter holding a large and heavy stone above his head in the blazing sun. It was brutal but effective.

'Bombardier,' I said one day, 'how did you come to be called Number One?' 'Ee be my fader, Sah,' he replied in pidgin, the universal dialect which we all spoke. 'Me, I go get nine brodders, Sah. Dey be, Number Two, Number Tree, Number Four. De las one, he be Number Ten, Sah.' I felt sure he was taking the mickey but he wasn't. The Grumahs were sensibly economic people, not wasting time thinking up names.

Totally different was Battery Sergeant-Major Kande. He was a copper-skinned Fulani, a practising Muslim, who performed his religious duties meticulously. Of all the three hundred or more soldiers we had, he was the only one who could easily have been employed as a sergeant-major in an English regiment. He was a superb, well-disciplined soldier, comparable to a Gurkha. His senior counterpart, Sergeant-Major Yakubu Wongara, was a delightful man, who had fought in Burma during the war, and who ran the place through a network of spies. As a result there was absolutely nothing he did not know. On one occasion he asked permission of our commanding officer to take a jeep to the nearest village and collect some expensive item of the CO's clothing which was about to be sold there in the market. 'That's impossible, Sa'rnt Major,' said the CO. 'It's in my house.' 'It was, Sah,' said the Sergeant-Major, 'until half an hour ago.'

Needless to say, he got both the jeep and the clothing! His one privilege (and misfortune) was to live in the most prominent property in the battery lines. He had four huts, connected by mud walls into a square compound where he lived with his four wives. All was well until one day all four set on him with pots and pans and chased him around the lines in front of all his men. It wouldn't have done for RSM Brittain but Wongara's reputation survived it since no-one dared to mention the event for fear of his spies.

Once a month I was visited by a Hausaman. These tall Nigerians, every one a white-robed Muslim with a white cap, arrived with a small boy carrying a battered suitcase on his head. One by one his pieces of ivory, ebony, carved wood and woven mats were handed to me. Even a second glance at anything sparked off the barter and the banter. 'Dis elephant he be foine, foine piece, Sah.' 'How much?' 'Dis one, e no go for less, dis one, dan foive pound. Dat good price, Sah.' 'I'll give you two bob.' 'Ayeeeh. Massa go joke too much.' Twenty minutes later we were both approaching 15s from opposite directions. Every price he dropped to was 'las price, las price'. It was always fun, we both played by the rules and once or twice I even bought something. My one regret, in that pre-ecological era, was that after a full year of bargaining, I never did buy one of those superb elephant tusks, carved into a bridge of small ivory elephants. When I think just how close we got – only a shilling or two in dispute – I feel sad at what I missed. Oh well, you win some you lose some.

One morning I was called by one of the African sergeants. 'Please, Sah, you go come see dis *giddah*.' It seemed a normal soldier's hut, circular, black-and-white painted, with a thatched roof and a door. 'Sah,' said my sergeant, 'ee be dis water, Sah.' I looked closely and noticed a tiny trickle of water, an inch wide and a quarter-inch deep, which ran almost invisibly down the slope, disappeared under one side of the door, reappeared at the rear of the hut and wandered off down the laterite surface. 'Sah, dis *giddah* go fall down, Sah,' said the sergeant plaintively. 'Nonsense,' I said with the confidence of European youth. He looked sadly at me and said, 'Yes, Sah, Sah.'

Two days later that tiny trickle had reduced the hut to a pile of mud, thatch and some bits of wood. I remembered a story Jesus had told about houses built on wrong foundations and the effect of wind, storm and water. My tribesman sergeant, for all his primitive ignorance, was a wiser man than I was. I felt, and rightly, that I was the fool in the gospel story. Not good for a subaltern's humility.

Quite the most exciting, and nauseating, event in our lines took place on Christmas Day. I was orderly officer on duty and heard a tremendous commotion. I marched over to the centre of the noise where a large crowd was ferociously bidding in an auction. At the centre, holding a large ladle, was Sergeant Sokoto. Dipping it in and out of a steaming cauldron he was offering the contents to the feverishly yelling mob. It looked like a piece of offal, a pig's heart, maybe. 'No, Sah,' called one of the soldiers. 'Dis one e be foine, foine, chop. E go pas all chop, dis one. You go buy 'im?' 'What is it?' I enquired. 'Dis one, Sah, e be cat's head!' I felt distinctly queasy recalling that some said that Sergeant Sokoto was prone to wander near the European houses nearby and had, it was alleged, been seen to walk about with dogs on leads of string. Whose much-loved domestic cat had purred his last purr, I wondered? Not my idea of Christmas dinner.

My chief extra-curricular pleasure was cricket. The ground was, being laterite, quite unsuitable so we had to play on coconut matting. It seemed to suit my bowling and I soon got used to batting on it. The season ran from October to March, avoiding the monsoon when rain came down in sheets. I had twenty innings for a couple of clubs, got a top score of sixty-seven and helped the battery to win the army cricket cup. In the final I got a not-out top score and took most wickets which was to be my launching pad into university cricket in the following English season.

In the midst of all this, I was sent off one Thursday morning with a Land-Rover and three large gun-towing tractors to go to Takoradi to collect three more Bofors guns, which had arrived at the docks. Accra, being on a coast battered by heavy surf, had no direct landing facilities for anything other than light cargo dropped into heavy rowing boats. Anti-aircraft guns could not possibly be unloaded there. There was no direct coast road so we faced a long inland detour through the forests. When we got back to the coast we passed the old slave castles of Cape Coast and Elmina. The vultures strutting about sent shudders down my spine and seemed somehow fitting sentinels for such places of long-gone horror. We spent that night at Takoradi, collected the crated guns and set off home. One by one, the guns, or their tractors, broke down until I was left, with no means of communication, shuttling from one to the next and finally returning to Accra to collect a couple of fitters. They did the trick, though the gun furthest away had been stuck in mid-forest and the driver, a very superstitious pagan, had paid a stray passer-by to sit with him in the cab all night to 'keep de spirits away, Sah'. I finally reached camp at noon on the Saturday having been without food, drink or sleep for thirty hours, and went straight to my bed. However, I was hauled out and torn off a strip by the battery commander for failing to stay and talk to his lunchtime guests in the Mess. I was utterly speechless.

Some weeks later I took my one leave in Kumasi, the inland capital of Ashanti. The journey by train, a wood-burning steam engine, took all day, but naturally, as all Europeans did, I travelled first class in a compartment with a large armchair. I stayed in a Victorian bungalow, part of the Officers' Mess, and the latter could have come straight from the Indian army. A huge single-storey building, with wide veranda and sweeping staircase, it made Accra look squalid and bare. I expected Rudyard Kipling to appear at any minute.

While there, I was introduced to an Englishman who was in charge of labour relations, and just off to see the gold mine at Bibiani, a hundred miles away. 'Want to come?' he enquired. 'You bet,' I answered and, a day later, I was twelve hundred feet down a gold mine, with a lamp on my helmet as the only light source and finding myself descending chain ladders through hundred-foot-deep chimneys in almost pitch darkness. Not again, thank you, but I wouldn't have missed it.

The labour officer, incidentally, quite shocked me. 'I used to be a campaigning Socialist as a young man,' he informed me. 'Not now,' he added, 'now that I'm well off I've ditched Socialism.' Not a Socialist myself, I found such cynical betrayal hard to accept. Perhaps with the idealism of youth I couldn't understand the sell-out mentality.

Also in Kumasi I was taken one evening to meet Ralph Amato. He was an opposition politician, married to a Swiss woman. I, who knew nothing about Gold Coast politics, was soon informed about corruption, tribalism and a host of worrying features. If Nkrumah took over, then Amato and others feared for their skins. A few years later Amato was dead in somewhat uncertain circumstances. I remembered that night and the way I was let out, in the dark, through a back gate, just in case.

While in Kumasi, I took a photo of a market woman and, to my discomfort, almost started a riot. She grabbed the camera, threatened to smash it. A large crowd assembled and I was reduced to very undignified pleading and a large pay-off in order to get the camera back. I've still got the photo and she looks very belligerent.

By now, March had come and in a few months I would be back in England. 'Lord,' I said, 'I gave you two years and you haven't said a word. What's going on up there?' That week a magazine arrived from my mother. She always sent me the *National Geographic* and the *Crusader* magazine. I read both avidly. Near the back of the latter was an advert for a college in Bristol. It taught theology and had as its principal a man whom I had heard speak in London once. Moreover it seemed to have links with the university. I decided to write, telling the principal that I thought my experience in the Gold Coast might point to a future life as a missionary in West Africa. Clearly I couldn't think of returning to the English Church Mission which was a million miles 'high' but what about the Church Missionary Society in Nigeria?

Before the end of the month, the Principal, the Reverend J. Stafford Wright ('Staffy' to everyone) replied and set the ball rolling. My Latin 'pass' in school certificate was a problem but it might be accepted. The odds were, he said, 'fifty-fifty' that I might get a place for October. I waited. Then came the news, 'Your references are satisfactory', and the University of Bristol Arts board had agreed to accept me.

My final three months in Accra were lived, not in my mud hut but in a pleasant small bungalow about half a mile from our camp, where I shared with an Englishman from Bromley who had been a member of Bromley Crusaders and Christ Church, Bromley. John Cooper knew some of the boys from Eltham College and he also knew Peter Dawes. John was not in the army but in a government job. He came occasionally to the Teshi church with me and we both went to the Wilmots on Sunday evenings. It was a great pleasure to have my own room in a modern bungalow and life was much more civilised – we even had running water and a flush lavatory. We have, for no reason, never seen each other again but I always valued his hospitality. It was the kind of brief friendship between two men, far from home, which today would automatically be assumed to have some homosexual basis. Such an idea did not enter and, I suspect, would not have entered, into either of our minds. Our sharing a two-bedroomed bungalow merely made sense at the time.

One day, in the wet season, there was a rainbow to end all rainbows. If I hadn't seen it I wouldn't have believed it. It was a triple bow. The first was stunningly bright. The second was more colourful than most English rainbows. The third was nearly three-quarters of a bow. Once in a lifetime but unforgettable.

Just before I left there was a small meeting at the Wilmots' home to lay plans to launch a Christian boys' camp. I was glad to share in that gathering, though I would never be involved in the project which was to be the source of a whole movement in the Gold Coast and, later, Ghana. Today, forty years on, I still meet people who came to a living Christian faith through the consequences of that small meeting. On such occasions one is very conscious of the mysterious ways in which God is supposed to move.

In August the return flight took off from Accra, ten hours late. It didn't inspire the passengers, all soldiers, wives and families, with confidence. We headed north-east for the River Niger and landed in early afternoon at Niamey. After a brief stop we then flew low alongside the river, watching hippos and antelopes, until we reached Gao, just east of the Niger's great bend. There, as dusk approached, we were taken to the only visible hotel, a mud building that both looked, and was, dirty and disappointing. I, being the only passenger who could even attempt a sentence in French, was required to interpret. 'There are no light bulbs, there are no this, that and the other,' I stumbled. The owner, a French-speaking African (Gao, now in Mali, was then in French Sudan), shrugged his shoulders in the Gallic manner and we settled down to an uncomfortable night. Nesting storks on the outside chimneys offered the only interesting subjects for conversation, the food was horrific (goat or camel – I never did find out which – not even when it convulsively reappeared on the next day's flight) and the bugs were voracious.

We flew low on across the desert and I was allowed into the cockpit. 'How do you know where to go?' I asked, seeing no evidence of instruments or compass. 'Look down below,' replied the pilot. 'Every couple of miles there's a black 44–gallon oil drum marking the road. We're following them.' He's having me on, I thought, until I looked and, lo and behold, there was the black drum just as he'd said.

El Aoulef was just as hot as last time (I later discovered in an atlas it had recorded the world's hottest temperatures – somewhere around 140 °F) but the boredom was relieved by the sight of a distant camel heading our way. Much nearer, I realised that it was a man on a camel. Even more interesting. When it reached us, five minutes later, it was a boy with a basket of figs. I had seen a kind of mirage. From that moment onwards, I never placed any value on the old saying 'Seeing's believing.' It turned out to be quite a useful preaching point when sermons were required. I would, without doubt, have sworn in a court of law that I had seen all three different objects.

Two days later I was home. It seemed very small after my plain, but large, mud hut. Mum and Dad welcomed me, the hero returned from darkest Africa. But who was this? I had left a dumpy, pre-pubertal, thirteen-year-old little sister. Out of the chrysalis, and out of sight, had sprung a curvaceous young woman, pretty, quite fragile in style. We'd had nothing like that in our home before. They told me she was Moira.

It was clearly time to go to university. Mum and Dad were

amazed. 'We didn't realise that you had the "go" to fix it all up yourself from Africa,' said Dad. They were also distinctly anxious when I mentioned the Nigeria idea of a missionary-to-be. They said nothing, judging it wiser to let things take their course for a bit. I had a couple of spare weeks and went to be a tent officer in a Crusader camp on the Isle of Wight. Unknown to me, God had another trick up his cassock sleeve, and it wasn't long before he played it.

Chapter Four

Bristol Fashion

I had never been to Bristol before, but, anxious to get the feel of the place before term started, I decided to attend the university's orientation conference for Freshers at the end of September 1952. In readiness, and with money in my bank account (all those 'captain's pay' arrears had suddenly turned up), I decided that I needed some suitable clothes. With the awful memory of the blue 'clurk's' suit, I headed for Harrods. There, in the 'Younger Man's Shop,' I purchased (for the large sum of £18) a charcoal-grey double-breasted suit and a buff-coloured felt waistcoat, the very height of fashion. Together with a rolled umbrella and a Harris tweed sports jacket I felt able to face the world.

The taxi from Temple Meads delivered me at the entrance to Tyndale Hall, an Anglican theological college facing the Downs at the top of Pembroke Road, in Clifton, Bristol's most fashionable suburb. Tyndale was a complex of five huge Victorian houses. The first, the principal's house, was semi-detached. The next two, Cranmer and Wycliffe, were semi-detached and interconnected; the main house, with chapel, offices and dining hall, was named after Ridley; and the fifth, also detached, was Latimer. The place seemed absolutely deserted.

I walked into the entrance hall of Ridley. Not a soul was in sight. It was all rather dark and gloomy and I felt a faint qualm. Was I really going to enjoy life in this atmosphere of faded Victoriana? I stood in the hall for some time, uncertain what to do, or where to go. Then I suddenly detected the distant sound of some voices. It wasn't from upstairs. There was quite a deep well, and nothing was coming down it. Nor was it from the basement. Nor from outside. I crept to the three doors off the hall, each in turn. Not from an empty lecture room. Not from the principal's office. The final, heavy door, said 'Chapel' and, very gingerly, I opened it an inch. I could see about fifteen heads facing away from me, with an elderly man addressing them and answering questions. Who were they? I closed the door and sat down on the stairs to await developments. I hadn't long to wait.

The chapel door opened and out walked a group of young men and women, obviously students. We stared at each other, then one of the men said, 'Who are you?' We introduced ourselves and thus it was that I met my future wife, her bridesmaid-to-be, and two future godfathers for our children. The group was, in fact, the core membership of the university Christian Union holding a pre-term conference, chaired by a husband-and-wife missionary couple from Burma, and the speaker, a brilliant Jewish-Christian Old Testament lecturer. 'Why don't you join us?' they enquired, and, explaining that I would need to double-head it with the university conference, all was agreed. Thus it was that I woke up after my first night as a student to have breakfast with the woman who was to share my life. Next day there was a group photo and guess who was standing next to me? It was, in reality, some years before either of us dug out our copies of the photo and discovered this unknown example of Freudian proximity.

Tyndale was, unknown to me, just entering a new, liberated, era. Stafford Wright, who had spent most of his life there as a lecturer, had only been principal for one year. His long-term predecessor was a brilliant, eccentric, and rather crabby man who ran the college in a very confined way. Hardly any women ever entered its doors, and although most of its students were ex-service men, back from the War, he treated them like schoolboys. He had four sons, all of whom I knew, one of whom became a multimillionaire and another a diocesan bishop.

'Staffy' was a great shock to me. I met him on my second day and suddenly realised that he wasn't the man I had remembered when I applied to the college. That man had, I thought, been a speaker at a London service which I, and Orpington YPF, had attended. It was his personality that had attracted me to apply to Tyndale. I was now to discover that my hero was nothing to do with Tyndale but was instead principal of Oak Hill, Tyndale's great rival college in London. I had, effectively, come to the wrong place. They had L.F.E. Wilkinson, Tyndale had Stafford Wright. Shock horror!

But not for long. Staffy was a marvellous man, winsome, fairly nervous, at least in mannerism, often lapsing into a soft, tuneless whistle. His interests were legion, including potholing, butter-flies, the paranormal (in a thoroughly healthy way) and, of course, his lecturing specialities of Old Testament and Psychol-ogy. He was a child at heart, shrewd yet innocent, with a conser-vative theology and a liberal ethos. He would attend retreats at Nashdom Abbey (and you couldn't get more Anglo-Catholic than that) and yet be totally respected by even the most extreme of the old-style conservative Evangelicals. He was, without a doubt, a one-off and greatly loved and respected by generations of Tyndale men. I soon joined their ranks in this regard for him.

The college in 1952 was by no means full. Able to hold about fifty-five, it had about thirty in residence, among whom, to my de-light, were Bob Beak and Peter Dawes. The atmosphere was full of fun, combining a totally serious and dedicated faith with a great deal of clowning. It was particularly notorious for its wa-ter-fights within and between houses and it was my proud boast that, like Augustus, who found Rome built of brick and left it built of marble, I found them throwing water about in cups and I left them geared to stirrup-pumps attached to bath taps. This was especially true of Latimer house where the main floor was tiled and the first floor was surrounded by a railed gallery and stairs. I still recall that gallery looking like a poor man's Niagara Falls as water came off it in sheets.

Both then and ever since, I have always believed that ordinands should be both free, and encouraged, to let off a great deal of steam. Most of their future lives will be under great pressure to be very proper and I am convinced that so long as the fun and fooling is not painful to people or destructive of property then it ought to be actively supported. Tyndale's water-throwing mostly took place in a house in which it did little actual damage.

It was, nevertheless, a considerable surprise when, towards the end of my first term, I was approached by the Principal and the Senior Student, asking whether I would take part in a rag they were organising. If a first-year student needed a green light this was surely it! My role was to be the postmaster general in the official opening of an internal telephone system between the houses. The creative mind behind this scheme was that of Raymond Parkinson, a little man with a bureaucratic moustache, who looked like the original clerk in any government ministry, and who was, if my memory is right, a trained telephone engineer. The equipment he installed would have been antique at the time of Queen Victoria's Diamond Jubilee and we were shortly to celebrate her great-great- granddaughter's coronation. All done up in a top hat, I was driven around the area, and, leaning out of a car window, doffed my hat to the worthies of Clifton, some of whom removed their headgear in respectful recognition. I still possess my speech of inauguration awarding Mr Parkinson a Master's degree. 'Parky phones' continued to work, erratically, for over a decade.

Daily life at Tyndale involved attending early morning chapel. Then, before breakfast, a half-an-hour personal 'Quiet Time'. After breakfast, for university students, a series of morning and afternoon lectures. Evening chapel was followed by supper and more study or whatever. Six of us were reading for the Bristol theology degree and our first year at the university included Hebrew, New Testament Greek, and two other subjects, of which I chose English and Philosophy. I much enjoyed learning Greek under Kenneth Grayston, a brilliant Methodist minister who would later become a professor. Hebrew I disliked very much. It seemed a crude and barbaric language alongside Greek but I slogged away at it for the one year that it was a mandatory subject and duly passed. English literature involved *Hamlet*, *Doctor Faustus*, and various poems. Philosophy required Plato's *Republic* as a set text, plus a course in Logic, which was valuable but frustrating since the lecturers were all militant Logical Positivists and we never once got to consider a single worthwhile concept, being forced to paddle in the shallows which that utterly trivial, but fashionable, school forced on us.

Life continued pleasantly and, for someone who had been out-side academic study for four years, remarkably easily. I enjoyed the work, the fun, the people, and the Christian Union (into which I threw myself wholeheartedly). I also joined the Anglican Soci-ety, which met at the vicarage of one, Basil Moss, alongside whom I was to work fifteen years later in Church House, Westminster, and who eventually became Provost of Birmingham.

But there was one snag. I was now twenty. I had never had a girl-friend and had felt no need of one. Throughout my teens, both at Christ Church and at Crusaders, the climate had marginalised the female of the species and her sexual attributes were hardly consid-ered. I had worked hard, played hard, soldiered hard, and apart from the irritating intrusions of Dumbelle, Goggle-eyes, and the Accra tart's small brother, I was simply too occupied to notice that there was a Second Sex. I had only a sketchy idea of what they looked like in the strategic areas and had never seriously kissed one. This, according to all the later guides to sex, should either have demonstrated to me that I was a homosexual, or forced me into a life of non-stop masturbation or both. It did nothing of the kind. In those far off days when kids and adolescents were largely left to grow at their own pace, not bombarded with pre-coital, coital, and post-coital messages, I simply wasn't ready. And had never, and this is the absolute truth, masturbated and only once seen it happen to someone in the school changing room, which had disgusted me. So what was the snag? The snag was that the great majority of students reading English were girls, very nubile, eigh-teen- and nineteen-year-old girls, and two of them were, in the jar-gon of the day, blond bombshells. For the first time in my life, my eyes developed a life of their own and not only my eyes. This was terrible for a fervent, chaste, possibly missionary-to-be, Christian, with a hunger for godliness. I went through six weeks of consider-able spiritual warfare, mental anxiety, and physical discomfort.

One day I was sitting in the college common room. I have no idea what the conversation was about or who was there, when, suddenly, David Woods, the Senior Student, laughed and said, out of the blue, 'Mike [they called me Mike in those days], what about Jackie Atkinson? I reckon she and you would make a good couple.' 'Yes, dear boy,' said a second voice, that of David Pytches (one day to be a charismatic bishop on the Anglican fringes), 'why, with your accent and her money, you'd be laughing.' I smiled and didn't give it a second thought.

Every Tyndale student was allocated a 'Sunday duty'. After Sunday lunch, we were farmed around local churches, geriatric hospitals, Sunday schools and the like, to get some pastoral experience under our belts. My job was to be an assistant to the leaders of Clifton Crusader class (which seemed obvious enough). The leaders were good, worthy, not-very-exciting men, most of whom belonged to the local Brethren Assembly. Among the boys, however, were two whom I was to meet in later years. One, Stephen Sykes, the youngest (and most brilliant) son of the retired Tyndale principal, was a terrible little know-all of an adolescent. I enjoyed pulling his leg about it, when, after being Regius Professor of Divinity at Cambridge, he was made Bishop of Ely, one of the cleverest theologians in the Church of England, and we met at a Buckingham Palace garden party. The second, a tall and fairly reserved young man in the sixth form at Bristol Grammar School, John Somerville-Meikle, was next to cross my path when he was church warden in Beckenham in the early 1970s and duly became second master at, of all places, Eltham College. Sadly, he died of cancer quite recently.

Christmas drew near and I, together with one of my fellow undergraduates, Brian Green, decided to accept invitations to go to the Christmas social at Manor Hall, one of the women's halls of residence. Brian was smitten by one of the 'English girls' and kept me waiting for some time while he said good night. We were already late and did not get back to Tyndale till after 'lock-up' time (in those days at 10.30 p.m.). He lived in Latimer, which was riddled with easy ways in. I, unfortunately had no chance of getting into Wycliffe and rang the doorbell which was answered by our South African Vice-Principal, Dr Philip Hughes, who had a flat in Cranmer, the other half of the building. He gave me a tremendous dressing down (it was 10.40 p.m.) and instructed me to 'see the principal' in the morning. It was all very prep schoolish. I dragged myself, deflated, up to the first floor. The bell rang again. Hughes appeared and let in Symon Beesley, the most ancient student and castigated him moderately. He came to the first floor and I told him of my crime. We laughed about it and the doorbell rang yet again. We both crept halfway down the stairs. Hughes appeared looking very angry. The door opened to reveal David Woods, the Senior Student. We all roared with laughter, Hughes saw the funny side of it and I was forgiven.

Back home, I worked for the Post Office doing the Christmas mail and as I walked the roads in Petts Wood I had time to consider. Was David Woods right? Jackie Atkinson was quite a tomboy. She had long hair down to her waist (well, I assumed so since she had a big plait, bent into a doorknocker on the back of her head). She was a bundle of energy, not exactly pretty, but with lots of character, a very determined girl. We seemed to get on all right. I wonder? I wonder? After Christmas I decided to write to her. She'd gone off to Austria with a party from the university, skiing in a place called Obergurgl, in the Tirol. She'd mentioned the hotel at the Manor Hall social. I'd never written to a girl before. What should you say?

I have searched the house high and low and I can't find it. I have a marvellous filing system and it isn't there. Jackie can't find it anywhere either. Yet we kept it for years and now it's gone. So I can't quote it accurately. What did I say? Whatever it was it sounded harmless enough to me. Nice and friendly. No more. Jackie, enjoying her skiing, thought it a very odd letter. It practically invited her to go off to Africa with me and wasn't that a kind of proposal of marriage? Anyway, skiing and *après*-skiing put it out of her mind and on the way home, during the long train journey, she got distinctly friendly with Tony, the secretary of the Christian Union. Nothing very improper, of course, but still, when the new term started I saw the two of them holding hands together and in 1953 that was a very public declaration of something. I went back to Tyndale and bled emotionally all over Symon Beesley. He was wonderfully sympathetic and promised to do all he could but the next week was simply torture. I had grown up listening to the Irish tenor, John McCormack, singing, 'Oh, have ye been in love, me boys, oh, have ye felt the pain? I'd sooner be in jail, me boys, than be in love again.' Now I knew what he meant and it was sheer hell. I was off my food and that was really serious.

The utter stupidity of the 'proper' pattern of Evangelical courtship in those days was that you couldn't ask a girl out for a coffee without it requiring a virtual proposal of marriage. The motive was very laudable. No cheap petting. No treating girls as amusement arcades. No 'experimentation' before marriage. It was all thoroughly worthy and responsible and it forced young men and women into the deep end before they had begun to learn how to splash about in the paddling pool. Moreover, once into the emotional and spiritual deep end and there was no way out without desperate pain to both boy and girl. I am very grateful that I was taught to treat boy–girl friendship seriously but I can't help thinking that we were extraordinarily fortunate not to have found ourselves trapped by the folly of what happened to us.

After a week, I could stand it no longer. I asked Jackie to let me see her. She invited me to call at her room in Manor Hall, during visiting hours. There I poured out my heart, my love, my hopes and left her to settle my fate. She asked for a week to consider and the pain grew worse and worse. At last she told me that she would drop Tony and go out with me. Paradise Lost suddenly turned into Paradise Regained. They all lived happily ever after. Like hell we did! But at least we had started. Before long we were holding hands. 'O joy, O rapture unforeseen.' I was on cloud 999. But godly young men and women must not, absolutely must not, overdo things. We laughed, we joked, we talked, we prayed, but we did not kiss. I must not treat her as a plaything. I must mean it, I really must. Weeks and weeks went by, six weeks in all.

Then, one night we decided to play squash. We booked the local university squash courts and had a few games. Neither of us were much good at it. Finally, we stopped and, for the first time, noticed that we had the whole place to ourselves. We sat looking at each other hungrily. How do you start? I could only think of one devious way to get things moving. 'Do you know that song in the *Mikado* which starts, "Were you not to Koko plighted?" ' 'Well, a bit,' said Jackie, smiling. 'Let's sing it.'

So we did. And when we came to the lines 'Let me make it clear to you, this is what I'll never do. This, oh this. Oh this. Oh this. This is what I'll never, never do' (repeat), we took W.S. Gilbert's advice and turned it into a kissing song. Soon we had stopped singing but we didn't stop kissing and, over forty years later, we haven't yet finished the song. If you're bashful and inexperienced try singing it. It can work wonders.

My friends at Tyndale naturally pulled my leg non-stop. Jackie began to attend Sunday morning chapel rather than go to a local parish church. The sermons were excellent, well geared to teaching future clergy but, up till then, only wives (and there were few of them) had been admitted. Jackie was, I think, the first 'woman' to be allowed in, and she was the first of many. She became almost an Honorary Member of Tyndale and this was especially recognised when the day of the university rag arrived. I, as an undergraduate, wanted to attend it, but it clashed with a college hockey match and I was a regular team member. On the preceding Wednesday, playing football for the college, I had received a particularly hard kick on the shin which was badly bruised. I told the Captain, Percy Ashford (later Chaplain-General of Prisons) that I couldn't play and he refused to accept it, calling in a trainee missionary, Peter Thompson, who had more medical degrees than a zebra has stripes. Thompson pronounced me fit and I pronounced him a bent quack. 'I am not', I said, 'playing.'

On Friday night, I sensed that something was up. Avoiding everyone, I crept up to the top floor in Ridley and kept my ears open in one of the bedrooms, whose owner had gone away for the weekend. Before long I heard some kind of hue and cry developing and a voice echoed from my room in the house facing, 'He's not here!'

I crept under the bed and heard the search continuing. Someone burst into the room, had a quick glance, and disappeared. 'He's not up here.'

I slept on the floor, under the bed, and crept out of the college in thick mist, at 6 a.m. Eventually I met Jackie. We went to the rag, then on to watch the hockey. Everyone eyed us expectantly with big grins but said nothing. Early in the evening we went our separate ways, she back to Manor, I to Tyndale. What I found in my room were all her belongings in her suitcases. What she discovered in hers were all mine in my tin trunk, labelled 'Honeymoon Flat, Manor Hall'. It took quite a time to sort things out and we reckoned honour was satisfied all round. So much for ordinands being solemn and virtuous.

Term was almost over but we still had the Bristol theological colleges football cup final to play. I had scored the winning goal in the semi-final against the Methodists – an extraordinary kick on the full, from halfway, which bounced in front of the keeper who was too far out, and went right over his head into the goal. The Tyndale supporters club, a wild mob of horn-blowing, masked and bewigged characters (mostly now sober, retired vicars), turned out to cheer us on and we won by a single goal.

During the vacation I had been invited to Jackie's home in Prestbury, near Cheltenham, right underneath the scarp of the Cotswolds, to meet her mother. I had taken the precaution, some weeks earlier, to send her some whipped-cream walnuts, which Jackie had told me were her favourite chocolates. She wrote me an impassioned letter of gratitude describing them as her 'dream of bliss' and added that 'I know I am going to like you.' She also offered me the inevitable word of caution about twenty-year-old students getting too deeply involved, since 'Jackie is the loyal sort, once she has made up her mind.' Being a widow, she was, quite properly, concerned about her only daughter's long-term welfare. She also, soon after, made it quite clear that there was none of the money that David Pytches had so mistakenly assumed.

Jackie's father, I had by now discovered, had died in 1945. He had been trained as a barrister, had served in the First War, then in the civil service, had written a few books, and compiled and edited about twenty others. He was well known in Gloucestershire, both through his long-standing links with the Territorial Army and the Cadet Corps and also with Freemasonry. His first wife, by whom he had two daughters, Grete and Bet to the family, had died in the 1920s and he had married Eileen Morgan later in the decade. She was also in the civil service and both were the recipients of an honour, he an OBE, and she an MBE. Jackie, born in Iver, had lived both in Eastbourne and Cheltenham where she was a pupil at the Ladies' College until her father's death. He had left her a small legacy, but there wasn't enough money to permit her to stay. Eileen, to whom it was a social disaster, regretfully sent her to Pate's Grammar School, a mile from their Prestbury home. Ironically, Jackie much preferred Pate's to the Ladies' College. The only evidence of past wealth was the world voyage to New Zealand which the three of them had made in 1936 and 1937. That had been paid for by all the royalties which had long since vanished.

The visit to Prestbury was enjoyable for Jackie and me but it was quite obvious that Eileen Atkinson was putting on a polite front and that everything I stood for, and, most of all, the 'missionary' possibility, was clearly distasteful to her. She, born in the Victorian era, had been brought up to the art of social dissembling and I was never sure in all the years before her death that I was hearing the truth, unvarnished, from her. It put Jackie in a difficult position, creating a conflict of loyalties initially, and later driving something of a wedge between her and her mother.

I went up early for the summer term to take part in the university cricket trials. I was selected for the first team for seven out of the sixteen games, with top scores of 76 not out and 55 not out. The university ground at Coombe Dingle was magnificently maintained (sadly no longer true) with a very fine wicket, and a certain young lady found her way there with considerable regularity. I didn't get to bowl for the First Eleven but fielded at cover and in the short legs so I was rarely out of the action.

I also passed my driving test, bought a 1934 Wolseley car, for the princely sum of £35, and was fully equipped for the joys of a mobile student life. The weather being generally warm, Jackie and I took a rug out on to one of the ledges high up on the Clifton gorge (now shut off as too dangerous) and tested each other's Old English and Hebrew vocabularies, punctuated by testing each other's tonsils at close range. Both of us had important exams which we needed to pass and, to my concern, Jackie's interest in academic work had considerably waned since I came on the scene. However, we both passed.

Needless to say, with so much lost ground to catch up, we

talked a great deal about our goals, our vision for life, our hopes, and about sex. One afternoon we were sitting enjoying the sun in a small park almost opposite the Bishop of Bristol's house. There was only one park seat and we had it to ourselves. Sex, or at least talking about sex, was top of the agenda. 'Darling,' I said, 'I assume we agree that sex is only intended for the purpose of having children?' I knew nothing then of the long, sad history of sexual attitudes fostered by the early church Fathers and pursued by their successors, who had taught exactly that. It simply seemed obvious to me.

Jackie did the best possible thing she could have done in those unpromising circumstances. She laughed. And laughed. And went on laughing. I was humiliated by this lack of respect for my wisdom, and, ever since, with hindsight, have been eternally grateful to her. She, with the experience of two mild friendships with young men behind her, was a proper little minx. Why, she had had to teach me, an ex-officer and gentleman, how to kiss. I never realised it involved more than a chaste, pursed-lip peck on the lips. She, the baggage, had other ideas (and, one had to admit, it was much nicer her way) and, now, here she was disturbing all my assumptions about sex and its significance. I decided that I should have to start reading up all this sex business. Fortunately, soon after, I discovered Edward Griffiths' *Modern Marriage*, already twenty years in print and in those days easily the best, most realistic, and most moral book on the subject. It was simply superb.

The Coronation took place on 2 June 1953, the week in which the exams were in full flush, but the college hired a television set and all who could spare the time sat round watching the black-and-white spectacle. For most of us it was the first sight of the box and we couldn't take our eyes off it. That night Bristol celebrated until the early hours and it seemed a suitable occasion for our courtship to develop a bit as we were now planning an engagement. Jackie's mother, Eileen, would not, I knew, welcome such a proposal before she was twenty-one, which wouldn't be until mid-August. My parents had come to the college to help me celebrate my own twenty-first with a party in David

Pytches' room, the largest of the student rooms in Tyndale, on 14 May.

Our actual engagement was a strange event. Jackie came to London on the day after her twenty-first birthday and I asked her to come with me to choose a ring. It would, I assured her, need to be properly sized and when that was done we would formally announce the engagement. She happily agreed and we entered a jeweller in Fenchurch Street which Dad had recommended. Surprise, surprise. It fitted perfectly. 'Thank you,' I said to the jeweller. 'Please wrap it for me.' He looked puzzled and Jackie was distinctly crestfallen.

When we reached Petts Wood at about five, I suggested a walk in the woods before supper. There, it being quite impossible to continue the slightly frigid farce, I properly proposed. She accepted. We came home and a happy evening was spent by all. My one anxiety was that Eileen would think that I had planned it to take place one day after her permission was no longer needed. I wrote to her to set the record straight and received a delightful, gracious, very straight letter asking me to consider the financial implications, to provide a proper life insurance provision, and to recognise the consequences of children for a marriage based on a small income. Finally, to my great relief, she expressed her delight at the engagement which had, she assured me, brought 'a new radiance' to Jackie and hoped that we should 'always be firm friends'.

With this under my belt, I began a six-week job as a ward orderly at Orpington hospital. I was allocated to a male geriatric ward where, under a sister, I worked with a Malaysian and the son of a local farmer. I was soon shocked to see how vicious both could be. Old men can often be querulous and irritating and two or three were rewarded with a quiet trip to the day room where my two colleagues beat them up. They never left marks on them but they frightened them. They frightened me into saying nothing, to my lasting shame. It was, nevertheless, an eye-opener to realise that such a thing could happen in a suburban National Health Service hospital.

I spent six weeks working there and nothing matched the very first day. Two old men were very ill and, in the afternoon, both died, an hour apart. I was instructed to assist in laying them out and discovered the inevitable, if distinctly unaesthetic, processes involved. No-one else died during my time there so it was deep-end stuff right at the start. I am glad that I had that unpleasant experience and a second one soon after. I knew the consultant surgeon, Stanley Farrant-Russell, well, since he was an ex-missionary, the lay reader at Christ Church and a good friend of the Crusader class. Plucking up my courage I asked him whether, while I was on the staff, I could be present at an operation in the theatre. 'Certainly,' he smiled, 'we'll find you an interesting one. Not an amputation,' he added, 'they're very obvious and boring.'

A couple of weeks later, one of our old men was booked to have a prostatectomy. 'That'll do,' said Mr Russell. I didn't even know what, or where, a prostate was but I soon found out. As they wheeled the old man in, anaesthetised, Russell said, pulling on his rubber gloves, 'If you feel ill, just go out without any fuss.' 'Oh, I'll be OK,' I said. He looked at me with a slight smile, too knowingly for my comfort.

The operation began. Unfortunately, it was soon clear that the haemostats, for cauterising the blood vessels, were not working. Blood was pumping out from the widely opened incision in the old man's belly. A sucker was inserted (like those things dentists put in your mouth) which kept the balance but I hadn't bargained on the combination of blood and ether. I crept out. Ten minutes later, with my head clear once more, I returned and watched fascinated for over two hours. Stanley Farrant-Russell's skill was a wonder to behold and not least since he was talking to a colleague almost all the time, hardly ever seeming to look at the work in hand. It did a power of good to my trust in the surgeons and, while I thank God that I have hardly ever been in a hospital as a patient, I was extremely relaxed when the day finally came for me to face the knife. Well, not perhaps 'extremely', but much less worried than I might otherwise have been.

Back in Bristol for my second, and Jackie's final, year I secured a new room in Latimer, much larger than my previous cell. I put two trophies on the walls, a tiger-skin and a stuffed alligator, both of which had been brought home from Malaya (as it was) by my Uncle Billy who had worked there before the War with a tobacco company. 'Intended, no doubt,' said Jim Packer, one of our lecturers, 'to give the air of a much-travelled man.' Such travelling was not unusual for Tyndale men of the late 1940s and early 1950s. The war, and later national service, had taken people all over the world and the temptation to talk about it was overwhelming. 'When I was in . . .' began someone and a cry went up, 'Swing the lights!' The nearest students reached up to the hanging room lights and set them in motion. It very effectively silenced the various bores, me included, and also taught us, for future use, the need to avoid the old clerical line 'When I was in my last parish . . .'

Jackie, for her part, had found a flat, which she shared with a Manor friend, June Badcock. June had recently come to the Christian faith while at university so it suited them both to team up. The flat was on the top floor of Royal York Crescent, Bristol's rather downmarket version of Bath's Royal Crescent, and offered a superb view right over the heart of the city and across to Dundry, the hill which formed Bristol's south-west horizon. Jackie and June were both facing their finals with all the emotional stress that it entails.

My second year began the real theological work. The course included Old Testament introduction, with Jeremiah as the set book. Then there was New Testament introduction. Our Greek set books were Matthew's Sermon on the Mount, Mark, Galatians and Philippians. Church History included both the Patristic and Reformation periods. Doctrine meant the person and work of Christ. Finally, there was Comparative Religion, looking at the world's other major faiths. I still have twenty-seven exercise books containing all the lecture notes which I took in those two years. Right at the start of that academic year in October 1953 I had to take a decision which was to have lasting consequences. Bristol was almost the only university that required undergraduates to take Hebrew in both first part and finals if they wished to sit for an honours degree. Most others required it in one part only, if at all. For my part, after a year's Hebrew, I knew that I both disliked it and found it very time-consuming. The alternative was to do an English set book (Jeremiah) and I felt sure that my future ministry, whatever it was, would benefit more from that, and from the extra time available for all the other parts of the course, than it would from a scraped lower second. So I opted for the pass degree course. My only regret in later years was that it ruled out all possibility of theological teaching. Good-bye Hebrew. Good-bye honours degree.

But there was a real plus which has only dawned upon me in more recent years. Nowadays students are mass produced in large classes with, in many cases, only the most peripheral relationship with their lecturers. I spent two years studying Jeremiah in one-to-one sessions with Stafford Wright. That was a tremendous experience and one which is virtually out of the question in to-day's cost-effective society. Little did I think at the time of the huge investment in preparation which Staffy so uncomplainingly lavished on me. One consequence was that I have never since then thought of Jeremiah as an old moaner, wallowing in bad news.

By half-term, Jackie and I had decided to go to Cambridge for the weekend. I would stay in the guest room at Caius (where David Maybury was studying after his national service in the Canal Zone as a field-gunner subaltern), while Jackie would do the same at Girton with her school friend, Pat Pearce, who was reading Maths. It was my first visit to Cambridge and the very different atmosphere from that at Bristol. It was probably then that I first experienced the attitude of effortless superiority endemic to both Oxford and Cambridge. Never having even thought of the possibility of going to either I had no sense of being in the wrong place at Bristol. It was a great university and one I was thoroughly enjoying.

Food and sweet rationing was coming to an end at last but restaurants had long been free from such control. Sadly, nearly fifteen years of serving up unimaginative food had created a 'take it or leave it' attitude and the customer was expected to put up with it, however tough or unpalatable the stuff on his plate. The first challenge to this 'eat up and shut up' view of culinary achievement came from Raymond Postgate, whose small *Good Food Guide* appeared on the bookshelves at that time. I bought one and have taken every issue since. In over forty years the *Guide* has sent us to disappointing restaurants on only two occasions (and they were back in the mid-1960s). The *Guide* has been an annual source of delight throughout and Jackie and I cut our teeth on many of the best restaurants in the Bristol area. There weren't very many but we found them and began to value the growing pressure for quality cooking which Postgate and his successors were exerting. The creative and artistic treatment of food has, since those years, been an art form which we enjoy whenever we eat out. With not much money available we have had to be occasional diners but, from student days, we have always thought expensive meals to be money well spent.

Around that time the university chaplaincy organised a mission to the university, with Joe Fison, later to be Bishop of Salisbury, as the chief missioner. It wasn't very memorable and had it not been for one of his assistant-missioners I should have entirely forgotten it. The chaplain was a glossy young man, a typically Establishment figure, and just the sort of clergyman who disdained the Tyndale tradition of Evangelical Anglicanism, which in those days was certainly a minority outlook within the Church of England. The assistant-missioner was a Franciscan friar, Father Michael Fisher, one day to become Bishop of St Germans, in Truro diocese. Fisher and the chaplain (so I have been told) were discussing where Fisher would stay during the mission. 'Have you any preference?' enquired the chaplain. 'Yes, Tyndale Hall,' said Fisher. 'Oh,' said the chaplain, hesitantly. 'Oh, I like it. Ha, ha. Now, where would you actually like to stay?' 'Tyndale,' repeated Fisher.

And he did. A friar in a distinctly 'Evangelical' college? Well, it worked and it worked well. Fisher liked us and we liked him. He had a gospel that we could recognise and before the week was out some of us urged the Principal to ask him to preach at a special chapel service. It was a great sermon. Finally the students crowned the week by dressing up as monks and friars and processed solemnly into the dining hall surrounding Michael as they intoned in plain-chant, 'I tort I tor a puddy-tat, a cweeping up on me . . .', and presented him with a signed copy of the Principal's new book. Michael was visibly moved and only a handful of our Ulster contingent found the acceptance of a friar too difficult to swallow in a good Protestant college.

At Tyndale, my closest neighbour was Geoff Hill. He was from Cumberland (as it was) and a great extrovert. We got on excellently and were generally involved in any fun and games that were on offer. Shortly before Christmas we decided, in great secrecy, to enter Ridley at the dead of night, and put hook-and-eye bolts on all the student bedrooms. The day before this escapade, I went up there when the house was deserted and prepared all the holes with a gimlet, disguising them with black shoe-polish. At about 1 a.m. we entered the basement (having left a door unlocked) and set off for the top floor. We bolted five of the eight and were about to start on the sixth when a light went on in one of the two still untouched. The door opened and a figure set out for the lavatory. We, unfortunately, were in a cul-de-sac with only the lavatory and the sixth room in which to hide. Gently we opened the bedroom door and crept in on hands and knees, at the foot of the bed. There was a sudden creak, and an agitated voice said, 'Who's there?', and a voice in the corridor said sleepily, 'It's only me, Pete.' A second 'Who's there?' followed a creaking of bed springs and, by means of a string and pulley, the light went on. Geoff and I, face downwards on the floor, by the door, were revealed. 'Boys,' said Peter Dawes from the bed, 'lovely to see you. Have a cup of tea.' The chain was pulled in the adjacent loo and in walked Derek Osborne. The tea party became quite hysterical and one by one the others were released from their rooms to join the party. It was by now nearly 2 a.m.

When, in the late 1980s, Jackie and I were present at the consecration of Peter Dawes as Bishop of Derby, in Southwark Cathedral, at the crucial solemn moment, when Peter was submerged by twenty consecrating bishops' hands, I could only irreverently hear him saying 'Who's there?' all those years before. I very much hope that Jesus has a developed sense of the ludicrous.

One of the college's great institutions was the bathroom. Each floor had its own bathroom which was the social centre. There, tea was consumed frequently and copiously. I have never drunk tea, but more theology was discussed, debated and approved or pulverised in the bathrooms than ever emerged in lectures. Quite often the bath itself was legitimately occupied during these bouts and the naked resident needed eyes everywhere as his colleagues sought ways of disposing of their tea dregs to add interest to his lustrations. Every Tyndale man rejoices in the bathroom tradition – it was the focus of fellowship, prayer, confession and learning and was, I think, unique in the story of English theological education. In fact, in almost every way, Tyndale gave the lie to the secular assumption that theological colleges were cheerless, ultrapious, monastic institutions, and the equally mistaken ecclesiastical view that it was a place of 'Fundamentalist' indoctrination. A more heterogeneous bunch of men it would be hard to find, including, in that era, a greengrocer, two miners, a cotton-mill worker, a shop steward, a parachutist, clerks, sailors, soldiers, airmen, would-be lawyers, accountants, a telephone engineer, two Jewish-Christian refugees from the Nazis, and a motley collection of graduates and undergraduates. Hardly a man fitted the 'dear vicar' image and all had thrashed out their Christian faith in the real world outside. It was a great place to be and its alumni have stayed loyal to it, even though its traditions have long since been merged into Trinity College, Bristol, which I was to help to create years later.

My 1953–54 Sunday duty was to assist in a ward service at Bristol's Homeopathic Hospital. I was, to be honest, glad that I wasn't a patient, having to endure the well-meaning half-hour of Sankey and Moody hymns and tract distribution. My job was to support the elderly quartet of Plymouth Brothers and 'their good ladies' in this virtuous activity. They were kind, warm-hearted, and living in a mental world long since vanished. I felt positively embarrassed to have to join in and be identified with this activity, as did Jackie, who came along for the ride!

One Sunday, the leader, a dear godly old gentleman, asked if he might have a private word. He was clearly uneasy but did his best. 'Forgive me,' he said in his beautiful Bristol dialect, 'Oi'm not a narrow-moinded man moiself, moind you, but Oi'm afraid some of the brothers and sisters aren't happy about yurr young lady.'

'Oh,' I said, surprised, 'what's she done?' 'Well,' he continued, 'Oi'm not saying it moiself but, you see, she did pray eout leoud when we were praying together and she didn't have a hat on.' Well, it was obvious that it wasn't one of the 'brothers' who was worried but one of the elderly 'sisters' who, like all good Plymouth Brethren, didn't approve of women praying aloud in any circumstances and, least of all, without a flowerpot-shaped felt container on her head. 'I'll tell her,' I said, and he beamed at me gratefully. 'It's not me, you underrstand . . .' Jackie quietly exploded when, in due course, I enlightened her. 'I hate hats,' she expostulated, 'and I'm certainly not wearing one just to satisfy these old . . .' I forget the word she used. I pacified her and she agreed to restrain her extempore utterances to the Almighty. Peace was restored. Well, we were their guests so we just had to conform once a week.

During the year, whenever possible, Jackie and I went on from the Homeopathic Hospital to the nave service in Bristol Cathedral. It was always conducted by the Dean, Evered Lunt, who was later to be Bishop of Stepney. He had earlier conducted a superb quiet day in Tyndale chapel on Isaiah 6 and I usually found his preaching stirring and thoughtful. His manner was strangely eccentric, since he pulled his chin in till he was almost throttled by his deep dog-collar and then peered myopically over his small glasses. One Sunday, as he was saying farewell at the door, I, in cocky student fashion, told him I could have got his sermon from the Chief Rabbi since there was nothing explicitly Christian in it from start to finish. He looked most surprised, stuttered a bit, and I was gone. I wrote to apologise for my ill-mannered behaviour but the point was still valid. He, like many Anglican dignitaries then and since, was making the foolish assumption that to use the word 'God' was to imply something Christian. I learnt an important lesson that day, even if I went about correcting it rudely. There's a lot more to Christianity than throwing the word 'God' about.

That spring the college was more aware than usual of London. We prayed for it fervently, including an all-night prayer meeting in the chapel. The Principal later said that prayer was so fast and furious that it took him half an hour to get a word in at 4 a.m. in the morning! The reason, of course, was the Greater London Crusade at Harringay Arena, which lasted for three months. Night by night, Billy Graham preached, Cliff Barrows led the singing, and George Beverly Shea, 'America's beloved gospel singer,' sang a mixture of Sankey spiritual songs and more modern, very sentimental, gospel music. Ten thousand people flocked to hear Graham every evening and I managed to get there twice when I was back home briefly. He had arrived to the sneers of the media and both the Liberal and Anglo-Catholic segments of the Church of England. By the time of the final meeting at Wembley Stadium over a million and a quarter had attended and 120,000 were present in the Stadium when Graham, flanked by the Lord Mayor of London and the Archbishop of Canterbury, Geoffrey Fisher, preached to them and to a second gathering of 65,000 at White City. London had seen nothing like it before and the evening papers cashed in with special supplements. The Crusade was to have a major impact on Anglican ordinand numbers for, perhaps, five years, and it launched Graham on a worldwide ministry which, forty-five years on, is only now drawing to a close.

It wasn't long before the cricket season came round once more and it was a disappointing one for me. I had been appointed Assistant-Secretary at the end of the previous season and was hopeful of a regular place in the First Eleven. In the event, and it was a real shock, I was asked to captain the thirds. I quickly scored eighty-one not out and was promoted to the seconds but it was a wet summer and many games were rained off. I didn't get another decent score and stayed outside the charmed circle for the rest of the term. I was, however, during the summer vac invited to play for Bickley Park, one of the top clubs in the Bromley area, and in my first match for them, batting well down the order, saved the match with an unbeaten thirty-seven. That assured me a place in their first team during the 1954 and 1955 vacations and I averaged twenty-five throughout.

Early in the term, I noticed an advert on the board in the Union building, 'Wanted. A cricketer to coach the school's cricket.' The address was a prep school near Clevedon and, with my car, it looked a feasible way of earning some pocket money pleasantly. I applied, was accepted and thus, in those days of 'Gentlemen and Players', unwittingly lost my amateur status. At £1 per afternoon, it seemed a decent arrangement when petrol cost 3s (15p) a gallon. Being a pro never became an issue (hardly anyone knew, anyway) but I suppose I ought to have emerged from a different door at the half-dozen county grounds on which I played.

Jackie safely graduated and made plans to return for one more year to acquire a certificate of education. She then went off on a parish mission in Southgate. Taking her to her hosts' home I pursued a particular car, as instructed, and when he emerged on to a main road, not known to me, I followed him, to be hit amidships by a Standard Vanguard. My old Wolseley was built like a tank and didn't sustain too much damage but it was expensive and a shock. I've never been involved in another accident of that kind in the intervening forty years.

One Sunday morning, back at Christ Church, Orpington, I and another local ordinand, Michael Baughen, noticed a figure sitting in the congregation. It was Colin Cowdrey, on the verge of winning his first cap for England. He was due to play in a cricket match nearby that afternoon and, unwittingly, was to be the means of removing half the Pathfinder Bible class boys, who all went to see him. I wrote to him, asking whether he realised what he had done and wondering whether he, as a practising Christian, could justify it. He replied with a thoughtful, but puzzled letter. He had thought about it a lot. 'How one spends one's Sundays is a serious issue to anybody who has made any start in the Christian life.' Was it an unacceptable compromise? He didn't really know. Michael Baughen and I appreciated the fact that he had replied. We two became close friends from then onwards.

My summer vacation job was a complete change. I was taken on by George Payne's, the tea and chocolate firm, in their warehouse by Tower Bridge. My job was to hump four tea-chests on a porters' trolley, which required a flick-of-the-wrist knack. I was to be instructed by Ginger, a not-too-bright Cockney. It took, he told me, 'a week to get the knack'. I successfully acquired it on the first day and on the Tuesday morning showed him. 'Yeah,' he said, 'well, you 'ave got it – but it takes a week, see.'

So, for a week, I wasted the firm's time and money. That, it seemed, was the accepted pattern for the working man, in those days. Actually, we only received deliveries about three times a day so our work lasted about two-and-a-half hours. The porters retired to the lavatory area to play poker. I lay on a pile of sacks in a corner, reading a book. A couple of days later the floor manager saw me. 'And what do you think you're up to?' 'I'm reading a theological book.' 'Oh, are you?' 'Yes, and when you stop them playing poker surreptitiously, I'll stop reading this openly.' He smiled. 'You've got a point,' he said and life returned to normal.

By now, I was growing increasingly convinced that God was calling me to serve in the Church of England's ministry. True, I had just preached my first sermon at Christ Church, Orpington. As you might expect from a young Evangelical, it was about the 'new birth' and the consequential changes needed in one's character and behaviour. It was 'correct' and unexciting (I still have the text) but, more to the point, a member of the congregation dropped dead on the way home, after it. Was that a hopeful sign for a would-be clergyman? Anyway, I decided to apply to CACTM, the Central Advisory Council of Training for the Ministry, and they duly sent me to Farnham Castle to a selection conference. I enjoyed it, and was impressed by the chairman, Canon Marcus Knight, a canon of St Paul's Cathedral, and soon to be Dean of Exeter. One day, unknown to me, I would follow in his footsteps at St Paul's. But, first, they accepted me, knowing that I was still hoping to go to Nigeria after a curacy. That was quite normal in the 1950s.

Life continued with its blend of lectures, discussions, prayer, both formal and informal, friendship and courtship. Jackie and I grew steadily closer, longing for a full sexual relationship, but absolutely convinced that it must wait for marriage, still well over a year off. We set ourselves goals and limits, enjoyed ourselves greatly within the limits, and found that life was tolerable if we both stuck to our rules. We've never regretted it. What's more we felt, and still feel, sorry for those who can't or won't accept that sex and complete commitment go together. We think the price that those who 'must have sex' pay is altogether too high and the damage done to the concept of lifelong marriage is all too evident.

Jackie had now got her own room in a house opposite Christ Church, Clifton, and close to the Suspension Bridge. She had inherited it from Sheila Runnalls, who had been a key figure in the Christian Union and had since left to teach. Sheila, later to be one of our bridesmaids and become a lifelong friend, married Michael Eastman, who was in due course to co-author a book with me. The landlady was a fearsome dragon, who stuck up warning notes all over the house about bathwater limits, loo paper, and so on. I kept well out of her way on my frequent visits to Jackie.

That autumn, now secretary to the university cricket club, I received a memorable letter from what we should now call a Sri Lankan. He was in charge of cricket at the RAF station at Pucklechurch, near Bristol, and sent me a 'Peter-Sellers-type' invitation to the university to take part, through our Third Eleven with their first team. A few phrases will capture the flavour. He wished to 'trespass upon your indulgence' and 'enlarging upon the liberty' confessed their wish to 'engage you in friendly encounter', and 'likewise expressing the hope' that the dates 'shall not clash with your commitments'. If they did 'I would no less voice my belief' that some alternative could be found, and would 'be equally appreciative if you could at the earliest opportunity, and irrespective of import, communicate a decision'. Sellers didn't need a scriptwriter. My Sri Lankan sergeant rolled his own phrases to order. The letter remains one of my most prized possessions. It naturally carries a full RAF reference number and is probably, in carbon copy, in some government archive to this day.

It was at about that time that the six of us who were starting our finals' year for the Bristol theology degree began to get anxious about our New Testament course. We had two lecturers, Denis Tongue who looked after the whole area of 'introduction', and the college Vice-Principal who handled our set texts from Matthew, Mark, Galatians and Philippians. We had no difficulty with Denis, who provided us with excellent material, but the Vice-Principal, John Wenham, a thoughtful and learned man, was nevertheless an unsatisfactory and slow lecturer and we were rapidly falling far behind our schedule. We set up among ourselves a supplementary course each of us lecturing the rest from whatever commentaries we could find. In that way we caught up the backlog while Wenham dropped further and further behind. By the time of our last term we were desperately behind and Wenham raced through Matthew's Sermon on the Mount in hopelessly superficial fashion. We all graduated but only, I suspect, because having lost confidence in him we did almost all the essential work ourselves. He was a good, able man and remained Vice-Principal for a further thirteen years but we warned our successors what to expect. To be a scholar is not any guarantee that one can lecture. To make matters worse, he oversaw our preaching course and advised us on how to do it, though I thought him to be a very dull and uninspiring preacher! I decided to ignore his advice on preaching and I thank God that I did. A bit of humility might well have ruined my preaching for life!

However, the serious duties of life did not spoil the lighter moments of Tyndale activity. One day, the Ridley members appeared at tea, prior to chapel, wearing very little indeed. I forget the reason but I decided to turn it to advantage. I quietly slipped out of the room, found their normal clothes in the common room and threw the whole lot down the college laundry chute. Keeping a very straight face, I entered the chapel and composed myself for prayer. Others came up from tea and did likewise, fulfilling the normal daily routine. Soon after, the first shouts and yells came from the direction of the Common Room. There were thumping sounds as men bounded upstairs. The service began in the usual dignified way, while for at least ten minutes, the chapel door opened and closed to admit latecomers. A surreptitious glance showed them to be in the strangest variety of garments, obviously grabbed or borrowed from any available source. It took them hours to find the missing clothes and no-one had a clue as to who had done it.

The university's Chancellor did not often appear at events in Bristol, but, four days before his eightieth birthday, Winston Churchill, still Prime Minister, came to confer degrees. He wore the robe which his father, Randolph, had worn in 1886 as Chancellor of the Exchequer. I was seated perhaps eight or ten seats away from the door as he arrived. I thought he looked a very fragile old man and although we cheered him it was, I believe, in appreciation of his great achievements during the war, and not because of his fading and nearly senile appearance in the 1950s. He thanked us for the gift of a silver salver to mark his birthday but, although he had eleven years left to him, I do not, with hindsight, think that Graham Sutherland's portrait maligned him. He was well past his sell-by date. That said, his very presence was memorable, the epitome of living history, a man who had lived so much of the eighty years in the very centre of world affairs. I was to admire him even more as the years unfolded and I read perhaps thirty or more books by, or about, him. 26 November 1954 was a day not to be forgotten and I can still recall parts of it most vividly.

Maurice Burrell, now a canon at Norwich, was the Senior Student that year and was engaged to Jill. They both came from Norwich and we occasionally saw her when she came to visit. She was, we knew, due for a minor operation and the college prayed for her on the day in question. That evening, Maurice rang and came off the phone white. 'She's very serious,' he said, 'I must go home at once.' He had already missed the last train from Bristol and could not hope to reach her before midday. 'Geoff,' I said to my neighbour, 'will you come with me and we'll drive him. I must have someone to talk to him while I keep my eyes on the road. I reckon we can get there by 6 a.m.' 'OK,' he replied, and we bundled him into my old car. It was going to be 220 miles, across country, and there were no fast roads in those days. Anyway, my top speed was about fifty-five m.p.h. unless we were going downhill. We could hope to average around thirty m.p.h., though the dark might help. We hadn't got beyond Chipping Sodbury when we hit fog, real fog. I drove into it, knowing that in college everyone was praying, even at midnight. That night we twice missed fatal collisions with big lorries by the skin of our teeth. I simply drove down the centre cat's-eyes and hoped for the best. We got there, fog or no fog, about 6.45 a.m. and dropped Maurice off.

Now what? 'Symon Beesley,' we chorused and headed for St Catherine's church, at Mile Cross.

We somehow discovered the address of Symon's digs and arrived at 7.15. His landlady came to the door and looked distinctly unsure about the two scruffy unshaven young men who demanded to see her lodger, the curate. 'I'm afraid Mr Beesley's still asleep,' she parried. 'So what,' we said, 'we're used to seeing him in his pyjamas.' She let us in and pointed upstairs to his room. We staggered in. 'Sym,' we shook him, 'wake up, you lazy slug.' His eyes focused, then a huge smile creased his face. 'What on earth are you rogues up to?' he enquired. He got up, pulled on a pair of long johns (to our amazement) and said, 'It's cold in these parts.'

By lunchtime the news on Jill was better and Geoff Hill and I drove back.

Many of my generation of Tyndale men reacted strongly against the gushy pietism of much Evangelical life. We hated the spurious 'language of Zion' that seemed to be endemic and which people had to learn if they wanted to be regarded as 'sound' or 'keen'. I remember quite consciously vowing that I would root it out of my vocabulary and talk English, whether to God or anyone else. On the whole, I think I was successful then, and I've never lapsed back into the awful artificiality. I can't understand the people who pour it out and I was treated, once, to a classic example at the university Christian Union's Sunday morning prayer meeting. When the time came for actual prayer (extempore prayer, of course) we had just fourteen minutes left. Anyway, the first prayer was by a Methodist ordinand and he went on (the exact phrase) for eight minutes. Without a pause, he was followed by a second Methodist ordinand who filled in the remaining six minutes. The first began (as did the second, later), 'O thou', long pause, 'that dwellest', further long pause, 'in *unapproachable* light.' Here he nearly strangled his tonsils to get the right sound effect. By the time the two of them had told God who and what he was the full fourteen minutes had vanished. Not one single petition from start to finish. Not surprisingly, the Tyndale contingent called them 'the Unapproachable Light Boys' and made sure that we got in first with actual intercessions at future prayer meetings.

A new and brilliant lecturer, Dr James Packer, had recently joined the staff. A theologian who had concentrated on the Puritan period, his lectures outshone all the others for their clarity and analytical framework. He and his young wife moved into the college and, although blessed with a dry sense of humour and a soft Gloucestershire accent, he soon showed signs of worry at the flippancy, as he saw it, of the chief jokers among the students. Needless to say, I was one. One Sunday he decided to preach about it. He took his text from the book of Proverbs, 'The laughter of fools is as the crackling of thorns under a pot,' and he graphically illustrated the theme from the life of the Bible's greatest fool, Samson the strong man. It was itself the sermon of a young man, for he was still in his twenties, and it made the great mistake of being directed, quite blatantly, at the small group of us. In particular, he referred to Samson's exploit when he removed the town gates of Gaza and set them up on a nearby hill. We, being soaked at that time in Goon humour, were almost in hysterics. 'I suppose,' he said, sarcastically, 'some of you think that was funny.'

We certainly did, and I still do. The sermon over, we decided that it could not go unchallenged. The annual college 'concert' was due very soon and we set out to make a taped version of the Goons, entitled 'Samsinge and the Gates of Gaza.' It took six of us twelve hours to produce a twelve-minute tape, with our (quite passable) versions of the Goon voices. The hero was, inevitably, Bluebottle, playing the part of the mighty Samsinge. On the night the college roared its approval and especially at the final moment. It was our practice to build large pyramids of empty milk bottles outside some lovesick student's door, in a dark corridor, then call him to the phone to speak to his girlfriend. The consequence was inevitable and the sound of bouncing bottles could be heard a long way. Samsinge, to everyone's delight, picked up the great gates, with groans and squeaks and . . . knocked over the milk bottles! Jim Packer had met his match and, much as we admired and respected him, we knew he wouldn't make the same mistake twice. He grew up, and so did we, but not till the following event ended our career of fooling about.

The last, and best remembered by all concerned, of the crazy

Tyndale rags was the painting of the goat. Our sister institution across the Downs, Clifton Theological College, now the site of Trinity College, was also in the Evangelical tradition and we shared lectures plus some good-humoured competition. One morning, some of our men returned to Tyndale with the news that one of their students (whom, for kindness' sake, I shall call Smith-Montague) had installed a goat in the grounds. This was, we thought, laying down the gauntlet with a vengeance, and we formulated plans to deal with the situation.

Two carloads of Tyndale vigilantes set out across the Downs at approaching midnight. As we left, a highly suspicious Irish student, Donald Cyprian-Marks (also a pseudonym) was seen entering the college telephone room. He rang Clifton, warned them of our coming and was told not to try taking the mickey out of them, thank you very much. So, like Stalin in 1941, no preparations to combat the invasion were made. Leaving our cars close to Clifton, we wandered through their desperately overgrown grounds, seeking by sound or smell, a goat. When we finally heard a low bleat, we found the animal, tethered to a post by a piece of string. His name was not George and his beard was not yellow, so we removed one half of the latter and painted his torso and legs in the green and black hoops of Tyndale football colours.

Next morning the story of the night's activity was relayed back to us from Clifton. A day later, at lunchtime, the phone went and I reached it first. It was Mr Smith-Montague and he sounded most distressed. 'Some of your men painted my goat the other night and the paint has caused her great distress.' 'Hang on a minute,' I said. 'These are very serious accusations. I think you should speak to our senior student. I'll get him.' I called Maurice Burrell to the phone. 'I'm terribly sad to hear this appalling news,' said Maurice. 'I can't believe that anyone from Tyndale would do such a thing.' (Maurice had not been in on the facts so he was just about skirting the borders of honesty.) 'I've had to take her to the vet,' whimpered Mr Smith-Montague, 'and it's cost me a guinea.' 'That's even more distressing,' responded Maurice. 'Look, we naturally admit no responsibility in this matter, but we can't see a brother-ordinand suffering, so we'll have a whip-round and send you the proceeds. Good-bye.'

We rapidly collected the 252p in coppers (the old guinea was 21s) and Geoff Hill and I were deputed to deliver the *ex-gratia* donation. Unfortunately, we had never met Mr Smith-Montague, who was the wettest wimp going, and when we finally found him and learnt that the paint-sores had been caused by the string which he had tied round the goat's neck, we had the greatest difficulty in keeping straight faces. The goat was, in fact, almost undamaged and it was Smith-Montague who was near to tears. We solemnly counted out the 252 coins, then 'accidentally' knocked the pile over, requiring him to recount them and sign a receipt for the '*ex-gratia*' payment which implied no admission of liability by anyone at Tyndale. How Geoff and I stopped ourselves from hysterical laughter while this pathetic and heart-rending performance ground slowly to a halt, I shall never know. We were so emotionally exhausted that we drove straight across the Downs to a cafe and had a second lunch.

The sequel was harsh. Donald Cyprian-Marks was surrounded, stripped, and painted in various strategic places. Months later he left the college and did not reappear. Smith-Montague was also never ordained. Student justice may seem harsh but all those of us involved felt that we had saved the Church of England from taking on two characters who might not have fitted happily into the life of a clergyman. Our one regret was not realising what an inadequate Smith-Montague was before we painted the goat, which in any case survived quite happily. Had we known, then perhaps the whole saga would never have taken place. I still have occasional twinges about it, not on behalf of the goat, but concerning wretched Smith-Montague.

At the end of March 1955 I travelled up to London to see the candidates' secretary of the Church Missionary Society in Salisbury Square. Canon Harry Wittenbach was a clergyman of the old school who, despite a somewhat gravelly style, did his best to set me at my ease while we discussed the possibility of Nigeria. All went smoothly until the question arose of my engagement to Jackie. 'Yes, well now let us see. You would have to complete a first curacy of three years, then two years at our training college in Chislehurst, followed by a first tour in Nigeria of five years. So, bearing in mind that you still have another fifteen months before ordination I think you could safely plan to marry in about eleven-and-a-half years' time.' To a man whose engagement had already lasted eighteen months his words came like a hammer blow. I said farewell as courteously as I could and reeled out. Half-an-hour later I was on the phone to Staffy. He found Wittenbach's proposal hard to stomach and suggested that I raise the whole matter with the Bishop of Rochester, whom I was to see on the following day.

I went by train to Rochester to meet the Bishop, Christopher Chavasse, who only had one leg. I heard him approaching down the corridor, ker-thump, ker-thump, ker-thump, and rose to meet him. He was a small, bald man, carrying a strange cigarette-holder attached to one finger by a ring. The interview was very positive, as he'd been in his earlier letter which began, 'My dear Mr Saward,' which contrasted well with the usual 'Dear Saward' letters from other bishops of that era. I told him about Wittenbach's plans for my marriage in 1966 and he exploded. 'Present 'em with a *fait accompli*, my boy. There's nothing they can do about it!'

I liked our bishop's style and humanity and we parted good friends. Later that day he wrote saying, 'I agree to the proposal that you should marry during the last year of your training for Holy Orders. I am satisfied it is the best course.' Jackie was pleased, Staffy was pleased, and I was ecstatic. I was also grateful to hear that my future training was to be paid for by the church since I had had to use up all my army savings to pay for my degree course. Kent Education Committee had given me a small grant but it was nothing like enough.

I decided that I had one other duty to fulfil while in Petts Wood for the weekend. I would go to both morning services at St Francis' church to see whether things were really as dull and dreary as memory suggested. I hadn't been there for almost ten years but the same vicar was still there. After two unmemorably frigid services I saw that he was standing near the door. Well, that was an advance. He'd never done that in the old days. I walked up and introduced myself. 'I used to be a choir-boy here.' Clearly he had no idea who I was. 'What are you doing now?' he enquired politely. 'I'm an ordinand.' His eyes lit up and he was suddenly all interest. He'd only ever had one ordinand before, a boy who had been a server in my time, Victor Cassam. 'Really,' he said, 'which college?' 'Tyndale Hall,' I replied. There was a pause of horrified silence. 'You wouldn't think of transferring to Kelham?' Kelham was his old alma mater, a rigorously monastic Anglo-Catholic institution, and the idea was, frankly, ludicrous. 'No, I'm afraid not,' I responded firmly. The die was cast. He drew himself up to his full five foot six inches and rasped ungraciously, 'In that case I must regard you as a failure in my parish. Good morning.' He turned and stalked away. I walked home not knowing whether to laugh or cry. I was going to be ordained into the ministry of the Church of England, as he had been, and this was his reaction. Farewell, St Francis, Petts Wood, and God help you.

And so to my finals. In the internal exams throughout the two years I had averaged 64 per cent, with 73 per cent in my Old Testament papers. This was upper-second territory in general, and first level for Old Testament. I carefully prepared over 100 possible answers in mnemonic form and from 109 questions had to produce only one unprepared response! Looking now at my heavily annotated question papers, it seems frustrating that, having discarded Hebrew, I could only get a pass degree, whatever my actual results. I duly collected it.

Wickets that summer were rock hard and in beautiful sunshine I managed to get twenty-five innings, eleven of them for the Firsts, not dropping to the Seconds once. The university played two two-day matches against Gloucestershire Seconds each year and that summer we beat them in the first match on the county ground at Horfield (unheard of) and almost made them follow on at Coombe Dingle. In the second match, stung by the earlier defeat, they fielded half the county side, but to no avail. My best score was sixty not out against Westbury, off whom I had taken seventy-six not out in 1953. After going down, I played six times for Eastbourne on the beautiful Saffrons ground, scoring freely, and five times for Bickley Park, including fifty-five against the Metropolitan Police. Right at the beginning of that innings I was hit in the throat by their red-haired fast bowler (no helmets in those days) and, honour needing to be satisfied, hit him for four next ball.

I have one especially vivid memory of fielding at backward short leg against RAF Innsworth when a young man called John Murray played a chanceless innings of seventy-six against the best the university could produce. He was, in due course, to be the Middlesex and England wicket keeper, securing over fifteen hundred dismissals, and he 'kept' behind me while I made a mere fifteen not out.

I also played a little tennis on the Tyndale courts and, to my surprise, found myself in the doubles final with Derek Osborne (the singles champion). One of our opponents was John Stanley, the College's best all-round sportsman, later to become Prolocutor of York Province and a Queen's Chaplain. Derek and I won and I informed Dad triumphantly of my achievement. When I got home he said, 'Come round to the recreation ground. I'll take you on for a set of tennis.' I was twenty-three and he was fifty-three. He beat me six–love and hardly moved at all. Honour was restored. He could never match me at cricket but at tennis I never dared to face him again. That afternoon was a distinct step forward in the humility stakes.

In late July we fixed our wedding date and Staffy agreed to tie the knot. Jackie, with the shrewd sense of a woman, insisted that it be at 2 p.m. on 3 April 1956. Why so precise, I asked. 'I want you to remember it for the rest of our lives,' she said, 'and 2 3 4 5 6, ought to fix it in your brain for ever.' So, at last, we had a horizon even if it did mean nearly eight months far apart in the interval. She had gained her teaching certificate and was going to teach at Strood, near Rochester, 150 miles from Bristol.

It was Staffy's idea that I should sit my General Ordination Exam in August. If you had a theological degree you only had to take seven papers and I had covered some of the ground in five of those already. That left Ethics and Worship to be mugged up. I only had any anxiety about the theoretical part of Ethics and skimming one small book sorted that out. The standards required were, frankly, very low and one only had to pass since there were no grades to achieve. 'GOE', said Bishop Stephen Neill, 'seems to me to be one of the gravest misfortunes that has ever befallen the Church of England.' He went on to add that 'It is one of those examinations which can be passed without having read a single, theological book.'

He was certainly right in my case. I vividly recall one useful piece of cynical advice from Jim Vincent, now a Truro prebendary. 'When you're doing history', he said in his lush Cornish accent, 'put yourself in each side's position, decide what they ought to have done and answer on the assumption that they did the opposite.' Faced with only one question about which I knew nothing (it was about the dissolution of the monasteries) I took his advice and produced a very satisfactory answer. I passed everything and was faced with a year to spend with nothing much to do. I started on an MA thesis (the university agreed that my BA results warranted the attempt) though I never finished it, and I can claim, somewhat disreputably, that I completed all that was legally required of an ordinand without ever having attended a single lecture on the GOE course.

One vital thing was achieved by my theological training. It opened my eyes to see a vast range of ideas 'out there'. Up till then I had assumed that simple trust, some prayer, churchgoing, Bible reading, and a moral life was the sum of being a Christian. Bristol taught me how small I was, how great the world of ideas was, and offered me the vision of a lifetime of mind-stretching discovery of God's truth in all its complexity. However long life was going to be I knew I should never get bored intellectually. I owe that to Tyndale Hall and it is one of life's great debts.

I saw the advertisement for a vacant curacy in the Church of England Newspaper at the beginning of November. It was in the parish of Christ Church, West Croydon, in those days part of Canterbury diocese, and the vicar, Philip Wood, was a very old friend of Herbert Taylor's whom I had met once at Orpington years before. I went to visit the place and we all agreed to it. There was a small terrace house and a teaching job for Jackie would be available in a nearby school. It would now be up to the Archbishop and he agreed to see me at Lambeth Palace on 16 February in the early afternoon. I little thought when I first entered the palace how many scores of times I should find myself there in years to come.

Geoffrey Francis Fisher, ninety-ninth Archbishop of Canterbury, was a genial but awesome figure. An eagle-lectern of a man, he had been a headmaster and knew how to keep a young man in his place. The interview proceeded well until I made the foolish mistake of disparaging Latin and the Classics. As an Oxford First in 'Greats' this was damnable heresy to Fisher and he wiped me up and down his study wall before releasing me to reel across the courtyard and out on to the banks of the Thames. Never again did I leave Lambeth in so deflated a state. Fortunately, Fisher had more important matters on his mind and the subject was forgotten, to my considerable relief.

There was just one final crazy thing left for me to do and, when I look back on it, I still feel the metaphorical shivers. One morning, at about 11, I decided, having no lectures, that I would have a bath. Someone came in to the Latimer top-floor bathroom, had a cup of tea, chatted for a few minutes, removed the door key from the inside, walked out and locked me in. As it happened, there was an empty clothes line there, so I tied it to the bath tap, put on some trousers, climbed out of the window, walked along the outside ledge, holding the rope taut in my left hand, and climbed in through the next window. My gaoler then threw a bucket of water over me. I get the shivers, especially if I ever go back, because the ledge was about 30 feet above a glass-roofed porch and it was about two inches wide. It was, I think, probably the most idiotically dangerous thing that I ever did. My forthcoming marriage, my forthcoming ministry, indeed my life, hung in the balance for those two minutes. I don't know to this day why I did it. I'm simply grateful that I survived.

Jim Packer, our Church History and Doctrine lecturer, was in those days an unashamed advocate of Calvinist and Puritan theology. His mind has always been dominated by both Scripture and logic and, in Calvinist terms, this had usually led to a very strictly ordered framework of doctrinal thinking. One of the classic tensions in Christian theology has been that between divine purpose and human free will and much Calvinist thinking has come down firmly on the side of the former. At breakfast one morning I asked Jim to help me in this. While broadly Calvinist in my thinking, as most Anglican Evangelicals are, I found it hard to accept the diminution of human free will within the Calvinist scheme of things. 'Wouldn't you agree', I put to him, 'that ultimately your kind of Calvinism turns man into a puppet?' He paused for a moment. 'Yes,' he finally said, and at that moment I knew I could never go down his road. I immensely respect him and like him, but cutting the Gordian Knot between divine purpose and human free will can never, to me, be a satisfactory solution. I cannot imagine that Jim in his maturity would have answered my question in so unsophisticated a manner.

Geoff Hill, to my disappointment, wasn't able to be my best man and I turned to my old friend David Mitchell. I should probably have asked him first anyway, but we were not much in touch. He had been a subaltern in the King's Own Scottish Borderers, served in Hong Kong, and was now at Oxford, where he affected a wild Gaelic manner and wrote obscure poetry. He despised my Evangelicalism and couldn't understand why I wanted to marry Jackie. 'Go to bed with her if you want to, but for God's sake don't marry the girl.'

Jackie and I ignored this sign of affection on his part and, in due course, I did both, but in the proper sequence. 2,3,4,5,6, it was, and at Holy Trinity, Cheltenham, with Moira and Sheila Runnalls in attendance as bridesmaids. In place of Wagner and Mendelssohn we had Walford Davies' *Solemn Melody* and the minuet from Handel's *Music for the Royal Fireworks*. Some of my friends thought both pieces highly symbolic of what was in store. Ironically, almost forty years later, I walked the length of St Paul's Cathedral to the same Handel, preceding the Princess Royal. I smiled on both occasions. Both women have real but different attractions for me.

We laid the most careful decoy plans to put our friends off the scent as regards our honeymoon plans and not even David got an inkling of what we were up to. Indeed, so engrossed was he in his duties as best man that he got left behind at the church and only just made it to the reception in time to make his speech. He doubtless knew what we would be up to, but not how, or where. We duly consummated the union in the Queen's Hotel in Cheltenham (just down the road from Jackie's home) and then went to the Castle Hotel, in Taunton, for a week. Taunton is not exactly Capri or Venice but the Castle had, in those days, the best food in the west of England (it still rates very high) and that was the second thing on our minds. We kept all the beautifully printed menus, underlined our own choices, and if you want to know exactly what we ate, you have only to ask. Taunton was a good centre for touring and we rented a Hillman Minx and ranged as far apart as Bodmin and Lulworth Cove. We then went to Philipps House at Dinton, near Salisbury, a National Trust manor house, for the final few days, while I recovered from a bout of food poisoning caused by a doubtful ham sandwich. I summarised our honeymoon in our wedding album as 'a host of timeless memories stored up from ten glorious days of exploration'. It was exactly that and it wouldn't have been if we had followed the urging of our desires for the previous two years.

And was it a successful marriage? Two tough customers who weren't going easily to say 'Yes, dear' to each other all the time are hardly ideal material for a smooth passage. Both of us are earthy realists, neither is given to sentimentality. So it would inevitably be quite a rough ride. A Christian union but hardly a bland or pious one. My disgracefully slanderous view is that, like yin and yang, we balance each other well. Jackie has many vices and few virtues and I have many virtues and few vices! Perfect equilibrium! In fact, Jackie is tenacious, loyal, prosaic, reliable, utterly discreet, never breaking a confidence, a woman who gets on with things and relaxes with soap operas. She is an excellent cook, a happy breeder of babies and mother of children, hospitable, someone who will get her hands dirty, prefers jeans and tee shirts to pretty, pretty clothes and doesn't mind being in the background. She worries incessantly about how much petrol is in the tank (she can't drive) and what the speedo is reading. She loves travel, entertaining, going to restaurants, and grandchildren. She has survived on a small income and few luxuries without grumbling, working in a supermarket for thirteen years to help pay school fees, and she's obsessed with Grand Prix motorsport. The marriage has merrily and grumpily roller-coasted for over forty years. We love each other and what's it got to do with you anyway? Mind your own business!

Jackie departed for Strood. I returned to Bristol with nothing much to do except play cricket before and after my ordination. I started with three games for the university Seconds, averaged over fifty, and was restored to the Firsts for my final eight games. I especially enjoyed taking part in a century partnership against our neighbours, Clifton College. These very big-headed schoolboys thought they were bound to win but Barry Auguste, from St Lucia, and I, scored over a hundred in an hour and we walked off smiling happily.

My very last game had one surprise left for me. Throughout my twenty-six games for the university Firsts I had regularly dropped hints that I could do with a few overs to prove my bowling skills. No-one took the slightest notice until we walked out into the field on my twenty-seventh and last match. At that point the Captain, Mike Dash (who was also our wicket-keeper), threw the new ball to me and said, 'Go on, have a go.' I set the field, walked back thirteen paces, came in on my nine-pace run and bowled the best ball of my whole cricketing career. It was an inswinger that cut back off the wicket. The batsman played and it fractionally missed his groping edge. The whole team turned to look at me. 'Wow,' said one of them, 'where have you been all these matches?' 'Well,' I said, 'it's too late now. You wouldn't believe me.' Good-bye, Bristol.

And with that happy retort, already three weeks on from his ordination as deacon, the Reverend Michael Saward set out for his parish, a student no longer.

Chapter Five

Pause for Thought (1)

He's twenty-four, he's just married, and he's a clergyman of the Church of England. We've just read all about his childhood and youth. Facts, facts, facts. But what about the real man behind it all? It's time for a little analysis.

Well, he's full of fun. Life has been easy and he can laugh and joke. He's oozing self-confidence and that irritates lots of people. No-one has got round to asking him why he's like that but they soon will.

He doesn't have any money and with his prospects he can't expect to have any. You don't become a clergyman if you want money and you certainly don't plan to be a missionary if you have pound signs in front of your eyes. So he's an idealist and fairly naive.

He has no idea about politics and isn't much interested. He has no idea about economics and only a rudimentary sense of social justice but, as a Christian, he thinks that justice is a good thing and he showed no trace of conscious racism in his time in Africa.

Like his father before him, he's a sporting type. He's played rugby indifferently, soccer a little better, hockey better still, tennis averagely, and cricket at top club and university level. He enjoys table tennis and can run and jump a bit, but not with any prospects. He's played the odd game of squash and a bit of badminton and he once tried one hole of golf. He got on to the green in two and took five putts to sink the miserable little ball. That was golf that was. He's never ski'd or skated and winter sports mean nothing to him.

He doesn't drink or smoke and never has, so he rarely goes into a pub. He can't dance and doesn't reckon he'll need to. He likes good food, but can't often afford it. He's never drunk tea or coffee in his life, for no obvious reason.

He knows next to nothing about painting, sculpture, music or architecture. He can sing and enjoys it but he can't read music and merely learns all the bass parts off by heart. He's never played an instrument. He likes poetry, hardly ever reads a novel but was gripped by a book on the American Civil War and, if he's going to read, will almost certainly concentrate on history, biography and travel. He's never been to an opera, a ballet or a concert and he doesn't possess a record player. He hardly ever goes to a theatre or cinema. He isn't remotely interested in the new rock 'n' roll craze that's just hit England and he's never worn a pair of these horrible blue jeans that are rapidly flooding the market. He has his hair cut short and likes it that way.

He's had two old 1930s cars and he sold the later one, plus his stamp collection, to get married.

Marriage? Yes, he's just broken the ice less than two months ago. He and his wife, Jackie, were virgins but were certainly not sexually ignorant. For the past three years they've been pacing themselves stage by stage, building up, you might say, to the consummation of their wedding night. That way the honeymoon was sheer pleasure. So much for the sex angle but marriage is a lot more than sex and they've been apart for the past month since the end of the honeymoon and it's not been fun. Neither of them has really begun to realise what actually living together means but with their temperaments there isn't a chance that wedlock will be a smooth experience. Not that they haven't realised that already. They've had a few explosive patches during their two-and-a-half year engagement and he's certainly agonised more than once as to whether this coming marriage is the right thing. But there it is. They've started and they mean to finish. They don't regard divorce as a live option, anyway, so it'll have to be survival or murder.

Everyone thinks he's gregarious and a natural mixer. As his dad says, he always seems to come out on top smiling. But he knows, even if no-one else does, that he has a very shy side and not

Donald, Lily and Michael Saward with Kim at Bude, 1936

Michael, Sgt Kenny and the guns of 8th Independent Light
Anti-Aircraft troop at Accra, Gold Coast, 1952

Tyndale Hall, winners of the Bristol theological colleges
football cup final, 1953

Michael with Jackie Atkinson on her graduation day at Bristol
University, 1954

Michael at the priests' ordination, next to Archbishop Geoffrey Fisher,
at Canterbury Cathedral, 1957

Bishop John Hughes, who provided this book's title

Gordon Harman, Michael and friends at Stoke Poges conference
house, 1960

"I gather it's a fellow called Saward."

Ian Barclay's cartoon in the *Church of England Newspaper*
lampooning 'On Top of My Column', 1966

George Hoffman and Michael at King Olaf's summer palace in Oslo,
1968

Radio and Television officer in Church House, Westminster, 1969

Ealing Parish Church in the 1980s

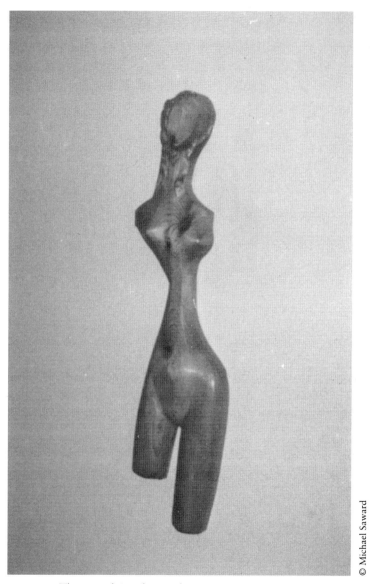

The carved wooden 'nudeWirgin Mary', 1979

In the Polygon after service, Ealing, 1980

The Caribbean 'talking point' mural in the study at Ealing Vicarage
1979

a little of the solitary in his character. To go into a room of people whom he doesn't know makes him distinctly uncomfortable and he has to work very hard to make himself willing and able to break the ice. He'd far rather sit down on his own and read a book.

Even on their honeymoon he requested, and got, an hour a day to be on his own. Jackie was puzzled and uneasy. Was there something wrong? No, nothing was wrong. He just needed time alone and he assured her that he'd come bouncing back to her with renewed fervour if he got his hour to himself. And he did!

So is he an introvert or an extrovert? He reckons that he's both and he likes the variety. What he certainly isn't is the kind of introvert who agonises over himself all the time. He agrees with Mozart who once wrote to his father Leopold, 'I like to enjoy myself but, rest assured, that I can be as serious as anyone else can.' So he takes life, and himself, philosophically. Seriously, but not too seriously. You win some and you lose some. He doesn't cry. Nor does he get overexcited. He's calm even when the pressure is on.

And, since he's a clergyman and a would-be missionary, what about the religious bit? Well, he's certainly an Evangelical and the core of his belief is a Saviour who died for him and whom he wants to follow, and proclaim, come what may. He has real confidence in the Bible's capacity to answer life's biggest questions and his four years of theological study have strengthened rather than weakened that conviction. But he isn't a Fundamentalist, though he's quite prepared to argue trenchantly (and he did so in his pre-ordination essays for Archbishop Fisher) that there are plenty of competent scholars who accept, as he does, a 'conservative' view of the Bible and its authority. So, he has made a practice of reading a passage from the Bible every day, and, for the past two years, he's written a page of comment on that passage every morning. He's coupled that with daily, private prayer.

On the other hand, he has never had much time for those brands of Christianity that lay the emotion on with a trowel. He feels almost physically sick at the tasteless exhibitionism which marks certain cults, both Catholic and Evangelical. He actively loathes heavy religiosity, the kind of 'look at me' pietism which oozes a schmaltzy sanctity and expects everyone else to treat such displays, physical or verbal, as essential requirements of authentic spirituality. To him, the Christian faith is, above all, about truth and if it isn't true then no amount of personal 'sanctity' matters one iota. So, he's aiming to grasp the shape of that truth and to become an expert professional in communicating it to others.

He knows that proclaiming, and defending, that truth is going to be a tough task. He knows that, because he is fast discovering the subtleties about a theology that can deal honestly with the realities of life, he must not knowingly cut corners in declaring that truth. Which means that he is all too conscious that one lot of Christians offer disgracefully simplistic answers while another lot have no real confidence that there are any answers at all. He knows, then, that he's going to have to carve out time to read books, and to study the Bible, analytically, so that he can master what it says and what it means.

And, lastly, because he's basically an orderly man, he's got to learn how to preach, to conduct services and to create a lifestyle, all of which have shape to them, both for their own sake and for his.

But – and it's a big but – Michael Saward has looked at himself in the mirror. Superficially, he likes what he sees and likes it quite a lot. But he has gone on looking – through his eyes into his own soul – and what has he discovered? In the words of C.S. Lewis, who put it best, 'a zoo of lusts, a bedlam of ambitions, a nursery of fears, a harem of fondled hatreds'.

Pausing for thought, then, has left him with an unresolved personal tension which he is going to carry into his life, his marriage, and his ministry. Externally he looks and feels very confident in his God, his perception of the truth of the Christian gospel, and his own ability to proclaim that truth competently and persuasively. Internally, he knows enough about himself and his human failings to recognise that there is only one posture appropriate when you are dealing with the living God and that is to be flat on your face. That's what humility is all about.

Chapter Six

Pale Young Curate

I was made deacon by Alfred Rose, Bishop of Dover, shortly after 8 a.m. on the morning of Trinity Sunday, 27 May 1956. One of nine, who were left in little doubt that this was deliberately a 'low-key' ceremony in a largely empty cathedral, I was faced with the strange experience of being, in the eyes of the public, a clergyman who was, however, in the eyes of the church, a distinctly second-rate animal. Later that morning, at 10.45, six other men were ordained priest and we lowly deacons stood by and were made to feel the contrast. They had the choir, the full cathedral, the Archbishop. Like the famous Miss Beale and Miss Buss, 'how different from us'.

Anyway, I had been duly licensed as an assistant curate at Christ Church, West Croydon, within the Diocese of Canterbury. And there's another weird anomaly! Why was Croydon part of Canterbury when it was a good thirty-five miles from the nearest bit of that ancient and primatial see? Ah well, that's merely because historically Archbishops of Canterbury had three palaces. The Old Palace at Canterbury was next to the cathedral; Lambeth Palace was the London home (and working office) of the primate; and, naturally, he needed a country residence close by, so Croydon (a fifteen–square mile lozenge of land) was his for keeps. That crazy arrangement was finally concluded in 1985 when the Dioceses Commission of the General Synod (of both of which I was by then a member) recommended the transfer of Croydon to Southwark diocese (which largely surrounded it) and the latter quickly gobbled it up.

So there I was, a freshly minted cleric, in Croydon. Well, no. Another anomaly. Some theological colleges in those days were geared up to Trinity ordinations (in May or June) while others mostly aimed at Michaelmas (in late September). I was made deacon at Trinity but my college term didn't end until the end of June, so back I went to Bristol to fill in a month. As already described, I completed my final cricket matches for the university, and was asked to act as invigilator for our college's men who were sitting their General Ordination Examinations. That came as quite a shock. Most of them, at that time of year, were non-graduates hoping to be ordained at Michaelmas and as they completed their papers and handed them in to me, I glanced at their answers. The general level was disturbingly low! These were my friends, soon to be ordained, and their ignorance was very worrying. Many of them would (and did) make excellent pastoral clergy but those capable of serious theological discussion and debate were a small minority. It is a matter of real grief to me that universal education has not, for the most part, created a church, lay or clerical, which asks for, or offers, serious mental effort. Simple answers to complex questions is what most people seem to want from their clergy and the arrival of the two-minute 'sound bite' has reduced attention spans to a level at which real teaching of the Christian faith can only be attempted for a small minority by an even smaller minority.

Cricket, invigilating and the frustration of having a wife 150 miles away teaching fourteen-year-old secondary-modern girls Shakespeare (which they hated), when all we both wanted to do was to make love long and often was, for a month, my lot! Jackie, in Strood, was coming apart at the seams. The children had no interest in English literature and she had great trouble in keeping discipline. After a two-and-a-half-year engagement, of which we had been apart for most of the last year, a ten-day honeymoon when all our emotions got nicely warmed up, and now a term apart, with horrible kids, weeks of separation, and tearful reunions – it wasn't an ideal way to start a marriage. Together we had carefully planned the next few years. A curacy for me. A couple of years teaching in Croydon for her (to bring in some money).

Starting a family, training for missionary service in West Africa. It was all nicely mapped out.

It didn't work like that. Before the end of term Jackie's nerve had broken. She couldn't, wouldn't go on teaching. She was a graduate with a teaching qualification and a year's probationary experience. And she absolutely hated it. She didn't have the right temperament or skills and she simply couldn't contemplate trying to teach young teenage girls who had got their lives inexorably mapped out, and Chaucer, Milton, Thackeray, Keats and T.S. Eliot were completely irrelevant to them. It was a shock. Financially we could expect a stipend of £450 a year, an old terraced house, some second-hand furniture, and now she was bursting to get pregnant. And we hadn't even lived under the same domestic roof as man and wife or slept together more than twenty or thirty times. Jackie withdrew from the planned teaching job in Croydon.

All the preparations for Croydon went ahead. Philip Wood, my vicar-to-be, was, as he wrote to me, 'very inefficient in many ways', and it worried him when I asked him for a contract. In doing so, I merely obeyed the urgings of the college staff who told us all to be sure to get 'something in writing' before you arrive. Clearly they had learnt of some of the bitter experiences which had come the way of curates in that era.

The day before I set out for my retreat (which culminated in the Trinity ordination) a letter arrived from Philip which shook me not a little. He took exception to my request for a contract, since, having 'checked up with several of his acquaintances' who hadn't come across such requests, he could only think of two reasons for it. One was that I didn't trust him and the other was that 'in a character which is hyper-efficient and business-like' there might be lacking the 'shepherd' virtues of 'patience, long-suffering, sacrifice, and self-giving love'. Ouch! Both suggestions seemed below the belt, not least when one had merely obeyed college orders and asked for some minimal guidelines. It was too late to do much about it and, in fairness, he had ended the letter with some words of encouragement. He meant them to be so, and I took them in that spirit, though looking back at them they were all about pain and suffering and the loss of what most people would see as their rights.

With the hindsight of what was to happen, they now seem prophetic. Philip was an former Lancashire farmer into whose soul
the iron had entered. He had an excellent theological brain, a dry
sense of humour and a deep pain which seemed to gnaw away at
him. Not long before his death, thirty years later, he would tell me
that he regretted having been ordained into the Church of England. He would, he said, have been happier in one of the Independent churches. I knew what he meant. He had always been
'agin the government', always a man at odds with those who
thought differently. He was brave, courageous, unafraid to pioneer and quite prepared to take on the world and the church, with
his strong streak of spiritual masochism. The latter became evident when he told me one day that 'he'd only had the Holy Spirit
for two weeks in his life'. With his theological brain he must have
known that such a statement was nonsense but his tough
soul-scraping conscience gave him little or no inner peace and he
could be as hard on others as he was on himself. He once dismissed the whole female sex with the Grumpy-like phrase
'women are queer cattle – especially wives'. He never ceased being
the hard Lancashire farmer.

His letter, fortunately, did make one concession. His fears and
anxieties had been slightly allayed by some words which I had
sent him, at his request, for the parish magazine. Jackie and I, as I
had written, were 'not seeking to commend ourselves but to seek
to point the careless to the Saviour, to encourage those who are
"young in the faith" and to learn, ourselves, from those of you
whose experience of the power of the Holy Spirit is deeper than
our own'. Even a hard man would have to acknowledge that such
goals were about as correct as any young curate-and-wife could
hope to reach and, fortunately, he knew that we weren't merely
mouthing pious platitudes.

The pre-ordination retreat took place in the Archbishop's
home, the Old Palace, in Canterbury, and lasted from the Thursday until the Sunday. It was conducted by the diocesan missioner
of Southwark Diocese, Canon John Hughes. I had never heard of
him but soon realised what a warm and godly man he was. His
preaching was biblical, and full of a spirituality which was quite

distinctively different from anything I had met among Evangelicals. He taught me more about conducting retreats than anyone else has ever done. I couldn't have asked for a better final preparation for the coming Sunday, though the long periods of compulsory silence were a new, and irksome, experience which I only later came to value. What neither I, nor he, knew, was that the Archbishop had invited him not only to conduct the retreat and preach at the priests' ordination but also in order that he could offer him the suffragan bishopric of Croydon, lately vacated by Cuthbert Bardsley. Bardsley, whom I came to know in later years, was a dynamic 'man's man' of a bishop, strong, aristocratic in style and bearing, and very popular. Hughes was utterly different, almost monastic, celibate, a smiling, strong teddy bear, gentle and warm, and rather lonely. He accepted Fisher's offer and we both arrived in Croydon within a few weeks of each other. I came to admire and deeply respect him (even when we disagreed theologically) while he managed once, at least, 'to find a faint streak of humility in me'. He was, I'm sure, far from pleased when he later learnt that I had enjoyed his 'put down' phrase and had marked it as a brilliant title for an autobiography.

Being ordained into the ministry of the Church of England does provide certain Gilbertian touches. You come away from both events (whether as deacon or as priest) clutching an imposing document, to which is attached the episcopal (or in my case the archiepiscopal) seal. On the authority of the Archbishop of Canterbury, no less, Michael Saward is to be acknowledged a man 'of whose virtuous and pious life and conversation, and competent learning and knowledge in the Holy Scriptures' the Archbishop has been 'well assured'. How about that? Not even the Prime Minister can produce testimonials like that. And I've got two of them, for good measure!

During the retreat, each candidate had an interview with the Archbishop. Remembering my disastrous experience at Lambeth Palace, back in February, I vowed to say as little as possible and I can recall almost nothing of what was said by either of us, with just one exception. Towards the end, I suggested, tentatively, that a new and dynamic Evangelical movement was beginning within the Church of England. 'That', said Fisher, with overpowering assurance, 'would be an absolute disaster.' Time has shown that I was certainly right in my prophecy. I leave others to judge whether Fisher was correct in his. He went on to castigate 'enthusiasm', obviously being aware (as I then was not) of the famous remark by his predecessor, Manners Sutton, who, consecrating T.F. Middleton, in 1814, to be the first Bishop of Calcutta, had told him that his job was 'to put down Enthusiasm and to preach the Gospel'. I was, at that time, totally mystified by the distinction.

The early service passed off quietly, though it was very meaningful for me. I recall the more magnificent priests' ordination chiefly because of the dominant presence of the Dean of Canterbury, Hewlett Johnson, notorious as 'the Red Dean'. A renowned Communist, loathed by Archbishop Fisher, he walked about the cathedral like a prima donna, smirking at his acknowledged significance. I thought him thoroughly repulsive, both ugly and oily in his person and manner.

After a brief family lunch and Evensong, at which I first heard Smith's 'Responses' (still my favourite), Stanford's 'Beati quorum via' and Howells' 'Mag and Nunc', we assembled for tea on the lawn of the Old Palace. My parents were both overawed by the friendly conversation they had with Geoffrey Fisher but, for all of us, the occasion was wrecked by Rosamund Fisher, a high-class battle-axe if ever I met one, who launched into Jackie. She, poor thing, had gulped at the wrong moment (nerves, probably) and Rosamund swung round angrily declaring 'you snorted at me'. Jackie who was dismayed, and caught totally off-guard, did her utmost to explain what had happened and apologise but all to no avail. From then on, I (and especially Jackie) avoided Rosamund Fisher like the plague. It certainly taught me that people in high places ought to be more sensitive to the fear which they can generate among those unused to conversing with the so-called Great and Good.

But the day was not yet over. Indeed, its most memorable event was still to come. I said good-bye to the family, doing my best to console a shattered wife, and went in to supper. Fisher, unlike most bishops, required all those ordained to remain until the

Monday morning. So fifteen of us, nine deacons and six priests, sat around a huge dining table, together with the chaplain, a secretary (later to become a bishop's wife), Rosamund at one end, and Geoffrey at the other. The conversation flowed easily for about an hour, Fisher telling us of the greedy eyes of liverymen at City dinners when he offered them his oysters, which didn't agree with him. Then, suddenly, he looked up to the far end of the table. 'Rosamund!' he barked, 'Take them all away.' Then, before we could even get up, he added, 'Saward, you stay here.' My heart sank. What was about to happen? Had the old dragon complained? Had I unwittingly said or done something criminal? What could he want?

It was almost sunset. Two hours later, in near darkness he released me. What had begun so fearfully got more and more relaxed. He initially did most of the talking. We, or rather he, talked about the church, about his work, about ministry, about a huge range of things. Bit by bit, I grew more relaxed and more confident. He was acting like a grandfather talking to a favourite grandson. My courage returned. It became a two-way conversation. I spelled out my hopes, my beliefs, my ignorances, and finally, I reached the point where we talked about, of all things, a quite trivial matter. One of the Anglo-Catholic priests had complained bitterly that he didn't know whether he was validly ordained because Fisher insisted on all of us wearing cassock and surplice but not, quite explicitly not, either scarf or stole. At that time the black scarf was certainly legal but the influence, for half a century, of the Anglo-Catholic movement, had resulted in many ordinands wearing a white stole. The legality of the stole was certainly a matter for dispute and the dispute was not finally settled until the mid-1960s. Fisher, to avoid controversy, declined to permit ordinands to wear either. To the Anglo-Catholic curate, made priest that day but not permitted to wear the stole (which he regarded as the symbol of priesthood), the question of the validity of his ordination was worrying. Fisher, when I told him, exploded. 'What utter nonsense!' he shouted. But I hadn't done with it. 'Then, why', I added, 'is the Bishop of London, Bishop Wand, refusing to ordain men like me, unless we agree to wear a white stole?' This was undeniable. Wand had declined to allow men, who rightly doubted whether the stole was legal wear, to be ordained in St Paul's Cathedral. He snubbed them brutally by only ordaining them privately in Fulham Palace chapel. Fisher exploded even more vehemently. 'Wand,' he snorted, 'Wand – that stupid old fool. I've told him he's a stupid old fool!'

I sat there transfixed. Here was I, one of today's new deacons, the most junior clergy in the Church of England, hearing the Archbishop of Canterbury, Primate of All-England, the most senior non-royal in the nation's order of precedence, slagging-off the Bishop of London, Dean of the Chapels Royal, third in seniority within the church, and calling him 'an old fool'. 'Remember this, word for word, Michael,' I said to myself. 'You'll never again, in all your life, hear such an indiscretion uttered by such an eminent person.' Little could I have guessed that one day I would be one of Wand's successors – not as Bishop of London but as Treasurer of St Paul's Cathedral. I slept well that night, secure in the confidence that Michael Saward, newly-ordained curate, and Geoffrey Fisher, the quasi-Pope of the Anglican Communion, had a delightful secret which they now shared. And Fisher, you remember, had been appointed a bishop on the day of my birth.

The following week I set off from college to conduct a mission to the massive RAF station at Stafford, together with Michael Ward and David Knight. The three of us (they were to be ordained some months later) lived in a caravan on a grass square in the middle of the station's married quarters. Two memories remain. One was the frantic (and fortunately successful) attempts by David and me to stop Michael wandering outside the caravan in only his underpants. He always has been slightly eccentric, as clergy go, but he could see absolutely no reason why such behaviour might possibly be damaging to the success of a mission to an RAF station. David and I were obviously more worldly-wise.

The other memory has always been somewhat enigmatic. I spoke at various 'home meetings', including one at the home of a very senior officer. At the end, his wife asked me to call round privately, a day or so later. I did so, and we had what I took to be a real heart-to-heart about the state of her soul. She was in her forties and obviously, because of service rank, a very lonely woman. Only in later years did I just wonder whether she had quite different motives. Clergy have to be realists and the prospect of a youthful and, hopefully, fairly virile young man of twenty-four in your home when you are in your forties might hold out entirely different possibilities. After all, a clerical collar in such circumstances is the safest camouflage of all, isn't it? I hope I'm only imagining it but when you're an enthusiastic evangelist in your twenties such thoughts don't enter your head. Time teaches you to be more cautious about people's motives.

The final few days of the summer term are usually taken up in theological colleges with visiting speakers who address the students on a whole variety of interesting but, often, peripheral subjects. One of our lectures was on trade unionism and was given by a one-time shop steward who had been ordained in the early 1950s and was an old student of the college. His name was Eddy Stride and he had just left Christ Church, Croydon, where he had been Philip Wood's first curate. I was, of course, about to succeed him so I listened with especial interest. Afterwards, he walked with me to the nearest bus stop, on his way back to Temple Meads and London. He was wearing what I came to recognise as his standard gear – a dirty old mackintosh and a trilby hat covering his bald head and owlish face. 'Well, boy,' he said to me, 'they'll murder you in Croydon, 'cos I can see for a start, you're a Tory.' I, for my part, was wearing typically student clothing of the period, grey flannel trousers and a Harris tweed jacket. Actually I wasn't sure what I was, politically, but I suppose he was probably right. Our paths were to cross again many times in the years ahead but his clothes never seemed to change.

That same week provided two further tangible pieces of evidence of long-term significance. A friend, whose parents lived in the college basement as caretakers, lent me a record of Beethoven's Seventh Symphony. Tired out, I lay on a bed and listened to it, the very first piece of classical music that I ever consciously considered. It was to transform a whole area of my life. Since 1956 I have never been without a growing (and now huge) collection of recorded music which moved from LPs to cassettes and eventually to CDs. For more than forty years I have accompanied all my deskwork with recorded music and as I write these words Mitsuko Uchida is playing Mozart's Piano Sonata, K280. I cannot imagine how life would have been, deprived of the sheer pleasure of a constant diet of the works, conducting and playing of countless great musicians.

Much more mundane, but just as useful, was the treasure which my father unearthed. At home, recovering from a minor illness, he went to buy a newspaper, saw a small ad in the newsagent's window and rang me. 'There's a dining-room table on offer in a house in Little Thrift,' he said. 'It's quite a large house and ought to be a reasonable buy.' Two days later, on my final return from Bristol, we walked the half-mile to Little Thrift, a nearby cul-de-sac. Dad, who knew wood, gave it a good inspection, while the lady of the house discreetly withdrew. 'It's mahogany, and there's no trace of worm. She only wants £4 for it – it's a wonderful bargain.' Madam returned, we made reluctant noises about the price, bought it, and carried it home, exultantly. The Saward family has been eating off it ever since. Apart from marrying Jackie (the licence cost 7s 6d, or 37p in modern money) it was the best bargain of my life and since, unlike Jackie, it never argues with me, it might be considered an even more desirable acquisition!

We moved our minimal possessions into our new home, 15 Chatfield Road, on Tuesday 16 July. It was a standard late-Victorian terraced house, about four hundred yards from Christ Church and half a mile from the vicarage. The only new item of furniture which we possessed was a small telephone table. Everything else was second-hand. To match (well, nearly match) our mahogany dining table, we purchased a set of six chairs (one carver and five chairs) from a local dealer for £14 and felt, at last, that we could begin normal married life.

Two weeks later we set off to Litlington, on the South Downs, to run the parish boys' camp. I was commandant and together with four or five other adults faced a small tribe of urban kids who were not at all used to life in bell tents on Sussex hillsides. Two slightly older potential troublemakers soon identified themselves but the announcement of a small number of sensible camp rules seemed calculated to keep reasonable order.

On the Sunday morning we all trooped into the village church where, at the local vicar's request, I preached the sermon. As we came out, he urged me to repeat it at his second village, Westdean, at the evening service. I agreed, and at 6.30 p.m. presented myself at the beautiful and tiny church, snuggling into the Downs. The congregation, including the vicar, Jackie and me, was six people. Two of these, in the front row, turned out to be Viscount and Lady Waverley. He, as Sir John Anderson, had been a member of Churchill's War Cabinet, and had given his name to the first civilian air-raid shelter. She, his second wife, was a widow whose first husband had been one of those who leaked vital secrets about comparative British and German air strengths to Churchill during the latter's 'wilderness years' in the 1930s. I knew none of this then, other than their names, but that was daunting enough for a curate preaching his first post-ordination sermon.

I preached for just over twenty minutes on *The Christian Athlete* based on St Paul's 'athlete' illustration in his first Corinthian letter, and linked it, inevitably, with the Melbourne Olympic Games and names like Zatopek, Chataway and Bannister. It was a sermon originally submitted to one of the Tyndale Hall staff and he had marked it 'excellent – I'm really delighted with it' so I was hopeful that it would hold even a tiny congregation's attention. Imagine then my dismay when Waverley composed himself for sleep, right in front of me, shut his eyes and was, as far as I knew, lost in the Land of Nod. His virtuous lady sat upright, hands in her lap, and frequently caught my eye. At one point, she fiddled with her fingers and a lordly slap was administered by the recumbent viscount. So the old rogue *was* awake! Both thanked me, in the porch, afterwards which could have meant anything or nothing. Well, I was learning.

Camp, however, produced its problems. The two ringleaders began to flout, quite openly, the minimal rules and encourage the younger ones to follow their disobedience. Finally, it came to a head when the only really important law was flagrantly broken and action was essential. The adults and I agreed that the two

ringleaders would have to be sent home. We took them to separate railway stations, put them on Croydon trains and rang their
disappointed parents. One came from a children's home and the
houseparents sadly concurred that, while they had hoped for
better, we had done the right thing. From then on camp was
thoroughly enjoyable. For my part, I had instantly acquired the
reputation of being a tough disciplinarian, which stayed
throughout my Croydon years. Since these were the early years
of rock-'n'-roll, Teddy Boys, and ripping up cinema seats, it was
just as well. Curates were assumed to be Wet Wimps and this one
clearly wasn't. The only person who wasn't happy was a strange,
myopic, elderly lady who ran the boys' Bible class and whose
boys could do no wrong. Since two of them were the camp ringleaders it didn't help. She hadn't been at the camp but she and I
were in polite collision from then on. Since we were joint leaders
of the Bible class, it wasn't a recipe for happiness and I profoundly disagreed with the way she ran it. She let them run rings
round her, was totally out of date and yet, to my amazement,
they loved her and that little class produced some excellent
ordinands. I chafed and chafed, constantly nagged the vicar to
ease her out but he, recognising that, despite everything, she was
loved and undoubtedly successful in her odd, incompetent way,
declined to act. Resentment began to build up in me.

On 26 August I preached my first sermon in Christ Church in
the morning service. It was the first of two on the letters to the
seven churches in the book of Revelation. I called it 'The Church
Redundant' and illustrated it with five of the seven letters. A
month later came the second, 'The Church Abundant', dealing
with the virtues of the other two churches. Both were fairly tren-
chant for a new boy but Philip sat in his stall smiling approval and
when I came to the section on morality, relating to the problems in
Pergamum and Thyatira, and asked whether the choice was between the 'prude mind' and the 'lewd mind', creating either the
'Grim-Prim mentality' or, in contrast, the 'Scanty-Panty mentality', he sat rocking with unconcealed laughter. I crowned it all by
referring to my recent discovery of a definition of the church as 'a
society of old women of both sexes, whose symbol is a cup of tea,

whose motto is "safety-first", and whose main occupation is gossip.' Tears were pouring down the vicar's face who knew only too well how close to the bone I was cutting! I'm not sure whether some of those 'old women of both sexes' ever forgave me.

Christ Church, Croydon, was, I soon discovered, a church with major problems. Philip had been there eight years and it had been an uphill struggle almost all the time. His predecessor had made little impact and the church had been locked into a time warp, looking back to Clifford Martin, the 'golden boy vicar', who had been a curate there, had returned as vicar, and would later be a kind and warm-hearted diocesan bishop. Everyone had loved him, he hadn't put a foot wrong, all was success. That was undoubtedly the superficial view but, in my opinion, he had left us the legacy of having failed to get to grips with almost every really important issue. The very people who were now leading the church had been allowed to go unchallenged in youth and early middle age and their attitudes were merely 'churchy' as opposed to genuinely spiritual in motivation. When, years later, in Liverpool, I met the 'golden boy' he couldn't have been kinder or more generous but, from his own mouth, it became crystal-clear that he had consistently avoided the 'cutting edge' of the gospel and bought widespread popularity and affection by agreeing with everyone all the time, except those who had unashamedly proclaimed the New Testament, including its tough as well as its gentle character. Such people he found unpalatable throughout his life and ministry. The gospel was, he told me, 'you thank God for what you are.' No message of hope there for a junkie, an alcoholic, or an adulterer, I thought.

His, then, was the inheritance which overshadowed Philip's years at Christ Church. His protégés ran the church. Both churchwardens had been in office for years and both strenuously resisted almost every change. Needless to say, Philip's sharp and challenging ministry had produced converts and almost all of them were thoroughly frustrated by the attitude of the wardens.

The church council, though divided, was dominated by the wardens. If they opposed new ideas (as they usually did) the council generally capitulated. Philip, no organiser or strategist, succeeded in pastoral or evangelistic things but was regularly wrong-footed when faced with a spineless PCC. I, and others, urged him to appoint a new vicar's warden at the 1957 annual meeting but he couldn't face the existing warden who openly boasted, 'Well, vicar, I've done twenty-one years and I ought to stand down but no-one else could do the job.' Philip wearily re-appointed him and he stayed warden for many more years.

To a brand-new curate, full of ideas and enthusiasm, the combination of a fine but exhausted vicar, a weird and eccentric Bible class leader, and a church council blocking most new proposals at the instigation of two not-very-spiritual but extremely powerful churchwardens was a recipe for first, amazement, then, frustration, and finally, thinly concealed anger. Again and again I would return from the church council meetings and say to Jackie, 'Give me a cushion to belt or I'll have to belt you.' She rapidly provided the necessary item of soft furnishing and I laid into it with a will.

My first Monday staff meeting was a shock. Prior to my arrival, for various seemingly good reasons, I had never entered the vicarage. Now, I walked into Philip's study and gazed in incredulous horror at the scene. Paper, in enormous quantity and disarray, was everywhere. The desk was almost invisible, swamped with paper of all kinds. The floor was totally concealed under a sea of magazines, mostly gardening magazines, and if there was a carpet I never caught a glimpse of it in the eighteen months that we worked together. I knew, in those first five seconds, that I would never have come to this parish if I had seen Philip's study earlier in the year. Philip began with prayer, chatted for a bit, and I then asked him to outline our parish strategy for the coming year. It was September so I assumed we should have some aims to carry us through to next July. 'I've no idea,' he replied. 'I suppose we'll just muddle along as we've always done.'

I went home for lunch in a continuing state of shock. What had I got myself into? How could anyone adopt such an *ad hoc* attitude? More to the point, how could I, an inveterate planner, hope to live with such a chaotic mess? It was obvious that this first curacy was going to be quite a different cup of tea from anything which had been foreseen at Bristol. Didn't the theological colleges, didn't the bishops, realise what they were letting young curates in for?

One more strange situation faced me. The church verger was (unique in my experience) also the treasurer of the church council. So I was to be paid by the verger? Odd, but not impossible. He was a pleasant little Welshman, not much blessed with imagination and certainly quite without financial vision. I asked him about my expenses of office which I reckoned would be about £7 a quarter. 'Aww,' he said, 'we aven' 'ad them before, see.' 'Well, you're certainly going to get them from now on,' I replied. He looked quite baffled but paid up. Months later he informed me that 'The chu-urch can' pay the phone bill, see.' 'Take it out,' I replied. 'Was-sat? Aww. Naw, we din' mean that, see.' 'Well,' I said, 'I can't afford it and I didn't put it in. Either the church pays or out it goes.' He looked staggered. 'But won' you need it?' 'Sure,' I said. 'I use it all the time on church business.' 'Aww,' he agonised, 'p'raps it'll 'ave to stay, then?' 'If the church pays,' I answered. 'Aww,' he concluded, and vanished, shaking his head all the way down the road.

Urban clergy spend quite a lot of their time at the local crematorium and I was no exception. In our case the Mitcham Road cemetery was adjoining the crematorium and we were on a rota system. It was pastorally an absolutely disastrous idea as you merely turned up and performed to order with no advance knowledge of what was about to land on your lap. One day I got a Beachy Head suicide with no advance warning. My very worst experience in the whole of my ministry was having to conduct nine consecutive cremations at twenty-minute intervals on one morning. I felt I was canning sardines and knew, to change the metaphor, that, after five, I was completely cooked. I staggered on trying to sound concerned for numbers six to nine. If you want to know what hell is like for a clergyman try mass-producing cremations for a morning. Thank God the clergy rebelled and such rota systems are, in my experience, rare exceptions today.

Actually, my first brush with corpse disposal came before that. It was, indeed, my very first burial. All went well until we reached the grave. Then, as the undertakers lifted the coffin to lower it into the gaping hole and I opened my mouth to speak, a moan from one of the women mourners turned into a scream. 'It's the wrong grave!' she howled. Panic. 'Stop everything,' I said. I almost lapsed into gunnery language which would have produced the order 'Stand Fast!' Anyway, the coffin remained in midair, then was slowly put back on the grass. The funeral directors conducted a discreet conversation with the family (no-one is more discreet than a funeral director) and quietly informed me that, unfortunately, the correct grave was six feet away and that both graves had the same family name on the headstones. 'I regret, Sir,' he added, 'that the two branches of the family are not on speaking terms.'

Two days later I returned and all was decently and correctly managed but, from that day on, I irritated every funeral director by refusing to sign 'in the office on the way in' that the disposal had taken place. 'Not this cleric,' I said. 'I've been caught once too often at that game.'

Philip's advice about funerals was daunting. 'God help you, boy, if you get a Surrey Street one.' Before long I got two of them. Surrey Street was Croydon's market and its community was a closed group of tough street traders. When one died, the rest spent huge sums on the funeral. A vast cortège of limousines drew up at the Croydon cemetery. Floral tributes matched the Chelsea Flower Show in quantity and far outdid it in vulgarity. The women all turned up in black and the chapel was packed to the doors, with many standing. As I began the service the women started to scream. Not just cry, but scream. And they continued, competing with each other, for the whole of the service. I gave up in despair. No-one could hear a word I said, so I heavily abbreviated it and completed the interment as quickly as possible. It was the most blatantly pagan event that I have ever had to face and two of them were enough for a lifetime.

Christ Church had a daughter-church, St Christopher's, in the middle of the Mitcham Road council estate. It was a fading brick, dual-purpose hall, with 'the church bit' behind a wooden screen. 'Curates usually like to run the daughter church,' said

Philip. 'Not this one,' I replied. 'I need to be learning from you. Can't we split our duties between the two?' So we did. 'By the way,' said Philip in my first week, 'I've put up a welcome poster at St Chris. You might be interested to see it and the estate's reaction.'

I cycled down the road, crossed into the estate, and there it was, a brightly coloured poster bearing the greeting 'Welcome to the Revd Michael Saward, our new curate.' Which wasn't all it was bearing. There, adhering to my name by its tacky contents, was a condom. 'Good grief,' I said to myself, 'I've never even seen one of those before and now the first one is sticking to me.' In those circumstances a good belly-laugh does far more for you than outraged self-righteous shock horror. I was learning and you certainly learn humility when a French Letter is obscuring your reputation.

Before long I was faced with my first wedding ceremony. I arrived well before time and the verger, the organist and I waited for the couple. And waited. And waited. No-one came. We made a phone call. 'Oh,' said the voice, 'didn't they tell you? They decided to have it at the Register Office six weeks ago.' I reflected. My first sermon (back at Orpington) had resulted in a death shortly afterwards. My first funeral had been aborted in midair. My first wedding simply didn't happen. I dared not contemplate my first baptism. One of my clergy friends summed it up admirably. 'Do you think Someone Up There is trying to tell you something?' I decided to soldier on, with the firm intention of 'having words' with Someone Up There at the first opportunity.

Baptism, incidentally, was, as practised at Christ Church, almost unique in the Church of England of the 1950s. Hardly half a dozen parishes in the whole of England attempted any serious pastoral discipline and infant baptism was administered quite indiscriminately throughout the length and breadth of the country. The assumption was made that the English were both Christian and Anglican and that they had a divinely appointed right to the baptism of their children. Never mind if they virtually never entered a church building throughout their lives or exhibited any knowledge of, or belief in, the Christian faith. Being 'English' put them into a special relationship with Almighty God and woe betide any clergyman who suggested otherwise. All babies were, in consequence, entitled to free orange juice, free schooling, free healthcare and free baptism. So the rule ran in the 1940s and early 1950s.

Philip Wood thought otherwise. He had been mightily impressed by Christopher Wansey, an Essex rector who had declined to baptise those infants presented to him whose parents had no intention of keeping any of the baptismal vows. Philip, unlike Wansey, believed in infant baptism and was very ready to administer the sacrament when offered some evidence that the parents were prepared to take the promises seriously. The vast majority, of course, were quite unwilling to do any such thing, merely demanding their right to 'have the baby done'. The matter came to a head in Croydon in the middle 1950s, shortly before my time, when Philip refused to baptise a child whose parents sent their older children (already baptised by him) to a Baptist Sunday school where, quite understandably, following Baptist principles, they were taught that their baptism was not the real thing and quite invalid.

The outraged parents contacted one of the tabloid newspapers, which, naturally, burning as ever for truth and righteousness, lambasted Philip all over its front page and called on the religious authorities to put right this manifest injustice. At which point another local vicar, a ludicrous joker of a man, promptly agreed, very publicly, to perform the rite. Philip, incensed at the disloyalty of a fellow-incumbent who was interfering in our parish, threatened to haul him up in front of the Archbishop for wilfully intruding across parish boundaries.

Eddy Stride, my predecessor, had fully supported Philip, and his pastoral style was probably, as far as I could gather, when I arrived, even tougher than the vicar's. Christ Church, Croydon, was therefore one of the very earliest parishes to face the hostility of an outraged populace. In those days, over two-thirds of newborn infants were automatically baptised, no questions asked, creating a pool of some twenty-seven million 'baptised Anglicans' in the nation. It is worth noting that today, forty years on, the number has dropped from two-thirds to one-quarter and in London Diocese the number is now below nine per cent. The pool has dropped to about twenty million and declines every year. Thus Christ Church, in Philip's time, was absolutely prophetic and led the way in the demand for a morally meaningful use of baptism and especially the honest application of the publicly taken parental promises. This inevitably meant that all baptisms took place in major Sunday services, again, years in advance of what is nowadays canonically quite normal.

One consequence of our baptismal practice was that we clergy grew quite acclimatised to irate parents flinging abuse at us in our own homes and even, on occasions, almost physically attacking us. I made it my practice to do all I could to explain gently, calmly and rationally, why we were asking parents not to perjure themselves before God, and other people, by taking promises which they had no intention of keeping. Few cared tuppence about it. They had no qualms about lying if it would 'get the baby done'. Fathers were, marginally, more willing to see the point but mothers fought like tigresses to protect their young from losing out on this sacrament. Every kind of superstitious reason was trotted out. Babies 'wouldn't do well' without it. Even worse, grandmas wouldn't have mother or baby in the house because they were 'unclean'. All my life I have come up against both clergy and lay people (always respectably middle class) who simply cannot believe such things ever happened. Believe me. I was there – and not just once or twice. The rude, superstitious paganism of working-class England in those days was horrific. Nowadays, it hardly exists because most young couples couldn't care less and know almost nothing about the Christian faith. One result is that infant baptism nowadays is generally treated seriously by the small minority who request it. The blood of the martyrs, like Philip Wood, is indeed the seed of the modern church. I'm glad to have been, all my adult life, someone who has fought for the principled use of infant baptism. I really do believe that the old indiscriminate and universal practice of infant baptism was the greatest single obstacle to the successful re-evangelisation of England in the years since the Second World War. Why? If you believe you've been 'done' and are thus 'a Christian' what need can there be to respond to a challenge to 'accept Jesus Christ as Lord and Saviour?' Not one of the various Anglican 'Missions', 'Calls to the North', 'Decades of Evangelism', and so on, has even begun to succeed because the English, and 'their' church, cannot or will not admit that most people are not Christians in our land today. Lots of people are certainly 'interested in religion', dabble in the occult, play at New Age ideas, but the need for a genuine conversion is ignored or shrugged off. Is it surprising that Britain in the 1990s is in such an appalling mess? It has long since pulled up its religious roots and there's virtually no theological or ethical cash left in society's bank.

Preaching understandably is one challenge all clergy face. It is said that John Robinson, later Bishop of Woolwich, once used the phrase 'the eschaton of history' in a sermon in a working-class parish in Bristol during his curacy and was puzzled by the remark from a member of the congregation that he didn't understand the reference to 'eskimos and history'. I was almost guilty of the same crime. I caught myself starting to refer to an 'anthropomorphic concept' but stopped, just in time. The trouble is, of course, that what I could say in two words took about thirty to explain in plain English. Doctors, lawyers and motor mechanics are allowed to use technical language. Clergy do so at their peril.

One really satisfying and creative area of life at Christ Church was the work which we undertook with the under-thirties. The teenage group in the Youth Fellowship was small – we usually got less than a dozen – but half a lifetime later I can see over half of them involved in Christian ministry. Four are clergy, two are clergy wives and one is a lay leader.

The second group, the Twenty Club, also produced clergy and wives, and both groups gave me real scope for teaching the Christian faith. Thirteen hour-long lectures covered the Bible, the Christian faith, personal spirituality, methods of Bible study, the church, liturgy, stewardship, personal and public evangelism, and so on. A novel idea was to charge each member for the course which encouraged good attendance and provided each person with a series of appropriate booklets as homework. Even more important was the sowing of ideas about how a church should be run and the consequential election of members to the church council. Eventually one of the stuck-in-the-mud churchwardens was ousted and morale began to soar. What happened next will be revealed in due course.

Not long after my arrival I came face to face with a real obscenity: the church jumble sale. A milling mob of grasping hands, traders, grandmas, all out to get something for almost nothing. This image of a church at work sickened me to the pit of my stomach. What could the world around see but a so-called Christian community trying desperately to raise a few pounds by selling off squalid, and sometimes filthy, old clothes? That day I swore a mighty oath that, come what may, I would never be party, as a Christian leader, to such an event. By all means give old clothes to the needy but never, oh never, let such an event portray our spiritual and financial nakedness to the local community. Since then I have preached, again and again, the need for genuine and sacrificial giving by the Christian community. And it's always worked. Set people real goals of financial commitment and jumble sales and bazaars shrivel on the vine while direct giving flourishes and the church can plan its finances accordingly.

Back home at Chatfield Road our marriage was settling down. Despite normal disputes and rows we were buoyed up with a blossoming and very pleasurable sex life. Bed was a sheer joy which contrasted with the unexpected and deeply painful sessions of counselling which I found myself plunged into with both teenagers and young couples. So many of these young men and women, single and married, were riddled with guilt, plagued by ignorance, and many of the married were missing out much of the sexual enjoyment that Jackie and I were taking for granted. Again and again I sat in my study listening to wives who had never known an orgasm, husbands whose techniques were in the Flintstones' class, kids who weren't sure whether they had had intercourse under the park bushes. No one had forewarned me about any of this. It wasn't on the curriculum at theological college! I was a curate, not a marriage guidance counsellor. But I learnt, and I learnt fast. I listened and listened for hours, especially to one or two regulars who seemed to come every week, pouring out their spiritual failures and their sexual guilt. Tears they shed in bucketfulls. They were all in the sixteen–thirty age range, they were all Christians, they were all seeking help. What really disturbed me was that we Christians were promising sexual bliss to those who reached marriage still virgin and a high proportion of these weren't finding it or were still single but guilt-stricken semi-virgins. Something was badly wrong and the answer wasn't to be found by either ditching Christian teaching about chastity or pumping guilt into struggling adolescents. Over a decade later I wrote a book about it.

Talking of books, I realised just how much these young men and women needed to read Christian books. Nothing could counter their lack of knowledge, on most subjects, faster than books. So, first, I built a church bookstall. It stood at the west end of the church and was much the most colourful piece of furniture in the building. Painted in pale blue, with hidden strip lighting, it set off all the books splendidly, so much so that the more irreverent took to genuflecting in front of it whenever they passed. We sold over £250 worth of books in our first year and that was to a 'non-reading' audience. In current terms, £250 seems little enough but translated into present day money that was £7,000. In one year, to a congregation of about a hundred adults in a working-class parish. Alongside that, Jackie became sales agent for *Crusade* magazine, the only illustrated Christian monthly, and built up the circulation to fifty-five copies a month, one of the largest parish circulations in the land. It was a tremendous joy to watch the impact of all this reading. People began to think for themselves, ideas permeated the church council, fresh and creative breezes blew. My sense of frustration began to dilute. There was hope.

Philip was undoubtedly worried that I might be trying to build up a 'curate's party' to compete with 'the council', and 'the vicar's party'. I wasn't, and I didn't, but the temptation was very great and some of the Twenty Club folk were spoiling for a fight with

the stuck-in-the-muds. My style was, I realise, very self-assured
and confident and one day, as Philip and I were driving to a meeting in Canterbury, he put it quite bluntly. 'Your self-confidence',
he said, 'doesn't sit easily with Christian humility. Doesn't it
worry you?' I paused. 'Can I tell you a story?' I said. 'When I was
sixteen I came across some words of St Paul in his Letter to the
Philippians. He told them that "I can do all things through Christ
who strengthens me." That day, Vicar, I took that as my motto
for life and that's why I'm so sure of things.' Philip looked surprised. 'And that's why you're so cock-sure?' 'Well, yes,' I said. 'If
he wants me to achieve things, he gives me the strength. I can't see
any reason to be hesitant. I trust him.'

Is that compatible with humility? Philip wasn't sure, though it
did give him a new insight into how my mind worked. It wasn't till
many years later that I realised that the old Authorised Version
translation was probably not really accurate. Paul was actually
saying that, whether rich or poor, hungry or full, in jail or free,
Christ enabled him to cope. Not quite what I had thought but
who is to say that the sense of deep inner security which it had
given me was wrong? It certainly built up my faith in a God who
gives whatever is needed to enable things to get done.

That attitude chimed in well with some words spoken to Jackie
and me by an old man in the congregation called George Carter.
He had, he told us, given away most of his possessions since, at
eighty, he knew that 'True happiness lies in the number of things
you can do without.' It took him a mere five seconds to say that.
It's stuck with me for a lifetime.

Talking of lifetimes, I could hardly have guessed that five members of that little youth group would stay our friends ever since.
Jean Green, a teenage tearaway from a family of ten kids, would
become the wife of John Place, who was to be my parish administrator in Ealing in the 1980s. Brian Lipscombe, whose siblings
were well known to the police and the social workers, came to live
with us and later married Yvonne Finch, also in the YPF. She, a
nurse, would become the vicar's wife when Brian was ordained.
Jennifer Sheppard, an unhappy foster-child with, nevertheless, a
twinkle in her eyes, married Walter Snook, the teenage church

organist who was later ordained. She became a godmother to Jill, one of our twins, and I became godfather to Lucy, John and Jean's daughter. Sadly, the Snook marriage broke up in the early 1990s and Wally later remarried. Jackie and I prepared both Brian and Wally for their theological training at Tyndale Hall by throwing a jug of water over the two of them when, late one night, they stayed talking outside our front porch and wouldn't go home even though we had gone to bed. We're still friends!

Although we largely lost touch with her, a sixth member, Anne Miles, eventually became a Methodist minister.

The existing church organist retired at the end of 1956 and there was no obvious successor. Philip and I discussed it and it was agreed that I should become choirmaster, with Wally Snook, only seventeen, as organist. The arrangement worked very happily though my method of choir training, picked up from John Ramell, the college organist, exposed one or two long-standing choir members as being incapable of singing a part after forty years in the choir. 'Sorry, I've got a bad cough,' said one elderly bass, every time we rehearsed the bass line. My policy was to rehearse unaccompanied, to wander around the church listening, to shout comments, and to go for simple material, well sung. It worked with Bach, it worked with Orlando Gibbons, and the choir did well. To my considerable amusement, one elderly soprano told the vicar that they were really trying hard but that I knew so much about music that they were lagging behind. What amused me was that I couldn't read music, but learnt everything off by heart in advance. Now that really is cocky self-confidence and not even I would claim much in the way of humility in that field. But – it worked!

The same month that I became choirmaster I also became, in expectation, a father. Jackie was over the moon at being pregnant and, at two-and-a-half-months, we told the world. Ten days later she miscarried (the first of perhaps four) and the world collapsed. Well, not really, but it felt like it to us. The next two years saw a monthly rise and fall of our hopes and the awful fear that we might be childless. Fortunately, it was the beginning of the era of subfertility treatment and I regularly trotted off to a Family

Planning Association clinic in Sloane Street. The prescribed treatment was crude but reduced us both to squeals of laughter and discomfort. Jackie did most of the laughing and I was left squealing. Twice a day I was required to submerge my testicles in a bowl of cold water. Simple arithmetic will show that I was forced to accept this torture on over fourteen hundred occasions and then, at last, Madam really was pregnant and not miscarrying. The utter bliss of success (and the end to the Arctic behaviour) was worth all the emotional and physical discomfort. But that is jumping the gun a little.

Meanwhile, in the church hall I was learning to put up with having to attend afternoon women's meetings. As a lifelong non-tea-drinker, my odd habit was the subject of regular chatter and gossip. They were a pleasant group of old dears, generally kind and thoughtful, but virile (or, in my case virile but not so fertile) curates were hardly living on the same planet. They, and especially their leaders, talked a whole language of pious platitudes which rang no bells with me. One day, in desperation, I went home and wrote some verses which I called 'Jarring Jargon'. I included every awful cliché and yards of pious verbiage and it really was an outrageous send-up of that type of women's meeting. At the next staff meeting I showed it to Philip, who guffawed knowingly, and passed it on to Sister Pescud who, being a classic jargonite herself, read it slowly then handed it back. 'Very nice' she said and I realised that she had taken it quite seriously.

I have never been able to come to terms with that kind of 'terribly spiritual' vocabulary. It isn't natural, people have to learn it, and all too many assume that it's a necessary part of being a Christian. And it has its dangers. One young, and not very bright, wife used to avoid all tough decisions by saying to the church council, 'I don't think we can settle that; I think we should just pray about it.' Month after month she played the same card and stagnation resulted. No-one knew how to counter such a 'very spiritual' attitude. Eventually that's exactly what we did but she went on complaining about our lack of real spirituality. 'We should have prayed about it,' she insisted, but by then we had realised that she only said this if the matter proposed was one she disagreed with.

Avoiding the need for reform showed itself in other kinds of issues. The Church of England, since 1919, has had an Electoral Roll of those wishing, and qualified, to vote in the annual parish elections. The roll at Christ Church in 1956 was 720 names. About 100 were regular churchgoers. Revising it was essential but few parishes ever bothered in those days. Jackie and I offered to do it, knowing that we must keep to the published rules which made removal of names not particularly easy. Philip and the church council agreed and in March 1957 we set about checking on the list. In just one month, and even keeping those tough rules, we reduced the roll to 280 names. The usual conversation at front doors was 'Joe Smith? He died thirty years ago' or 'Mary Jones – no, don't know that name. We know the names of the six who've lived here before us. She wasn't one of them.' Jackie and I thought we'd done well, getting down to reality. 'Don't like that,' said one of the churchwardens. 'The Archbishop expects to see 700 on our roll. We've always had that sort of number.' It dawned on us that truth was far less important than window-dressing.

Parish life, for urban clergy who take their ministry seriously, is a seventy-hour-a-week business. Philip hardly ever took a day off and it showed. I carefully guarded my weekly day off but, even so, Jackie stuck a note in my diary some weeks before 3 April which said, tersely, 'First wedding anniversary. Keep this day clear or else!' I did. In fact, we haven't missed celebrating birthdays and anniversaries from that day onwards.

Just before that, Jackie went to Bristol for a weekend. As I went to my first lonely bed, I glanced at Brian Lipscombe's bookshelf. Brian, having moved in with us, was away doing his National Service. I picked out a book by Aldous Huxley, *Brave New World*. I had heard of it but knew nothing about it. I settled myself in bed and couldn't put it down. I finished it at five o'clock the next morning – one of the three or four most gripping and influential books I have ever read. From then on I knew that I couldn't afford to ignore books. I was hooked. Two years later I began to keep a complete list of what I've read and now, forty years later, that list contains well over two thousand four hundred titles.

Clergy were expected to spend time in 'house-to-house'

visiting. I never found it a very creative use of time, especially as, increasingly, no-one was at home in the afternoons as more and more women were doing part-time, or full-time, jobs. 'A house-going parson makes a churchgoing people' was the cliché. Not anywhere I've been. Many lay people won't believe this and assume that, if only clergy would visit, churches would be packed. One spring we planned a parish visitation and with clergy and lay teams we visited eleven hundred homes. Not a single person came to church in consequence. One lay visitor was so shocked at the total indifference he met that he left the church. So our eleven hundred visits reduced our congregation by one! I'm glad to report that he did eventually return.

Outside the parish there was also plenty to do. The Croydon chapter of clergy met regularly and I almost always attended. Philip rarely went, 'such a bore', but I enjoyed getting to know those of very different traditions. Most were either 'Central' or 'Anglo-Catholic' and I cut my first debating teeth when Henry Cooper, the Prolocutor of Canterbury, the most senior elected clergyman in southern England, came to speak and made very dismissive remarks about 'Evangelicals'. I seemed to be the only one present so I took him on and wasn't totally worsted. That, in fact, was the first of countless occasions in the years ahead when either I was the only Evangelical present at some meeting or the only one willing to put his head above the trench. In that way I acquired a reputation for enjoying controversy. It wasn't actually true but I simply couldn't stand by and watch the things I believed in being regularly betrayed by silent complicity on the part of too many who were watching their professional chances of preferment. Certainly it seemed to me that it could only be that or sheer ignorance and fear. From those days I vowed to be as professionally competent as possible, always ready 'to have an answer for the hope that is in me'.

This soon showed itself in the post-ordination training course at Canterbury at St Augustine's College. Generations of clergy have been required to undergo 'potty training.' Many have hated it. I thoroughly enjoyed mine. For three years, we travelled by train, once a month, for a day in Canterbury. The journeys, for those of us in Croydon, meant about ten of us meeting at Bromley South and talking our heads off there and back. We were tutored by Kenneth Sansbury, later to be Bishop of Singapore and General Secretary of the British Council of Churches, and the debate was sharp-edged but very friendly. As I recall it, the three leading protagonists were Tony Bridge (an ex-atheist artist), later to be Dean of Guildford, Kenneth Jennings (a Liberal-Catholic academic), who became Dean of Gloucester, and me. We regularly slogged it out. I faintly remember one of the quieter men, Eric Evans, who made little impact then, but, in later years, sat alongside me as both a General Synod member and a Church Commissioner, and with whom I was ultimately to work happily in the 1990s when he was Dean of St Paul's.

Philip preferred to attend the local ministers' fraternal. These were almost all Free Church Evangelicals. I went once and got talking to a Pentecostal minister who told me that, to be a Pentecostal, 'you had to receive Christ as your Saviour, then get rid of him to let the Holy Spirit in and so become a real Christian.' I was outraged at such a heretical doctrine and told him so. I didn't go back! In fairness to Pentecostals, those I have since met have all been equally appalled at such a travesty. At one interdenominational prayer meeting, I met a senior Salvation Army officer. 'We don't have Holy Communion in the Salvation Army,' he told me. 'Come to think of it, we don't have the Lord's Supper either.' Had he really said that? Yes, he had. He honestly thought they were two quite separate events. After the same meeting, which had pummelled the Almighty with interminable extemporary prayers, I invited a fellow-curate, Michael Cooper, back home for coffee. A delightful, gentle 'high churchman,' he said quietly, 'There's a lot to be said for the Anglican collect.' I said nothing but it made me value the concise prayers of the Church of England. They say exactly what needs saying, they don't waste a word, and they discourage Christians from being hijacked by exponents of long-winded exhibitionist jargon. I may be an Evangelical but I honestly wonder whether God isn't sick and tired of Evangelical prayer meetings. On and on they go, utterly convinced that a torrent of words is a sure guarantee of the superspirituality of those mouthing them. God help God! He must have unbearable ear-ache.

One afternoon I came back from the vicarage with a small blue booklet called *If*. Philip obviously thought I needed to be 'done good to', and suggested I read it. I shut my study door, sat down, and opened it. It began with the instruction, 'Do not read this book in the usual way. Take one page at a time and meditate upon it.' 'No way,' I thought, and flipped through it. It was an odd book. It only had one sentence at the bottom of each page. A very pre-ecological waste of paper! Then my eye caught the words, 'If I covet any spot on earth except the dust at the foot of the cross, then I know nothing of Calvary-love.' Some words of Amy Carmichael, a missionary in India. What happened next was not, I suspect, a 'vision' in the usual sense. It was, I think, in my head. Yet I saw a cinema screen and in it a hill, back-lit, with three crosses. The camera zoomed in slowly, the hill went out of shot and so did the side crosses. The upright of the centre cross re-mained in close-up, just the foot of it. I was transfixed. There I was at the foot of the cross. Slowly the 'vision' (or whatever it was) vanished.

What did it mean? What should I do? I told no-one, not even Jackie, for five years. It was too precious for words. Slowly I real-ised that I had always thought of the crucifixion as having been 'over there' in space and time. Two thousand years ago. Two thousand miles away. And so it had been in reality. But now, and for the rest of my life, that objective reality would always be com-plemented by my having knelt in 'the dust at the foot of the cross'. I was no longer a distant onlooker. I'd been there.

Almost before I had realised it, my priest's ordination was upon me. This time, Trinity Sunday fell on the 16 June, and, as be-fore, there was a pre-ordination retreat. This one was conducted by George Reindorp, Vicar of St Stephen's, Rochester Row, in Westminster, and just appointed to be the Provost of Southwark. In due course he would become Bishop, first of Guildford and, later, of Salisbury. The contrast between the soul-searching spiri-tual quest under John Hughes and the glib chatter of George was most disturbing. When, in some desperation, I sought him out for some personal advice (my relationship with Philip, was, at that stage, under stress) he revealed himself to have no more than a handful of chirpy clichés. To crown everything, he urged all of us ordinands to go out and buy his latest book, which I duly did. I read it on the Saturday night, including a sermon 'for an ordination'. Next morning, he got up in the pulpit of Canterbury Cathedral and read it out word for word. I often met George over the years, took the mickey out of him whenever I dared, but never really forgave him for his inadequate cock-sparrow behaviour which so sadly diminished the ordination. George, of course, was a very 'successful' clergyman and bishop!

Strangely enough, I wasn't upset by Geoffrey Fisher's cheeky comment as we awaited the service. Having ten minutes to spare he used up the time explaining how we could all give assent to the Thirty-Nine Articles 'without actually meaning it'. I thought this was a bit outrageous for an Archbishop of Canterbury but he went on to say 'and that was all for Saward's benefit'. Since I was one of a handful present who *did* actually and genuinely assent to the Articles, I thought it was a low blow. We grinned at each other and I silently vowed revenge!

One afternoon the doorbell rang and a sixty-year old woman stood there. Seeing my collar she gulped, then launched into her prepackaged Jehovah's Witness spiel. She certainly had courage so, against my better instincts, I asked her in. She gave me the full works, hardly drawing breath for about ten minutes. Naturally, she cheerfully denied the divinity of Christ. When, finally, she paused, I asked her, politely, 'Since you've been quoting Greek at me, could I ask you what you think the word *morphe* in Philippians 2, verse 6, means? You know,' I added, 'being in the *morphe* of God and all that.' She floundered and I pressed her. It was obvious that she hadn't a clue that the word described Jesus as being of the 'essential nature of being' of God, as St Paul meant. Eventually she capitulated. 'Actually,' she ruefully admitted, 'I don't know any Greek.' 'Funny,' I said sharply, 'you quoted Greek at me when you thought I didn't know any.' Then I gave her both barrels on Christ's divinity and the relevant Greek words. She leapt up. 'Look at the time,' she gasped. 'I must go.

Anyway, I'm right and you're wrong. Good-bye.' And off she went. When a teenage Jehovah's Witness later tried the same game on me in Edgware I reduced her to tears. It seemed cruel but I wanted her to know and face up to her cocky ignorance. Since then I've rarely shied off giving the works to Jehovah's Witnesses. They scare, or bore, so many people but they are no more than puppets mouthing tape-recorded loop messages. Mormons, in my experience, aren't much better and I once travelled on a TGV train from Paris to Nice with a Mormon couple. Charming, sweet, naive, and programmed.

Being a highly organised animal I have always kept statistics. I can tell you my batting averages since I was ten. So it was that I knew that in my first year of ministry I had given 134 talks and sermons, and conducted 53 cremations and funerals. In recent years such figures would have been quite impossible. First-year curates are now governed by strict rules and I doubt if they could speak or preach as much as once a week. No-one thought to consider us in those days. You were a clergyman? Get on with it!

Around that time I began to play clergy cricket for the diocese and proved myself with both bat and ball. One result of the cricket, the chapter, and the Post-Ordination Training was that I already knew one-third of the diocesan clergy, at least by sight, and since the vast majority were not of my tradition I discovered the value of having friends from all schools of thought.

In mid-July Jackie and I set out to lead a party of about twenty adults to Austria. We had been accepted by a Christian holiday organisation called Pathfinders (not the children's group of the same name) and found ourselves years younger than everyone else, which was a trifle disconcerting. Never having been to Salzburg or the Tyrol before, I had to keep one jump ahead of everyone but all seemed to go well. We took a coach trip to see the magnificent Grossglockner, saw the famous Salzburg marionettes in a Mozart opera, toured the Salzkammergut lakes and did it at an exchange rate of 72 schillings to the pound, nearly four times better than today's rates. We spent our second week in Kirchberg, near Kitzbühel, and woke up one night to discover the innkeeper's whole family (including a geriatric grandmother) building a new wing, in pouring rain, by floodlight. We couldn't imagine anyone in England working so hard to better their family's prospects.

On the journey home our party had to cross the frontier into Germany at Kufstein railway station. I had the party ticket, shepherded my charges into the train for Munich, and suddenly realised we were two old ladies short. Jackie and I dashed back to the barrier where a little piglike German policeman was blocking the way, maintaining loudly, 'Zis lydy kinnot inter Zharmany.' The lady and her companion looked non-plussed and my German was almost non-existent. 'Warum?' I asked. He pointed out that her passport was six months out of date. Amazingly we had crossed six frontiers and no-one had noticed. But there was no question about it. It was out of date. At that point our train departed with our party, all unaware of the drama at the barrier, and I with the ticket, Jackie and two stunned old ladies, was left to watch it vanish. Do angels exist? I don't know, but at that point a Canadian angel arrived, speaking fluent German. He discussed the matter with the intransigent policeman, got him to take me off to his office, above the station, where I could phone the British consul in Munich, get temporary passes, 'covered in official stamps, please', and arrange for someone to meet the train in Munich and keep the party together while the four of us came up on the next train. Luckily, we would still have time to catch the Munich–Ostend express. With this plan in mind (which duly succeeded), I set off with Little Piggy towards his office.

Still uttering 'Zis lydy kinnot . . .' and so on, we reached a dark stairway. He ascended, humming a snatch of Beethoven. I whistled the next few notes, asked 'Lieben Sie Beethoven?' (or something equally improbable) and we entered the office. Little Piggy was beaming. Nothing was too much trouble. All was solved. I learnt a lesson. Never try to beat a German at rational, legal logic. Tickle his emotional underbelly with some sentimental words or music and you're home and dry. And, a few hours later, we were. I later discovered that the lady had been warned to renew her passport but couldn't be bothered.

Two weeks later I started (but never finished) a correspondence course in journalism. My first assignment was to write a brief autobiographical sketch. Back it came with comments. 'You reveal an engaging style, clear and readable, free from defects, and never overloaded with ornament . . . an eye for the oddities and idiosyncrasies of people that will stand you in good stead. Please send two guineas.' I sent the money and, lacking all humility, decided I didn't need any further teaching. Nine books and hundreds of articles and reviews later, who is to say that I wasn't right? What's more, if you've got this far into this book, who are you to argue?

Michael Brown, then a selection secretary in Church House, Westminster, had been my tutor for my priest's essays and he urged me to attend the International New Testament Congress at Christ Church, Oxford, during September. I agreed and found it very stimulating. One night Geoffrey Fisher came up from London as chairman for a session to be addressed by a soon-to-be French Cardinal (who later dropped dead in a French brothel – 'just a pastoral visit' they announced). Fisher began his speech of introduction with the words 'as I was wondering in the car what to say to you . . .' and there was a stunned hush. Here was the cream of the world's New Testament scholars (plus hangers-on like me) and the Archbishop of Canterbury hadn't even bothered to prepare! You could hear the sound of his dropped clanger in Rio de Janeiro. Fortunately, Michael Ramsey, Archbishop of York, had provided a magisterial paper two days earlier, colliding with Rudolf Bultmann's destructive thesis and he upheld the honour of the Church of England. Ten years later it was my memory of that paper which finally got me on relaxed terms with Ramsey, after nearly a year as his radio and television officer. None of my small talk had broken his silence but his defeat of Bultmann cracked the dam of this shyness and we were friends from that day onwards.

Back at the ranch, I was in trouble. Philip had just announced that he was moving and I wrote to various clergy inviting them to preach during the coming interregnum. One letter produced a chilly response. Bertie Rainsbury, Vicar of Emmanuel, South Croydon, an Ulster Protestant of extreme views, declined to preach. I had, he declared, 'abused his pulpit in his absence by attacking both the Inter-Varsity Fellowship and the Keswick Convention' in a sermon on Pharisaism. Needless to say, I had done no such thing but he had been so informed by 'a number of mature Christians whose judgement I respect'. I rang both his curates, who had been present, and each denied that I had made any such remarks. I remembered that after the sermon, a significant number of people had congratulated me saying 'we really needed that', so I went straight to Philip and told him what had happened.

He read the text of the sermon (full notes, not a verbatim script) and kept saying, 'No, you didn't say that? Whoopee! Just what they needed at Emmanuel', but we agreed that I should write to Rainsbury, regretting any misunderstanding, agreeing to see him, mentioning the support of both Philip and the curates, expressing surprise that he had said nothing for over two months, and declining to retract anything I had said in the sermon. I was invited to his gloomy vicarage and was clearly 'on the mat'. Looking at my text he kept groaning (he was a master of the 'holy groan') and saying, 'Do you not see?' 'No,' I said, 'I merely talked about the danger of Evangelical Pharisaism and my remarks about the IVF and Keswick were in no way disparaging.' I mentioned his curates but he dismissed their opinions out of hand relying on the 'wound' I had caused to an elderly gentleman who had walked out halfway through (I had assumed he had a weak bladder!)

Eventually it all blew over but not before I was told that I would never occupy Emmanuel's pulpit again. At least three others have since been incumbents there (including two of my friends) but in that, at least, he was right! Ironically, even twenty years later, people came up to me, elsewhere, saying, 'Wasn't it you who preached that splendid sermon on Pharisaism at Emmanuel in 1957?' You can't win 'em all, can you?

Just before Philip's departure, the subject of Canon Law revision came to the boil. The Archbishop agreed to meet both Christ Church and Emmanuel church councils and did so on 9 December. He swept into the Emmanuel church hall, virtually ignored both Bertie and Philip (both of whom he disliked) and, in the silence, roared out to me at the far end of the hall, 'Saward, you keep your mouth shut tonight!' 'Of course, Your Grace,' I said smarmily, knowing that I wouldn't and that he knew I wouldn't. He talked for an hour and, finally, called for questions. I apologised, hesitantly, for disobeying his instruction but asked for his advice. 'Last week, Your Grace, you said that the final authority in religious matters was the voice of the Holy Spirit, speaking through the Church. Tonight, you said it was Holy Scripture. Could you clarify this, Your Grace, I'm afraid I'm simply not clever enough to reconcile those statements.' I sat down. There were forty-five minutes left and Geoffrey didn't stop talking or take another question. Needless to say, he completely ignored my point. A couple of days later, his chaplain, Michael Adie (soon to marry the Archbishop's pretty secretary and eventually to be Bishop of Guildford) wrote to say that the Archbishop 'appreciated my question'. Old rogue, I thought. He may be a magisterial politician and a delightful person but he's got no idea about theological integrity. He'll merely say what he thinks he can get away with.

There was one delightful sequel. Soon after I was with a group of clergy when Fisher came up and started talking about Canon Law revision. 'I've had hundreds of letters about it,' he said, 'but the best came from the church council at Christ Church, Croydon. Isn't that your parish, Saward?' 'Yes, Your Grace, it is. And I wrote it.' Fisher pealed with laughter. 'Listen everyone,' he said and retold the story.

Philip left for an Area Secretary's job in the west Midlands. He was drained after ten years' attritional battling. I only wish I had worked with him in his earlier years. By my time, he had grown disillusioned. To every idea I offered he merely said, 'It would never work.' Now, with what promised to be a long interregnum, we should see. So I tried them all out and they all succeeded beyond my wildest dreams. I learnt another lesson. 'Never' and 'always' are killer words. They kill all initiative. Croydon was swamped by 'we've never done it this way' and 'we've always done it that way'. Not in my time, I thought. We'll soon change all that. We did. And it worked. In those nine months I created regular vestry hours, daily prayers in church, marriage preparation courses, large-scale public baptisms, and, best of all, a mid-week Wednesday evening biblical exposition. I started that with twelve people and by September there were forty – nearly half the adult congregation. Week by week my expositions got longer and longer. The final one lasted seventy minutes! More and more people came. Make what you will of that.

Pastoral problems didn't decrease. One night a teenage member of the YPF gulped down a bottle of aspirin and arrived at our front door. We were up half the night while the hospital did a thorough pump out. Another YPF member, John Cleaton, woke up one morning blind and paralysed, in due course diagnosed as multiple sclerosis. The church rallied round and I persuaded a local factory to give him a tape recorder – not free, mind you, but I bullied them into a discount. He, poor kid, was in complete shock and God and the church were entirely to blame. Then, to make things more complicated, he wanted to be ordained and that was pretty well out of the question. The Bishop, John Hughes, helped him a lot. Imagine, then, my delight when, thirty-five years later, an article appeared in the *Church Times* telling his story and showing him in a dog-collar. He had finally been ordained, in 1992, far away in west Dorset, still blind, still with multiple sclerosis, but now a prison chaplain. Soon after, he wrote me a long letter, recalling those far-off days in Croydon and telling me of his recent work in the ministry. If ever a man learnt faith through terrible suffering it was John Cleaton. I thank God that we were able to play just the tiniest part in that process even though he probably still feels that we let him down.

A second tragedy struck when an elderly woman of about sixty went into the local mental hospital. I called, and we sat outside on a garden seat. She looked very strange. 'There's nothing you can do,' she said. 'Satan came to me in the night and told me that he had claimed my soul. I'm doomed. You can't help.' This happened long before charismatics started exorcising 'possessed' people and I felt impotent. She was in a hospital, under medical care. I couldn't start trying out exorcism, even if I knew how. I prayed for her out loud but she shrugged it off. 'You're wasting your time. I'm damned.' A couple of weeks later she came home and hanged herself, leaving a note to say that she had committed the sin of Judas Iscariot and must pay the same price. She had been a Sunday school teacher almost all her adult life. I still don't know what happened but she certainly looked like a woman possessed. Failure stared me in the eyes and it looked to be mine, not hers.

Terrible tragedy like that, as it was, goes hand in hand with memorable idiocy. I vividly recall visiting a Mr Chamberlain, close to John Cleaton's home, who told me that he couldn't believe in Christianity because the 'Dead Sea Squeals' had disproved it. No, that isn't a misprint. He really did call them the Dead Sea Squeals. How I kept a straight face, I'll never know!

Tragedy, idiocy and brutality. There was this kid of about fourteen who was a violent thug and non-stop trouble. After weeks of his disruptive behaviour I told him he couldn't come on a Bank Holiday ramble. So he did. We kept him screened by older boys, well away from the main party. He was impossible. Finally, on a common near Epsom my patience gave out. I waited till everyone was out of sight, grabbed him by neck and trousers, and chucked him head first into a gorse-bush. His flow of language would have turned a drill sergeant's cheeks pink. But he never again caused any trouble. Quite unjustifiable behaviour. Today I should be 'done' for child abuse. But it worked. And I'm not one bit penitent.

Occasionally I found myself reaching what I learnt to call 'pinging point'. The stress was getting too much and I decided to drop everything and go away alone, for twenty-four hours. I walked on the South Downs, getting all the steam out of my system, and it worked. Over the years I've only come close to pinging point three or four times but, first, recognising the symptoms and, secondly, getting away alone have been the effective cure. Once, when in Liverpool, I walked over the fells from Shap to Sedbergh and then via Dent to Kirkby Lonsdale. I hardly saw a soul and treasure the memory of sitting in the cleft of rock a thousand feet up in the hills, holding an open umbrella above me to keep off the torrential rain. If only I had a photo.

In the summer of 1958, Jackie and I took off on a Lambretta

scooter, which we had recently bought, for a holiday in Austria. We crossed the Channel on a Bristol air-freighter to Le Touquet, and rode in one day to Chalons-sur-Marne. *En route*, we crossed the old battleground of the Somme and I got my first vague understanding of the slaughter as we passed military cemetery after military cemetery. Eventually we crossed the Brenner Pass into Italy drawing knowing leers from Italian frontier police who scanned my passport photo (me in a dog-collar) and saw a man in a red shirt, an incipient beard, and a young woman riding with him. To Catholic cops the picture was all too obvious. Grins and obscene gestures. And I wondered what they meant!

We spent a week in an inn on the Millstättersee in Carinthia, where for £5 each, full board, we could lie in bed, look up the lake's ten-mile length to the line of the Austrian Alps and wallow in the beauty of it. The inn is still there today, but highly commercialised, and the simple, bucolic nature of the place has long since vanished.

Returning to Salzburg, in pouring rain, we climbed the Pass Lueg where the bike's gear cable jammed in first gear and a tyre punctured at the summit. The bliss of sitting on wet gravel mending the tyre in pelting rain and feeling the seam of one's overtrousers rip for about twelve inches with the resulting soaked bottom can be easily imagined. I steered the wounded bike for eighteen sodden miles to Salzburg in bottom gear and then faced the indignity of hotel after hotel declining to find rooms for two bedraggled rats. My copy of volume one of Churchill's *History of the English Speaking Peoples*, which I was reading on the trip, still bears the stains of the rainwater on its dustcover.

Eventually we reached home, wiser, poorer, but hugely enriched by all that we had seen of France, Germany, Austria, Italy, Holland and Belgium. On our last night we were so broke we slept under a road bridge and at 6.30 a.m. consumed a bowl of steaming vegetable soup in a dirty *estaminet* on the French-Belgian border. We were cold, tired, but desperately happy. We never had much money but travel was ten times more valuable than being surrounded by new furniture. And by travel we meant all the cheapest and most uncomfortable means of getting around. The

Germans, Austrians and Italians may have hated the victors of World War Two but they needed us badly and we were the fortunate benefactors of their relative poverty in those years. We slept in clean linen sheets in peasant houses for what, in today's prices, was less than 20p a night for the two of us.

My last encounter with Geoffrey Fisher that year was when I wrote a very polite letter complaining of a sneering and destructive review, in the official diocesan periodical, of John Stott's book, *Your Confirmation*. The editor presumably thought he could say what he liked and get away with it. Fisher's reply, to a young curate, was generous in the extreme. He had read the book, he had read the review, and 'I think your protest was entirely justified. The review was one-sided and by no means did justice to Stott's book.' Stott's theology, he added, 'has an entirely acceptable place in Anglican theology and . . . deserves respect.' Having given me admirable support, he kept me neatly in my place by saying that 'anything I say to [the Editor] about the review is my affair and not yours.'

John Stott, later to become a very good friend, was relieved and delighted by the correspondence since, as he put it to me, he had been 'rather distressed by the review'. Did Fisher rap the editor's knuckles? Who knows? Someone close to both of them later said that he knew that Fisher had made his displeasure evident in no uncertain fashion. By keeping my head and being polite, I had won the battle. With Fisher, politeness was always the way through. He had, he once told me, physically thrown out an Evangelical clergyman from Lambeth Palace who had been rude to him. I got away with massive, and regular, cheek because I never crossed the line into rudeness and Fisher appreciated it.

Then the new vicar was appointed. His name was 'Perfect'. But, sad to say, he turned out to be the most stupid and thick-skulled clergyman I have ever met. I had nine months of absolute hell. He broke his promise to the church council that he would follow Philip's baptismal policy. He sacked most of the organisation leaders within a couple of weeks. In the space of a couple of years he lost two curates, one lay reader, one churchwarden (the new one inevitably) and did almost irreparable damage to the church. I could have sued him successfully for libel and he nearly drove my successor out of the ministry in his first year. He scrapped all my successful policies at a stroke and everything lapsed back into lethargy. Dick dropped dead in the street of a heart attack. Christ Church was saved and the new vicar, Derek Osborne, carefully cleaned up the mess and rebuilt the church. Harsh words, after so many years? Perhaps, but no-one ever caused me, and many others, so much pointless and unnecessary pain. The really hurtful thing was that he had blackened the reputations of six successive curates in two parishes and I, for one, went through many months of grief trying to find a second curacy and discovering that no-one wanted me because of Dick Perfect's slanders (and they were slanders) about my ministry.

Thank God, one man didn't believe them. He had followed Perfect, in his earlier parish, as vicar and knew from bitter experience what kind of man he was. Don Smith was no fool, later became an archdeacon, and recommended me to the Rector of Edgware, as a good man to fill the vacancy there. On 1 September 1959, mightily relieved, Jackie, now plumply pregnant, and I, moved into 8 Elmer Gardens, a typical suburban semi, and began five of the happiest years of our lives. What's more, we not only had a baby on the way. We had a Lambretta motor-scooter and we'd been half round Europe on it.

Chapter Seven

Up the Edgware Road

Twelve miles up the old Roman road from Marble Arch is the unspoilt little village of Edgware. Handel was reputed to have written his 'Harmonious Blacksmith' at Canons, the large house nearby. The ancient High Street has a sprinkling of Tudor buildings and the parish church goes back to mediaeval times.

Then the process of suburbanisation caught up with Edgware and by the time the Underground got there Edgware had become typical outer-suburbia and what was left of the village was swamped. Thus from the 1930s to the end of the 1950s Edgware was a comfortable area of English middle-class affluence. But a tidal wave was about to sweep over it and by the middle 1960s. Five synagogues had appeared, and the whole social and religious balance was transformed. The inexorable movement of Jewish people, decade by decade, from Whitechapel via Stoke Newington to Golders Green, had eventually reached the sylvan shores of Edgware and Stanmore. Whereas in the 1950s there had been one Jewish family in each road, by the mid-1960s there was only one non-Jewish family in the same row of houses and many of the front gardens had been covered with tarmac hard-standing for the Jaguars, a guaranteed symbol of well-to-do Jewry.

When Jackie and I arrived in 1959, the process was only just discernible. St Margaret's, though a slightly enlarged mediaeval village church, had been running two crowded morning services, plus a busy evening service, to get everyone in. The church was flourishing, a daughter church was already over twenty years old, and there were embryonic plans to build a second one on a small new estate right on the edge of the green belt. St Margaret's was the most flourishing Evangelical parish between Northwood and Finchley and people flocked there from miles around. The Young People's Fellowship had anything up to eighty attending every Saturday evening, and St Andrew's, the daughter church, had its own YPF of about thirty to forty. By the early 1960s, Edgware had three curates, a full-time London City Missionary, and a part-time worker from the CMJ (the Church's Ministry among the Jews). It also had a flourishing Scout group, with the best Scout band in North-West London.

When I wrote to the Bishop of London, Henry Montgomery-Campbell, telling him of my appointment, he (notorious for his mordant and scathing wit) replied to say that he was glad to hear that 'you are planting yourself on the Parish of Edgware'. Not much warmth there, and very different from John Hughes' good wishes, coupled with a request to 'Come and see me whenever you care to; it will always give me pleasure even though we shall know that we shall regard each other as in part *heretics*!' Add to that Geoffrey Fisher's farewell comment that 'I shall deeply regret losing you from the diocese' since it has been 'a very healthy and good thing to have had you amongst us and we shall all be the poorer without you ... God go with you' and I was conscious that, although hugely relieved to leave Christ Church and Dick Perfect's baleful presence, I was saying good-bye to real friends. Certainly, as I settled into Edgware, I soon realised that Canterbury had been a diocese with a very human face and a total contrast to the frozen and ecclesiastical tundra called the Diocese of London.

St Margaret's was humming with life, exhibiting the kind of vision and faith that seemed so lacking at Christ Church. The attitude to money was a marked contrast. Gone was the pinch-penny approach, and the breathtaking 'Restore and Build' appeal, launched by Melville Scutt the Rector, raised £10,000 in the month of October. I simply didn't believe it possible (remember, I was earning about £400 a year in Edgware) and Melville's faith was a lesson to me which I never forgot. Even allowing for the fact that he had a tame, and generous, donor hidden away in the wings of Hampshire I was, as they say, gobsmacked.

All seemed set fair. A new kind of ministry was opening up. It was exciting, demanding and hugely satisfying. Then, one afternoon, Melville asked me to go to see him at the vicarage. To my surprise, and puzzlement, he began to ask me a whole series of questions about Croydon. What was my attitude to this? What had I done about that? In what way was I involved in the other, and so on. I answered all his questions frankly and fully but couldn't think why he should suddenly be so interested. At the end he apologised for being so intrusive but 'I wanted to hear it from your own mouth.' 'Why?' I asked, 'Isn't it history now?' 'Well,' he said, 'I'm glad you've told me and I believe what you say to be the truth.' 'So why ask me?' I added, still nonplussed. Then it came out. Dick Perfect had written him a long letter in which he had blackened my character with a whole series of allegations. Without knowing what was going on I had successfully, to Melville's mind, refuted every one. 'That's all right,' he concluded, 'we'll forget it. I can't imagine what made him write like that.' 'I can,' I said ruefully, and told him the whole story of broken promises, lies and slander.

I don't believe that Perfect was an evil man. He was simply a small-minded, arrogant fool with a shocking memory who bullied anyone who would let him. I couldn't let him get away with what he had done and in the correspondence which followed he flatly denied having made any such accusations, even though Melville had read them out to me! He wrote saying that he had no 'evidence that you have a clue of what the Holy Spirit commands', and explaining that he had deleted a phrase from my farewell 'thank you' in the parish magazine in which I had hoped that 'we taught you a little more of the counsel of God – you certainly enriched us by your concern for us' on the grounds that it 'was patronising'.

He finally maligned almost everything I had done in Croydon. For a man who regularly boasted that he hadn't read a book since he left Cambridge, thirty years before, and whose sermons were, in their final five minutes, virtually the same every week, it was breathtaking. Then I remembered how, in his first week, he had announced that 'no curate would ever be allowed to disagree' with him and it all became clear enough. He believed in his own infallibility and I, foolishly, had been unwise enough not to take it seriously. So ended, as I thought, my unhappy experience of the Perfect vicar.

The Edgware Young People's Fellowship had been founded in 1936 and was a wonderful training ground for any curate. It met every Saturday night and had been deliberately chosen for that evening to put the maximum challenge in front of teenagers on the night when most secular entertainment was at its peak. If you could gain their allegiance on Saturday to what was a very formal meeting, in an unattractive church hall, in serried ranks of chairs, with a chairman and an outside speaker talking for about half an hour – if you could succeed in that, then you were really getting somewhere. And succeed they had for more than two decades. They had produced ordinands and missionaries and their goal, as I saw it, was to create lots of mini-Billy Grahams.

To my mind there were two weaknesses. One was the simple fact that our real goal was to produce treasurers, secretaries, churchwardens, PCC members and organisation leaders for the Church of England in the nineteen-seventies, eighties and nineties. To aim for Billy Grahams was quite unrealistic. We wanted lively, spiritually adventurous, lay and clerical men and women, who wanted to be both faithful witnesses to Christ and church-builders. So, the programme and its goals needed to be redirected into the training of well-equipped Christians and that meant quite a significant shift.

The other weakness was the problem of a rapidly ageing, and mostly self-selected leadership. The committee were almost all in their late twenties, some even in their thirties, and yet the great bulk of the members were in the fifteen–twenty-three age-bracket. No-one seemed to have thought of any system for avoiding the top-heavy pattern, indeed no-one seemed to have given much thought to system, structure or administration. You didn't need such things in a YPF did you? I spent a lot of my first six months planning a complete restructure and, although I ran into some flak, some of the key people like Peter Liddelow (later both ordained and a Justice of the Peace) gave my proposals tremendous support and we launched a greatly revised package within the year.

The first major YPF event, a month after I arrived, was a youth mission conducted by a famous retired Guards' officer and evangelist of the 'stiff upper lip' variety. Himself a charming and delightful man, absolutely presentable in society's highest echelons, Major Bill Batt was renowned for his ability to 'win converts' wherever he went. I inherited his mission (and probably wouldn't have chosen him myself) but he arrived and proceeded to 'win converts' both in the local schools and in YPF-sponsored gatherings. Four days into the mission, the YPF leaders came to me. 'These converts,' they said. 'He's asking people to "receive Christ" and he hasn't given them any reason or grounds. He hasn't mentioned the cross or resurrection once.'

The ball was firmly in my court. I asked to see the major. 'Sir,' I said (he was the sort of man you automatically called 'Sir'), 'some of the YPF leaders are a little anxious.' I told him why. 'Now, Michael,' he said, exuding upper-class *bonhomie*, 'you don't want to get into all that theology business. I just tell people "receive Christ", and they do. That's all you need.' As a young curate, and ex-subaltern, I felt distinctly wrong-footed by this Deputy Lieutenant of his county. After all, everyone said he produced converts by the barrow-load. I would have to be patient. 'Thank you, Sir,' I said, entirely unconvinced.

Saturday night came. At the end of the YPF's meeting I saw that three young scallywags, known local troublemakers, were talking to him. He brought them up to me. 'Michael,' he announced, 'John, Bill, and Tom, here, have all "received Christ" tonight. However, they are due in court on Tuesday. Will you go and give them a good character? Tell the magistrates they've been converted, you know?' I drew him on one side. 'Major,' I said, 'I can't possibly do that. You know, and I know, that they're rogues.' 'But they're converted,' he expostulated. 'They'll be all right now.' 'Well,' I said, 'the most I can do is to go to court and say what they've said to you. I need a bit more evidence, and time, before I go putting my reputation on the line with the local magistrates.' He seemed very disappointed. 'Sorry,' I said, 'but

I'm surprised that you, yourself a magistrate, are asking me to do this.'

The major's mission ended. He had clocked in fifty-four converts in the local schools, and fifty-five in the YPF meetings. Within two months seven of them were still in contact with us, linked with our follow-up work. Needless to say, no church got a sniff of John, Bill and Tom. I was absolutely appalled. Five years later I was involved in a university mission at Cambridge at which the Major was an assistant missioner at one of the most prestigious colleges. He clocked in twice the number of 'converts' of any other missioner. Did they last? Anyone who preaches 'conversion' without any attempt at explaining the meaning of the gospel of Jesus Christ denigrates, in my assessment, the whole challenge of Christian discipleship. But he was such a charming man and, years later, such a caricature of Colonel Blimp when he was a member of the General Synod. All too often, when he got up to speak, the members walked out to the tea room. The sad thing was that while a godly, kind, well-meaning man, he was also a predictable old bore.

In those first four months as we settled into Edgware it was agreed that I should be chiefly the parish church curate, looking after the YPF and conducting a Sunday evening service in the Spur Road community centre. My fellow curate was Ian Stephenson who, with his wife Pat, a wonderfully warm, sensible and no-nonsense woman, had been trained at Tyndale and was, in that respect, my exact contemporary. Ian was a rugged, prickly character who had been a sailor and had knocked around in some pretty seedy places. He had had a very striking conversion and could establish a rapport with those whose needs were similar to his own but he and I were temperamentally poles apart. We had had rooms next to each other in college and had clashed quite often. In Edgware the clashes continued but, fortunately, most of our duties kept us well apart from each other. He got to Edgware a year before me and left a year after, so for the whole of my more than five years there we were forced to come to terms with each other. Strangely, we have kept in loose touch ever since, not exactly friends but never, I think, enemies. It is one of the strange and compelling things about the Christian gospel that while it doesn't solve everything at a stroke (as some of the naive pretend) it does seem to help those who have little naturally in common to recognise their loyalty to someone beyond themselves. Ian and I were, and still are, like that. I doubt if we could ever work happily together but each recognises something to respect in the other. We did, indeed, on occasion find common ground, strikingly demonstrated when we unitedly browbeat Melville Scutt into agreeing that the parish should take part in the annual Christian Aid house-to-house collection. 'Christian Aid?' said Melville. 'What's that got to do with the gospel?' There was a stunned pause while Ian and I took in this extraordinary remark; then we both fired two barrels apiece and Melville reeled under the combined artillery and capitulated, and the collection took place.

Melville, a bluff man of no great brain, was like that. At my very first public meeting he said how glad he was to have a curate with a lot more theology than he had and he said it with genuine humility. He was, as we've already seen, a man of vision, of faith and tremendous vigour. He was an 'old-school' Evangelical who believed in evangelism, a weekly prayer meeting, and simple preaching. One of his earlier curates called him a 'clown in the pulpit', and went home in tears after a particularly banal sermon. But, and to me it was a huge plus, he had welcomed me, given me a job with tremendous scope and I could live with his eccentricities (for the most part) when I compared him with what I had been saved from in Croydon.

Elsie, Melville's wife, was a total scatterbrain. A fluttery lady, she never once got Jackie's name right in the ten months we worked together. Usually she called her 'Katie', but there were various other equally misguided attempts to introduce her. Where Melville blustered, she dithered, and to hear either of them answer a telephone made one cringe for the unknown on the other end. Melville gave everyone the impression that you had interrupted something supremely important and that you could have a maximum of ten seconds of his time. 'Hello! Yes, yes, yes, yes, good-bye, good-bye, good-bye.' He slammed the receiver down. Over the years Melville had acquired the reputation, within St

Margaret's, that the last person to get to him before any decision had to be made, would get what they wanted. Melville simply didn't know how to say no and the sequence was only broken if someone of social importance exercised pressure. They always won!

I only suffered the consequences of this once. For months I and the 'wardens' representatives' at Spur Road had planned a stewardship campaign for that small but excellent congregation. It was to be launched at a special meeting and I had mentioned it over and over again at our weekly staff meeting in the rectory. The Spur Road congregation was well aware of it, fully support-ive, and praying earnestly for its success. Then the blow fell. On the very morning of the planned meeting Melville announced that it was entirely unacceptable and that he and the churchwar-dens were absolutely opposed, not least because I had given no warning and they didn't approve of this newfangled 'steward-ship' idea. No warning? I blew up! 'You've been fully aware of this for months and months and you've never said one word of criticism.' 'Well,' said Melville with the voice of finality, 'it is not to take place!' 'Then you come and tell them,' I replied. 'I can't possibly let them down in such circumstances. It's quite outra-geous.' Needless to say, one of the churchwardens had put the blocks on it at the last moment and Melville had succumbed tamely as usual.

The Spur Road wardens' representatives and the whole con-gregation were incensed. All the printing had been done, every-thing was ready for lift-off and now, with no reason, the Rector turned up, stopped everything, and walked out. I was left to try and calm everyone down, to be a loyal curate, and so on. It was one of the hardest nights of my ministry.

A week or two earlier, Melville suddenly announced, 'I'm afraid you're going to have the same trouble as you had in Croydon.' My heart sank. What now? 'I've accepted the living of All Saints, Woodford, in Essex.' Huge relief flooded through me. What on earth had possessed him to tell me in such an insensitive way? Well, it didn't matter. All was in order and Melville and I could easily survive each other for a few more months. On balance I had enjoyed working with him and I would never forget his trust in me when Don Smith had put my name to him, when my life was at its lowest ebb.

Quite unexpectedly an invitation arrived from Les Brown. Les was a Scot, a qualified pilot in his twenties, who had, in a period of unemployment in early 1959, worked at a chocolate factory in Croydon where he had met Brian Lipscombe, filling in some time between National Service and university. Les had, largely through Brian's influence, come to faith and this would eventually lead to his being a pilot in East Africa with the Missionary Aviation Fellowship. Les had joined Christ Church and had often been in our home. 'Would we', he wrote, 'join him at a concert at the Royal Festival Hall as part of the Beethoven Festival?' Otto Klemperer, in his eighties, was making his final London appearances as conductor.

Jackie and I took the tube and met him on the South Bank on the twelfth anniversary of the Queen's wedding. Les had got three excellent stall seats and we settled in as the Philharmonia Orchestra played the Prometheus Overture and, after the interval, the Seventh Symphony. Both were very enjoyable, even if taken at the usual Klemperer tempo. Between the Overture and the interval, Henryk Szeryng played the Violin Concerto. I had never heard it before and wasn't sure that I should like a solo violin piece, even with orchestra. It began with the four measured notes and proceeded in the normal way. Slowly I became aware that something very strange was going on. I was sitting (or so it seemed) a yard above my seat and experiencing what I can only describe as perhaps twenty minutes of orgasmic ecstasy. It was fantastic. Utter, utter bliss. Nothing like it had ever happened to me before. Nor would again in the succeeding years. It was, and remains, virtually indescribable. Heaven had touched earth in the Royal Festival Hall and I was at the very point of meeting. It was the rainbow's end. It was, you realise, Experience Number Three. First, my conversion in the tent at Studland Bay. Second, much more recently, the Dust at the Foot of the Cross, in Chatfield Road. Now, third (and lastly, as far as I can judge), Ecstasy with Violin on the South Bank. The first two weren't too difficult to understand. God had spoken to me in unmistakeable manner and I had responded as best I knew how. In both events, the crucifixion of Jesus Christ had been absolutely central. But what was this third experience? What should I make of it? I honestly didn't know. Certainly it had been wonderfully satisfying, a washing over my soul with music that had caught me up into the emotional clouds and held me there for what seemed an eternity. And how very very strange because I'm just not the sort of person who goes round looking for 'experiences' and generally distrust the claims of those who do.

For twenty or more years I simply recalled the experience with pleasure but didn't know how to interpret it. It didn't seem to have any obviously 'religious' significance, at least not in overtly Christian terms. Then it slowly began to dawn that perhaps God, in his love and mercy, had given me two striking demonstrations of his redeeming work on the cross and completed this trinity of revelation with a taste of his work as creator of all that is beautiful, dynamic and worthy of praise. Yes, indeed, utterly 'religious,' but this time speaking of his majesty in the universe which he had made, goes on sustaining, and fills with his life force, the Holy Spirit, who draws out of humanity an infinite range of talent, skill and glorious creativity in artistic works. All a load of sentimental maundering? Quite possibly, but just as possibly the self-same reality perceived by Elizabeth Barrett Browning's words:

> Earth's crammed with heaven,
> and every common bush afire with God,
> but only he who sees takes off his shoes.

Anyway, I've taken off my shoes and, in so doing, I have been enabled to worship. Each of my Three Experiences has done something to me that hasn't felt self-indulgent. Each has taught me something new about God, about myself, and about his power to change people. Each in its own way has radically changed me and it certainly seems, at least to me, to have been a change for the better. All three happened between the ages of fourteen and twenty-eight and nothing remotely comparable has taken place since, nor have I sought such experiences in the intervening years.

I am profoundly grateful for all three, willing for more, but not expecting or requiring them. To have had three in a lifetime seems a luxury to someone whose temperament is much more cerebral than emotional.

It was a crisp and icy morning when Brian Lipscombe and I set out early, on the Lambretta, to go to Cambridge where I was to present a paper to the Tyndale Fellowship Church History study group on 'The Missionary Strategy of Alexander Duff 1830–40'. We reached Baldock quite safely, then, among the wide open expanses of windswept country on the road to Royston, I hit a patch of black ice. I was travelling at about 45 m.p.h. and the bike turned on its side and continuing, like a bobsleigh, slid for maybe a hundred yards along the road before slowly coming to a halt. Fortunately, both of us had hung on, and we were completely unhurt. Despite the unpleasant shock, once we had realised that there was no traffic heading for us we had let nature take its course and actually enjoyed our version of the Cresta Run. To turn from that to a paper on Alexander Duff in fever-stricken Calcutta was no small contrast. In due course the paper was published in an academic periodical, the *Evangelical Quarterly*, but I never did finish the thesis which was originally aimed at a Bristol Master's degree.

By this time I knew that, while I could write, I was not going to be an academic writer. If I had any gifts with a pen they were largely in the journalistic direction and were aimed at the popular market. At my lowest point, in the spring of 1959, I had gone on a 'New Writers' conference' in Eastbourne and met, among others, a young teacher called David Winter who was about to become the editor of *Crusade* magazine. Would he be interested, I asked, in a series of six articles, fiction based on fact, about the early church? Yes, came the answer, he certainly would and needed the first one for publication in March 1960. It would need to be in his hands in January. So began the six 'Retrospect' articles with which I launched my literary career. They ranged from the Rome of Hippolytus in 217, the persecution under Diocletian in 305, the Council of Nicaea in 325, the work of Jerome in Bethlehem in 406, the life of a Benedictine monk in Monte Cassino in 534, through to Alfred the Great's translation of Bede's History of England in 885. They covered ground rarely, if ever, included in popular Evangelical periodicals and it gave me a good starting point from which to begin my writing career.

Looking back, I recall that these early articles were motivated not only by a desire to write but also by the somewhat desperate conviction that this was the quickest way in which I could hope to rehabilitate myself among the leaders of the Evangelical constituency. In the light of what I did, in fact, write, it made my name among the younger Evangelicals but some of it caused even more anger among the older men, though, as it happened, they didn't actually link my name to the newspaper articles which were chiefly written under pseudonyms. The first of these was a closely guarded secret known only to John King, the editor of the *Church of England Newspaper*, and me. It was to take the form of a letter, 'Dear vicar', from a curate who was distilling the experiences of twenty-five curates whose disheartenment the letter expressed. It created a minor explosion. Here at last, out in the open, were the deep wounds inflicted by incumbents on inexperienced, well-meaning young curates. Scores and scores of curates, it seemed, had faced something similar and the letter touched a nerve all over the country.

Not surprisingly it didn't go unnoticed by the 'Dear vicars', one of whom wrote a hurried and angry reply to the *CEN*. To my solemn-faced amusement, I saw that the signatory was one J. Melville Scutt, Rector of Edgware. He, of course, had absolutely no idea that I had written the article and I had to keep a very straight face and play a very straight bat for weeks afterwards as battle raged in the correspondence columns. In after years, as an incumbent myself, I made it a practice to read 'Dear vicar' once every five years to remind myself of what a curate could feel. Luther, you remember, had said that 'the calf cannot imagine what it will be like to be a cow and the cow cannot remember what it was like to be a calf'.

Melville had always edited *Challenge*, the Edgware parish magazine, and though it had a striking, if rather confused front cover, the interior was a real jumble of bits and pieces. Early in my time I suggested a few small changes, which he ignored, but when the November issue appeared I went through it with a toothcomb and found thirty or forty misprints. 'All right,' he responded, 'then you edit it in the New Year.' Having done that for almost a year in Croydon, till you-know-who had instantly removed it from my care, I was delighted. For the rest of my Edgware years I was either editor or, later, consultant editor, during which years it was transformed, became the first parish magazine in England to have colour on every editorial page, made a profit (usually thought impossible) and won first prize in a national parish magazine competition. It gave me the entrée into one or two theological colleges to lecture on parish communications where, as I later learnt, one George Carey, an ordinand, had had a sharp disagreement with me over some matter of policy on the subject. George Carey? I didn't remember him, or the event, until in the early 1990s his wife Eileen said, at dinner in our home, 'Don't start having an argument with George; the two of you began it in the early 1960s when he was an ordinand.' Me? Argue with an archbishop-to-be? Never! (I only argue with actual archbishops!)

Edgware General Hospital was a mere four hundred yards from our home and when the pains began Jackie was rapidly taken into the labour ward. In those days my suggestion to the hospital that I might be present at the birth was treated with total disdain. So, I went back home and set about chairing a YPF committee booked for 8 p.m. Halfway through, the phone went. 'You've got a daughter.' I went back into the living room. 'We've got a baby girl, Rachel,' I announced. 'Will you chair the meeting till I get back?' I said to someone, walked across to the hospital, kissed Jackie and returned to the committee. Unbelievably, when Jonathan (Joe to everyone) was born eighteen months later, I was in the middle of chairing a YPF committee!

One morning the phone rang. 'Could I talk to you, Michael?' said an unknown voice. Well, almost unknown. It was Norman, my successor at Croydon. He asked me, in pained tones, why I had so unkindly ripped out the bookshelves in the study alcove at Chatfield Road. It seemed, he added, such a thoughtless thing to do as he would have been very glad to have them himself when he had moved in, months back. I was taken aback. 'Norman,' I said, 'I absolutely agree. I explicitly asked Dick Perfect whether you wanted them and, after enquiring from you, he had told me that you didn't need them and that I should take them out.' Norman's voice was weary and heavy. 'He never asked me,' he said. Then he poured out his pain. I, at least, had been in office when the Perfects arrived and could stand up for myself. He, a brand-new deacon, had been bullied from pillar to post and, in only a few months, was ready to leave the ministry. 'Go and see the Bishop of Croydon,' I said. 'How can I, after so short a time?' he groaned, and soldiered on.

The months dragged by. He often rang, bruised and hurt. At least, by now, the Bishop knew. He was allowed to move, after just two years. And he wasn't blamed. At last the various authorities had caught up with Dick Perfect. Six miserable curates. Well, at least, the official penny had dropped. Five of us had been made to carry the can. Thank God no-one else was permitted to go as his curate.

Melville's institution at Woodford was scheduled for 1 July and there is usually quite a long interregnum. The legal minimum, in those days, was twenty-eight days. Our new man came on the thirtieth! He had been appointed in late March and his name was Gordon Harman. It was not a little ironical that one of the churchwardens had said to me shortly beforehand, 'I don't mind who we have so long as it isn't the man who was once a curate here at the beginning of the war – Gordon Harman.' Poor churchwarden! He eyed me with considerable embarrassment when the new rector's name was announced. Gordon had been a missionary in China, had been imprisoned during the Communist revolution, and on his return had been rector of the large parish of Cheadle in Cheshire where he had worked with a series of outstanding curates, one of whom had come from my home church at Orpington. He at once wrote me a thoughtful, caring letter which left the future open but in the most reassuring way. I wrote him a long, frank letter offering my resignation (the etiquette required that in those days), and expressing willingness to stay and my wish to do so.

Jackie and I went to Westmorland in Easter week to stay with Geoff and Jenn Hill and returned via Liverpool ('We'll work anywhere but there,' we said innocently as we left) and called in at Cheadle to meet Gordon and his wife Mildred. She was the daughter of Fred Mitchell, a famous lay Christian leader who had been killed in the Calcutta Comet aircrash some years before. Gordon, very tall and thin, had a tinder-dry sense of humour which I couldn't initially fathom. Mildred was a Bradford lass of impeccably proper Keswick Convention style. I wondered how we should cope. So did Jackie. She and I are earthy, Goon-show trained, and generally ready to say exactly the wrong thing to see how people react. I decided that I couldn't be sure when Gordon was being serious, and when not, so I would say outrageous things all the time and see how he and Mildred coped. Months later he told me that he couldn't believe that an Evangelical Christian (never mind a clergyman) could be so outrageously flippant and began to doubt if I was really a Christian at all. It was an interesting exchange and, once the ground was cleared, he went on 'doing me good', while I went on 'taking the mickey', and we've been friends (even if mutually amused or puzzled by each other) ever since.

Shortly after Gordon's appointment, I was approached by John Cordle, a Member of Parliament, who happened to be Melville's brother-in-law, asking me to meet him at the House of Commons. On the terrace, he invited me to become, in effect, the sales manager of the *CEN*. A few days later I wrote declining: I didn't think that I had been ordained to sell papers. I would, however, I added, be delighted to go on writing for the *CEN*.

Cricket continued to be one of the few effective ways open of getting to know clergy from outside the deanery. My first game for London diocese put me firmly in the driving seat. I scored 69 and then took six wickets for 14 runs, being 'taken off' twice in the course of this. It was, I suppose, the high point of my clerical cricketing career though, over the years, I had the unusual experience of taking part in three *Church Times* cup finals (one for Canterbury and two for London) of which we won one and lost two. Between 1960 and 1964 I played a mere 14 games in five seasons, scoring 373 runs at an average of over 26. In one match against Southwark, at the Oval, I opened the batting as usual and made just over 40 in half an hour. In the same five years I collected forty-four wickets for just under 13 runs apiece. Considering how few games I got, I was happy with my results and greatly enjoyed playing with my brother clergy.

Parish life continued as usual and we decided, with everyone's agreement, to take our summer holidays shortly before Gordon's arrival. Jackie and I, Brian Lipscombe, and Yvonne Finch (by now his girlfriend), and two other married couples, would all go by train to Munich, rent a Volkswagen microbus and drive all over Austria for a couple of weeks, camping as we went. It wasn't the most successful of holidays. It rained too much, one couple's marriage was virtually at breaking point (and ended two months later), and it was crowned by one of the drivers (not me) turning the bus over on a mountain pass. Jackie and I returned feeling that we had been a cross between nurses and psychiatrists but long-term friendships seem to have survived the traumas. The one vivid recollection which has stuck was being in Salzburg when the Russian President Nikita Khrushchev was there on a state visit. The city was swamped with police motorcyclists and helicopters, and we caught only the briefest of glimpses as Himself swept past us in a high-speed motorcade.

On our return, Montgomery-Campbell, the Bishop of London, turned up to institute Gordon. No-one could discover whether or not he would be bringing a chaplain so I was deputed to occupy that onerous role ('Carry yer pastoral staff, Guv?') should no-one else have been instructed to appear.

The episcopal limousine drew up smoothly outside the church. Saward sprang smartly to attention. 'Have you brought a chaplain, my Lord?' Episcopal grunt. 'I have been asked to do it, if you haven't.' The Bishop emerged from the back seat, looking his usual gaunt and waspish self. He looked at me with ill-concealed contempt. 'It appears I have no alternative.' Vintage Montgomery-Campbell.

As the autumn began, the reshaped YPF started in earnest. I now had two assistant leaders, a secretary and a treasurer, the same range of visiting speakers, two annual rambles, a well-attended house-party weekend, a biweekly Bible study, interlocking with a teenage confirmation course, and a Sunday evening after-church social gathering. Membership was about eighty and Saturday evening activities were carefully preplanned, conducted by the members, with the curate acquiring fame as 'the man who gives the notices out'. Once a year we held an annual business meeting, which (said the oldies, knowingly) 'will never work'. It was, in fact, better conducted than the adult annual parochial meeting and drew almost as many people! So, we were on the way to creating the new generation of my hopes. What's more, people seemed to enjoy it, came regularly, and were more than willing to participate in two Young Churchmen's Fellowship rallies, in central London every year. I wrote it all up in my first full-sized book *Christian Youth Groups* which I co-authored with Michael Eastman (by now our bridesmaid Sheila's husband) in 1965.

The YPF had very few rules. My view was that, like a good school, morale and behaviour was in the hands of the 'prefects' and the inherited traditions. People behaved as was expected of them and didn't need to be bossed about by 'the masters', though 'the Head' had the final say. The only firm rule was 'no snogging during YPF activities'. It was a remarkably effective rule. Of course, youngsters will kiss and cuddle but that must be in their own time. Not on our premises, not at our activities. Since 'snogging' unchecked is like an epidemic – once allowed it would dominate everything. It sounds harsh but it worked well and I've never heard a former YPF member complain.

One key change had taken place. All teenage candidates for confirmation were now required: to attend either the Saturday YPF or a Sunday Bible class; to attend weekly the confirmation class, which (every other week) was also the YPF Bible study; and to attend the annual YPF weekend house-party. They had to commit themselves to this, in advance, and by so doing, gradually, for the most part, became integrated into the youth group before their confirmation. In this way we avoided the endemic problem faced by the Church of England of losing candidates from the church, immediately after their confirmation.

Working among teenagers can often bring you face to face with their sense of guilt. One YPF girl came to see me, shortly before her 'A' level exams. 'I feel spiritually drained,' she moaned. 'I'm not right with God. What should I do?' I gave her an armful of holiday and tourist brochures from France, Germany, Austria and Switzerland. 'Spend an evening looking through those,' I said. She looked puzzled and slightly shocked. A week later she returned, in smiles. 'You were right,' she said, 'it wasn't a spiritual problem. I just needed to relax and put my exams at arm's length.'

My three tasks, as curate, were now becoming quite clear. To run the YPF. To edit *Challenge*, the parish magazine. And a third had emerged. To organise, with Jackie, all the St Margaret's marriage preparation work. To these, of course, were added a normal Sunday preaching duty. Marriage preparation was very much our idea. Jackie and I had, in Croydon, begun to arrange courses of three or four evenings for couples wishing to marry in church. At first we asked the local Marriage Guidance Council to provide a couple to speak at the evening dealing with sex but to our surprise and disappointment, they were coy and far from competent and we decided we could do better ourselves. The courses in Croydon were oversubscribed and in those days many, if not most, of the couples were either virgins or sexually very inexperienced. Sex was only one of the subjects. We discussed the meaning and purpose of marriage, the finances, the marriage service and, finally, I would see each couple for a personal interview before I married them.

In Edgware we had between fifty and seventy weddings a year. In no time we found ourselves running half a dozen courses a year of, usually, up to six couples. These were very popular and we had had approaches from couples marrying in other parishes which, obviously, we couldn't allow or we should have had angry clergy complaining. Even as late as the early 1960s it was clear that the 'sex' and 'contraception' evening was providing information to many couples who were quite without experience of intercourse. The contrast with the 1990s, where most couples are cohabiting before marriage, is very marked. Our 1960s courses would be quite pointless today where any understanding of a Christian view of chastity as a positive virtue is almost non-existent outside the church (and, sadly, sometimes within it).

In my early years as a curate I spent a good many hours discovering and buying as many of the best commentaries on the Bible as I could find. Then I started making my own analyses of St Paul's letters and other sections of the New Testament. Slowly, bit by bit, I began to 'get on top' of the meaning of the Bible and its great themes. I worked especially hard on the letter to the Romans, Paul's 'Gospel', and in the following years expounded it seven or eight times, either in parish pulpits or in midweek groups. Before long I was familiar with its argument and could describe its teaching without a Bible in my hand. I went on to do this with other biblical letters and realised that far too many people saw the Bible as no more than a ragbag of 'texts' and 'quotes'. To discover it as a whole series of developed ideas, many of them interrelated, was a tremendous liberation. Those hours of early study have been repaid a hundredfold over the ensuing years.

One Sunday morning, the rector was away and I was awaiting a visiting preacher, Teddy Saunders, from Finchley. He didn't turn up. So we started. We finished the psalm. We ended the lessons. We said the creed. Still no Saunders. We prayed the prayers. Then, early in the hymn, I went up into the pulpit and knelt down. I wrote three words on a scrap of paper and preached a sermon of John Stott's from memory and the three words. I had heard Stott deliver it over ten years previously! At the end of the service I went to the porch. 'Lucky you had that sermon with you!' said two chirpy elderly sisters. 'What sermon?' I asked. The penny dropped. 'No?' they said. 'Yes,' I said, 'there's a God in heaven.'

Preaching at St Margaret's was generally a great joy. The congregation was appreciative and large and had one almost unique tradition. The YPF members sat in a large block just below the pulpit, in the side aisle, and many of them took notes of the sermons. In so many churches it was very different. The teenagers in such churches would congregate right at the back and sit in giggling groups, avoiding all serious interest in the service. Edgware produced high-quality leaders for the future (my era in the YPF provided eight clergy and one lay missionary, not to mention a galaxy of lay talent) and I have little doubt, in human terms, this was because we set them high standards, made great demands on them, and engulfed them in a strong corporate tradition of Christian behaviour and expectations.

All this, though, happened under the eagle eye of Mildred Harman. Mildred sat right at the back by the centre aisle, in the rectory pew. There she agonised. If I mentioned, let us say, 'Burma', in a sermon, she worried herself sick over the reaction of the Burmese present. If I said 'Patagonia', she felt deep anxiety for the feelings of the Patagonians. It would have been just the same if I had said 'Pitcairn Island'. Mildred had been trained to worry about 'the weaker brother'. How would such people feel? Caring about people's feelings is a good, selfless virtue. Mildred carried it to quite ridiculous extremes. There never were any Burmese, Patagonians or Pitcairn Islanders within a hundred, probably even ten thousand miles, of Edgware. Mildred still worried in case there just might be one, hidden behind a pillar. Would I have hurt their feelings? She was a lovely, kind, virtuous lady and I ragged her wickedly, knowing she would rise to any and every bait. She suffered from diabetes and died in the 1970s while still only in her late forties. She was a godmother to Joe and we still miss her.

Our parish boundary was also the diocesan and county boundary and stretched right out to the middle of Elstree, not too far from the film studios. On our side of the boundary were a few very large houses, rented by film stars while filming there. That year, one of them was taken by Sophia Loren, to whom (it is no secret to all my friends) I have been utterly faithful in my loving admiration since she first hit the cinema in the 1950s. Tragedy struck, however. While living in our parish, during the filming of *The Millionairess*, she was robbed of her jewels, worth, according to her husband, £200,000. Two men, Peter Scott and Ray Jones, have both, years later, boasted that they were the thief. Neither mentions the other! I, foolish, lovesick boy, missed my one big chance. She was our parishioner. And I failed to pay her a pastoral visit. How I would have consoled the lady! How I would have soothed away her pains! I have had to be contented with a photograph on my study wall, before which I burn metaphorical candles. O Hagia Sophia, how I rue the day I failed you! Jackie grunts in the background, resigned to her old man's libidinous phantasy.

Elsewhere I was, I suppose, beginning to make a name. It was in 1961 that I first received regular outside preaching invitations in the first instance to Durham where I was to occupy the pulpit at St John's College, Cranmer Hall, and St Nicholas church (later to become George Carey's parish). By 1962 I had been to Exeter and Reading Universities and a particularly interesting day run by the King's College, London, Joint-Christian Council at which I met Lawrence Bright, a Dominican friar, who opened my eyes to the explosive reforms about to burst upon the Roman Catholic Church in Vatican II. We both presented our respective traditions to the students, then travelled back to London together from Chigwell where the conference was being held. I could hardly believe my ears.

A major matter of interest at the time was the publication of *Lady Chatterley's Lover*, following the trial. On the day it came out, Gordon, Ian and I got copies, read them, and I prepared a statement, which we all agreed, for *Challenge*. We were far from shocked and our statement was a very cool and moderate judgement. I remember this because the widespread assumption was that our sort of Christian would be horrified by Lawrence's explicit descriptions and coital language. We weren't.

The Metropolitan Police created a Cadet Corps at Hendon around that time and I was invited to become one of the visiting chaplains. I was much the youngest selected, and I served there for almost four years, conducting weekly padre's hours. Today some of my cadets are Chief Constables and, although I have not kept in touch, my occasional links with the police have always been warm and friendly. When I needed a reference, the Commandant, Andrew Croft, a former Royal Marine Colonel, embarrassed me (and that's not easy!) by his fulsome comments. One phrase, 'young in outlook, mature in judgement, tactful, energetic, capable and enthusiastic, he is ideally suited to a major role . . .', and so on, seemed certain to secure me the post being advertised. It didn't. In those days, the word 'Evangelical' was a lethal description and I soon realised that it was going to be a millstone in 'career' terms. For the first ten years of my ministry it killed all chance of serious preferment. Clearly there were many people, and certainly many bishops, who gave credence to Thomas Arnold's long-since obsolete canard that an Evangelical was 'a good Christian with a low understanding, a bad education and ignorance of the world'. The choice was stark. Drop it, or pay the price. I consciously decided to pay the price. That isn't paranoia – I've good evidence to support that judgement, as will become apparent.

In the late summer I had a phone call with John King and put a proposal to him. Would he consider a pilot series of half a dozen pseudonymous articles which might, if successful, develop into a regular column? Yes, he would. What exactly did I have in mind? About four hundred words each week, loosely entitled 'It's a problem,' but over the pseudonym 'Qoheleth'. Qoheleth is the Hebrew title for the 'Preacher', the alleged author of the Old Testament book Ecclesiastes, who was a writer of a somewhat agnostic, not to say, cynical turn of phrase. Try it, said John. We agreed to keep it highly confidential. I wanted the freedom to speak straight, rather as I had done in 'Dear vicar' the year before. The *CEN* published the first 'Qoheleth' on 15 September 1961. Within six weeks I had a regular column, a distinctive style (which I've never really changed) and an avid readership, cheering or jeering, depending largely on whether they were the 'old' or 'new' brand of Evangelicalism.

As the months went by the 'Qoheleth' column practically sold the paper. It certainly filled the correspondence columns and was one of three regular columns in the paper. One was by Eddy Stride, my Croydon predecessor. One, called 'Through a Glass Darkly' was by Richard Allen, with whom (unknown to me) I was to work in Liverpool a few years ahead. Each was quite different and mine was the gadfly. I ran it for exactly twelve months, ending on 14 September 1962. It ranged all over the field, touching raw points left, right and centre. Before long, my closest friends had a pretty good idea who was writing it. No-one (except John King) knew for certain but Philip Wood wrote at the halfway point saying that his sides were aching with laughter. 'Surely', he went on, 'there is only one man with this style in the whole church of God.' He added that, if his guess was right, he found it rather challenging to have been associated with two men (Eddy and me) who 'regularly scorch the paper' with their pens. As for the older YPF people, in their twenties, they read it and constantly dropped hints. The curate smiled, and said nothing.

Two weeks after 'Qoheleth' was launched, a new curate joined our team. His name was Patrick Claridge and Gordon somewhat tactlessly told Ian and me that he was the finest potential clergyman he had ever met. Being Gordon, and blamelessly incorruptible, it wouldn't have occurred that this might raise the odd trace of jealousy in his assistants. Ian and I waited, sceptically, for the paragon to show his face. We went to St Paul's Cathedral for his deacon's ordination on the day of the third 'Qoheleth' article and met both him, a big, rotund, jolly, friendly Devonshire farmer and Barbara, his wife who seemed bright and terribly enthusiastic, don'tcher know!

Since Pat was to take over Spur Road from me and to live in the new St Peter's parsonage, overseeing the building of the new church, which I had played a significant part in designing, it was important that we got on well and quickly. We, by now, had two toddlers, Rachel and Joe (known initially as Sproggs and Podger) and they had Michael, a curly-headed, good-looking boy, not much older. Despite my instant reaction to Barbara, we soon settled down and all became the best of friends. Often in each other's houses, or going out on day-off picnics, the Sawards and the Claridges looked set for many years of friendship. Rachel, struggling to get her tongue round 'Claridge,' could only manage 'Candy' and 'Auntie Candy' and that is what they became. Out of the mouths of babes these things come and for the past thirty years Barbara has been known to everyone as 'Candy' Claridge.

Soon after Pat's arrival we acquired a new archdeacon and in a short time he was made Bishop of Willesden. His name (eventually to have an ominous ring to it) was Graham Leonard. He was a quite outstanding and pastorally most caring man, replacing his much-disliked predecessor, George Ingle. Ingle it was who told me, just before that, 'I couldn't give tuppence for what happens to you. Your sort can find your own little bolt-hole!' 'I thought you were my Father-in-God,' I protested. 'Couldn't care less about your lot,' he said, dismissing me from his premises. 'No jobs for your sort.'

Edgware, like Croydon, soon revealed its pains and once again many of them were sexual ones. I sat listening to a young homosexual, sobbing his heart out. He hated his many one-night stands. All he asked of me was that I supported his need for a long-term lover. 'Surely, that must be better? It must be right?' 'Better? Yes,' I said. 'Right? No! Ask me for practical advice, I'll give it to you. Ask me for moral advice, I'll give you that. They may not be the same. Loyalty is better than promiscuity. I agree. Sodomy is sodomy. Don't ask me to call it "right" because I can't, and you know I can't.'

As for heterosexuals, once more I came across the same problems as in Croydon, especially among the young married couples. I spent six months trying to help one couple. He was lacking in imagination, she was longing for excitement. One day I walked into a room in the church area. Planets were flashing out of her eyes. 'It's happened?' I said. 'Oh, yes,' she gasped. It gives one enormous joy to know that your counselling may have caused that to happen in a marriage heading for holy deadlock. I never sought such a ministry. It landed on my plate and went on for years and years. Eventually, I was persuaded to write a book about it.

The year that the YPF had its Silver Jubilee was, I suppose, the year that I started writing hymns. In those days youth groups had very little to choose from. There were the old hymns. There were hundreds of children's choruses. Latterly there were American-inspired 'gospel-songs' which went with a swing but lacked much theological content. My first five hymns were deliberately geared to fill gaps. Two were eucharistic. One was an attempt to treat the Holy Spirit as the source of life and vitality as distinct from the Victorian maiden-aunt who 'checks each fault, and calms each fear, and speaks of heaven'. The fourth was about Christ as the Lord of life, and the fifth, and best known, 'Christ

Triumphant', was a credal hymn, latching on to the many, and vital, titles of Jesus in the New Testament. I little realised how many hymns I would eventually write or how much editing and lecturing they would lead to in years to come.

By this time I had already topped my first thousand talks and sermons, and conducted over two hundred funerals, a hundred and thirty weddings, and three hundred services of Holy Communion. Since baptism was now being treated with the same respect in Edgware as in Croydon (Ian and I had persuaded both rectors to do this) I had only conducted about sixty baptisms.

On the subject of preaching, things had changed radically since Gordon's arrival. From chirpy, superficial chats we had moved to the other extreme. Gordon took his cue from the famous Puritan preacher, Martin Lloyd-Jones, who drew huge congregations to the Westminster Chapel to hear his hour-long expositions of Paul's letter to the Romans. Gordon didn't preach for an hour but he did set out to work his way through Peter's first letter and that meant sixty-nine sermons (almost consecutive) followed by a further thirty-five on the second letter to Timothy. Ian, Pat and I made three or four attempts to persuade him that we had gone from one extreme to the other and that the congregation simply couldn't cope with it but Gordon was absolutely adamant. Expository preaching was *real* preaching and it must be the order of the day – at least for him, if not for us. It was, I still believe, a pastorally disastrous decision, simply not taking account of the fact that congregations like Westminster Chapel's were self-selecting nomads from all over the greater London area, whereas Edgware (like most churches) had its own parish to think of and the great majority of such churchgoers were not geared to concentrated blocks of teaching of this kind. A whole range of issues, not least that of the Jewish influx into the district, affected the church and were contributory to its decline between 1960 and the 1980s, but I have little doubt that the preaching policy was a factor in the slow erosion of those years. The most vivid commentary on this was provided by Philip (now the Revd Philip) Robinson, a regular at St Margaret's who, looking at the notice-board which announced next Sunday's 1 Peter sermon, concealed by Gordon's title, said with a hard edge to his grin, 'It doesn't matter what he calls it, it's still bloody 1 Peter!'

Gordon was not a man to bend. His integrity was one of his great virtues. It was almost impossible to imagine him being influenced against his better judgement and the virtue had its obverse and reverse sides. He could be persuaded to change his mind (infant baptismal policy was an instance) but it was a tough and usually fruitless operation for his curates. First, in Cheadle, then in Edgware, Gordon's curates, almost to a man, revered and respected him as an outstanding curate trainer. He gave all of us (and there were about sixteen or seventeen) great freedom, which was rare in those days. He offered you a job, left you to get on with it, and didn't interfere. He was always available for help and advice, would occasionally, and quite sharply, draw attention to your unchecked vices (or what he took to be vices) but both expected loyalty and gave it in return. Of the five incumbents with whom I worked (one still to come) he was the one from whom I largely discovered 'how to', as opposed to 'how not to', do the job. And yet, strangely, he wasn't a model vicar. He was intransigent, austere, unaware of the pressures of normal domestic life. Not having any children, he and Mildred gave themselves unsparingly to the parish, but both lived in a world where the clock ruled and the disruptive effect caused by children had never percolated. On one occasion, he publicly rebuked a young mother of two small children who had arrived five minutes late for a midweek Bible study, puffing and gasping from having got the children to bed, got her husband's supper, and run all the way to the church hall. 'We start at eight o'clock,' he told her. That was the only time, in all my years of ministry, when I was seriously tempted to get up and punch a clergyman on the nose.

Gordon was, then, a tough man, a splendid trainer, an earnest preacher but a man who lived in his own ascetic world. His sermons were worthy, but illustrated, for the most part, with terribly dated anecdotes and quotes revealing a pious world which certainly wasn't mine. Rachel, aged three, walked home from church one day with me, having sat through a service. 'Did you listen to the rector's sermon?' I asked her (trying to make conversation). 'I heard him,' she said wistfully. 'I didn't listen, I only heard him.' I knew the feeling and suspected she wasn't the only one in church who had felt like that. It was sad, because he was far and away the best of my five incumbents and easily the most approachable for a curate. I used to write impudent verse to him, of which the following lines are an average sample:

> O figure tall, to whom I call,
> with head halfway to heaven.
> What can it be that marks this day?
> How many years have passed away?
> He answered, 'Forty-seven.'

> . . . our greetings come, yet we beseech
> thee, after Sunday last's long speech,
> how many minutes must thou preach?
> He answered, 'Forty-seven.'

I don't know whether Wordsworth would have approved of the parody but Gordon clearly enjoyed it. I was still sending him up in verse when, more recently, I, and all his former colleagues, celebrated his eightieth birthday.

One interesting contrast about incumbency styles was the difference between Philip Wood and Gordon Harman when you entered their study. Philip's was chaos. Gordon's was like an operating theatre. Not a piece of paper out of place. It was clinical. Mine has always been closer to his. However, by the autumn of 1963 I knew that I was in danger of drowning in paper. I decided to create a filing system. I invited Gill Townshend, a trainee librarian in the YPF, to help me and, together, we sat on the floor at Elmer Gardens and brought it into being. It has been revised a few times but since then I have sold it to over nineteen hundred clergy and ordinands within the Church of England. It is, wrote one vicar, after using it, 'my saviour from galloping paralysis'. The Michael Saward Filing System has probably been one of my most useful contributions to the Church of

England, used by anything up to one in seven of the clergy over the years.

That same year Jackie and I began our practice of sending out an annual Christmas letter, instead of Christmas cards. Such letters are now quite common but ours was probably the first within our circle of friends. To us it seemed obvious enough. Many on our Christmas list were people that we almost never saw. A letter provided news, which cards didn't. We enjoyed getting them when others took up the idea and ours was deliberately geared to being 'unparsonical' and, sometimes, deliberately outrageous in the style we adopted.

Those years, in the early and middle 1960s, were both exciting and exhilarating. Reform was in the air in every direction. Among Radicals it was lurching off into wildly secular paths, among Catholics it was the extraordinary goings on at the Second Vatican Council in Rome, while even among Evangelicals (potentially the most conservative group of all) new ideas were blossoming. John Stott's re-creation of the old, long-defunct, Eclectic Society, in 1955 had given to many of us a forum for debate and, in due course, actions which were to transform the whole Evangelical Anglican movement and set it, within thirty years, in the forefront of English Church life. But great rivers all start with tiny trickles and it was my good fortune to be in at the start of a number of these bubbling streams. Gordon had invited John Stott, Rector of All Soul's, Langham Place, then just over forty, to preach at a special guest service in St Margaret's. We publicised him as an 'internationally renowned preacher' (as indeed he was), and I requested permission to produce a revision of Evening Prayer which would make more sense to those we were trying to reach on that occasion. Gordon rashly agreed (remember that in those days Evangelicals were still locked into defending the Book of Common Prayer against all comers) and I came up with a mildly revised version whose moderation could hardly have worried anyone. To my astonishment, I was bombarded at least once a week for the next eighteen months with requests from all over the world for copies. I had obviously touched on a sensitive nerve.

A second area of concern related to church architecture and the way in which furniture could teach or deny aspects of the faith. In both 1962 and 1963 we had spent our holidays first in Austria and then in West Germany. Quite by chance, initially at least, I discovered eight post-war Roman Catholic churches which had, in varying degrees, expressed the teaching of the Liturgical Movement (about which I, and English Evangelicals, knew absolutely nothing). I came home and wrote up my findings in eight illustrated articles in the *CEN*. While few clergy ever have the chance (as I was about to) of building new churches, many are able to set about the reordering of traditional buildings and I was anxious that both openings should have some principles by which clergy might be guided in the design and building of St Peter's, in Edgware, resulting in a 'poor man's version' of what such a building might be. This involved especially questions of the placing of font, pulpit and holy table in relation to the seating of the congregation and within the overall framework of the building itself. I was especially influenced by the churches of St Christophorus in Niehl, an urban suburb of Cologne, and Pius X, Neu-Arzl, the Winter Olympics village outside Innsbruck. Both were stark, austere, but entirely adaptable to good Evangelical ideas or worship and opened both my eyes, and those of others, to how much the Liturgical Movement could creatively change English Evangelical thinking. The chief problem was that such Roman Catholic churches were usually centrally funded by dioceses which were willing to spend money creatively whereas most English parishes were up against committees trying to save money at every opportunity. It was said, in the late 1960s, that there were more really good modern churches being built in both Cologne and Basel than in the whole of England since the end of the War. St Peter's was just such an instance. Being almost entirely parish-funded, every corner was cut to save money and what could have been a stunning church ended up as a box, showing ideas, but lacking the artistry to fulfil them. Well, I tried, and I certainly made the right noises to those willing to listen.

Closely linked was the question of what is known as 'the westward position'. To most people the phrase is meaningless. Let me put it this way. Go into a church in the 1940s or 1950s and the clergyman (unless he was one of the Evangelical minority) conducted Holy Communion with his back to the congregation (the 'eastward position'), facing what he called 'the altar.' Many still do it today. Only the Evangelicals (and not all of them) stood at the left-hand end (what the Prayer Book calls 'the north side of the table') and conducted the communion at right angles to the congregation. Did it matter? It certainly did in the late-nineteenth century when court cases had been bitterly fought over such issues, going right up to the Privy Council. The mediaeval 'eastward' position had been ditched at the Reformation, when altars were removed from Anglican churches, and did not reappear (for the most part) until the Anglo-Catholics reintroduced them in the 1870s and onwards. It was all to do with a particular doctrine of priesthood.

By the 1950s, most Evangelical parishes had their clergy appointed by patronage trusts like the Church Pastoral Aid Society and men were only appointed, and curate grants were only available, where the 'north side' practice was in operation. This was true in both Croydon and Edgware.

One of the incidentals of the Liturgical Movement (and not unimportant either) was its phrase 'the Lord's People, round the Lord's Table, on the Lord's Day.' Inherent in this, and in all consequent Roman Catholic reform, was the adoption of the 'westward position', in which the priest faced the people, from behind the altar, and conducted the Mass, if possible in the vernacular, not in Latin.

The vast majority of Evangelical Anglicans were totally unaware of this but, to a tiny handful, it was seen as the way for the future. Almost certainly the first to attempt it was William Leathem, Vicar of the newly-built St John's church in Harborne, Birmingham. Convinced that he was rediscovering the practice of the primitive church (which, indeed, he was) he took 'westward' in the new church, which had been built for it. The holy table was well out from the east wall and, naturally, he conducted communion from behind it, facing the people. His curate's grant was immediately withdrawn by the Church Pastoral-Aid Society. Leathem's Evangelical pedigree was undoubted but, in this instance, that didn't count! He was, in fact, a visiting lecturer at Tyndale Hall, my old theological college, but that didn't count either. Leathem was simply treated as a liturgical freak and was ignored.

So it was that on 2 February 1962 (months before the first of the continental church-crawls), 'Qoheleth' Saward called, in the *CEN*, for a serious review of the 'westward' possibility. He was, at once, attacked but, fortunately, on such foolish grounds that he was able to win the first skirmish. But nothing was done. He was, however, joined by Dr Philip Hughes, a South African scholar, and editor of the *Churchman* magazine, and by Dr Leon Morris, a prolific scholar of equally unquestionable Evangelical bona fides and an Australian. Saward was a midget alongside these two giants but I had two small advantages – I was building a 'westward' church, and I was occasionally taking 'westward' at weekend house parties in order to test the thesis. I had also discovered that, in 1893, counsel's opinion had been sought by the Church Association (later to be the Church Society) and 'westward' had been given a clean bill of health.

To counter all this, the Church Pastoral-Aid Society proceeded to issue a booklet, effectively rejecting 'westward,' in favour of 'north side'. But the dam had burst and, before long, Evangelicals were welcoming, and taking up 'westward' all over the country. Eventually the CPAS quietly fell into line with their grant policy and by the 1980s everyone had forgotten it.

Articles and reviews had poured out from me but now came the chance of some booklets. The first was to be for teenagers on the subject of leisure. One of a series of four *Christian Viewpoint* booklets published by the Scripture Union, it attempted to provide some basic principles about how youngsters should spend their free time. Activities, it suggested, should be tested by four questions: (1) Is it beneficial to me? (2) Is it harmful to others? (3) Have I got it in perspective? and (4) Can I ask God to bless it? I dare say that my opinions have altered over the years with regard to the details but these principles weren't, and still aren't, a bad set of guidelines for anyone to adopt.

Falcon, the publishing arm of CPAS (with whom I have had a bumpy relationship for forty years), asked for a small booklet entitled *What is the church here for?* and published it with some excellent illustrations, not least its delightful cover picture of Peter Sellers, as the vicar in the film *Heavens Above!*

Then came the first larger book. Scripture Union wanted a 192–page paperback *Christian Youth Groups*, which Michael Eastman researched and I wrote. Based on our joint experience as youth leaders in Romford and Edgware, it received highly complimentary reviews which ranged surprisingly from the ultra-Protestant *English Churchman* to the trendy Radical *New Christian*. The latter called it 'excellent and refreshing' and the former 'a must'; while Michael Baughen, later Bishop of Chester, described it as 'invigoratingly fresh', with a 'wide variety and range of splendid quotations', and he highlighted various sections as 'clear, succinct, and helpful – first-rate – of great practical value'. The book sold out, which was a good sign.

A completely fresh challenge was provided when the radical magazine *Prism* promoted a national competition for a tabloid newspaper treatment of the Gospel narratives. As a biblical conservative (which at that stage, *Prism* hadn't realised), I was both amused and delighted to be declared the winner. The initial project was for three issues, one on the nativity, one on John the Baptist's preaching, and one on his murder. Each included background history, adverts and feature articles, all with a factual basis and all set in something approximating to the style of the *Daily Mirror* (the leading tabloid in those days). Figures of some eminence like Hugh Montefiore and David Edwards gave the project their backing and the publishing go-ahead was given. Sadly, and flat against my own wishes, the three papers were printed on glossy paper rather than newsprint, had artists' drawings rather than photographs and were laid out in 'school' rather than 'newsdesk' style. Much of their 'tabloid' impact was diluted though letters poured in congratulating me. One from a public school chaplain said, 'Wonderful effort – this has had rave reception in the school. Virtually everyone has thought it excellent – even prefects have liked it, and younger boys want to buy it.' He added, 'I do hope you're allowed to do the whole dozen.' It was not to be. The publishers had a fire, most copies were lost, they didn't reprint, the idea drifted into obscurity. Only years later did

I realise that the proprietor was a certain Robert Maxwell. Ah well, you win some, you lose some.

Frank Williams, the actor (the *Dad's Army* vicar), was a good friend and he has lived all his life in Edgware. Now a very decided Anglo-Catholic, he grew up at St Margaret's, and was already making a television reputation when we were there. We went to see a performance of one of his own plays at the Watford Playhouse and he took us to *Beyond the Fringe* at the Fortune Theatre. It was a huge success and launched the careers of Jonathan Miller, Alan Bennett, Peter Cook and Dudley Moore. I watched Bennett's famous sermon ('My brother Esau is a hairy man, but I am a smooth man') with the amused, and slightly wounded, eye of a professional under attack. Well, after all, I *had* nearly landed an 'anthropomorphic concept' on Christ Church's artisans so one couldn't be too careful.

The local cemetery and crematorium at Hendon was set in beautiful woodlands on the lower slopes of Holders Hill. There was a goldfish pond, squirrels, and an atmosphere of quiet peace. So, when I was taking cremations, we quite often took the children and they and Jackie quietly enjoyed the landscape. We were intrigued by the horror with which some adults discovered this strange behaviour. 'We're getting them acclimatised to the reality of death,' we said. 'Why should we hide it from them? They really enjoy the place.' They did indeed and to our considerable amusement began to 'play funerals' at home. 'What are you doing?' we asked. 'We're playing feenals,' they said. 'Here comes the coffin.'

For two years I was wondering about a move. I had gone to Christ Church planning to go on to train with the Church Missionary Society for work in Nigeria. Somehow, timings never seemed to link up and jobs in Africa fell vacant, just after I had gone to Edgware. Then a real opening emerged. There was a vacancy for a theological teaching post in Kenya, in Nairobi, and I was short-listed for interview in London by Noel Davey, whose daughter, incidentally, was an occasional attender at the Edgware YPF. He knew of my West African experience and since Kenya had a thoroughly Evangelical tradition things looked quite hopeful for this important provincial post. Davey was famed for his part in a scholarly work on New Testament Introduction and as director of SPCK (the Society for Promoting Christian Knowledge) he had been given the task of interviewing likely candidates by the Archbishop of East Africa, Leonard Beecher.

The interview was an experience I should not like to repeat. It was over in just seven minutes. Davey asked me just two questions. To the first, 'Are you a Fundamentalist?' I responded, 'You tell me what it is and I'll tell you the answer.' He did not reply. The second was, 'What is your attitude to the East African Revival Movement?' and I said that I hadn't liked what I had seen of its English supporters but had been impressed by what I knew of the Africans' behaviour during the Mau-Mau period. And that was it. Out. 'Good afternoon – we'll let you know.'

They appointed a Radical of aggressively political leanings who was ejected later by the Kenya government for interference. I was really angry. A major job in an Evangelical province, for which I was very adequately qualified, was given to an unsympathetic young man because I declined to give an instant reply to an undefined but heavily loaded question and clearly wasn't 'anti' those who had been the chief group of martyrs during the Mau-Mau. I never knew whether Archbishop Beecher, and the province, had any idea what had gone on but, clearly, Davey had no intention of recommending any kind of Evangelical. If an Evangelical couldn't get appointed in an Evangelical province, what hope was there in England? And what kind of so-called Evangelical archbishop was it who put such an appointment into the patronage of a Liberal-Catholic?

Just to make matters worse, at the same time I was asked by the secretary of the Crusaders' Union (under whose umbrella my conversion had taken place) to consider becoming their first travelling secretary, charged with promoting the work of Crusaders throughout Britain. I saw him in his office, right opposite St Paul's Cathedral, and suggested that being ordained into the ministry of the Church of England wasn't a natural qualification for an undenominational job, with no direct church links at all. An Anglican clergyman might give Crusaders 'status' in the eyes of headmasters and clergy but it would leave me in complete limbo. In responding, Jack Watford (the secretary) hurt me deeply. 'Well, of course,' he said, 'if the church means more to you than Christ does, you wouldn't be the right man for us anyway.'

What a dilemma! Not acceptable, being too Anglican, for Crusaders. Not acceptable, being too Evangelical, for the province of East Africa. Thank God I've never wanted to be a 'party man' for any group, just a committed Anglican who happens to held Evangelical convictions. Back, then, to Edgware, and keep soldiering on. Somewhere, sometime, God has something on ice. We'll just have to wait. Most curates were into their first livings by five or six years. I would have to wait eight and a half for mine, and then it would be a task of very uncertain prospects.

In all, twenty different possibilities flitted across the horizon in those four years. Nine were incumbencies, most in back-street urban parishes, six in the north of England or inner London, and I was glad to have Gordon Harman's wise advice. 'Don't go to that kind of job,' he said. 'All the gifts you have will be wasted there and they will want you for skills which, on the whole, you haven't got.' He was right, although it cost me hundreds of pounds in lost extra stipend, by staying a curate when, frankly, as a family we needed the money. One offer was to be a missionary in Chile. The secretary of the South American Missionary Society had been enthusiastic. 'Yes, there's an important job to be done. No. No accommodation, but you'll easily get some. Well, I can't say what you'd be paid, but I'm sure you could do some broadcasting and earn a bit. Yes, it is all a bit vague but I'm sure the Lord will see you through.' I wasn't worried about the Lord but I was very concerned about the slovenly approach of some of his servants! The thought of being dumped on the quay at Valparaiso, knowing no-one, not speaking Spanish, without a roof over the head of a wife and two small kids, no income, and a so-called Faith Mission approach, which effectively blames *your* lack of faith if it's a disaster, didn't appeal one bit to me. The secretary, not surprisingly, went off to be a bishop!

Another missionary society wanted me as Publications Secretary. Their publications budget was minimal, one-fifth of that recommended to such societies by an independent consultative organisation. I didn't say a direct 'no', but they weren't willing to pursue the matter so it lapsed. I was also unsure of their forthcoming appointment of a new General Secretary, whose influence would be absolutely crucial. At that stage, understandably, they couldn't tell me who it might be.

Out of the blue, I was asked to do a once-a-week part-time lectureship in church history at the Mount Hermon missionary training college in Ealing. This was a challenge and Gordon, who had partly engineered it, was keen for me to take it on. Early church history for young, single, mostly Baptist, women missionary candidates looked like being a tough assignment. Their principal was a lovely, gracious, elderly ex-missionary lady of warmth and sympathy. I said 'yes', and did four terms of it. At the end I felt fairly sorry for some of the recipients of these young women's ministrations in the Third World. A few were going to be splendid, a real gift to their churches, but some were humourless, hard, frustrated spinsters-in-the-making who objected to my deliberately swashbuckling style (the only way to get them interested in church history), complaining that I was basically flippant and 'not spiritual enough'.

Jackie and I loved our years in Edgware. We loved the YPF, the churches, the many friends, and, not least, our relationships with our neighbours, our doctor and our dentist, all of whom were Jewish. The neighbours, of our own age, would probably have become Christians had they not been of Jewish blood. They had little time for, or belief in, Jewish religion, but their families would never have understood. Our doctor, a Russian Jew who had Anglicised his name from Zermanski to 'Manning', was a delightful and very direct medic, whose skills we were much to admire. One day, in his surgery, I joked about a brief encounter I had with a condition he described as 'epididimitis-orchitis'. 'What a marvellous thing to have,' I said. 'I'll be famous with an illness like that!' 'You're the first man who's ever laughed about it,' he replied. 'Swollen testicles and blood in your semen – you must be mad.' 'Well,' I joked, 'you assure me it isn't going to last and with a title like that it'll certainly help to sell my autobiography one day.' He shook his head. How does any good Jew, even an atheist like Manning, understand a *goy* cleric who can smile at such things – my life?

Michael Maybaum, our dentist, was unique. Son of the local Reform rabbi, Ignaz Maybaum, who had come on the Vienna, Frankfurt, Amsterdam, London circus, Michael was tall, black-bearded, sockless, in open-toed sandals, a string vest and corduroys. A roaring extrovert, you could hear him from the waiting room, laughing, shouting, the archetypal image of a volatile Jew. He will always be my image of Jesus, a Jew in a million. He played about in my mouth, we both talked theology, and when he charged me for dentistry, I threatened to send him a bill for theology. He gave one month each year to work, free, in Israel, for their army in the Sinai. He taught me to see a new side to the Pharisees, his heroes, who weren't exactly top-of-the-gospel-pops. I loved that man more than any Jew I've ever met. I admired him for his unashamed love of, and cynicism about, his own people. He never made any attempt to conceal his understanding of just how provocatively awkward Jews are, and just how much fun it was to slog it out verbally with a Christian priest as both laughed at their own and the other's foibles and failings. We two Michaels had an instant and long-standing charge of electricity uniting us. He'd never have done any dentistry while I was around, arguing theology, if he hadn't had a good Jewish Mamma as receptionist. Only recently did I learn that he had died a relatively young man. *Shalom*, Michael Maybaum, I miss you.

After five years in Edgware I really felt I had begun to understand anti-Semitism. I went there, not feeling a trace of it in myself. I left, well aware how easily it could develop and fester. The cleverness, the talent, the business acumen, and the sheer aggressiveness of so many, not least of the senior rabbi who, frankly, couldn't be trusted when Christians were around. On one occasion, it being the duty of the minister, or rabbi, on a rota, to arrange for the printing of the annual order of service for the Remembrance Sunday gathering at the War Memorial, it was recognised that the first part was Christian, and the second Jewish, and yearly it was printed thus. Not on this rabbi's turn. He omitted every single Christian reference from the first part and thus effectively forced the clergyman to insert them all 'on the hoof'.

With rabbis like that who finds anti-Semitism surprising. He positively invited it!

Then there was the volatile Mr 'Malachi'. He was a very noisy estate agent who, for some forgotten reason, came to our house one night and, once inside, pulled out a revolver (loaded, he said) and wagged it about threateningly. Why, Jackie and I never discovered. He wasn't out for us, but he certainly frightened both of us.

Utterly impossible to forget was the row in the big supermarket. Screams of abuse tore through the building. 'You dirty old cow . . . You filthy old bitch' and other choice epithets resounded from wall to wall. I could only faintly imagine the consequence of such a contest between two non-Jewish suburban wives. Never, never, would either speak to the other again. All respect would have vanished. But not so for our Jewish ladies (and they were very much 'ladies'). These were Jewish mothers. And I had no doubt whatever that within twenty-four hours they would be hugging and kissing and laughing and being, well, being Jewish.

I admire the Jews. I don't admire their self-righteousness or their very understandable capitalising on the horrors of their national agony. I find it hard to cope with their almost complete unwillingness to accept any responsibility for the sufferings that they have undergone or to acknowledge that they, when in power, are hardly angelic. I cannot easily understand their willingness to accept atheist Jews, Marxist Jews, crooked Jews, any kind of Jews, except Christian Jews. Most of all, I can't see why what I have just written should be regarded (as it doubtless will be regarded) as anti-Semitic. It's no more than an attempt by a Christian who is proud to be 'a son of Abraham', even if not by birth, to analyse why it is that hostility can exist between Jews and Gentiles, with all the blame being on one side. I wouldn't have missed my five years in a largely Jewish suburb. I wouldn't have missed the rabbi, or Messrs Malachi, Manning and Maybaum, and all the others. They were human, like all the rest of us, and their flaws were sometimes our flaws, and sometimes their own. So I don't feel anti-Semitic and I would do all I could to help them to feel secure in this country, as a full part of British life. Just don't ask me to pretend that they, alone, are the world's special goodies, innocent, moral virgins. They aren't and they make life harder for themselves if they won't admit it.

I worked with Gordon for four-and-half years and he gave me every opportunity. I was, I suppose, a fairly senior curate by then. I felt free to speak my mind since we rarely disagreed on matters of substance. People began to say, 'We've got two rectors in Edgware.' We hadn't, and there was never the slightest chance of the cuckoo usurping the nest, but it was becoming obvious that I should move. Edgware needed a new curate and I needed a new challenge.

Early in 1964 I was unexpectedly approached by Richard Allen (the *CEN*'s 'Through a Glass Darkly' columnist) who, having been appointed to lead a new 'group' ministry in Everton (actually, in later terms, a 'team') was looking for more clergy to join him. Jackie and I looked at each other. 'Not Liverpool', we both groaned. It was the third Liverpool offer within a few months and we decided that God was totally unscrupulous and not to be trusted. In 1960 we had said 'anywhere but there' and now the pressure was really on. The job sounded interesting. I should be largely free of parish responsibility, would be creating an 'inter-church centre' based on a Georgian church close to St George's Hall, and we should have a large house, completely restored within, an incumbent's salary, and a more senior status than that of 'curate'. The group needed six clergy, working together but each having quite separate areas of responsibility. It certainly appeared to have more unusual features than most jobs for which I had been considered and, by mid-May, we accepted the challenge.

Then came some terrible news. Pat Claridge had not been feeling too well that spring. He consulted Dr Manning who sent him for tests. These appeared to be satisfactory but Gordon Harman, somehow, learnt of the real diagnosis and felt morally bound to leave Pat in little doubt that he was dying of a form of leukaemia. I shall not easily forget that night. Pat returned from the rectory in a state of shock, told Barbara, and together they rang me with the news. Could I come at once? Of course. Jackie realised that this was no five-minute affair and indeed I stayed talking with them all night. They were stunned by the sudden manner in which they had been given the news and were still far from clear as to the exact diagnosis and timescale facing them. Both Pat and Barbara, individually, as well as together, needed a tremendous amount of love, encouragement, sympathy and reassurance and I spent many hours with them in the ensuing weeks. In the event, Pat had over two years to live, but Barbara had been warned that the disease would possibly transform him, making him far more difficult in his behaviour as it took its slow toll. This terrible, nagging, sense of nemesis was the backdrop to our final Edgware months.

One night we all went together to the South Bank to see a special showing of Paul Czinner's brilliant film of the 1954 Salzburg Festival production of Mozart's *Don Giovanni*. Conducted by Furtwängler, the performance was outstanding and the singers were superlative. Those who know the opera will be aware of just how the tension builds up to the climax of the Don's death and judgement and I had the strange, and enigmatic, experience as I sat between Jackie and Barbara while the emotional pressure mounted. We had not, when we booked our seats, grasped just how far the sense of impending death was to influence that summer evening.

Money being short, Jackie and I planned a cycling holiday in south Germany. We took the bikes to Koblenz, on to a Rhine steamer to Rüdesheim to cycle towards Heidelberg. From there we rode alongside the River Neckar, stopping at inns for the night. East of the river is, or was, utterly unspoilt Germany, deeply rural, with never a tourist in sight. We paced a weasel along a country lane, hid from storms in barns, and climbed up hill and down dale in blazing heat, our tyres beginning to clog up with melted tar from the road surface. Carrying your luggage on a bike, when the brake blocks jam up, is no fun however stunning the scenery. I was violently sick after drinking two litres of *Apfelsaft* and Jackie was distinctly queasy each morning. You've guessed it. So did she. She was three months pregnant with twins. Not the most intelligent time to be pumping female legs up and down on a bicycle. We reached the sightseeing paradise of Rothenburg-ober-der-Tauber, caught a train, first to

Dinkelsbühl, and later to Nördlingen. All three towns, on the so-called *Romantische-strasse* more than lived up to their name and we didn't see a single British or American tourist for two weeks. Once more we put the bikes in the guard's van to Stuttgart alongside a deer's carcass heading for a restaurant and another memorable holiday was over. The pregnancy certainly wasn't.

Our final Sunday came on 22 November. We said our fare-wells, grateful for such full and stimulating years. Two babies born in Edgware, baptised at St Margaret's, and two more now awaiting their birth, but conceived in Edgware. Creative and ex-citing work done in a superb YPF, supported by a splendid team of young leaders. A dozen or more marriage preparation courses, out of which I had personally married 99 couples. Over 100 fu-nerals, 45 baptisms and 1150 talks and sermons. As we set out for Liverpool a few days later we went believing that life was much richer and our memories much happier than on the day when we had arrived from Croydon.

What kind of a place was the land of Beatlemania? It didn't take long to find out.

Chapter Eight

Missionary 'cross the Mersey

The city burghers modestly franked the 1964 postage stamps 'Liverpool, pacemaker of the '60s'. Liverpudlians, never slow to laugh, howled with derision and the slogan was rapidly changed to 'City of Change and Challenge'. Well, yes. It needed change desperately, and it couldn't face the challenge. Pride in the past prevented action in the present, while there was still time. Alan Bennett calls Liverpool 'that sentimental self-dramatizing place'. How right he is.

There had certainly been action. What Hitler hadn't bombed, the City Council had demolished. Vast inner areas were looking like Pompeii and hurriedly replacing the old 'back-to-backs' – monstrous tower blocks themselves to be demolished within twenty years – not to mention the horrors on the outskirts like Kirkby, Cantrill Farm, Speke and Netherley.

Shielding Liverpudlians from the disaster all around them, and the incompetence of their civic authorities, was the vast success of their football clubs and the even more cosmic reputation which the Beatles had created. Alongside them Cilla Black and Gerry and the Pacemakers were midgets. Shout, in chorus, 'We are the champions!' long enough and loud enough and you will, indeed, in your own self-estimate 'never walk alone'. You'll also be infinitely blind to the humiliating crash which all non-Scousers could see a mile off. Your commercial, industrial and shipping base is collapsing all around you and you're heading, fast, for widespread unemployment. Disaster is just out of sight but you won't listen to anyone because John, Paul, George and Ringo are bigger than Jesus Christ and Bill Shankly is seated at the right hand of God. You may have two cathedrals but the temple, scene of the most committed weekly worship, is at Anfield (if you're a Red) or Goodison (if you're a Blue). Football is God Almighty. To hell with the rest. In the 1960s it provided just about the most polluted atmosphere in Britain and, in consequence, the most adenoidal dialect, to go with it. It was a memorable place, with its twin-towered port building, its liver-birds visible for miles, and the deep-throated baying of the last few Cunarders, slipping their moorings and heading out into the Irish Sea. Once heard, those great foghorns are never forgotten.

Liverpool was emerging, thank God, from one of the worst of its legacies. Welsh and Ulster Protestant and Irish Catholic had lumbered into each other and the ultimate conflict had been endemic, regionalised, and bloody. Ritual events were the excuse for mob violence and even as fighting died down in the late sixties there were those who bemoaned the exhausted cessation. 'More's the pity,' was one response to my polite enquiry about whether the fighting was not, at last, ending. The speaker was an elderly lady, not exactly your archetypal Belfast bully-boy. The Church of England was far too gentlemanly to get its fingers dirty in the fighting. But not a few Anglicans were in the Orange Lodges and the Diocese had grown up with a strong Protestant tradition. Even in the 1950s, 'Liverpool Evangelical' was a distinct subculture of its own and it was one of the reasons why I had been so unenthusiastic about the thought of working in such a place. Never mind the fact that my mother had been born in Anfield. 'Liverpool,' said Jackie and I, 'anywhere but there!'

The Anglican leaders in Victorian times had been clever. You had to give them that. When the great building era began to swamp the hillside along the Mersey, the Anglicans built churches and named them not, for the most part, St John, St Paul, St Peter, and so on. No, they picked all the names of the great early church Fathers and completely upstaged the Irish Roman Catholics. Liverpool's Anglican parish churches, unique in England, are dedicated to Ambrose, Cyprian, Chrysostom, Polycarp, Athanasius, Clement; to lesser-known biblical characters like Timothy,

Philemon, Nathanael, Cleopas, Barnabas and Stephen; or to ancients whose origins were distinctly not Reformation-oriented, like Lawrence, Anne, Francis, Benedict, Nicholas and George. Even Celts like Cuthbert, Bede and Columba were represented. Only Patrick and Dominic were left for the Romans. No-one was left in any doubt that the Church of England was maintaining its claim to be the ancient Catholic church of the land.

But what was I supposed to be doing? When Richard had begun the Beacon Group of churches he had found himself with St Timothy and St Ambrose, both in the 'Pompeii' area of Everton, together with the Shrewsbury House mission (known locally as the 'the Shoosy') of which Roger Sainsbury was the Warden. The Shoosy was a traditional back-street mission club founded by Shrewsbury School and it had been linked into the Beacon Group. Roger and I had often opened the batting for London Diocese so we were no strangers to each other. Two other churches nearby were loosely linked, St Polycarp, to the north, and Holy Trinity, to the south. All four churches were in a straight line covering about a half-mile and, with the demolition, were virtually visible to each other. Polycarp's was a hideous building, the interior having white tiles immediately reminiscent of a public lavatory. Holy Trinity was the oldest, a Georgian, galleried church built in 1795. It had seating for a thousand, a congregation of twelve, and a parish which was ninety-nine per cent Liverpool Irish Catholic. Only one member of the church still lived in the parish, Phoebe Higgins, with her mother and brother, in a squalid tenement block where, every so often, notes would come through the door saying, in illiterate scrawl, 'Get out, bloody Protestants, or we'll burn you out.' Holy Trinity was a vicarage large house, 67 Shaw Street, once built for doctors and lawyers but now the only domestic premises in a long terrace of warehouses and doss-houses with holes in wall and roof.

Richard's idea, supported by the Bishop, Clifford Martin, was to use Holy Trinity as an ecumenical, or 'Inter-Church', centre and fund it with the Holy Trinity stipend. The man to be appointed would live in 67 Shaw Street (duly renovated), take Sunday services at Holy Trinity, but not be technically the incumbent. This, then, was the job he offered me. I could choose my own title (I called myself 'Warden'), be paid a vicar's rate for the job, and, if later agreed, become secretary of the soon-to-be-created Liverpool Council of Churches, and city organiser for the virtually non-existent branch of Christian Aid. Beyond that I would be a member of the Beacon Group and almost anything else which took my fancy! For an Evangelical clergyman to take on an ecumenical job (and I was the first in England to do so) was to court the kiss of death in Evangelical circles. So, before accepting, I cleared my path with a wide range of friends and got their general support. In those days most people in our tradition believed in a doctrine of the 'invisible church' and regarded events like the Keswick Convention, which proclaimed 'all one in Christ Jesus', as quite sufficient evidence of 'spiritual unity'. The ecumenical movement, stressing the need for a more visible unity of 'all in each place' was gravely suspect, since it attracted 'Liberals' and was open to, though not supported by, the Roman Catholic Church.

Fortuitously, and quite without pre-planning, I preached myself out of the former, and into the latter doctrine of the church during a sermon on Ephesians 4, in September 1964, from the St Margaret's, Edgware, pulpit. As I preached I realised, and explained, that it seemed that St Paul, while calling for 'unity of the Spirit', had linked it with 'the one body' which was surely the most visible and tangible of all metaphors. Moreover, he had done so by linking all to God in Trinity. Thus all things – one Lord, one Faith, one Baptism – were exhibited in one body. It was as well that I made that exegetical discovery when I did for it gave solid foundation to both the work of the next three years and to the doctrine of the church which has increasingly been at the root of Evangelical Anglican ecclesiology in the ensuing quarter of a century.

In the same month I had called, together with David Edwards, publisher of *Honest to God*, a gathering of Radical and Evangelical clergy, in Church House, Westminster, to see what, if anything, we might have in common. We met in David Paton's room on 28 September and, as I recall, we included names like Michael

Green and Bob Jeffery. This gathering took place just two weeks after the British Council of Churches' first Faith and Order conference in Nottingham, which I had attended, in anticipation of the coming Liverpool job, as an official Church of England delegate, at the instigation of David Paton, the Secretary of MECCA (the Missionary and Ecumenical Council of the Church Assembly). That was the conference which called for 'union by Easter 1980' and I found no difficulty in voting for that, as it proved to be, wildly naive prospect. Thus, then, I set out for Liverpool, England's hardest nut (in ecumenical terms) with some very crucial contacts under my belt.

The house was, inevitably, nowhere near ready. When we had first walked round 67 Shaw Street, in the early summer, Jackie had emerged in tears. The area was, or rather felt like, a bombsite and Jackie, being a prosaic woman, not much blessed with anticipatory imagination, could only see, and dread, the thought of bringing up a family in such an unattractive tip. I did my utmost to reassure her. 'The Bishop has promised us £1,000 worth of redecoration and renovation,' I said. 'That's a year's salary. It will be a really beautiful interior by the time we move in.' She sobbed quietly, unable to envisage what it might mean. I, having been blessed with a very vivid imagination, knew exactly what was to be and was excited by the prospect. It would be really quite grand and would certainly make our little Croydon and Edgware rabbit hutches fade into insignificance. And so it proved to be. But builders and decorators the world over always underestimate the time needed and Mr Duckett, the St Timothy's churchwarden, was just such a local builder. He was a month overdue and we, arriving in late November, could not move in until 6 January 1965.

We were saved from living on the streets in cardboard boxes by the generous hospitality of John and Elaine Stanley. Both had been fellow-students at Bristol and they had accepted the parish of St Cuthbert's, on the Everton hill, shortly after we (surprise, surprise) had declined it, earlier in the year. Their vicarage was right opposite Anfield football ground and, provided you could bear the noise of the vast crowds, you could sit in their attic and see a third of the pitch for free. Having little choice, we dumped our two children with my parents in Petts Wood, and gratefully accepted the Stanleys' hospitality. They had five children, so we were nine living in that vicarage. Jackie, by now, was aware that she had twins on the way and we just had time to get the house in order and move in before, on 14 January, the twins weighed in at almost fourteen pounds. How a girl as slim as Jackie had been, not much over seven stone when we married, could have produced four children, aggregating twenty-nine pounds eleven ounces, and one of them a month premature, never ceases to amaze me.

To crown it all, a letter arrived urging me, at very short notice, to accept an invitation to become an assistant missioner at Cambridge, for their triennial mission, in the absence of Michael Whinney, who had gone down with meningitis. What on earth should I do? To work with Dick Lucas on that mission was a great privilege but I had a new job, a vast house, and four children under five, plus an exhausted wife. There could only be one realistic answer for any decent husband. 'Go,' said Jackie, 'my mother will come and we'll survive for ten days somehow.' So I did, she did, and they did. The house, incidentally, was quite beautiful, and, provided you didn't look out of the windows, you could have assumed yourselves in a mansion. Our drawing room, on the first floor (and you couldn't call it anything less grand), was complemented by a superb dining room on the ground floor and a magnificent study. Even the children had a playroom of about 200 square feet in area. The drawing room had three, shuttered, floor-to-ceiling windows and we had to buy a complete bale of curtain material just to provide for the six curtains. The room measured (as did the dining room) twenty-six by eighteen feet and was thirteen feet high. We felt like a couple of French aristocrats moving into Versailles. The salary was the only thing that didn't match the splendour. It was, in all, a strange contrast. Greater comfort than we had ever known in the worst and most derelict district in which we were ever to reside. We ought, perhaps, to have been embarrassed but we used that house well, for hospitality, and for all the church meetings (such as they were). Duckett, for all his recalcitrant dithering, had done us proud. I wasn't used to churchwardens who could call the clergy 'looky boogers' but before long I grew accustomed to Liverpool vicars whose vocabulary was equally colourful.

So, off I went to Cambridge. In those days it was possible to change trains at Bletchley and Sandy on what was a rambling route, and with an hour to wait for the Bletchley connection I stood outside a television shop and watched, minus sound, as they carried Sir Winston Churchill into St Paul's Cathedral and conducted his funeral there in great and solemn splendour. The mission too was a great occasion with large crowds and some superb preaching by Dick Lucas. I was working in Pembroke College and first met a young rugby player, Barry Morrison, who would in due course be one of my Edgware successors. I also had my first experience of preaching in an Oxbridge college chapel and dining at a High Table. As a recent escapee from teetotalism, I was particularly impressed with the College's Pouilly Fuissé, a wine whose price has generally limited my enjoyment of its pleasing dryness.

On my return, I found a wife who had coped very well but who couldn't get her mother off the premises fast enough. Eileen Atkinson was bossy, would run her fingers around the woodwork meaningfully, and had no idea how to make herself welcome in a daughter's home. She finally departed after a decorous pause, and as the taxi bore her away to Lime Street station I ran up all forty-six stairs of the main part of the house singing the 'Hallelujah Chorus' at the top of my voice! She was always helpful, either visiting us or when we went to Frinton, but the price was generally much too high for our comfort. Her last three homes at Eastbourne, Cheltenham and Frinton sum up the lady's style and character perfectly.

I had hardly begun to think about work when a letter arrived from Edgware. Gordon Harman had sent me a list of his sixty-nine sermons on 1 Peter. Oh, not them again, I thought, having heard most of them once round. The letter was, however, quite clear. Could I, being expert at 'catchy titles', provide him with a new set? Well, all right, I'd have a go, I thought, and rapidly knocked off sixty-nine new fairly gimmicky titles (even if they were still 'Bloody 1 Peter').

He replied by return, sending a quite unexpected cheque, and congratulating me. 'I think they're excellent,' he said, 'but I believe one of my mine is better. It's 1 Peter 5 verse 7. The verse is "clothe yourselves with humility as with a garment". You've called it "Humble Piety". I prefer my title. I call it "An attractive Piece in the Wardrobe".' I could just imagine the gusts of laughter from Edgware passers-by, seeing on the churchyard notice-board that the Rector would be preaching next Sunday about 'An attractive Piece in the Wardrobe'. It promised to be French farce at its best. Did he ever actually use the title, I wonder. I've never dared to ask him.

I began at last to look around at Liverpool and see what I could make of it. On the one hand there was Holy Trinity and the Beacon Group. Then there was the diocese and the almost moribund Evangelical Fellowship. Lastly there was the ecumenical task and its related work with Christian Aid. Further afield I would need to travel regularly to London for the monthly committees of the Bible Churchmen's Missionary Society (to which I had recently been elected) and there would be plenty more London events linked with Christian Aid and the British Council of Churches. One little extra. The Bishop had asked me to become the clerical member of the city's Round Table which meant a regular luncheon with a group of the up-and-coming businessmen who, it might be hoped, would have the needed imagination to see the way ahead for an increasingly bogged down city.

What hope was there for Holy Trinity? I had quite unreal visions of it becoming a city-centre church but even with the support of a group of university students we never had a serious chance. I had grandiose plans for a major reordering (the diocesan architect said, 'What do you want me for – you've done all the basic work yourself?') but no-one had a penny to spare and, anyway, though I didn't know it, the City Council was proposing to knock it down and build a major road right through it, which they duly did after I left. Holy Trinity was, in short, a total non-starter but it took me two years to find that out for myself.

One advantage Holy Trinity had was that every bus and coach coming in from the north passed it and I had a huge space for a poster, about ten feet square, facing the road. I used to put up striking captions which often drew comment. Perhaps the best was 'Wanted. Penitent Sinners. Apply Within'. The *Liverpool Echo* quoted it and delightfully capped it with 'First come. First saved. Had I been vicar in the 1970s I would certainly have tried 'Christ refreshes the parts even Heineken cannot reach'. Vulgar? Of course, but most people are vulgar. That's what the word originally meant. My aim was to present the church with humour and imagination, not so that people would drop everything and come in (they won't) but so that when they did need a church, the penny would drop – 'That's the kind of place I could go to.'

As to the congregation, twelve people in a thousand-seater is not a recipe for high morale. On my first Sunday morning I stood in my stall. No choir. No organ. A man on a small harmonium who slid on to one right note in every five. We would have been better without him. The other 11 people were scattered around the five hundred seats in the pews which occupied every square inch of floor. I said, 'Good morning,' and added, 'You know I'm not your vicar though we'll be together for some time. So,' I continued, taking a deep breath, 'I am not proposing to start this or any service from now on unless all of you are sitting in the front three rows close to me. I hope that is clear.' Then I sat down and waited. And prayed very hard. And waited. Whose nerve would break first? An old lady got up and slowly walked forward. One by one they all followed. They all squeezed into those front three rows. Thank God for that! For almost three years until the day I left, and they closed the church (at the same final thanksgiving service), we all sat in a small area and were a real, if tiny, congregation. We even grew a little. There was a magnificent, tall pulpit once used by the famous first Bishop, J.C. Ryle. I never used it until that final service when the two hundred from all over the Group, and elsewhere, gave me the needed excuse. Normally, I preached from a small central lectern and talked, well, chatted really, to them. I really enjoyed those services. We were not a bunch of scattered individuals. We were the People of God, together, few, but a real family.

The church council had eight members. It met in our drawing room. The church hall was so dark, disgusting and awful that I never entered it after my arrival. What we did, we did in church or at home. Prayer groups, Bible studies, all were at home and we relaxed together. The eight PCC members came from all over Liverpool. They all worshipped at Holy Trinity because of long-past family associations. Not one was a troublemaker but all could see the writing on the wall. When we finally faced the ultimate need for closure not one voted against. Three abstained because they couldn't bear the thought of actually voting to close the church but otherwise all the rest bit the bullet. They were a great group of Christian men and women and I was proud of them. It's not often a vicar (or quasi-vicar!) has closed a church with a congregation in good heart.

The two churchwardens, Bill Challen and George Linforth, were plain, ordinary, working men. Not manual workers, but 'lower-middle-class' clerks with their own dignity. Bill had the imagination to think of standing for election to the old Church Assembly and I virtually wrote his election address for him. He was duly elected and served for two years until one Sunday morning he had a heart attack in church, and died later in hospital. It was a terrible blow to that tiny congregation, just three months before we closed the church.

The Beacon Group was a very unsatisfactory affair and Richard Allen was a strange man. He was one of the very few geniuses I have ever met and like most geniuses a weird mixture of brilliance and incompetent oddness. He had never been an incumbent when Bishop Clifford Martin asked him to chair a group of four churches and a club, and he had absolutely no idea how to do it. He would never give a lead – 'They must reach their own decisions' – but none of the people had ever had to make such decisions and had no idea how to start, nor could each church ever agree with the others. Two new deacons were given no instructions or advice and left to drown. It was the most ridiculous mess I ever met but Richard was convinced that we must all go through this Slough of Despond if the Group was to have any future. One church pulled out of the Group (St Polycarp's), incensed that the clergy would not affirm publicly that a glass of beer was, in itself, sinful. It was not much good telling them that they were Manichaeans, not Christians, since they had grown up with the Band of Hope and alcohol was inherently diabolical! It was quite a big enough matter to split the Group. I groaned with despair.

Roger Sainsbury did an excellent job at the Shoosy and let the rest of us squabble. Neville Black and I, the planners, were almost distraught with frustration. Eddie Neale beamed at all of us, and drifted from pillar to post, once treble-booking himself to speak in Liverpool, Manchester and London, at the same time. Richard, whose marriage was slowly collapsing, was unwilling to accept any formal planning and by 1967 the Group came apart at the seams. He left both the Group and Mollie his wife. Olivia Abbaye, the Group's woman worker, went off to the South Seas, and Rita Langman, our hard-working and competent secretary, moved to another job.

I was saved by having such a range of tasks. Even if two didn't survive, I could find real fulfilment in the others, and I did. Within the diocese, my jobs took me all over the city and in every parish in the Liverpool Archdeaconry. I saw the extraordinary situation of a diocese with an allegedly Evangelical bishop and more than 150 clergy of that tradition who had no coherence. The diocesan Evangelical Fellowship had about 20 on its books and an attendance of about 8 to 12 people. My old Tyndale colleague, Brian Green (leading the Toxteth Team Ministry) and I came to the conclusion that a revolution was needed. We went to a DEF meeting, complained, and were invited to do better. The chairman (who had been in office for about twenty years) handed over to Brian, and the secretary, for the previous ten years, gave me the paperwork. It amounted to a tiny paperback notebook and 20 names.

I wrote to 150 clergy, telling them that we were about to create a new dynamic group, inviting top-class national speakers. We should meet at the cathedral, would require a sensible subscription, and would not bother them again if they didn't reply within ten days. The result was electrifying. I suddenly became, in effect, the shop steward of a group of 130 fairly like-minded clergy, got outstanding speakers (mostly from London) like David Winter and John Stott and found myself with the funds to pay them decent expenses and fees. We so used, and exhausted, John Stott on a long weekend when he spoke fourteen times, that I sent him back on the first-class Pullman. I'm willing to bet no other diocesan Evangelical group has ever done that, before or since. Attendances varied between 100 and 140. We were, suddenly, the largest group of its kind in the country.

Alas, when I moved on, the whole thing collapsed. My successor had no idea how to continue or capitalise on it. That was always Liverpool's problem. They hated these southerners who came and took over and showed them how to do it but often they lacked the drive and know-how to do it themselves. It's hardly surprising that I often say, not entirely facetiously, that my three years in Liverpool were my 'missionary service for the Church of England'. It was certainly the biggest culture shock of my life.

The ecumenical task was not easy but it was perhaps an era when such jobs had reasonable prospects of success. There had been a moribund 'Merseyside Council of Churches' and when Edward Patey arrived as Dean of Liverpool he saw at once that something new was needed to try to capitalise on the Faith and Order conference at Nottingham. My arrival, soon after his, gave him the chance and he soon used his past Coventry Cathedral experience to good effect. I wasn't perhaps, his natural choice (he was a Liberal-Catholic) but maybe he saw that I was: first, willing; second, in post; and third, able to touch a large part of the Liverpool Anglican community which would not view him with much confidence. He was keen to build new links with Roman Catholics (concerning which I was open but for obvious reasons cautious) and laid foundations which were later wonderfully capitalised by the Heavenly Twins, David Sheppard and Derek Worlock.

With Edward as chairman, and me as secretary, the new Liverpool Council of Churches began its life. Both of us were aware that one vital element must be the link with Christian Aid, and Edward, being a good friend of Janet Lacey, the national director, was able to arrange a meeting between the three of us. Liverpool's contribution to Christian Aid had been a mere £1,100 in 1964 for the whole city and she saw at a glance that a part-salary and a free car were essential elements if this was to change. Thus I became a part-time member of Christian Aid's staff and received a new Morris 1100 (purchase price £600). Within the year I had tripled Christian Aid's income from Liverpool and in that alone justified my appointment.

Travelling all over the city led to some fascinating encounters. In an area traditionally hostile to non-Roman Catholics I went to an RC church on the ring road, Queen's Drive, for a meeting and tentatively asked the priest, a very Irish character, whether it might be possible to end the meeting with the Lord's Prayer. That would have been out of the question a couple of years earlier. 'Ah well now,' said his Reverence, 'dat's an interesting tought.' Then, before I could respond, he added with a smile, 'But you'se will come across to de presbytery for a little drap o'whiskey, won't you'se?'

Stories about Irishmen are legion and sometimes aggressively racist. (West Indians in Liverpool were known as 'Smoked Irishmen'.) However, I promise faithfully that the following event happened on my own doorstep. Paddy wanted his baby baptised but 'de Farders' wouldn't do it. It seemed that he was divorced. We talked and eventually I said that I was more interested in whether he was a Christian than whether he was either Catholic or Protestant. I knew what they were, in Liverpool terms. 'Sorr,' he said firmly, 'oi'm not interested in bein' a Christian – oi'm a Cattolic.' Believe me, he really did say it.

One afternoon, I was grateful to receive an invitation from the Jesuit priest at the local Roman Catholic church of St Francis Xavier, 'SFX' for short. In their parish, I was the nonconformist. They were the Ninety-Percenters between Scotland Road and Shaw Street. We talked amicably in post-Vatican Two manner until one elderly priest asked me about the kind of 'experiences' that Evangelicals often claimed. As gently as I could, I described my own Three Experiences, not pushing them, but simply letting them stand in their own right. As the others moved out of earshot, he said softly, 'I envy you, young man. I've been a Catholic for seventy-two years and a priest for nearly fifty and I have never had any kind of personal evidence that it's true. I just keep going and grit my teeth.' I felt no sense of satisfaction that afternoon but I did feel sad for him. He was celibate, he was obedient, he was poor, he was faithful, but he had never, not even once in a lifetime, had the slightest flicker of personal experience to reassure him. Christ, he knew, had died and risen but he didn't know what was meant when people said that Christ had died for them.

My job left me very little time for clergy cricket and I only played about half-a-dozen matches for the diocesan side. Against Chester, I found myself up against a young curate called Max Wigley. Not only was he, and he still is, one of the funniest comics in the Church of England (he could do it professionally at top level) but he had also been a Yorkshire colt as a fast bowler and those were days when Freddie Trueman was around. Max bowled two balls to me. Both were, I thought, half-volleys just outside the off-stump and I drove each for four. So I thought. Actually the first hit me on the thigh and I had the bruise for weeks and the second took my off-stump. The experience was an exact repeat of what had happened to me at Bristol against one of the Gloucestershire young fast bowlers. To a reasonable club and university player like me, county fast bowlers were simply a yard faster than anything I ever met elsewhere.

A letter came, out of the blue, from Gordon Harman. There had been some pressure from within the YPF to change the traditional pattern. My successor, George Hoffman, was uncertain but, like Gordon, broadly sympathetic. What did I think? That's an awful question. The relationship between a clergyman and, first, his predecessor, then, second, his successor is always fraught with problems. To be asked to make his decisions is a real hiding-to-nothing and I wasn't about to start that. 'You decide,' I wrote. I had spent over a year urging Gordon to appoint George Hoffman and nearly as long pestering George to accept, and I wasn't going to get involved now. In the event, they did reorganise things and the circumstances of those days probably required it. Certainly the youth climate was radically changing. It's quite possible that I might have agreed to those changes had I had to take the responsibility but I didn't. The fact is, and I offer no-one any blame, when I returned to Edgware YPF for a meeting in 1970 I was shocked by the chaotic mess of the Saturday meeting, so disorganised and unplanned. When, years later, in 1985, I rang the then rector to ask what plans he had for the Golden Jubilee in 1986 he said, ruefully, that they had had to close it down since no-one attended anymore.

It is one of the sadnesses of life in the ministry that circumstances, and sometimes one's successors, seem to take a delight in destroying actively, or by indifference, the work into which one had put so much time and effort. I have certainly had to come to terms with this on four or five occasions and it always hurts. Doubtless, there are times when change is vital but it is amazing how often the reason seems no more than the arbitrary desire to be shot of someone else's shadow.

Far into the future there was to be one great consolation. Thirty years, to the day, after I left Edgware YPF, I and my former leaders, David and Freda Ward, Tony Charles, Richard Wilkins, Romy McCabe and Peter Liddelow, sponsored a reunion at which over eighty former YPF members turned up. Two came from Australia, one from western Canada, and dozens from all over the British Isles. We held a memorable weekend get-together, with much nostalgia and re-creation of old friendships. One of the greatest satisfactions for me was to see how many were in leadership roles in their local churches. Of course there were sad stories, divorces and deaths to report, but I was especially thrilled when they gave St Margaret's £500 towards the creation of a new youth work following its collapse in the 1980s. There are few greater fulfilments for a clergyman than to see his efforts continue to mature and flourish in later decades. In Edgware YPF I was so blessed by God.

As the year passed, I received an invitation to the Third International New Testament Congress. I had greatly enjoyed the first two in 1957 and 1961 so I made plans to attend the next one. Then it dawned on me. The congress wasn't just aiming at the big scholars with the famous names. There was plenty of opportunity for presenting papers at the more popular level. Take your life into your hands, Saward, and offer them 'Teenagers, Tabloids and the Gospel Narratives'. Tell them how you came to publish 'Eastern Star'. There'll be plenty of teachers there. Maybe they'll be glad to hear about it. Well, I've never been a shrinking violet so off went my application to Christ Church, Oxford, and back came confirmation from F.L. Cross, the Lady Margaret Professor of Divinity.

On the morning in question I went for coffee to a small café on The High, and was introduced to Professor William Barclay, the Scottish biblical commentator. To him I confided my anxiety about my 'cheek' and he burst out laughing. In broad Glaswegian, he reassured me that most people had no idea what the academic scholars were talking about and prophesied that my meeting would be packed out. 'You'll be right on target,' he declared and boosted my morale enormously. I crossed the road to the Examination Schools, found my room and was amazed to find that it was packed out. The chairman moved us to a larger hall and we went on well over time, with a host of questions. Full marks to Willy Barclay! He made my day.

One afternoon I was called urgently by Joe, whom we were still calling 'Jonathan' in those days. 'Daddy, Daddy,' came the excited voice of a four-year-old from the walled yard behind the basement which did duty for a garden. 'What is it?' I called. 'Quickly, quickly, I've found a little animal and it's dead.' 'Is it a mouse?' I enquired. 'No, it's smaller than that.' 'Well, is it a beetle?' 'No. It hasn't got a guitar.' He was, I remain certain to this day, quite serious.

Our part of Liverpool was full of characters who might have come straight from early *Coronation Street* even though that is set in Salford. Every street had its Ena Sharples and its Albert Tatlock and the show's initial success was clearly because of the reality of its denizens. The older women, especially, lived lives of an amazingly circumscribed nature. Our street, halfway up Everton hill, was about a mile and a half from the Pierhead and we could see the buildings from our rear windows. Yet I met not a few women who had hardly ever been that far and whose normal lives never took them more than half a mile from home in any direction. When the children (and especially the daughters) got married they lived as near to 'Me mam' as was possible and that was usually less than eight hundred yards.

One consequence of this was the fine social gradation of the Everton hill's streets. From Scotland Road the streets ran in close parallels to Shaw Street, halfway up the hill. Above that were more streets not quite so exactly parallel until St George's Church (where my grandfather had been married) topped the hill. The upper half of the population were 'Protestant' and below Shaw Street lived the 'Catholics'. (Actual religious understanding of those terms seemed quite minimal – the divide was tribal.) To Jackie and me, living at the mid-point, the social distinctions seemed totally meaningless. It was opaquely Liverpool working class from top to bottom. Not so to the residents. The higher up the hill, the 'better' the class. The 'ruff' lived below Shaw Street and the 'really ruff' lived down near Scotland Road. It wasn't then, surprising, to find that our first-floor drawing room offered, like the Home Office balcony at Trooping the Colour, the best seats in Liverpool for the annual Orange Lodge march, celebrating the Battle of the Boyne in 1689. We might have been in Belfast, there on Shaw Street, as the procession trailed on with all the bands and stick-twirling, the bowler hats and the 'sash my father wore', straddling middle-aged bellies. We watched it during our first year but came so to dislike all that it stood for that we ignored its aggressive posturing in our later years. What it patently lacked, thank goodness, was a focus of the kind which Ian Paisley came to provide in Ulster in the 1970s onwards. It was so obviously dying on its feet while we were there. One great bull of a man stood out, carrying the scars and cauliflower ears of earlier encounters but we never even discovered his name.

For two weeks in November, the D'Oyly Carte company came, with the usual repertoire of Savoy operas, to the Liverpool Empire. We saw, first, *Ruddigore* and, later, *Princess Ida*, and I took the extraordinary step of writing to the leading soprano, Ann Hood, to congratulate her on her performance. Not being by nature a stage-door-Johnnie, I quite surprised myself at my nerve. She replied, a few days later, from the Theatre Royal in Newcastle-upon-Tyne, saying that we had seen her first-ever performance as Ida which was 'nerve-wracking'. Having seen most of the D'Oyly Carte stars for fifteen years, I thought she was the best of the sopranos and told her so. Sadly, my judgement wasn't that of the management who dropped her quite quickly. Her reign was the shortest of all and it is rare to find a photo of her in the large library of books about Gilbert and Sullivan operas. Looking back, I suppose I owe my love of classical music to Sullivan, who provided me with a bridge from the world of Glen Miller and Bing Crosby, in which I had been brought up.

Henry Kendall, my grandfather, died on Tuesday 30 November in the Trinity Hospice at Clapham Common. He was ninety-one and his lifespan exactly matched that of Winston Churchill. As he was in his last minutes, so we were told, he relived a shipwreck or similar and it seems likely that it would have been those terrible moments when the *Empress of Ireland* went down, under his command, after the collision in the St Lawrence estuary, fifty-one years before. Of all the fearful events at sea in his early life that was the one he could never face and which, in that last seeking for breath, he met once more.

I preached my first cathedral sermon in January 1966 during the Week of Prayer for Christian Unity. It was inevitably in Liverpool Cathedral and gave me the quite unusual experience of speaking to more than four hundred people who, in that vast auditorium, appeared to occupy no more than half-a-dozen rows.

A week later I went to Leeds University as an assistant missioner working with John Stott. No man has had a greater influence on my ministry than John, right from the time I first met him in 1955 and immensely enjoyed his first book, *Men with a Message*, which had been selected as the then Bishop of London's Lent Book. His name will keep reappearing in this book for he moved from being an idol to a warm personal friend. He remains, though now in his late seventies, a figure worthy of enormous respect to hundreds of clergy in my generation. To work with him, and hear him preach nightly, at the Leeds mission, was a great privilege.

Nearly five years had passed since my 'Qoheleth' column in the *Church of England Newspaper* and 1966 saw me climbing up a second column which was also to last for exactly a year. This time I forswore pseudonymity and occupied a single column of newsprint, topped by a head-and-shoulders photograph surmounting a Doric pole entitled 'On Top of My Column'. One of my friends, Ian Barclay, a gifted cartoonist, responded with two elderly clerics, surveying a displaced Nelson, in front of a Saward-topped version of the centre of Trafalgar Square. 'I gather,' one said, 'it's a fellow called Saward.' This delightful cartoon appeared alongside column number 3.

As with 'Qoheleth', the column was provocative and provided plenty of material for letters to the editor. Perhaps the most memorable exchange related to one, Nicholas Stacey, the Rector of Woolwich in the heyday of South Bank Religion. Stacey, an ex-Olympic sprinter and a gifted publicist, spent some years in Woolwich, concerning which he extracted enormous media mileage. He and his talented team exhibited South Bank 'religionless Christianity' to the nation by trying every means that they could think of. His congregation grew a little bit, chiefly drawn from 'wealthy areas outside this working-class parish', as he put it. Amazingly, his failure to achieve his goals, which coupled 'a maximum of faith' with 'a minimum of dogma', led to two articles by him in *Readers' Digest* and the *Observer*. When can the story of 'failure' have been given so much 'self-publicity' in such hugely influential outlets?

I took up the issue in my column and asked whether, since he claimed to have 'played every card in our evangelistic pack', he had thought of trying the King of Hearts? Stacey was incensed and wrote an angry letter to the editor calling me a liar. He had not 'admitted defeat' in his articles (one of them entitled 'The Failure of a Mission') – he had merely admitted that 'We have achieved virtually none of our aims.' He did not answer my implied charge that he hadn't preached the gospel, and in a second column I contented myself with pointing to the fact that, in the digest article, he had never once mentioned the name of Jesus Christ. Not long after, Stacey, to whom no-one would, it seems, offer another job in the Church of England, left parish ministry. My own postbag was full of letters congratulating me on, as one put it, 'trouncing the impossible Nick Stacey'. I was especially delighted to receive two warmly supportive letters from Canon Charles Smyth, the eminent Anglican historian, and ex-chaplain to the Houses of Parliament, and a further note from the editor John King, saying that Smyth had written to him saying that 'I thought the way in which Saward stood up to Nicholas Stacey was indeed admirable.' My real crime had, of course, been, as a correspondent pointed out, 'to criticise anything the South Bank People see fit to do or say, be it ever so outrageous'. They 'feel free to attack and destructively to criticise anybody and anything, but they themselves must be inviolable'. 'Do not', concluded the writer, an Anglo-Catholic clergyman, 'hesitate to denounce in the Name of the Lord this wretched Neo-Christianity.'

I tangled with another Radical with rather less success. Harry Williams was a clerical don who later became a monk. I was asked to review his book *The True Wilderness*, and gave it the briefest and harshest review of the hundreds which I have published. I thought it was a quite appalling book and later said that 'it denigrated almost all religious certainty except his own certainty about uncertainty'. His was 'a certainty that if there is a God then he must want us to mill about in the wilderness learning to "be" '. It was, I added, this 'so-called "Radical doubt" which is emasculating far too many ministers today'. I went on to quote, with approval, some words by Bishop Stephen Neill, one of the twentieth century's greatest Anglican thinkers. Writing about the certainty of knowing the 'new birth', he added that, for anyone who has not had such an experience, 'it is no use pretending that some other will do as well'. 'If that central experience is lacking', he continued, 'you may be able to do many admirable things in the work of ministry, but one thing will be missing . . . the proclaiming of redemption through Christ, with the quiet authority of the man who knew, by experience, of what he speaks.'

Having accepted two roles in the ecumenical world I, not surprisingly, found myself frequently meeting with extremely Radical Christians who were well dug into the structures of both the British Council of Churches and Christian Aid. Here, indeed, I was living right on the frontiers as they were perceived by many Evangelical Christians, and well beyond them in the eyes of others. It was an uncomfortable territory, being shot at from both sides, and although I defended myself, both in speaking and writing, I was glad to be able, in most cases, to enjoy getting to know some of the people involved. Throughout my life I have struggled to distinguish people from opinions and have only rarely failed to keep on good terms with those whose opinions I found myself abhorring. David Edwards, Trevor Beeson and Bob Jeffery were all, in their time, vocal Radicals and there is something wryly amusing about their having occupied, between them, the deaneries of Norwich, Winchester and Worcester, plus canonries at Westminster and Oxford, and the office of Provost of Southwark (perhaps slightly more in character!). I have, I think, crossed swords with all of them and like all three.

John Robinson, in his time the most improbably notorious of all the Radicals, was best known to the general public for his little paperback *Honest to God*, written from a sickbed. John, whom I didn't know, though met once, was a shy scholar. I do, however, remember the gales of laughter at an ecumenical conference at Swanwick when Sydney Carter, the songwriter, in John's presence, sang one of his choruses taking the rise out of Anglican Radicals (Sydney was a Quaker) with the words 'Glory, laud and honour to I really don't know who, but keep on swinging the censer round the way we always do.' I can do business with men, however heterodox, who have that kind of sense of humour. Indeed, years later, I wrote a prize-winning hymn for the BBC, tailored to the tastes of one of the judges, the same Sydney Carter.

Attending conferences and committees became a major feature in my life during my Liverpool years. I travelled to London fifty-four times (in those days four hours each way), went on ten Christian Aid conferences, eight ecumenical conferences, plus nine other conferences at Swanwick. I had missions or speaking engagements which took me to Leeds, Manchester, York, Oxford, Keele, Bristol, Birmingham and Londonderry (and to some of these two or three times). In those years there were not many motorways, and a 60–mile 'gap' in that between London and Lancashire. I discovered that, in the little Morris 1100, outside rush hour, I could do the two hundred miles from Apex Corner in Mill Hill to Shaw Street, in exactly two hundred minutes and could plan Liverpool to Swanwick, in Derbyshire (across country almost all the way) to within three minutes! Indeed I spent so many nights at conferences in Swanwick – twenty-three nights in twenty months – that I facetiously asked for residential terms.

The majority of my London visits were to monthly committees of the Bible Churchmen's Missionary Society, which gave me a continuing international perspective. By now I had realised that overseas missionary work wasn't going to be my life's chief ministry, as I had once thought. Nevertheless, since BCMS worked in India, Burma and Ethiopia (until expelled), Morocco, Kenya, Uganda, Tanzania and, eventually, Spain and South America, it seemed that my African experience, and dozens of new contacts, would all help to keep my vision a good deal more worldwide than that of most of my Liverpool neighbours.

Two successive secretaries of BCMS greatly influenced me. Canon A.T. Houghton (pronounced 'Hawton'), after serving in Burma before the Japanese occupation, became General Secretary in 1945 and lifted the society's reputation to a high level. It was he who persuaded me to serve on the general committee not least because, when I joined in 1964, he hinted at his likely successor, Alan Neech, who had enormously impressed me. He had served in India for twenty-five years. These two men, outstanding, shrewd and warmly godly, gave a new image to the society and they, more than anyone, gave me the confidence to believe that I could contribute to BCMS at a serious level and help to rebuild the society, which had (fairly or unfairly) acquired a very narrow reputation. In consequence, I served on both general and the executive committees between 1964 and 1976.

A completely new door opened, just once, into Walton Jail where I was asked to preach. It was an extremely stimulating event, one of the only two or three in a lifetime at which a sermon drew heckling. It wasn't hostile, merely a loudly posed question, in mid-flow, but it provided me with the kind of interruption which, perhaps regrettably, is not often given to Anglican preachers.

Something not dissimilar occurred on my birthday, 14 May. The diocesan authorities had planned the summer meeting of the diocesan conference to take place that afternoon, being a Saturday, many months before. Unfortunately, they had not thought to take note of the fact that Everton were playing at Wembley that afternoon in the FA Cup Final. Needless to say, thousands of Everton supporters with tickets were there (doubtless including not a few Diocesan Conference members). Virtually nobody wanted to be at a large hall in St Helen's at a Diocesan Conference. Nevertheless over 100 loyal members turned up to be greeted by the new Bishop of Liverpool, Stuart Blanch, smilingly promising up-to-date information from a transistor radio, whenever it could be smuggled on to the agenda. Everton, I am glad to report, won the Cup. The Diocesan Secretary never made the mistake of fixing future conferences on Cup Final day. Stuart, from that day on until his sad death in the early 1990s, remained one of my heroes. A plain, very 'unclerical', man he was one of the Church of England's greatest, and most unsung, leaders of the twentieth century, first in Liverpool and, later, as Archbishop of York. He had the common touch and he blended it with quality scholarship and a delightfully direct, and modest, personality. When Stafford Wright, my college principal, heard of Stuart's appointment to Liverpool in 1966 he said it gave him renewed confidence in the Church of England. I was to thank God for Stuart's wisdom many times as we grew to know each other over the next fifteen years.

Two weeks later, on Whit Sunday, I was invited to conduct the half-hour BBC Radio *People's Service* from Holy Trinity. It was my first appearance on a live broadcast and Peter Firth, later Bishop of Malmesbury, produced it, offering me much valuable professional advice. We used one of my hymns, 'Wind of God', for which I wrote an extra verse and, appropriately, we sang it to the tune 'Everton'. Some weeks later, I won a Southern Television *Hymn for Britain* competition with 'Through all our Days, We'll Sing the Praise, of Christ the Resurrected', to the tune 'Greensleeves'.

One day our Rural Dean, Edwin Young, Vicar of Liverpool, invited the Archbishop of Dublin, George Otto Simms, to speak to the clergy chapter. Simms was half-German and half-Irish and wasn't blessed with a great sense of humour. In the question time, I mischievously suggested that there were the nations of the world and then there were the Irish and that the latter would not be comfortable if they felt that they lived in the same century as the rest of us. Would he care to comment? Young was in stitches, the rest of the clergy smiling, and His Grace solemnly spent fifteen minutes trying to answer the question. It's very hard on the nerves watching someone like that failing to grasp the impishness of some clergy.

At much the same time, I discovered a completely new and very enjoyable leisure activity. It wasn't cheap and it was widely assumed to be of dubious moral propriety. I'm talking about a sauna and massage. Liverpool had such a place, with an excellent plunge pool and a masseur of real skill. A couple of hours or more and you came out feeling a new man. Since then I have been in saunas, and the occasional Turkish Bath, on many occasions, and only twice have I ever been the object of an improper proposal. These days expensive health clubs, with magnificent facilities, are available but I've still to find a really top-class masseur, like the man in Liverpool thirty years ago. Perhaps you have to be a professional footballer to benefit from top-class massage. Even so, if I could afford only one real luxury, on a regular basis, it would be to have regular treatment from a skilled masseur. That, sadly, looks like being one of life's unfulfilled ambitions.

In early June, Jackie and I left the children in the care of our respective parents and flew to Italy to conduct another holiday tour on behalf of Highway Holidays, the successor to the earlier Pathfinders. Based at Cattolica, on the Adriatic, we spent time in Venice, Florence and Urbino, seeing such treasures as the Uffizi (on a stiflingly hot day) and the magnificent marquetry made for the Montefeltro family of Urbino, plus the occasional painting by Raphael. It was our first visit to Italy and combined those elements of the raffish, and artistic brilliance, which make that country such an extraordinary place. It whetted our appetites for future visits, though, strangely, they have been few and far between. It was, incidentally, to be my last tour with Highway. Their goal was to be a blend of holiday and evangelism but virtually the whole party on this occasion was made up of fully paid-up Christians and I used the evenings to expound the letter to the Romans. It seemed only sensible to provide Christians with real food but, unfortunately, one of the national committee was on the party and he wanted to hear evangelistic talks. These not being on offer he reported back that I was not a suitable leader and no further invitations were forthcoming. I did three in all in 1957, 1960 and 1961 but found that they rarely reached the kind of 'customers' for which an evangelistic holiday made much sense. A good idea, but unsuccessful through the organisation's failure to get to its target audience. I shed no tears.

On our return, we discovered that time was running out for Pat Claridge. A mere thirty-eight years old, he was slowly shrinking from his bucolic, rotund self, 'expiring inch by weary inch' as I was later to write in an 'In Memoriam' piece from the 'Top of my Column'. He spent his last few days in the Middlesex Hospital and, just twenty-four hours before he died, I saw him there. He had lost many stones of weight and I was unprepared for the gaunt face. I have, ever since that day, been grateful that all my memories of Pat are of the big, happy man and only the faintest trace of that shadow dying in front of me. My last act was to promise him that whenever Barbara or Michael needed me I would do my best to look after them and for fifteen years, until circumstances gradually made it less necessary, I tried to fulfil that pledge. He died on 5 August.

Rachel, at six, decided to come to Holy Trinity on Sunday mornings. The only child in the congregation, it was her own decision and, while it can hardly have been exciting to be one small girl among a dozen adults in a huge building, she seemed evidently to be sad to have to miss it. One older lady took her under her wing and brought her to the communion rail so that she wouldn't feel out of it. That was an almost unheard-of practice in Evangelical churches in that era.

Our four small children had only our backyard in which to play and two sides of that were bounded by twelve-foot-high brick walls. One night, in a gale, a large section of the wall collapsed. We thanked God that it hadn't happened in the daytime or we should have had four tiny corpses buried under tons of brick rubble.

Television had not, until 1966, been part of our domestic scene

but its arrival turned Jackie into a soap-opera addict almost overnight. Life for her was dominated by the house and the children
and the chance of making friends was very limited. Having such a
splendid setting for a dining-room we arranged a whole series of
dinner parties for people around the city but hardly anyone ever
invited us back. It wasn't, as far as we could see, because we were
not wanted, but simply that such events didn't form part of most
people's lives and they, especially the clergy, chose to have almost
no social lives in the evening. Parochial clergy in cities are, admittedly, up to their necks in evening meetings but, even when they
weren't, dinner parties were not on their agendas.

What was high on many people's agenda was the Greater
Merseyside Crusade. Conducted by Dr Eric Hutchings, an English evangelist, it was held in the Liverpool Empire, and lasted
throughout the month of October. Taking its model from Billy
Graham it drew very large crowds from all over both Liverpool,
the Wirral and the outlying districts. Eric Hutchings asked me to
serve on his committee and I told him that I doubted whether our
'styles' were very compatible but that, since I was hobnobbing
with Radicals, Roman Catholics and a wide range of ecumenical
enthusiasts, I could hardly stand aside from the work of a fellow
Evangelical in seeking to evangelise a city with Liverpool's problems. Two days before the Crusade began, the planned accommodation for John Grant, Eric's 'song leader', fell through, and he
came to live with us for the whole period. Thus, Jackie and I got to
know the chief team members, Eric, John, Russell Mills (and his
American wife, Betty Lou) and despite our differences (which
weren't in any way personal) we valued their friendship. Eric was
a northern ex-businessman, a small, smiling character who was in
his element in Britain's provincial cities where he conducted many
Crusades throughout the fifties, sixties and seventies.

The day after Hutchings finished, we went to a quite stupendous performance of Benjamin Britten's *Burning Fiery Furnace* at
the cathedral. It was, I think, only the second after the Aldeburgh
première and I was so impressed that I referred to it in the week's
column:

In almost total darkness, a procession of theatrical monks moved through the Nave to the inclined spiral stage where, after a short session of plainsong, they launched into the story of Shadrach, Meshach, and Abednego. I don't find Britten easy as music, but coupled with the brilliant spectacle and superlative lighting, not to mention a procession of the sackbut, psaltery, and half Portobello Road, round the cathedral, the general effect, and the simple message of faith triumphant in trial were both striking and convincing.

I went on to contrast the 'singspirational' music of the typical 'crusade' with Britten's – not to compare them which, I said, 'would be both futile and stupid', and to wonder when Evangelical musicians 'might really grapple with the Gospel and translate it into the Britten idiom?' It has never ceased to sadden me that Evangelical religion makes so little attempt to present its message to 'the more aesthetically sensitive and more culturally sophisticated' in our land.

With the advent of television, I began to watch a whole range of programmes which greatly widened my awareness of the world around. Working, as I was, for Christian Aid further opened my eyes to the horrific suffering in many parts of the Third World and a combination of all these factors undoubtedly challenged my theology. Most Anglican Evangelicals have a broadly Calvinist framework to their thinking and, for me, this had created a mental capacity to explain almost everything quite tidily. I certainly did not feel much pain until the combination of television and Christian Aid shook me out of my comfortable theological lethargy. That, I realised, was exactly my problem. My brain could tidily explain it all. Tears didn't come to me. I could rationalise everything.

But there was a difficulty. Virtually everyone I met in Christian Aid and in the ecumenical world was strongly committed to the political 'Left'. In British terms, Labour could do no wrong and the Tories were fascist pigs. It was absolute death in such circles to suggest, even tentatively, that this was far too simplistic a stance for an intelligent person to adopt. After all, the media (apart from the hated *Daily Telegraph*) were all hostile, or so it seemed, to the despicable Tories, now out of office after, in Harold Wilson's phrase, 'thirteen years of Tory misrule'. Coupled with this went the conviction that America was the Devil's own country and that liberal values were being disseminated by the good old Communists across Asia, Africa and Latin America. Only one place was worse than the USA and that was South Africa, together with its lickspittle allies in Rhodesia.

How should I react? I was an uncommitted, unpersuaded Tory. Eddy Stride had been right all those years before. I had always voted Conservative but never out of any strong conviction. The truth was that I had always voted for the least worst party but now, here I was, surrounded by people who had an absolute conviction that it was quite impossible to be a Christian and not be on the political Left. I talked one day about it to John Collins (not the St Paul's Cathedral and CND one, but the Holy Trinity, Brompton, one). If ever I saw a smooth, public school Tory it was him. And he amazed me. 'Well, in national elections', he said, 'I always vote Conservative because the country's safer in their hands, but', he added, 'locally I vote for whoever will do the best for the community.' I looked puzzled. 'You mean, you've voted both Labour and Conservative?' 'Oh yes,' he said. 'When I worked in the Medway docklands, I voted Labour without any hesitation, in the borough elections.' It was a totally new idea. There I was living in Bessie Braddock's constituency, one of the toughest Socialists in the land, and there was no doubt that she had done a tremendous job for her constituents. Voting Tory there was a complete waste of time. She waltzed home with huge majorities.

Gradually, over the years I became convinced that the best place to be on the political spectrum was just to the right of centre. I could never be either kind of extremist and those just to the left of centre seemed to be failed revolutionaries who hadn't the courage of their convictions. Just right of centre meant you cared about tradition, you valued continuity and you would go as far as you could modifying them as need arose. So, from that time on (though I once voted for Bessie Braddock's local sidekick) I have been a left-wing Tory, though, as a clergyman with a duty to all my parishioners, I have never made it public before.

Being a member of Liverpool Round Table No. 8 opened up a world of young businessmen who lived, both mentally, and geographically, poles apart from Bessie Braddock. Lawyers, doctors, accountants, and so on, they mostly lived in the Wirral, up towards Southport, or in the Childwall, Woolton and Mossley Hill triangle. In those days the city boundaries had excluded almost all the monied middle class who worked in the city but paid their rates elsewhere. Thus Liverpool was about four-fifths working class and had very little comfortable suburbia. Round Table meant weekly lunches with these young men, though it was recognised that my job would rule me out from most of the social events. I enjoyed getting to know them, saying 'Grace' at all the obvious occasions and even speaking at one lunch. As Christmas approached, they arranged a special lunch with a greater variety of guests than was usual. These, a closely kept secret, turned out to be fishnet-stockinged-dancers from one of the theatres and they were not overdressed anywhere else! The committee had not only invited them, but one or two photographers as well, and, wearing my clerical collar, I was obviously a high-profile target. Two very luscious young ladies approached me with seductive smiles. 'Can we sit on your knees?' they enquired guilelessly. I could see the photos, already, in tomorrow's *Liverpool Echo*, so I had to think fast. 'You're both gorgeous,' I said, 'and I could eat the two of you for lunch. But I'd hate to damage your reputations. It wouldn't do your careers any good being seen around with a vicar. Bye for now.'

Round Table also taught me how a well-respected Christian after-dinner speaker could handle an audience of men, used to bawdy, and sometimes quite obscene, stories. One well-known Baptist layman used a limerick that neatly bridged the gap:

There was a young lady of Wantage
of whom the Town Clerk took advantage.
Said the Borough Surveyor,
'Of course you must pay her
you've totally altered her frontage.'

He went on to add that no-one in life is absolutely useless. If they could do nothing else they could always serve as a bad example.

One Sunday a funny old man turned up at church. He was lonely, he lived in a dosshouse, he had no friends or relations. He was willing to do anything. Could we help him? The churchwardens and I talked about it. We could only pay him peanuts, almost an insult. He didn't mind. Anything to occupy his time. So we gave him a cleaning job in the church and he was totally honest. He got to know our older kids and they liked him. His name was Albert Page. He was so reliable, so deferent, so lacking in any confidence that we even used him as a baby-sitter at home and later he became our 'daily'. His health was indifferent. He landed in hospital. There, as I visited him, he decided to become, consciously, a Christian. It was so improbable. It was so inevitable. Nobody pressured him. Nobody really thought he understood what we were up to in church. But he knew and I learnt a good lesson. The weak, the poor, the lonely, the have-nots, the not-so-brights, in short, the Albert Pages of this world, have souls capable of needing to know a Saviour. In the few years left to him, scruffy, run-down Albert tied his tie a little tighter, combed his hair a little more tidily, smiled occasionally through his deeply creased old face, and served Christ in any way that was open to him. He was one of my few real legacies to Liverpool.

I decided one night to go and see Richard Burton and Elizabeth Taylor's new film *Who's Afraid of Virginia Woolf?* It was a blistering experience of domestic controversy and I reeled out of the cinema, bludgeoned by the violence of the relationship, the language and the implications. Ten minutes later, I opened the front door, rushed up to the drawing room and burst out with 'Darling. You must go and see that film. It'll show you what we're heading for.' Jackie looked somewhat pained but, a few days later, went herself. Our marriage, which had always been a rollercoaster of a union, was not looking its best at the time. Taylor and Burton did us a favour by showing us what domestic hell an unhappy marriage could be. Since then I have always called that film 'the intellectuals' *Tom and Jerry*', portraying characters who can't live with, or without, each other. Jackie and I both know what that feels like!

A considerable surprise came in the form of an invitation for me to pay a ten-day visit to Londonderry in Northern Ireland in order to preach night by night in the cathedral and all the city's Anglican churches. This took place in the first ten days of March and gave me some real insight into life in the province of Ulster, prior to the later years of pain and disaster. I immensely enjoyed the generous hospitality though the ambience within the churches seemed to be about a century behind London and the service in the cathedral was so archaic and stilted that I was grateful to have been placed in a stall behind a pillar – how I kept a straight face I do not know.

My host took me out for a day off into the wilds of Donegal (some of the tinkers living in sod-huts with children like wild animals make that word appropriate) and coming back, miles from anywhere, we stopped at a small Anglican church where I discovered that the church bell, shining from much polish, bore the name SS *Laurentic*. 'How did that get here?' I asked, to be told that it had come from a sunken ship off the coast. 'That sunken ship, and that bell, crossed the Atlantic in pursuit of Dr Crippen in 1910,' I replied. 'It carried the Scotland Yard detective who captured Crippen, on my grandfather's ship *Montrose* in the St Lawrence estuary.' What an odd coincidence, that I should find it in the only church in Donegal that I have ever entered!

A college friend invited me out to lunch in Londonderry. 'What do you do in your Donegal parish?' I asked, adding, 'You'll be telling me you play croquet.' 'Now it's a funny thing you mention that,' he said. 'I've just ordered a set.' His world was the world of Jane Austen, 150 years adrift from mine.

Throughout my time in Liverpool I had been closely linked with the university's Christian Union, speaking on many occasions. Now came my fourth university mission (following on from Durham, Cambridge and Leeds) and I found myself working with Leith Samuel, an independent minister from Southampton. He had been at Cambridge, before the War, with Gordon Harman and the two were not only of a very similar type, they were also tall, lean and hungry-looking characters. I felt that, knowing one, I knew the other.

A second very surprising invitation arrived at much the same time. Would I address the university's Student Christian Movement group? SCM's influence in the universities was fast collapsing because of its capitulation to Radicalism and to be asked to speak both to the CU and the SCM, in the same term, was almost unique.

Edward Patey and the Council of Churches' committee looked for ways in which we could fulfil a social as well as an ecumenical role in the city. I was deputed to meet some of Toxteth's black leaders and find out, first, what they thought was wrong, and, second, what we could do together to put it right. It seemed an admirable idea and, in the best sense, a thoroughly liberal piece of thinking. I found this handful of black Liverpudlian leaders in a cellar in Toxteth. They, I was told, were the key people, trusted by the black community. 'So what you want?' said the leading leader. I told him what we had in mind. 'Go away, man,' he said, 'leave us alone. Your sort will only bring trouble to us.' 'Why?' I asked, genuinely alarmed at this hostile reaction. 'Surely there must be some racist things in Liverpool which we could try to put right?' How naive can you get? 'Look, man,' he said, 'there no racism in Liverpool. We been here for years and years. No trouble. We don' want no trouble. You go look for it, it come. Go away, man.'

I went back to my committee. They looked at me with evident disappointment. There *had* to be racism in Liverpool. If there wasn't, we would have to find it. I had really let them down. 'I'm only telling you what their leaders have said,' I responded. A decade or so later that very street where I had met them was at the centre of the Toxteth race riots. Oh, there was racism all right. But those old leaders reflected accurately their generation's attitude. Talk about it and it will erupt. So keep quiet. But the white Liberals wouldn't and the Black Power new generation wouldn't either. All hell broke loose. So who was right. I don't know the answer to that. I just know what happened.

Watching late-night television, as I now did, I was a regular viewer of BBC2's *Late Night Line Up*. This live programme nightly invited three guests to discuss the evening's earlier material and, if it went well, could last an hour or so. One night I watched a debate on some religious issue in which, as it seemed to me, the Christian viewpoint had been virtually abdicated. I decided, after midnight, to write an angry letter to the producer. Then a better idea occurred. I would say how disappointed I was and that obviously they had had to scrape the barrel to find competent speakers. 'Scrape a little further', I said, 'and you will find me.' This, I calculated, might be just the right approach to get myself invited on to the box. And I was right. The reply said how glad they were to learn of my existence and that they 'would be in touch'. Then, nothing. Three months went by. Nothing. So I tried again. 'That was a much better programme,' I wrote, 'but you still haven't scraped down to me yet!' The phone rang next day. 'Sorry,' said the producer, 'we lost your name and address. Can you come next Wednesday?'

It being Easter week, we were taking the children to Petts Wood anyway, so it suited us very well. 'Glad to,' I replied, and my TV career was launched on 29 March 1967. The chief subject for discussion was a long play *A Breach in the Wall*, all about the consequences for Anglicans and Roman Catholics if Thomas à Becket's remains were to be discovered. The other two with me were Edward Carpenter, of Westminster Abbey, and Joseph Christie, a Jesuit from Farm Street. Joan Bakewell was the interviewer and I knew, just before she got to me, that I had nothing to say on the question, which, instinctively, I knew she would ask. I went through thirty seconds of purgatory. I'd pushed myself on to this programme and now I was going to be struck dumb. She turned to me and asked exactly the question which I had foreseen. 'Well,' I said, buying three seconds of breathing space. Then, crisply and clearly, I answered it. The relief was unimaginable. I didn't say a lot more because Carpenter talked incessantly and I only got one more chance. 'Can you come again on Monday 17 April?' asked the producer. 'Delighted,' I replied.

That time the play was a parody of Cain and Abel, jointly-produced by the BBC and the Australian Broadcasting Commission, with Keith Michell in the lead role. This time my fellow guests were Russell Braddon (the journalist and former Japanese prisoner of war) and Ann Sharpley, of the *Evening Standard*. I got a better deal from them and Braddon and I shared a taxi back to central London. I mentioned the previous experience to him, saying how badly I had done. 'I saw that one,' he said. 'It's true that Carpenter talked a lot but then I remember what you said and I haven't the faintest idea what he was on about.' Perhaps he was just being kind but it certainly did my morale a power of good.

The BBC paid me £15 for each appearance (which is far more than, pro rata, you would get today). I decided, before the second one, to be really rash and go to the restaurant on the top of the Post Office Tower for dinner before the programme. Years later, a bomb scare closed it to the public but in those days it was new, and expensive. I had cold duck and salad and a sweet and it cost 32s 6d. In today's money that is £1.62p and in reality it would cost about £25.

In between the two programmes an event occurred which was, though I didn't know it, to change the whole direction of my life. This was the First National Evangelical Anglican Congress, held at the University of North Staffordshire, or Keele. To become one of the key gatherings in the history of the Church of England in the twentieth century, Keele was initially the idea of a group of clergy from the north-east, of whom Raymond Turvey was the catalyst. He, Vicar of St George's, Leeds, discussed the possibility of a national congress with London leaders like John Stott and Peter Johnston, Vicar of Islington, and together they received the support of all the major Anglican Evangelical societies. By the autumn of 1966 plans were well advanced, involving some nine hour-long addresses, plus a welcoming speech from the Archbishop of Canterbury, Michael Ramsey, and a concluding sermon from the Bishop of Liverpool, Stuart Blanch. A parochial preparation course was underway and all seemed comfortably settled.

However, the large group of younger Evangelical clergy who belonged to the Eclectic Society, founded by John Stott in 1955, were meeting at the first national conference at Swanwick in mid-November. I had been invited to join Eclectics in January 1959 and it had quickly become the single most significant influence on my ministry. It had few rules – you had to be under forty, you had to accept the Bible's supreme authority, and you had to attend regularly. By the mid-1960s it had divided, amoeba-like, creating new groups as membership in each topped forty. It was my good fortune to be in the right places as each new group came about and I was, in consequence, a member for almost fourteen years which was, in those days, almost a record.

On the final night at Swanwick, 16 November, a small group of us – Gavin Reid, Eddie Shirras, Frank Entwistle, Philip Crowe, George Hoffman and me – stayed up talking until nearly 2 a.m. Jackie had come in at 1 a.m. with two small twins bouncing about in sleeping bags but failed to persuade us to go to bed until we had completed our plans. We were convinced that Keele must be opened up to its thousand participants by having the addresses pre-published and then discussed in groups and, secondly, by having a statement, in draft, for debate. This was my idea, derived from the document similarly handled at the 1964 Faith and Order conference. We took these proposals to next day's plenary where they were approved, virtually without dissent.

A few days later Gavin Reid presented these proposals at the Keele congress committee meeting in London, where they were warmly welcomed. Two or three of us were drafted on to the Keele committee and in no time I found myself both congress Press Officer and Secretary for Observers caring for over thirty of these 'observers' as well as running a press office with daily media briefings.

On the first day, 4 April, my most colourful task was to welcome Athenagoras, Archbishop of Thyateira and Great Britain, the Greek Orthodox leader, and most senior of the observers. He was quite a lurid character and confounded me within the first few minutes by fishing in his filthy cassock pocket and bringing out a piece of chewing gum which he kindly offered me. I wasn't in the habit of using chewing gum, even from a heavily bearded Greek Archbishop, and we had a witty encounter about the disgusting transatlantic customs which he had picked up while in Canada in earlier years. We were to meet on various later occasions, usually in strange locations.

Keele for me was a golden event. Almost everything I touched was tremendously successful and I came away exhausted but thrilled at the way the congress had captured minds across the churches and especially within the Church of England. The statement had publicly committed Evangelicals to a full role within the national church and its long-term consequence were far-reaching and are still with us. I still treasure a letter from John Stott, the congress chairman, who congratulated me on having done 'an extremely good job', with your customary conscientiousness'. My two tasks were, he added, 'extremely strategic' to 'the whole congress'.

A week later, during a parish house-party weekend in the Lake District, for a church in Wigan, I reached my two-thousandth talk or sermon. They had taken less than eleven years, the first thousand being reached in five-and-a-half years, and the second taking almost exactly the same time. Succeeding thousands were to take much longer, ten years to reach three thousand, another seven to four thousand, and a further ten to five thousand (reached on 2 January 1994 in Key Biscayne, Florida).

By the early summer of 1967 I was absolutely clear that the Liverpool job, as regards the Beacon Group, was leading nowhere. I had, earlier in the year, had a friendly letter from the Bishop of London, Robert Stopford, offering to 'keep an eye open' for any suitable vacancies but it wasn't until June that two possible posts were advertised in the church press and I applied for both and was short-listed.

A couple of weeks prior to these advertisements I had sent a note of congratulations to Geoffrey Fisher on his eightieth birthday. He had retired at seventy-four and was living, in some splendour, in Trent Rectory near Sherborne, where he acted as priest-in-charge, with some vigour! His reply was a duplicated postcard which had doubtless gone to hundreds of correspondents. To it, however, he had added in his own hand a warm personal note saying, 'Your letter specially delighted me. I so *enjoyed* your friendship at the ordination times. Biblical Conservative? We all are – we all start from there and always come back there again to get fresh vigour! How I should enjoy an argument with you again!'

In the same post came a copy of the Rochester diocesan news

(I'm not sure why) which contained an absolutely delicious howler in relation to a vicar who had recently died. I cut it out and have kept it ever since. James X, it said, 'after a full morning's work, ministering to his parish, returned home and died almost without warning. This was typical of his whole ministry.' I hope the archdeacon who wrote that lived down the embarrassment.

Eventually the two job interviews took place. The first, for Peter Firth's post in BBC Manchester's Religious Broadcasting Department, was chaired by Gerald Ellison, Bishop of Chester, a prince-bishop if ever there was one. He, in those days, was still soberingly pompous and I did not find it surprising when I learned that I hadn't succeeded. It was, as I came to realise later, a very great blessing in disguise. The second post was that of Radio and Television Officer in the Church Information Office at Church House, Westminster. It had two elements. The first concerned the work of the church as a whole, and especially as it related to the Church Assembly (which was, in 1970, to become the General Synod). The second aspect was to act for the Archbishop of Canterbury and both to advise and arrange for his broadcasts.

I was faced with three interviews. The first on 26 July was with the Chief Information Officer, Major-General Adam Block. Adam was a typical senior army officer, honest and honourable, an 'officer and a gentleman' whose leisure pursuits in his Hampshire home were, predictably, 'huntin', shootin' and fishin' '. More to the point, he was a gunner, and, faced with an ex-gunner subaltern as a possible aide, it was really no contest. The other short-listed candidate wanted to keep his city incumbency and work part-time for CIO and that was never a serious starter. A further big plus in my favour was the fact that Adam had attended the Keele congress and later told me that my handling of the media there had settled the matter as far as he was concerned. One fence jumped, two to go.

The second was the Archbishop himself. I presented myself at Lambeth Palace on 4 September (everyone naturally had holidays in between), conscious of that awful time with Fisher in that same palace over eleven years earlier. Michael Ramsey and I sat in armchairs, on opposite sides of a large fireplace in his study. Thirty years earlier, Hensley Henson had described Ramsey as 'a heavy fellow with a fat face, and a cumbrous manner, not prepossessing, but improving on acquaintance'. The description was uncannily accurate, I thought, and he did improve, I was to discover, on acquaintance.

The so-called interview was farcical. Ramsey had no idea what to say and after half an hour of long silences punctuated by a question here and there, and my answers, I was becoming really concerned. Was this silence a diabolical technique to see whether I would talk, and talk? Well, I didn't. He was the boss, wasn't he? Let him set the pace. Let him provide the agenda. But thirty minutes of almost nothing left me no alternative. I must make my case. 'Your Grace [we still said that in those days], I should very much like to do this job if you will have me.' 'Er-er-er-er, ye-e-e-s. Good, good. It is, er-er-er, of course, er-er, m-m-m-my decision.' 'Oh, naturally. I fully understand that,' I replied, 'but I didn't want you to think it was of no great concern to me.' 'Oh-oh-oh-oh, no, no. Un-un-understood, un-un-understood. It-it would be your task, er-er-er, to tell me, to tell me, when er-er-er, I should, and-and-and-and when I should *not*, appear on the tele-vis-ion, m-m-mm.'

At the end of forty-five minutes, of which about fifteen had been total silence, while his eyes bored into me, we parted. He seemed satisfied but how could one know. His chaplain, John Andrew, one of the smoothest operators in the business, was giving no clues. Even so, three days later, I was taken into the Church House torture chamber and grilled by the Secretary-General, Sir John Guillum-Scott, and four or five others, including Adam Block.

The one memorable moment was when one of them produced the most extraordinary question: 'Bearing in mind your particular churchmanship, would you find it possible to have any dealings in your work with agnostics?' This was so ill-informed a question that I almost exploded. 'I don't think I've ever been asked so outrageous a question,' I responded. 'I spend most of my life talking to people who are, in all probability, agnostic in one way or another.' There was a slightly embarrassed silence and, in that pause, I am sure that the job was made secure. Any sensible clergyman of any churchmanship was meeting agnostics everyday of his life and the idea that Evangelicals lived in some secluded bolt-hole was, frankly, insulting. The job was mine and I now had to settle the salary and some accommodation. The initial offer, for someone needing a London home capable of housing a wife and four children, was unreasonably low and I had no option but to say so. Without awkwardness, they upped it and we were on the house-hunting trail. I had a month in which to make all the arrangements and it wasn't enough. Jackie and I needed somewhere in easy commuting distance and we found a row of new town houses in Beckenham, in a cul-de-sac called Ellesmere Avenue. At £6,975 we could just afford a very generous mortgage from the Central Board of Finance so we signed the contract. There was a snag. We couldn't move in until just before Christmas. There was also a solution. Sheila Eastman's parents were off on an extended holiday to Australia. We could rent their house in Ewell at a very reasonable price. So we did.

John King's response, on hearing of my appointment, was heartwarming. 'An absolute dead-end job,' he said. 'I can't imagine why you've accepted it.' Time, I'm glad to say, proved him well wide of the mark.

Saying good-bye in Liverpool wasn't too difficult. We had many acquaintances all over the city but, apart from the Stanleys and the Greens who went back to college days, we had few real friends. It hadn't been that kind of a job. Richard left just before us so the group was breaking up. Holy Trinity was closing. We combined its closure with my last service. About two hundred people turned up from the Beacon Group and all over Liverpool. I preached, as I had promised myself I would, from Bishop Ryle's ten-foot-high pulpit. Then they pulled the church down and built a dual carriageway over the remains.

My last task was to find Albert Page somewhere to live and the only other thing which my diary tells me happened is that I either met or telephoned a Derek Hatton not long before we moved. Well, well, well.

By late October I wasn't even a memory to the churches of Liverpool and none of them has ever asked me back. Our 'missionary' days were over. Civilisation was beckoning.

Chapter Nine

Doing the Lambeth Walk

I presented myself at Church House, Westminster, at 9.30 a.m. on Monday 23 October 1967 to find that I had been allocated a shoebox of an office on the first floor and that the decent desk used by my predecessor had been removed in the brief interregnum. So, it was the law of the jungle from Day One! I had no secretary but a pleasant girl called Robina Elliott would look after me until she took over as Adam Block's new secretary in a week or two's time. I played myself in.

The Beckenham town house was brand-new even though for six of us it was a real squeeze. We filled the garage full of spare furniture, boxes and bicycles and never even considered buying a car. One Saturday in Bromley we saw a limited-edition of a print of the Houses of Parliament by Oskar Kokoschka. It was priced at £100 but we knew we desperately wanted it and it has been the centrepiece of all of our subsequent homes. We have never tired of it.

Beckenham to Westminster was a daily commute and it taught me how easy it was for parish clergy to forget just how weary men are after a day's work and travel. The vicar's brilliant evening meetings, committees, Bible studies, and so on, lose much of their attraction. Busy mums doubtless feel much the same and television assumes seductive shape in such situations. It was a good, if hard, lesson to learn.

My first real duty was to be present at the filming in Lambeth Palace, one week later, of a discussion between Michael Ramsey and John Betjeman. It had all been arranged beforehand and I merely stood and watched, in growing embarrassment, as these two men, both in their sixties, sat together on a sofa and giggled and simpered. It was distressingly camp and I could see, at once, why C.S. Lewis had so disliked Betjeman (who had been one of his students at Oxford in the 1920s).

One of my first routine tasks was to arrange for the next group of participants to be selected for the coming Churches' Television Centre courses at Bushey in Hertfordshire and to see that those already chosen for the next one were ready. I decided to analyse the lists since the courses had begun and found to my surprise that of the hundreds of participants (all clergy) only about a dozen were Evangelicals. I went straight to Adam, put this fact before him, and asked permission to rectify the situation. I wanted to be quite open about this, not to do it surreptitiously, and he gave me the green light. When, some months later, I spent a day with David Skinner (the previous Radio and Television Officer), I very tentatively raised the matter of the principles applied in selecting names and was intrigued to be told, 'Oh, I assumed, like politicians in power, that you picked your friends and your "party". That's what I did.'

Well, it wasn't my way. I made sure that I played fair with all the traditions, subject only to trying to restore the imbalance created quite cynically by Skinner. After five years, the list looked much more 'across-the-board' Anglican. It did teach me a lesson, which was that my 'honest and fair representation' view was certainly not the usual one applied by many Anglican men in positions of power. They played it just like party politicians and 'packed' their own people in. On the whole, Evangelicals haven't done this when in power in the past thirty years but Catholics and Central men frequently have, to their discredit. Many Evangelicals simply don't think in political terms, in 'power' terms, and quite a number of recent Evangelical bishops have fallen over backwards not to make appointments of their own associates. Some have completed ten-year episcopates without appointing even one fellow-Evangelical (however competent) to a senior diocesan post. That kind of oversensitive extremism is as foolish as the other variety and each of these dioceses has suffered accordingly.

The television centre at Bushey had been founded and funded

by J. Arthur Rank (later Lord Rank), the Methodist business tycoon, and he and his associates had appointed as director a weak and incompetent Methodist minister, named Cyril Thomas, who ran the centre for years. He grew increasingly out of touch with the real world of television and thousands of pounds were spent in preparing men who would never broadcast, for programmes that would less and less be made. Cyril Thomas was what I, perhaps unkindly, used to call 'a Methodist auntie', a phrase which appealed to Michael Ramsey. When, eventually, Robin Woods became chairman, he sacked ('retired' I think the phrase was) Thomas quite brutally, having chopped him up in small pieces at a crucial meeting which I attended.

What was to be my actual job? It took sometime to get to the heart of what was needed and eventually I defined it as 'part bureaucrat, part diplomat, and part spy'. The first part was easy enough. It was the interrelationship between the second and third that was to prove tricky. The Church of England had been, for centuries, part of the power structure of British society and assumed that it could remain on even terms with press, radio and television, all playing fair with each other. Certainly as regards radio, and its adolescent offspring television, the Reith era had seen its role as supportive of society's institutions, of its religious and moral values. Radio, to a great extent, had continued to be a purveyor of religion and virtue, with only the occasional maverick programme (Margaret Knight's 'morals without religion' had created a minor storm in its day). Television, once ITV had arrived (very much against the church's wishes), was to be quite a different matter. The powers that be, in appointing Hugh Carleton-Green as Director-General, were not blind to his attitudes and they gave him a great deal of rope with which to hang himself. He, and his senior television executives, appointed a group of highly talented young producers, presenters and journalists, whose attitudes were frequently anarchic and whose influence was to be out of all proportion to their roles. Anthony Jay, a former BBC executive, was quoted by Max Caulfield, as saying that the BBC was loaded with 'people whose social, political, and moral assumptions are opposed to the majority of the country'. It was hardly surprising, then, that the 1960 Pilkington *Report on Broadcasting* had commented that 'Television portrays too often a world in which the moral standards normally accepted in society are either ignored or flouted.' One consequence of this was that thirty years later many of these 'normal' moral standards had been replaced by those of the television world, to the nation's enormous disadvantage and damage.

Walking right into the middle of all this, in 1967, I found a largely Liberal church leadership, quite unable to grasp that a revolution was under way and that Christianity was going to be one of the chief victims. Why, these BBC chaps had been to Winchester and Shrewsbury, Marlborough and Westminster, Christ Church and Trinity. They were just like us, a bit rowdy perhaps but, basically, decent chaps. As to the ITV fellas, well a lot of them, at least the officials and producers, had quite good backgrounds, as well. Nothing really to worry about, even if those noisy characters like Frost and Levin and a few of the 'Lefty' playwrights did go rather over the top. Well, actually, we're too involved to see too many of these TV programmes ourselves but no harm's likely is it?

The one really dangerous person around, as the Liberals saw it, in 1967, was a Midlands schoolteacher, a Mrs Mary Whitehouse. She was unfortunately stirring up a lot of illiberal reaction from dreary middle-class people like herself. Whatever else happened at the local level, national church leaders must publicly distance themselves from her sort or they would be smeared by the media, and attacked by the church's young Radicals.

Now, not all the bishops thought like that but hardly any dared disagree openly. Coggan at York played it very low-key, and everyone knew that Ramsey was a lifelong Liberal, so 'stum' it was. When I was appointed I was quite explicitly told by the Chairman of the Archbishops' Advisers, and his fellow-advisers, that I must not, repeat not, meet Mrs Whitehouse in any circumstances whatsoever. I expressed some anxiety at this, believing that I ought to be free to discuss media issues with anyone interested but it was made absolutely clear that to come into contact with Mary was more than my job was worth. I obeyed this extraordinary instruction for eighteen months, then finally demanded the right to meet her. Grudgingly this was allowed. We met on Paddington Station, had dinner together ('early, so that no-one will see you'), in an obscure Marylebone restaurant and remained in contact, but by no means always in agreement, for the next three-and-a-half years.

So, I was bureaucrat and diplomat. But it soon became clear that I would have to become a spy. Flushing out what was actually going on was a very different matter from believing what you were told by the men in the expensive suits in the executive offices in Portland Place, White City, Brompton Road and the ITV Company boardrooms. It was their job, and in their interest, to encourage the nation's major institutions, and not least the churches, to believe that all was well in their hands. True, Lord Reith was dead (I went to his memorial service in the Abbey) but although things *had* changed, 'nothing really radical would happen'. These remarks went side by side with the dubious assurances that everything was changing and, anyway, 'religion was really as broad as life', which kept coming from the producers, presenters and religious advisers. Spying was vital if I was to do my job effectively and keep the Archbishops and other interested parties aware of what was happening, and, even more, of what was projected for the future. It certainly wasn't going to be a world that Reith would have liked, indeed he had plainly indicated as much in a television interview before he died.

For many months, then, I had my opulent lunches (mostly at their expense) with Penry Jones and John Lang, from the BBC's Religious Department; with Christopher Martin, from the Independent Television Authority (as it then was); with Guthrie Moir, of Thames TV; Bill Allenby, of ATV; and, on one occasion, with five BBC executives from Television Enterprises who thought I could sell their product throughout the churches. I had a very 'executive suite' lunch with Kenneth Lamb, in Broadcasting House, when he was Secretary to the Corporation. I discovered the inside of the Cavalry Club, the United Universities' Club, the Army and Navy Club, the Savage Club, the Arts Theatre Club, and (what would one day be my own club) the Athenaeum. And it wasn't only clubs. I discovered Rules, Simpsons, the Gay Hussar, Wheelers, and a good few more West End restaurants. In that first year it was all 'diplomat' socialising. The 'spy' bit came later.

With all this socialising going on, it was just as well that I had consciously decided, in the mid-1960s, to stop being a teetotaller. On holiday in the Mosel I had discovered wine and though I never drink beer (and rarely spirits either) I have since come to develop quite a palate, especially for French wine. I also took to drinking coffee, initially white but later black, which I had never done before. I drew the line (and still do) at tea which I regard as looking, smelling and tasting, indescribably horrible. Lastly, I began to eat cheese. Blue cheeses, especially Stilton and Cambazola, and soft cheeses. Again, I drew a distinct barrier as regards hard cheeses. I don't like their taste, smell or consistency.

In the midst of all this, another world broke in. In mid-November, his 'All-Holiness' Athenagoras, Patriarch of Constantinople, and entourage, flew in to Heathrow. Television, recognising the value of an elderly, long-bearded Greek in a flat-topped black hat, asked for an interview at Lambeth Palace. We set it up for *Panorama* in the Lambeth state drawing room and His All-Holiness was scheduled to be questioned by Stuart MacKenzie, the Canadian. 'Roll,' said the director and the first question was fired. His All-Holiness undid a kind of scroll and proceeded to read out a prepared statement. 'Cut,' said the director. 'You can't do that on British television!' and an unseemly squabble began between MacKenzie, the director and some highly aggressive Greek priests. It wasn't my party so I walked away and left them to it. They were obviously in for a long session.

The Patriarch wandered off and sat on a low stool-like chair conversing with sundry bodies. John Satterthwaite, an unctuous canon, later to be Bishop of Europe, came to me. 'Have you met his All-Holiness yet?' he enquired in a voice that implied that this Greek was more-or-less God. 'No,' I said. I didn't mind meeting him (his namesake at Keele had been quite fun) but there was no way I was going to call any man, however eminent, 'Your All-Holiness'. Constantinople could out-pope the Pope as much as it liked but I regarded his title as blasphemous, nothing less. 'Come with me,' cooed Satterthwaite, and I walked over slowly. 'Your All-Holiness,' oozed Satterthwaite, 'may I present the Reverend Michael Saward to you?' A long pause, at least fifteen seconds, ensued while the Methuselah-like Greek looked me up and down like an art critic facing a might-be Rubens. Finally, as it was almost becoming embarrassing, he spoke. 'He is a *good* boy?' he enquired of Satterthwaite. At thirty-five, I thought I deserved better but John effusively assured him of my moral probity. 'Oh, indeed, yes he is,' he said with complete conviction. The elderly wizard stretched out a thin hand. 'How do you do?' he said in measured tones. I have no idea how I answered or how the programme turned out but I know that, while I have been within three feet of a pope, I have held the hand, briefly, of an All-Holy patriarch. Not many people know that.

A week later I interviewed a young lady in her early twenties, Rosanne Dill, as a possible secretary. A member of the Stewards' Trust (a series of Bible study groups founded by John Bickersteth, Michael Alison and Tim Royle, all known to me), she (like them) came from a very 'county' background. Her grandfather had been Chief of the Imperial General Staff in the earlier part of the Second World War and she worked for me for about eighteen months. She was a delightful girl and I later got to know both her cousins, Serena and Suzanna Cole.

My first return visit to the north in early December involved: speaking at Manchester University; preaching for my Orpington friend Michael Baughen at Holy Trinity, Platt, nearby; meeting the Anglican Adviser to Yorkshire TV (Fenton Morley), later to be Dean of Salisbury; and finally seeing the Archbishop, Donald Coggan, at Bishopthorpe Palace, outside York. Quite a weekend.

Three days later I had supper, in his Chelsea home, with Sir John Lawrence, Editor of *Frontier*, and his rather strange, arty wife Jacinth, who cooked us a very odd supper. John had been very enthusiastic about Keele, which he had attended as an observer and had asked me to write a piece for *Frontier* which I duly did. As a couple, they were archetypal old Chelsea, he being a descendant of the John Lawrence of Indian Mutiny fame.

Adam Block, being the kind of soldier who couldn't imagine anyone going to church except on duty, and on best behaviour, was interested when I suggested that he ought to see what was happening at St Helen's, Bishopsgate, in the City. We went for the weekly Tuesday lunchtime service and could only just get inside the door. About seven hundred to eight hundred businessmen were there and Adam was stunned. We stood for almost an hour. He had never seen anything like it.

The following day, he, Michael De-la-Noy and I went to Lambeth Palace for the first meeting of the 1968 Lambeth Conference preparatory committee. This committee, whose job was to organise the forthcoming conference, was a heavy commitment in the following nine months. Ralph Dean, Bishop of Caribou in western Canada, was to be the organising secretary. Ralph was a fun-loving go-getter with a great capacity for work, who eventually became Archbishop of British Columbia.

As the old year ended, Michael Ramsey did a brief televised New Year message from All Hallows, London Wall, in the City and he and Joan Ramsey invited me to stay the night at Lambeth since it would be a very late finish. At around a quarter to one, as we were about to go to bed, she offered me a hot drink. 'I would really much prefer a glass of cold water,' I said, unaware that it would take her nearly a quarter of an hour to find it! She seemed to have no idea where there was a cold tap in the palace. She didn't forget that event, and nor did I.

In my room, I found headed Lambeth notepaper. This was really too good to miss so I wrote to three clergy friends, in very scrambling writing, saying 'Dear "Smith" (or whatever), It gives me the greatest pleasure to offer you (at which point at the page was turned) my best wishes for 1968. Yours sincerely, Michael [but not the right one].' What a rotten thing to do to a fellow-clergyman! Still, they stayed friends, I think. Just.

At home we decided to attend Christ Church, Beckenham, about half-a-mile away. The Vicar, Herbert Cragg, had been there since 1956 when he left a northern parish, (thereby stranding one of my best friends, his newly ordained deacon, after only a few weeks who, I suspect, never forgave him. It helped to under-

mine my friend's subsequent ministry). On our arrival, his opening words to me were, believe it or not, a quotation from an
obscure part of the Old Testament, 'Hast thou found me, O mine
enemy?' He could hardly have made us less welcome, but we
stuck it for almost eighteen months until Rachel and Joe went on
strike. 'That Junior Church,' they said, 'is really bo-o-o-o-ring.'
And they were right. It was. We had all attended it as a family in
the Church Hall and the 'rite' had been invented by an earlier
vicar, in the 1920s. I used to 'go on' to the adult service in church
and was never once greeted (I wore collar and tie), in eighteen
months, other than by curates or churchwardens. The church had
a 'name' but it was utterly stuffy. Finally, Cragg insulted some of
my friends at a staff coffee party. They (in other parts of the country) needed defending and it became clear that, on both sides, the
Sawards ought not to stay. We left and joined St John's, Eden
Park, a mile away, where we were welcomed with open arms. The
contrast between the 'famous' and the 'unknown' Evangelical
churches was a lesson I have never forgotten. Herbert Cragg,
almost the only senior Evangelical to defend the Anglican-
Methodist reunion scheme, was promptly made an archdeacon.
Was there another lesson there?

If Cragg didn't want me, others certainly did. I began a
pre-Lent series of lunchtime lectures at St Giles, Cripplegate, in
the Barbican (Oliver Cromwell's church), and the first of a set of
talks and a weekend house-party for the Twenties group at All
Souls, Langham Place. Then Archbishop Coggan's sister, Norah,
a kind slave-driver of a woman, arrived at my office inviting me to
become the first national chairman of Message, a Christian telephone service. You didn't say no to Norah Coggan and I served in
that role for four years.

April and May were busy months. The Independent Television Authority sponsored a large conference at Canterbury at
which Michael Ramsey spoke and proposed a superb definition
of what did and did not constitute 'religious' television. His
definition did not please the radical ITA religious programmes
officer, Christopher Martin, who tried to avoid its impact. I, by
contrast, quoted it throughout my time at CIO. The radical view

was that 'Religion equals life. Therefore all programmes are religious.' This delighted the secularists, the humanists and the commercial operators, because it played right into their hands. All programmes, on this basis, were 'religious' so they could get away with anything – and they did. One senior television bureaucrat did his own reputation no good at the official dinner, when, in the Archbishop's presence, he sprawled, dead drunk, across the high table during the admittedly overlong speeches. How he survived in the job after that was hard to understand. His was, in my judgement, and not mine alone, a damaging influence to the churches' cause at a very crucial point in the history of religious broadcasting. Years later, with this underlying their concern, the General Synod's report *Broadcasting, Society, and the Church* urged that this particular post should only be of a seven-year term, and should not be filled without close consultation with the churches. The Independent Broadcasting Authority ignored the recommendation.

That year, my parents, Donald and Lily, moved from Petts Wood to St Giles-in-the-Wood in north Devon. My father had worked in the City for forty years, not counting his time in the army during the War, and after two heart attacks early in his retirement it was clear that he needed somewhere quiet. They found a converted Georgian stable in a ruined manor house, a quite delightful square of such houses, a mile from the nearest public road, and lived there until a few weeks before their deaths. It was a beautiful and safe place for the children to go on holiday, midway between Dartmoor and Exmoor, and an easy drive to the sea. Both our family, and my sister Moira's (when later she married), greatly enjoyed visiting them.

At the end of April, the American members of the Lambeth Conference media team came to scout out the ground. They stayed at, and dined us at, the Hyde Park Hotel, and one of them, a young blond-haired New Yorker of my own age and length of service in the ministry, Bob Libby, started a friendship with me that has gone on, and deepened ever since. He ran the radio and television operation for the Episcopal Church so our posts were in close parallel and we enjoyed the same kind of earthy sense of humour.

Another interesting person who invited me to his office a couple of weeks later was John Trevelyan. John was the key man at the British Board of Film Censors, in Soho Square, and we had a fascinating discussion about the principles by which he was governed and the pressures which came upon him almost everyday. This was the period in which sexual explicitness was more and more coming into vogue and John explained to me just how far he was prepared to go. At that point not one wisp of pubic hair had been seen in a British cinema but he knew perfectly well that he was going to be pushed by the French, the Italians and the Japanese, not to mention the Danes and the Swedes, all of whom were making films with nothing much left to the imagination. So far he had generally held the line on violence and drugs but the changing climate in Britain was clearly leading towards greater freedom in sexual issues. In a year or two the dykes would be breached, in his opinion. 'Are you depressed?' I asked him, adding, 'Has your Board got a future?' His answer was explicit and prophetic. 'I do feel depressed, very depressed,' he said. 'Organisations like this', he continued, 'ultimately cannot be a King Canute. We'd be out of business. Having said that and, in effect, undercut the very *raison d'être* of the Board, he bemoaned the 'deplorable stuff I see here ... I wouldn't want my children to get standards of morality entirely from the cinema. If you get enough violence, people get used to it.'

Later in the same week I landed one of the most 'in' events possible. For three or four years the mark of having 'arrived' on the London scene was to be asked to a small group breakfast with David Frost. This was better still. This was a private breakfast, alone with him, in his Egerton Crescent house in South Kensington. At 9 a.m. I presented myself, well aware that I was no more than a possible entry point to a programme between Frost and Michael Ramsey. In the event we talked little about that but, at his request, a great deal about why I was a Christian. He put me through the hoop, assuming that, like most clergy he met through the BBC, I would be a South Bank Radical of the Nick Stacey kind. The fact that I wasn't, that I seemed to believe in, and was quite ready to defend, the great credal doctrines, fascinated him. He wasn't sure whether he was a Christian, probably not, but he certainly believed in some kind of God, and found it hard to understand how a man could be a clergyman and hold lightly to the historic Christian beliefs as so many that he met did.

Four days later, in the middle of the 1968 Paris riots, I was invited to go to Alexandra Palace, where the BBC had a TV news studio, first, to watch the evening news, and then, later, give a 'Postscript' on the night's events. It was the first time I ever used an autocue (they called it a 'teleprompter' in those days) and I found it a great improvement on having to learn one's lines in advance. I took up the challenge of mob violence and the mindless slogan-chanting which accompanied orchestrated battles with the police. I also questioned the problem of 'the System' which so easily and impersonally could take control and against which the ordinary citizen felt so impotent. Christians, I added, were for 'law and order' in principle but not necessarily as applied by harsh governments. Then, in accordance with the programme's format, I prayed for all those involved.

Oliver Hunkin, son of a former Bishop of Truro, and an Anglican clergyman, had produced the programme, as a BBC staff member. He left me in very little doubt, though he was never quite explicit, that taking a balanced position was all wrong. The correct solution, in BBC eyes, was to throw all my weight behind the rioting students. Needless to say, I was not invited back. I was not entirely surprised, but still shocked to discover Old Etonians taking up so irresponsible a stance. I was, you realise, still naive enough to believe that members of the Establishment class would support the legal authorities. Not in the BBC in 1968.

Needing a break before the busy weeks of the summer, Jackie and I took off, with rucksacks, for Luxembourg. We spent our first night under the walls of a floodlit château in Clervaux and trained, bused and walked all over that little country. We had driven across it, quickly, in 1963 but now we were to give it a good inspection. Luxembourg city had, in its day, been a northern Gibraltar but its ducal palace took our breath away. The guards were comic opera characters and the front gates were flanked by a corsetière on one side and a fish-and-chip shop on the other. Buckingham Palace it wasn't. At dinner, Jackie consumed the *menu gastronomique* but we both avoided the 'grilled lamp shops'. These barbaric foreigners! In bed that night I read a new and thrilling publication, the *Revised Canon Law*. I followed this with Alan Bullock's *Hitler: A Study in Tyranny*. Travelling north, we came to Esch-sur-Sûre where we spent three days during which the sun shone for a full three minutes.

We ended our time by walking about twenty miles across the frontier, on a disused railway line, to Bastogne, centre of the 1944 Battle of the Bulge. Always on the lookout for evidence of battle-fields I was intrigued to see American tanks still, symbolically, guarding the town from eastern marauders coming out of the Ardennes.

A mere forty-eight hours later, I caught the plane from Heathrow to Oslo, as an English representative to the conference at which a new, amalgamated organisation, the World Associa-tion for Christian Communication, was being formed. We stayed at the University, intrigued by the road sign nearby saying 'Psychi-atric Clinic', which seemed somewhat prophetic. George Hoffman, my Edgware successor and now just launching TEAR Fund (a relief organisation) was also present, as was Douglas Brown, the BBC churches' correspondent, both of them good friends. We soon realised (all being journalists of one kind or an-other) that some horrific things were going on and the conference was spilling blood in all directions. The platform had been, meta-phorically, overturned. The Germans, being law-abiding, were threatening to go home. The English, Dutch and Canadians were enjoying the revolution and the French and Italians had no idea what was going on. The two most enjoyable memories were eat-ing reindeer in a high-class restaurant at the BBC's expense, and walking among the hundreds of nude statues by Wiegeland in the city's main park. I decided that the Scandinavians must have a fix-ation about nakedness. There was also a third event, a tea party for delegates in the King of Norway's summer palace. I still pos-sess a photo of George Hoffman and me helping ourselves to the superb delicacies on offer.

I returned by way of Copenhagen, Hamburg and Amsterdam, in all of which cities the evidence of burgeoning pornographic industries was only too obvious. In Copenhagen, even the W.H. Smith-type shops in the main street, were dominated by coloured photographs on glossy magazine covers, which were tastelessly obscene. These were not conventional 'girlie' photos – these were reminiscent of butchers' shops, in close up. I am not remotely prudish but Copenhagen, in the course of one evening, left me with no desire to return.

Back in Church House, CIO had at last moved to larger offices on the third floor and room 356 became mine (as it has been for my successors ever since). I decided, slightly tongue in cheek, to put up a copy of a Cranmer portrait on the main wall by my desk. 'That', I thought, 'should provide some interesting reactions.' So it proved. Two or three days later, Eric Treacy, Bishop of Wakefield, wandered in, stopped in front of the picture, and growled, 'What have you got that creep Cranmer up for?' I liked blunt Eric, and he got it straight between the eyes. 'When you've been burnt at the stake for your faith, you can call him a creep!' I replied. 'Huh,' grunted Eric aggressively, then smiled. 'You've got a point,' he said. We became very firm friends from that day. A Yorkshire bishop, he liked straight speaking, and he always got it from me. He delivered 'my' first speech in the House of Lords, a year later and signed 'my' first letter to *The Times* just before. 'You get the facts right, and I'll make the public noises,' he growled. He was as good as his word and, if I needed to get some points across in the media, Eric was my megaphone. It worked well. He needed the research and I needed the mouthpiece. He used my office as his private *pied-à-terre* from then on. They don't make bishops like that these days.

In quick succession, a young man named David Dimbleby rang me to enquire about the Lambeth Conference and a possible interview, and a not-so-young Malcolm Muggeridge met me. He and I would meet again and correspond on various occasions.

At last the Lambeth bishops arrived. There was a mini-row about the Lambeth booklet because Michael De-la-Noy had included, quite reasonably, some London restaurants in it. The puritan-end of the newspapers (such hypocrites) screamed at the lavish entertainment being encouraged and some clergy rose to the bait.

Then it was my turn. I had an excellent seat on 25 July in the organ loft at Canterbury Cathedral, 'bishop-spotting' for the television commentators. Ironically, it wasn't quite as good as the one I had had in Canterbury for Lambeth 1958 when, as a curate, I had found myself four feet from Michael Ramsey, at the very west end of the rows of diocesan clergy, right up against the various archbishops at the east end of the great steps leading to Augustine's Chair. Next day I was marshalling Donald Coggan, Trevor Huddleston and George Reindorp for another programme and two days after was in 'the gods' at Westminster Abbey for the opening London service on the Sunday. Like ham in a sandwich, the Saturday was chiefly taken up with a huge garden party at Lambeth, attended by 460 bishops and their wives. It was said that one American bishop was deeply offended because his mistress was not invited! I'm sure that story is true.

In the palace gardens, a huge queue formed of those wishing to pay their respects to Geoffrey Fisher. Geoffrey, the only bishop present wearing gaiters, apron, and a clerical top hat with strings attached, looked like a refugee from *Alice in Wonderland*. The contrast between the old and new episcopal worlds could hardly have been more strikingly demonstrated.

As the afternoon drew to its close, Jackie and I joined the 'Fisher-queue', now down to four. Eventually, the very last, we stood facing him. Eighty-one years old and an absolute pain to Michael Ramsey, his successor, Geoffrey's memory had been working full-time all afternoon. He saw me, paused, 'Now don't tell me,' he said pointing his finger. He looked again. 'Ah yes, got you,' he smiled. 'You're that young curate with whom I had all those arguments, ten years ago. Saward? Saward. That's it.' I told him what I was doing, what I had been doing. I gently pulled his leg by reminding him that, ten years before, I had been on holiday in Austria just before Lambeth '58 and had sent him a 'wish you were here' postcard to cheer him up. He bellowed cheerfully but obviously had no idea what I was talking about. We would only be in contact once or twice more before his death. Shortly before he died he signed a photograph of himself, Ramsey and Coggan, taken in 1961. All three signed my copy, probably the only signed photograph in existence of three consecutive Archbishops of Canterbury. I was moved four years later when I attended his memorial service at Canterbury, and, later, by his simple grave at Trent, in Dorset.

One more 'first' followed on the Monday. The Queen always gives a Buckingham Palace garden party for the Lambeth bishops, a far smaller number than the thousands at her annual summer garden parties. I attended, obeying instructions, in a black cassock. While walking around the garden, Jackie and I met John Capon, just appointed to succeed John King as editor of the *Church of England Newspaper*. We chatted amicably and I mentioned that George Hoffman and I had been to King Olaf's tea in Oslo, four weeks earlier, where the food had been magnificent. What happened next is in dispute. John duly published in the *CEN* that I, 'looking every inch a junior Lord Soper' in my cassock, had been complaining about the poor quality of the Buck House food. I questioned the veracity of this libel and wrote to the Queen's Press Officer, Bill Heseltine, apologising for what was a complete distortion of my remarks. Heseltine, as an Australian journalist himself, invited me to 'dismiss the episode from your mind' since 'nobody here noticed' or took it amiss. 'I know', he concluded, 'how difficult reporters, even old friends, find it to resist the temptation to crack a joke of this kind.'

The Lambeth Conference took place, for the most part, in Church House, so I sat in on a good deal of it. It was the subject of over a hundred radio and television programmes in Britain, and Jackie says that I have never recovered from finding four archbishops queuing outside my office to see me. If any man's humility is to be tested, how's that for starters?

The radio interview I best remember was one which I organised with Radio 1, late one evening, with Bishop Bill Frey, then of Guatemala, and later of Colorado. Bill, possessed of a richly 'dark brown' Texan accent, had once been a disc jockey and the BBC's pop channel couldn't resist having him on the programme. 'Why, Bishop,' said the interviewer, 'did you give up being a DJ?' Frey's reply convulsed the studio. 'Well, when I realised', he said, 'what an utterly stupid and futile job it was, I packed it in.' Without question, Bill Frey was the only bishop in the world who could have got away with saying that. It was a priceless moment in the history of broadcasting.

We all had one weekend off and I took Bob Libby away by car on an ancestor-crawl to Ross-on-Wye. We spent a night at Tyndale, in Bristol, and returned via Stonehenge. As we reached London, he asked whether I thought Michael Ramsey would autograph a cartoon he had drawn. 'I'll try it on him,' I said. The next time I was with the Archbishop I showed it to him. It showed Ramsey, with a mitre, askew on his head, reacting to a speech by Ted Welles, Bishop of West Missouri. Welles spoke incessantly at the conference, on every subject, prefacing his remarks in the approved manner with 'name and number'. His was 309. Libby's cartoon archbishop was saying 'M-m-my G-g-god. N-not 309 W-we-welles, W-we-west M-m-missouri, again!' Ramsey looked at it quizzically, even with some distaste. Then he said (and these were his actual words) 'Em-em-my. Gee-gee-god. En not 309 Doubleyou, wee, welles, Doubleyou, wee, west Em em Missouri, again. Not very funny.' He signed it and pushed it at me. One thing I knew for certain, Michael Ramsey, like most English (and unlike most American) bishops, would never have said 'My God' in that manner. Americans say 'my God' all the time and it grates on English Christian ears. So, objection number one. But what really intrigued me was the thought that Ramsey, by saying it all phonetically, just possibly didn't realise that he stuttered. What a thought! I've wondered about that ever since.

Lambeth was, without warning, up-staged by the publication by Pope Paul VI of his encyclical *Humanae Vitae* right in the middle of the conference. It was, ecumenically, extraordinarily tactless to produce the world-shattering repudiation of artificial contraception at such a moment, and it pushed Lambeth right off the front pages. The only consolation for Anglicans was that it allowed our bishops to distance themselves from Rome in no uncertain manner.

There is only one sensible thing to do after a gruelling Lambeth Conference and that is to go to the Oval for the final test match. That is exactly what I did on the Tuesday afternoon. It was one of the most astonishing last days in test history. Australia needed 352 in the final innings, but were 86 for five at lunch. I raced across from Westminster and arrived just as a freak storm inundated the playing area. The chance of further play seemed minimal but the sun came out, the ground staff started mopping up and half the spectators (or so it seemed) joined them in a desperate attempt to make play possible. The match restarted at a 4.45 p.m. with seventy-five minutes left. No wicket fell until 5.25 p.m.. The Australian opener, Inverarity, was the last to go with just five minutes left. Derek Underwood had taken four out of the last five wickets, taking seven for 50 in the innings. It was compellingly exciting and put both the Lambeth Conference and the Pope's encyclical back into perspective.

The Archbishop and I went to Bushey for the day on 1 October. I had given them a very clear indication that they were not to be sycophantic but to give him a 'normal' day course and be as critical as necessary. Cyril Thomas (he was still there at this stage) had said, 'We Methodists have no fear of an Archbishop of Canterbury – of course we'll be as tough as is needed.' On our way, I mentioned in the car that Thomas was what I called a 'Methodist auntie' and Ramsey repeated the phrase somewhat quizzically. The day was a disaster. Thomas and his assistants oozed oil over Ramsey, said the equivalent of 'Darling, you were marvellous,' and I was left to make the only critical remarks offered, which they immediately tried to minimise. I was privately very angry because Ramsey had gone there looking for some solid, and probably critical, advice and had been totally let down. This fiasco was to play its part in Thomas's eventual sacking.

As we drove out of the gates on our way back to Lambeth, Ramsey started to chuckle. 'Methodist auntie, Methodist auntie, mm-mm-yes, yes, quite right, quite right.' I apologised for the disappointing day but all I got was further repeats of 'Methodist auntie, Methodist auntie' and a broad grin.

John Andrew, his chaplain, moved on after Lambeth and (the bishops having urged the appointment of a bishop to the chaplain's job) was succeeded by Geoffrey Tiarks, who also became Bishop of Maidstone. He was older, quite delightful, and mischievous in a very cheerful way. He was quite capable of sending you into the Archbishop's study and telling you an excruciatingly funny joke as you appeared in front of Ramsey, which reduced you to helpless laughter.

Andrew's going did, however, leave the childless Ramseys lacking a 'crown prince' and, to many people, it appeared that Michael De-La-Noy had set his cap on claiming that role. One by one, person after person at Lambeth and in Church House was alienated leaving them with the feeling that he was slowly empire-building at everyone else's expense. This went on for over eighteen months before the axe eventually fell.

In the meantime, the Archbishop continued regularly taking part in radio and television programmes. Many were in studios but some were filmed in the palace. One such piece of filming nearly brought disaster. Colour television was in its infancy and, in any case, television needs plenty of colour to use its potential. On the morning in question I arrived at the palace to discover that Joan Ramsey had allocated a room for our use which had been decorated pretty well all over in white. This was absolutely useless for colour television and I knew that the producer would, when he arrived, take one look and call the whole thing off. I couldn't take that chance and I only had about half an hour to play with. At Lambeth there was one piece of fixed advice which all the staff obeyed without question and which all newcomers, me included, were told on our appointment: 'Don't ever try to get Mrs Ramsey to change any room allocation. There is no way she will and you will probably end up with blood on your nose if you ignore this.'

What on earth should I do? I made a decision and I made it quite deliberately. I would attempt, metaphorically that is, to seduce Joan Ramsey. I would flirt with her, flatter her, make her feel an important and exciting woman, and I would do it in less than fifteen minutes. Now believe it, or believe it not, that is exactly what I did and in just under fifteen minutes I got her to change the allocated room for one whose colour scheme and decorations were more appropriate. The programme went ahead as planned,

Joan Ramsey smiled sweetly at me and never stopped doing so from that day until her death. I only hope she didn't realise what I was up to.

Adam and I were asked to organise a Bushey course for diocesan bishops which we duly did in late October. We got about fifteen of them, ranging from the pompous to the racy. One of the former, Basil Guy of Gloucester, arrived at the retreat house in St Albans where we had our overnight accommodation and proceeded to launch into me for the discourteous way in which I had addressed him in the invitatory letter. I had begun it with 'Dear Bishop' rather than the traditional 'My Lord'. I explained politely that Church House was using the new formula since this had been requested by the recent Lambeth Conference and we were merely obeying orders. 'That's nonsense,' pontificated Guy. 'I intend to be, and expect to be, addressed as "My Lord" till the day I die, so don't you forget it, young man.' He stormed off to get himself a drink.

Somewhat shaken, I was accosted by a younger bishop, John Trillo (whose daughter-in-law has typed this book) who grinned and said, impishly, 'And I thought that dinosaurs were extinct.' He cheered me up no end. Incidentally, one bishop in my curacy days had replied to a 'My Lord' letter which ended, as was the old custom, 'I remain, Your Lordship's obedient servant,' that he wouldn't like to put that statement to the test. Well, there's no pleasing some bishops!

Church House assembly hall was, in mid-October, the scene for a meeting organised under the auspices of the Evangelical Alliance. Very few press representatives were present but a pretty young journalist from the Press Association was sitting up in the gallery next to the CIO seats so I sat next to her and explained who and what I was. She asked me a question. 'These Evangelicals,' she said, 'are they snake-worshippers?' I've been asked some strange questions in my time but that was probably the most outrageous. Snake worshippers? She got a comprehensive introduction to Evangelicalism and I then wrote, or vetted, most of her story.

Occasionally I found myself uneasy about a speech or sermon from Michael Ramsey which our office was required to publicise.

On one occasion I went to see the Archbishop and, taking my life into my hands, told him that a sermon about to be preached had no distinctively Christian content. 'I could have got it from the Chief Rabbi,' I said. It felt strangely like a rerun of my comment to Evered Lunt, the Dean of Bristol, back in the early 1950s. The only difference was, I suppose, that now I had some measure of responsibility for advising Ramsey, which hadn't been the case earlier. He looked slightly taken aback. I pursued my point. 'You refer to God,' I said, 'but nowadays the word "God" isn't limited to Christians. Many Anglican leaders think that to mention "God" is to make a Christian statement. It might have been so in the Europe of past centuries. It certainly isn't today. We must have more of a Christ-focus.' Ramsey stayed silent for a few seconds. Then, 'Er-er, mm-mm, yes. Yes, I'll add something, add something. Yes, yes.' And he did.

On a later, not dissimilar occasion, I went even further about an exposition of a passage from one of St Paul's letters to the Corinthians. 'Archbishop,' I said tentatively, 'are you sure you are right to interpret it that way? I've looked up six or seven major commentaries and none takes your view.' Discussing theology or the Bible was never a problem with Michael Ramsey. He would have done it all day and every day, given the chance. 'Yes,' he agreed, 'yes, lots of them do take that view, but I think, yes, yes, I think, you will find, you will find, erm, erm, erm, that the new *Peake* takes my view, takes my view, yes, yes, yes,' and he smirked triumphantly.

I looked up the new *Peake* and it flatly disagreed with him, offering the standard interpretation. Even I hadn't got the nerve to tell him that. He had, after all, been Regius Professor of Divinity at Cambridge and though he wasn't the only one of them that I tangled with, I had to draw the line somewhere. What was so enjoyable was the realisation that he wasn't even remotely offended at a young clergyman putting him on the spot. In that respect he and Fisher, otherwise so temperamentally different, seemed to welcome an attitude that was combative, so long as one was polite.

Shortly before Christmas I travelled to Belfast by air, to take part in a weekend house-party for Queen's University chaplaincy, organised by Cecil Kerr. On the Saturday, Belfast was the scene of a large civil rights march, one of the unwitting triggers for the quarter-century's violence which was to follow. I preached in the university chapel on the Sunday, then flew home, hardly aware of what a significant date it was to be in Ulster's history.

An event that stands out vividly took place on the evening of Sunday 5 January 1969. David Frost, avid for national publicity, organised a great party for some two thousand of his friends and acquaintances at the Alexandra Palace. This enormous building had within it a vast fairground and all the 'attractions' were free. I still possess a magnificent photograph of Bishop Mervyn Stockwood, recklessly driving a 'dodgem' car, with, as his highly apprehensive passenger, Lord Longford, looking as miserable as any man in that fearful situation might. Stockwood was attended, as was his custom, by two young clergymen in black ties and dinner jackets, whose task was to keep him vertical and drive him home, his reputation for the copious consumption of hard liquor being notorious. On that occasion, one of his 'flankers' was Michael Whinney, later Bishop of Southwell, and the other was probably Michael Mayne, lately Dean of Westminster. *Tout le monde*, if not exactly *tout le demi-monde*, were present. Jackie and I tried just about everything, recognised large numbers of the very famous and the would-be very famous, and returned home with a cuddly toy of huge proportions which I had won with my skill at the shooting gallery.

Forty-eight hours later, Tony Waite and I conducted a crowded memorial service for Richard Allen, in Church House Chapel. Tony had been his vicar at St George's, Leeds. Richard's life, since Liverpool, had drifted for eighteen months, until one day, driving on the motorway, he fell asleep at the wheel, and was killed. That, at any rate, was the verdict and as no-one will ever know exactly what happened, it seems the most likely cause. Richard had, prior to his four uneasy Liverpool years, been the creative mind behind the crypt centre for down-and-outs in the basement at Leeds, and he was an amazingly gifted and creative man. He and his wife, Mollie, were a highly improbable couple. She was an Irish doctor and they had married quite late. How or why their marriage came apart I never knew but they had been separated for many months before his death. All in all, it was an especially sad memorial service because, however hard it had been to work with Richard, no-one could doubt his genius.

Talking of creative genius, Irving Allen Ltd., the film producers, recognised mine by offering me, in mid-January, a contract to be 'Technical Adviser for Religious Questions' to the coming film *Cromwell*, which they were about to make. They paid me £250 (worth perhaps ten times that in today's money) for which I did remarkably little and every single thing that I did by way of 'technical religious advice' they totally ignored. I received scripts, as revised, from 'first' to 'final shooting', and then 'paperback of the film'. The factual errors which I pointed out, repeatedly, were as evident in both film and book as in the first script. People, long-since dead, made speeches. King Charles I conversed with Cromwell, long before they ever met. The churches were furnished quite improbably, and major pieces of such furniture were hopelessly confused. I learnt one important lesson which was that rewriting history was as much done by Hollywood as by the Soviet Union, and that the former were just as cynical as the latter when it came to crucifying truth. 'It doesn't really matter,' they told me. 'Hardly anyone will know.'

One Friday evening in late April I was standing at the window of our house in Beckenham when suddenly a yellow-greenish ball of light flashed across the evening sky. I rang the *Daily Mail* (why them I can't recall) to report it and the story made the next day's front page. It was, so the Royal Observatory claimed, either 'a big meteorite or a piece of old space ironmongery'. Another skywatcher claimed that it was Russia's Cosmos 265 satellite burning out as it re-entered Earth's atmosphere. The remains of it landed in north Wales. I thought no more of it until months later someone sent me a cutting from an American newspaper in which I was quoted by name as having seen 'a UFO'. It implied that I was claiming it as some kind of space-ship. They didn't actually say that I had seen little green men but their readers could well have presumed that a London clergyman was supporting such an appearance. Was this, I wondered, the way in which such stories are fabricated? All I had said to the *Mail* was that 'I thought it was a comet.'

On 8 July 1969, the Church Assembly and the Methodist Conference both voted on the proposals of the Anglican-Methodist reunion scheme. The Methodists voted for the union but the Anglican vote fell well short of the required seventy-five per cent. It was my job to put through the telephone call from the Archbishop to the Secretary of the Methodist Conference in Birmingham and I surreptitiously tape-recorded Ramsey's end of the conversation. He did his utmost to play down the failure (which unknown to him was to be repeated even more disastrously three years later). Eventually he asked to be put through to the President and added, 'By the way, who is your President?' I was stunned. We were at the crucial point of a possible merger and the Archbishop didn't even know the name of the Methodist President.

Back in the world of television, especially in Independent Television, the 'clever' men and women in the various religious departments were either bright postgraduates, being given a chance to shine where success or failure didn't much matter, or old warhorses being put out to grass before retirement. Religious convictions, especially among the former, seemed to be of no consequence. I found myself in a particularly tricky situation. As the only 'official' Church of England character around, I was presumably supposed to interpret the views of the hierarchy to those in senior positions. This, on formal occasions, I did but my more difficult job was to keep in some kind of creative relationship in the world of Independent Television with the company-appointed Anglican Advisers. These were all appointed, with fairly minimal consultation with the church authorities, and given (or so it seemed) limitless contracts. One of them, appointed in 1968, was still occupying the same advisory post twenty-five years later, despite the plea of the General Synod report for their contracts to be limited to seven years.

My relationship with those Anglican Advisers was very uneasy in most (but not all) cases. To my mind, many of them (like my predecessor David Skinner) were only too obviously merely endorsing the increasingly radical, or secular, programme policies of their company employers but, perhaps not too surprisingly, they were hardly welcoming to my anxious and, occasionally, critical comments in this respect. One of the more sympathetic ones wrote pointing out that the hostility of those particular advisers was resulting from the fact that they 'know that you are right but don't like you being so aware of it yourself!' This group, he said, 'assume that you are bound to be engaged in some form of low intrigue, because the television world abounds in low intrigue!' He concluded, 'Keep on coming, and let them growl.'

The undercurrent of religious and commercial company politics reached a significant point in a series produced by Tyne Tees Television, a small regional company, in 1969. I was present in Newcastle when some of the programmes were being made and stayed up half the night discussing religious issues with the stars of the series – Cliff Richard, David Winter, Cindy Kent, and others – all of whom were excited and very positive about the storyline. Entitled *Life with Johnny*, the six programmes retold Gospel parables with Cliff Richard, a major entertainer even in 1969, indeed as he had been for the previous fifteen years, as 'Johnny'. The series had been made with the Independent Television Authority's encouragement and had involved Tyne Tees in a major investment. The programmes were far better quality productions than was then normal for 'closed period' religious material and functioned at a level, and with a style, much closer to teenagers than was usual.

The time came to show the series and the four 'network' companies declined to show them – these companies, London Weekend, ATV, Yorkshire and Granada, transmitted to all the major areas of population and their attitude had large financial implications not only for Tyne Tees but also for the livelihood of other regional companies investing large sums in religious programmes which wouldn't get 'networked' by the 'big boys'.

The result was that an excellent 'biblical' series, 'featuring an internationally famous Christian singer', as the *Broadcasting* report described it, 'was lost to network audiences'. The religious press asked all the right questions and the ITV companies and the ITA executives gave evasive answers. What had happened? According to one ITA executive, 'The network people saw it and didn't feel that it reached the required standard and their panel of Religious Advisers didn't question this decision.' At that point the ITA's annual report was published and tried to gain credit by calling the series 'a notable event' (not mentioning its non-transmission by all the network companies). Asked to comment on this piece of hypocrisy, the ITA executive said that 'notable event' did not 'imply success'. I asked the executive why he thought it was that a dozen Anglican bishops, shown the series, thought it was 'first class' and deplored the limited showing? Their view, said Mr ITA, was 'subjective'. The 'ITA advisers didn't agree'. But, I pursued him, 'the Bishops are much more representative of church opinion' than your advisers 'who weren't appointed by the church'. ITA's response was to say that mine was 'a tendentious reading' of the situation. 'Well,' I concluded, 'it's a view widely held in the church.' These quotations come from notes made at the time and are verbatim.

I cite this incident in detail because it illustrated the degree of politicking going on. Some months later an Anglican Adviser, who had been present at the key meeting, told me that the network companies, the 'big boys', had deliberately killed *Johnny* as a commercial prospect, because they didn't want a small regional company to muscle in on their territory with a successful religious series. In this they were aided and abetted by Radical Anglican Advisers who didn't like the 'open-and-shut religion portrayed by the parables'.

David Frost, soon after, referring to similar attitudes in religious television, said to me, personally, 'I try to bring God into my programmes but these people are trying to keep God out of religious programmes.' Again the words are verbatim.

Months later, I was discussing some of these issues with Bernard Sendall, the Deputy Director of the ITA. I suggested that the Authority and the Companies were concealing their real (and frequently commercial motivation) behind a smokescreen of moral platitudes intended to deceive the churches. 'You amaze me,' he said. 'I thought Christians were supposed to believe the best about other people?' 'No,' I replied, 'we believe in original sin, and think we can recognise its implications when we see them.' He walked off angrily.

As the months went by I realised, more and more, just how much the broadcasting organisations were, as it appeared, consciously deceiving the church and its leaders into assuming that their motives were of the highest, and thoroughly Reithian, when in reality their philosophies were, in the case of Independent Television, ruthlessly commercial, and in the case of the BBC constantly forced into a ratings battle, in which the traditional values of religious and ethical organisations were slowly eroded by the war to get maximum audiences.

In September 1969 *The Times* published a letter from me on the subject of television violence, prompted by my having seen a pre-transmission presentation of BBC2's version of Kazantzakis' *Christ Re-crucified* in which, as one member of the studio audience put it, the camera 'lingered lovingly' on the horrors of throat-cutting, emasculation, and quartering. As a result of the private audience's objections, the BBC cut the most horrific elements from the publicly shown programme. This wise editing was objected to by the critic, Michael Billington, in a *Times* review, to which I replied. My objection, I said, was to the overstepping by the BBC of its own published code on TV violence. This letter was the first of thirty-nine of mine published in *The Times*.

By this stage it was becoming increasingly clear to me that I was a 'voice in the wilderness' and that the Church of England needed to speak at top level if these issues were to be heard at national level. Two things followed. I was invited to speak to the Royal Television Society and did so, trenchantly, with the 'personal authorisation of the Archbishops of Canterbury and York, the Bishop of London, and the Church Information Advisory Committee'. My paper put its finger on most of the key issues and while it provoked, in expected quarters, an unfavourable reaction, this, I was told, was because the broadcasting executives present, 'although they recognised the authority with which you were able to speak, didn't like hearing it from someone of your "status" '. Reading it in print, 'a lot of people were most impressed by it'. Further evidence that, however correct my points, and however 'authorised' they were, 'top people' would only take them, if at all, from the church's 'top people', of whom I clearly wasn't one.

My next stage was to urge the setting up of a major debate in the Church Assembly on broadcasting, out of which would come a commission and a report, which could form the basis for the church's submission to the inevitably forthcoming government commission or committee which would be needed in readiness for the new BBC Charter and Television Act due in 1976.

The debate took place in 1970 and the General Synod Broadcasting Commission was set up under the chairmanship of Sir William Hart, formerly Director General of the Greater London Council, and met twenty-six times prior to the publication of its report in 1973. It received written oral evidence from a mass of organisations and individuals and its *Broadcasting* report was far and away the largest document of its kind, before or since, to come from the Church of England.

It makes sense to complete, at this point, the story of the *Broadcasting* report, although it will take us well out of our chronological sequence. The members of the Commission were chosen to form a cross-section of Anglican life, both in churchmanship and in general 'cultural' style. Those giving evidence included members of both Houses of Parliament, nineteen members of the BBC (including the Chairman of the Governors, the Director of Public Affairs and two Heads of Religious Broadcasting), eleven members of the ITA (including the Chairman and two Deputy Directors) and Network Companies, and a huge range of national organisations (including the British Humanist Association and the National Secular Society), plus fifty-seven individuals. Naturally, a wide range of bishops, clergy, lay readers and church bodies also submitted evidence.

The balance of opinion on a number of crucial issues moved quite decisively as interviewing took place. The Commission began with no clear stance *vis-à-vis* the various broadcasting authorities but the evidence from critics and the mandarin attitudes of senior broadcasting executives moved almost the whole Commission to take up a more critical stance. In particular, Kenneth Lamb, a senior BBC executive, under polite but sustained questioning, lost his temper with the Commission and did considerable damage to the Corporation's credibility in areas of major policy. The view developed that if such an attitude could exist at this level of discussion then allegations of dismissive and rude behaviour adopted towards less prestigious individuals and organisations seemed likely to be authentic. The report was, as a result, moderately critical.

It was, however, on publication in mid-October 1973, generally well received in the religious press but was then either ignored or treated dismissively by both sides of the broadcasting world. Almost the only hostile treatment in the serious press came from *The Times* Religious Affairs Correspondent, Clifford Longley, who was later to report the Synod debate in a very loaded way. Synod debated it on 8 November, when sixteen speeches were made. Ten of these welcomed the report with varying degrees of support, three others spoke in general terms. Only three were hostile, and the speech from Robert Runcie, Bishop of St Albans and Chairman of the Central Religious Advisory Committee (the key committee appointed by the BBC) had, almost of necessity, to be a defence of the BBC.

The most damaging speech of all came from the newly appointed Bishop of Durham, making his maiden speech in the Synod. Dr John Habgood launched into a speech of great hostility. My own view, listening to it, was that he had probably been 'nobbled' by someone senior in the BBC. His speech alone, out of the sixteen, caused considerable disquiet and when he urged the Synod not even 'to receive the report' (the normal procedural motion), only a handful took that extreme advice. The report was commended for diocesan discussion in their synods by a substantial majority (162 votes to 108), though a further motion seeking financial consideration of a series of consequential recommendations about training and an advisory system was not passed.

The report, being the fruit of all my work between 1967 and 1973, while accepted and passed to the dioceses, had effectively been wrecked by John Habgood's attitude and I have always found it hard to forgive him. When in 1994, a young BBC official, quite unaware of the report's existence, read it at my suggestion, he came back saying how prophetic it had been.

To add insult to injury, the chairman allowed Habgood to speak for a full fifteen minutes (ten is the maximum permitted), an extension of time virtually never granted to a Synod member. In his speech he, in his own words, spoke 'heatedly', accusing the report of 'inaccuracy' and 'serious bias', and arguing that there was 'no case for saying . . . that there has been a radical change of philosophy in the BBC'. His final insult was to accuse the Commission of 'deliberate distortion'. Such gross offensiveness was not acceptable in General Synod debating and he was forced, at the end of the debate, to 'unreservedly withdraw' the word 'deliberate' which he had uttered, he explained, 'in the heat of the moment'. He did not apologise.

I at once wrote to *The Times*, which had given substantial coverage to Habgood's hostile remarks, in a piece by Clifford Longley. As one of the Commission's secretaries I had hoped that they would publish a corrective but, although the editor set up two-thirds of my letter in print (which he sent to me) he did not carry it in the paper as they were, he said, 'very pressed at the moment'.

The report, generally welcomed by the religious press, remains in my judgement a largely accurate document which was unpopular among Liberal churchmen because it was far too explicit in its criticisms of the radical and materialistic dominance all too evident in the major broadcasting organisations of the time. I believe that John Habgood and, to a lesser extent, Robert Runcie, whether knowingly or not, misled the church and played into the hands of the mandarins in the BBC, IBA and ITV companies. The general unwillingness of these organisations to permit the report's charges to be debated on television showed them as they all too often were – liberal to all except those who disagreed with them.

As the ultimate originator of the need for a commission and a report, I have to recognise, sadly, that I lost that battle. In those days the Liberals were simply too well-placed and well-connected to permit an orthodox Christian view to gain a fair hearing. But it was not only the church which lost, once more nation was sold short on its Christian heritage – religious, ethical and traditional –

in the name of 'enlightenment', since much of what the report prophesied has come to pass and Habgood and Runcie need to carry some of the responsibility.

Soon after, Kenneth Lamb was appointed Secretary to the Church Commissioners, following his time with the BBC. When this was first announced to a Commissioners' plenary meeting, I asked, perhaps tactlessly, whether he would be a suitable candidate for the office if he could not control his temper and I cited the Broadcasting Commission's experience. Bishop David Say, a senior diocesan bishop, who was a close associate of Lamb's, was obviously far from pleased with me for asking such a question. From then onwards for years he treated me with disdain. I don't doubt that Lamb was soon made aware of the incident. He had a very long memory and I never made the mistake of trusting him in his years at 1 Millbank. He was always charming in public but I had no confidence that he could be relied upon to act dispassionately. The incident with the Broadcasting Commission had revealed a deep flaw in his character and it was not the only one.

My one consolation in all this was that my own stance, and the report on broadcasting, were consistently endorsed wherever and whenever I spoke to ordinary church people and massively supported, in essence, in a debate on broadcasting in the London diocesan Synod. The voting was 168 in favour and 12 against, with only one contrary voice raised in the debate.

Around that time there was a heated controversy concerning grants made by the World Council of Churches to what were variously described as 'terrorists' or 'freedom fighters' depending on the speaker's political stance. To my surprise, for reasons I cannot now recall, I found myself conducting a telephone conversation, on Michael Ramsey's behalf, with Albert van den Heuvel, the World Council's man in Geneva. I had seen something of Albert in religious television conferences and seminars and knew him to be one of the most extreme Dutch Radicals working for the Council.

'Why', I asked, 'did not the WCC ensure that it made its grants to bodies on both sides of the political spectrum? I know the Archbishop would have found it easier if this had happened.' Van den Heuvel was clearly very surprised. Then came an extraordinary admission. 'We gave grants to those in right-wing countries fighting for their freedom simply because no-one needs to fight for freedom in left-wing countries. Surely that's obvious, isn't it?' That, in one sentence, just about summed up the bias so dominant in World Council circles. I hope van den Heuvel was still around to see the end of the Berlin Wall and the collapse of Communism and Socialism in Eastern Europe.

We must now return to my day-to-day life. Rosanne went off on a world tour and she was replaced by her cousin Sue Cole. She worked as my secretary for almost all my remaining time at Church House.

One major aspect of my job naturally concerned Michael Ramsey's broadcasting. He was a strangely ambiguous character. Put him in an interview with someone like Ludovic Kennedy, who was as sharp as a razor, and his answers were brilliant, even if he sometimes seemed dithery and eccentric. In the five years that I worked for him I can hardly recall any occasion when what he said was not incisive, coherent and, in Christian terms, totally orthodox. Listen to him carefully and he was compellingly persuasive. Indeed the closer people got to him the more they admired, respected and loved him.

It was my task to advise him about which requests for radio and television interviews he should accept. As a general rule the top men got him and the others didn't but on three occasions I took a big risk with unexpected consequences. All were in the early 1970s. The first came when I was invited to lunch in a Beauchamp Place restaurant with Simon Dee and Barry Took. Dee had made his name as a disc jockey of a very trendy kind, whose stock-in-trade was lightweight interviews with typical show-biz personalities. An old boy of Shrewsbury School, his actual name was Carl Henty-Dodd. As the lunch progressed he and Took presented their case for a long and serious interview on London Weekend Television in which Dee would be simple Joe Bloggs, the man on the Clapham Omnibus, asking the kind of questions about ordinary life, human behaviour and religious belief, which never got asked by the top-level political interviewers who were usually out to trap their guests. I warmed to the idea and, after much debate, so did Ramsey. It would be unhurried and transmitted at a peak audience time. Together they made the programme and it was one of the best interviews he ever did. Dee made no attempt to trick him and he put many of the queries which ordinary viewers would find just to their taste.

Then the 'politicking' started. London Weekend didn't like Dee. They wanted him out. They certainly didn't want him associated with archbishops or any other national heavyweights. In next to no time he had gone and the ITV network was faced with the embarrassment of a major, full-length interview with the Archbishop of Canterbury, which they didn't wish to transmit. In the event, if my memory is right, they put it out in competition with a major international football match which ensured it a minority audience. Dee virtually vanished overnight and has never made any major reappearance on television.

The second event proved to be a fiasco, though an amusing one. A conference 'American Women in Media' was held in the Royal Garden hotel in Kensington and, as a gesture to transatlantic goodwill, Ramsey agreed to do a short interview. We took the lift to the top floor to a huge room overlooking Kensington Gardens and Ramsey sat down facing a lady of indeterminate age. The cameras began to roll and she launched into her first questions. After thirty seconds I interrupted and said, 'Excuse me, but who do you think this is you are interviewing?' She looked surprised and said, 'It's Adam Faith, isn't it?'

The Archbishop and I moved to another set where a second lady of indeterminate age and a similar lavender rinse set out to coax him into some indiscretion. 'Orchbishop,' she croaked, 'we just love having you on our show. Why, I do remember the las' time you were with us in Las Vegas you said what ay beautiful city it was . . .' 'N-n-no,' said Ramsey, 'I think y-y-you will find that I said what an "in-ter-est-ing" city it was. Yes, mm-mm-in-ter-esting-yes yes.' The interview slid slowly to a halt. 'Goodbye, goodbye, mm-mm.' And we left.

Some months later, the third risk involved the Archbishop in appearing on Yorkshire Television's hugely popular, but controversial, spoonful of sugar called *Stars on Sunday*. Its audience was easily the largest for any allegedly religious programme, often reaching fourteen million Sunday by Sunday. The brainchild of Jess Yates, it was described by the Broadcasting Commission's report as 'sentimentalised fantasy . . . a pretty world of sweet girls and handsome young men, in gothic-arched chapels' where 'angelic children hug elderly ladies' knees to the strains of . . . *Take thou this rose*, cowboys sing American gospel songs to their horses and serried ranks of West Riding policemen in bow-ties thunder out the Hallelujah Chorus *fortissimo*'.

Let me own up. I wrote that section of the report so I'm quoting myself. It was, then, with eyes wide open, that I urged Michael Ramsey to take part in *Stars on Sunday*. Archbishop Donald Coggan of York had already done so, as had the Roman Catholic Cardinal Heenan. Others strenuously urged Ramsey not to descend to such banality but he agreed to participate. Jess Yates sat him in a huge upright shiny leather armchair and handed him a beautifully bound, but archaic, Authorised Version of the Bible. It was massive and perfectly geared to the pseudo-mediaeval set. 'No,' said Ramsey, 'I've brought my own New English Bible.' Yates fought for five minutes but Ramsey was absolutely adamant. So, New English Bible it was. The plain green binding. Poor old Jess. He wanted schmaltz and he oozed syrup but his heart was a lump of toughened steel. In Michael Ramsey he met his match.

Talking of Yorkshire Television, I went one day to their Leeds studios to meet their Anglican Adviser, Brandon Jackson, who had got his job partly on my recommendation of him to Archbishop Donald Coggan. As I entered through the revolving door I came within two feet of Eartha Kitt who was standing there. It was a mesmerising experience. Kenneth Tynan once described her as 'a coloured singer with the daintiness of a wax figurine and the arrogance of an Arab pony'. What an understatement! I have never, before or since, come within touching range of a woman who radiated such raw sexual power. I had long enjoyed her singing, had some of her records, been aware of her feline humour, but that was as nothing alongside this pulsating volcano, steaming with erotic heat. Wow!

Mary Whitehouse was another powerful lady. Not exactly Eartha Kitt but no slouch either. I twice went to Birmingham to sit in, incognito, on her annual rally at the Midland hotel. On one occasion her chairman, a senior policeman, called on all present to vote on a motion denouncing a recent BBC television play. As a large number of hands rose, I called from the back of the hall, suggesting that it would surely be wiser to discover how many people had actually seen the broadcast before they voted to condemn it. He tried to dismiss my point but I reminded him that the press were present and that it would presumably not be to anyone's advantage to call for a vote until the number of viewers had been established. Very reluctantly he agreed, asked for those who had seen the play to identify themselves. About six hands rose. 'Mr Chairman,' I said, 'I think I've saved you and your organisation from making fools of yourselves.' He wasn't best pleased at my intervention because he had made a complete fool of himself. Needless to say, the press descended on me. I refused to identify myself so they didn't get the story they were wanting.

A year later I went again and this time returned in the train to London with the main speaker, David Frost. We had a compartment to ourselves and well over two hours to talk as the train ran late. He had gushed all over Mary in the meeting but was vitriolic about her to me. I like David and have since enjoyed being on his programme but I was not impressed with his Januslike performance on that day. I frequently disagreed with Mary but respected her courage at standing up when all the odds were against her. She was terribly naive when she started out but she learnt fast and deserved better from church leaders who were mostly terrified of being identified with anyone who resisted the radical Liberalism of the 1960s and 1970s.

The members of the religious press group met on a regular basis. Mostly they were staff members of the Christian newspapers but others, like me, were encouraged to join them. On one occasion, their chief guest was Charles Curran, Director-General of the BBC. Controversy had been raging about visible signs of sexuality in BBC drama. 'Where', enquired one of the more pious journalists (and there aren't many of them), 'do you draw the line on bosoms, Mr. Curran?' Curran, a practising Roman Catholic, hesitated only briefly. 'Well, it depends', he said, 'on the bosom.' I'll remember that, I thought, and I have. I doubt if Mary Whitehouse would have settled for such an evasive answer.

I was due to attend a special meeting in Chester of the 'Call to the North' programme, sponsored by Archbishop Donald Coggan of York, and I stayed the previous night with Sue Cole's sister Serena Campbell-Lambert and her husband at Burlton Hall, just north of Shrewsbury. Early on the Monday morning, 13 July 1970, I was in the bath when John, the husband, banged on the door. I emerged dripping water and he handed me a transistor radio. 'Your wife's just rung to ensure that you listen to the Radio 4 news.'

I returned to the bath and a few minutes later heard that my colleague, Michael De-la-Noy, had been sacked by the Archbishop of Canterbury. He had written an article for *Forum* magazine, a so-called counselling magazine dealing exclusively with sexual matters. I was not surprised for I knew that almost all De-la-Noy's associates both at Lambeth Palace and Church House had become heartily sick of his general behaviour and would weep no tears at his going. Indeed I had little doubt that the *Forum* article was simply the last straw.

Then a quite different penny dropped in my brain. My last act on the previous Friday night had been to place on Adam Block's desk the final typed draft, completed by Sue Cole that day, of my latest book *And So to Bed?* All hell would break loose with De-la-Noy's dismissal: the press would besiege Adam and the Church Information Office and the first thing that he would discover on his desk was a completed book on sex by Michael Saward, the second of his two lieutenants, while he was fighting off problems caused by his other assistant, also a Michael, on the subject of . . . sex! At top speed I leapt out of the bath, grabbed some clothes, discovered the phone, rang Sue and urged her to get from her Chelsea flat to Westminster at top speed to remove, with all haste, my book from Adam's desk. She did so, Adam was none the wiser until, weeks later, I told him to his considerable amusement. He was happy with my book when he read it but extremely glad that it hadn't appeared on his desk on the day of De-la-Noy's swift departure.

De-la-Noy ('just a scribbler' – his own words) hurriedly cobbled together a book about his time with Michael Ramsey, entitled *A Day in the Life of God*. Ramsey was shocked by its tone. 'A thousand pities,' he said to me, 'a thousand pities that it was ever written.'

That was just one of many comments as we drove around London on our way to various broadcasting studios. The others that I recall from that time relate to the appointment of bishops in the days when prime ministers did not have a Crown Appointments commission to advise them. 'Who actually chooses bishops?' I asked, perhaps tactlessly. 'I do, in the southern Province; Donald does in the northern Province; we tell each other, then propose the name to the prime minister.' Others claim that Michael Ramsey gave them quite different answers. I can't comment on that except to say that I am reporting verbatim what he said to me.

I remember thanking him for the appointment of Maurice Wood as Bishop of Norwich. 'I know that the Evangelicals greatly appreciate it,' I said. Wood was the first of our number to be so appointed. 'Yes,' he replied, with the twinkle in his eye, 'and how long will it be before they repudiate him?' He knows our lot, I thought, remembering the tendency of certain Evangelicals to write off anyone made a bishop. And then came the waspish punchline. 'Not', he stuttered, 'a very great brain, I think.'

On the third occasion we were passing the Cenotaph in Whitehall. He was grumbling away about so-called Evangelical bishops (none of whom seemed to be so to me). 'They simply won't stand up and be counted,' he complained. Later, as we returned, I mentioned my good friend John Stott, Rector of All Souls, Langham Place, but never given any further preferment, despite his worldwide eminence. 'Stott,' said Ramsey, 'I do find that man so intransigent.' 'Well, Archbishop,' I replied, 'this morning you complained that so-called Evangelicals wouldn't stand up and be counted. You really can't have it both ways.' He gave me a very sharp look and subsided into silence. The point had gone home.

For our summer holidays that year, Jackie and I agreed to do a holiday chaplaincy in France. Maisons-Laffitte and Versailles were twinned and I accepted the post for three weeks in July and August. The children went to their grandparents and we took over a mini-château in Maisons-Laffitte, the home of the Malaysian cultural attaché. He had a massive and superb collection of long-playing classical records and we played about eighty of them, hearing symphonies at full blast with no fear of disturbing even the closest neighbours who were about a hundred yards away. Our one problem was the plague of mosquitoes from the nearby Seine which, in the days before effective repellents, ruined our sleep, night by night, with high-pitched whining dive-bomb attacks reminiscent of the old German Stukas of the Second World War.

After the holiday my first task was to go and see a notorious play which had just opened as the Criterion Theatre. Entitled *Council of Love* it was the most appallingly blasphemous thing I have ever had to endure. I can usually control my emotions but I came nearer to standing up in the dress circle and shouting the odds than on any other occasion. It was simply sick and, to a Christian, repellent in the most offensive manner possible. I wrote a detailed report for the Archbishop as I did for many other films, plays and television dramas. He, being the recipient of many complaints, needed such information for his replies. His constant problem was to decide whether he should complain publicly (which would give huge publicity to the offending piece) or keep quiet and appear to give tacit approval. I did not envy him the task. Whichever he did was bound to cause offence.

Ten days later my sister Moira married Rick Fordham and they held their reception in the Bishop Partridge Hall in Church House. This was a rare privilege and only available because I worked there. When I enquired about the possibility, the manager, a Dutchman, asked me, 'Is your sister a church institution?' Whatever else Moira was, or is, I don't think she has ever deserved to be called 'a church institution!' Having assisted at the wedding service, I made the family speech at the reception. I gave my brother-in-law a whip and a carrot, as he would need both, and described Moira in glowing French: 'Elle est toujours fraîche, tendre, savoureuse, aromatisée.' I explained, 'I got those words off a tin of frankfurters.' It was a fairly riotous speech, one of the best, I think, that I have ever made.

Year by year Jackie and I attended, first, the Eclectics Society national conference and later (when we were over the forty age limit) the Senior Evangelical Anglican clergy conference. In 1970 the overall theme was that of 'authority' and I organised and led the sectional conference on 'Authority in the Arts'. It drew the largest audience and was later described by Michael Baughen, the conference chairman, as 'a magnificent job . . . easily the best and most worthwhile group'. He congratulated me on my 'outstanding gifts . . . and the care, preparation and expertise' which had gone into it. I had immensely enjoyed the conference and the major paper which I had written for it but, even so, it was pleasant to receive such appreciation. My fellow-Evangelicals rarely use such language about me so it was flattering to my ego. I was also gratified that Michael Baughen made a special point of congratulating Sue Cole, who had done much of the behind-the-scenes work for me. She was not only very easy on the eye – she was competent at the job, which mattered even more.

Six days later the Queen opened the newly constituted General Synod in Church House. As I stood in the entrance hall awaiting her arrival, Maurice Wood, Bishop of Norwich, entered. 'Hello, Michael,' he smiled, 'looking as if you own the place, as usual.' 'Only because I've taken lessons from you, dear bishop,' I riposted.

The Queen arrived and I stood on one side with John Miles, the successor to Michael De-la-Noy. 'How long before we get the first complaints about the Synod?' he whispered. 'Six months,' I said, and, sure enough, it was six months to the day.

Two days later I accompanied Archbishop Donald Coggan and Ian Ramsey, Bishop of Durham, to 10 Downing Street, where they spent two hours with the Prime Minister, Edward Heath. I sat outside the Cabinet Room increasingly aware of the lack of security. It was a very different story when I next entered the place over fifteen years later. It was my job to take Ian Ramsey on to a BBC studio for an interview on that first occasion.

In the same week, Mary Whitehouse sponsored a special lunch at the RAF Club in Piccadilly where her organisation was handing out prizes for reputable television programmes. I met Malcolm Muggeridge briefly and then found myself sitting next to Hank Marvin, the pop-guitarist, who had often worked with Cliff Richard in the days of The Shadows.

Malcolm Muggeridge invited me to his cottage in Robertsbridge later in November. He and Kitty ate a few lettuce leaves while I was regaled with rather more. Then we went for a walk in the fields. They were wet and heavy but at least he lent me a pair of Wellingtons. Throughout the visit he assumed that I was a 'Southbank Radical' and nothing I could say or do would persuade him that countless Anglican clergy were no such thing. He was a delightful man, with his rotating jaw-line almost cracking as he agonised over every sentence, but he seemed to me to be the archetypal extremist. He had been an extremist politically as a young man. He had been an extremist sexually and he was a religious extremist. I quite liked him and very much liked her but his motto seemed to be 'moderation in nothing'. When his religious conversion came it was once again an extremist position that he adopted. So, while I appreciated his generous hospitality, I found him a very unsatisfactory man, a kind of adolescent fanatic, a journalistic Peter Pan.

John Trevelyan, the Censor, put my name forward to the Nottingham University Union to defend censorship in a debate with Peter Watkins, maker of the notorious film *The War Game*, which the television authorities had refused to transmit. I had recently spoken to the Christian Union there and had had an audience of over two hundred students. The Union debate drew the massive attendance of 11. It wasn't much consolation to win, as I did, by six votes to five. At least I had the satisfaction of knowing that the Christian cause was flourishing even if no-one was interested in censorship.

Two other areas of importance occupied my time as the 1960s ran into the 1970s. The first came about when a group of us started writing and editing new hymns for use in churches and youth groups. We produced *Youth Praise I* and, later, *Youth Praise II*, in which I had three and six hymns respectively. Then we turned our attention, as a group, to the Psalms and spent four years (1969–73) preparing *Psalm Praise* which contained metrical versions of psalms and canticles. I wrote nineteen of these, including, on one extraordinary evening, Christmas Eve 1971, a series of six. Six hymns in one day must constitute some kind of record? Doubtless Charles Wesley exceeded that but not, I think, often. The group of us met regularly and, in later years, formed ourselves into Jubilate Hymns Ltd., a title which was, I think, my invention. We were to continue writing throughout the seventies, eighties, and into the nineties.

The other area of activity concerned the future of theological education. Between 1964 and 1976 I was a member of the general and standing committees of the Bible Churchmen's Missionary Society (BCMS), later to take the name Crosslinks. The Society was closely associated with Tyndale Hall in Bristol, which it had founded in the 1920s. I was concerned with the plan for a merger between Tyndale and Clifton Theological College which was being seriously proposed in the late 1960s. Clifton had been founded in the early 1930s but the two colleges had grown closer and had shared lectures in the 1950s and 1960s. In 1965 the Clifton council had sacked about half of their staff (mostly Tyndale-trained men) and they were, as a college, very vulnerable in the late 1960s.

In 1968 the two councils announced a forthcoming merger, with Michael Baughen as the principal-designate. Baughen had a tremendous record behind him, though he was not academically well qualified. This was not, by any means, in those years, a disqualification for principals of theological colleges. The first six months of 1969 saw a growing swell of opposition to the merger and tempers were rising. In particular, the fact that Dr James Packer had not been appointed was a cause for much anger. Packer was recognisably one of the ablest, if not the ablest, Evangelical theologian of that period and he was assumed by many to have been the obvious, if not the only, candidate. By the early summer the opposition was so strong, especially among the BCMS-Tyndale constituency, that the whole merger plan was at risk.

The matter reached a head at the BCMS executive committee in June. As I recall it, there were seven voting members. Three were in favour. Three were against. I was the seventh. Before the vote was taken I asked the chairman of the Tyndale council, who was present, whether Packer's name had been considered. He said that it hadn't. I said that whereas some wanted Packer and some did not, my only concern was whether he had been considered since he was so evidently a major candidate. To be told that he had not even been considered forced me to vote against the merger since I could not see that such a procedure could possibly be defended. I added that I was faced with, effectively, voting against one of my closest friends, Michael Baughen, against whom I had absolutely nothing. I had, nevertheless, to take one of the hardest decisions of my life. I voted against the merger, which collapsed. Michael Baughen and I have stayed friends, despite that decision.

The Tyndale council resigned, as did Stafford Wright, the Principal (who had married Jackie and me). An interim working party was set up, of which I was a member, and we successfully saved the college, which was at the point of collapse. There were two important elements in this. The first was the creation of a new constitution in which the council-to-be would be created by an electorate rather than, as previously, a self-appointed oligarchy. A layman, Peter Lefroy-Owen, and I, created this constitution and 'sold' it to the working party and the new principal, James Packer. The second key decision was to spend a quite disproportionately large sum on a top-quality brochure. That brochure, designed by Alan Wagstaff, was a better and more confidence-building production than any theological college prospectus, before or since. I was adamant that we needed such a publication to put all our eggs in the shop window. If we failed to save Tyndale the money would be of no use but if such a prospectus could catch eyes all over the Church of England we might pull off the needed resurrection. Constitution, prospectus and the appointment of Packer kept the ship afloat.

Within the year the new college council was exploring a second merger with Clifton and Dalton House, the BCMS women's college close by. Tyndale made most of the running, supported by Dalton House, whereas the Clifton council, chaired by an elderly bishop, Russell White, was cautious, suspicious and dominated by a small group who wanted to continue to be self-appointed and largely unanswerable to anyone. The merger proposals were virtually torpedoed by their intransigence and distrust and only the last-minute intervention of Oliver Tomkins, Bishop of Bristol, who was brought in to chair a small working party, saved the day and led to the creation of Trinity College, Bristol, in 1972. The final compromise was the decision to create three co-principals – Alec Motyer, Joyce Baldwin and Jim Packer – who, as friends, succeeded in working together, and the eventual agreement to employ Colin Brown on the staff. Brown had spoken out after the Clifton 'sackings' in 1965 and Russell White was determined to make him a scapegoat. To my amazement White had said to me, with a smirk, 'It is expedient that one man should die for the people,' quoting from the Gospels. I felt physically sick and lost all confidence in White's ability to act rationally. Thank God the merger went through, largely on Tyndale's terms, and I was proud to become a member of the new college council from 1974–78. Since those days the college has gone from strength to strength and its second principal, George Carey, is now Archbishop of Canterbury.

On the domestic front, we were tightly crammed into our Beckenham town house. With four growing children and a garage jammed with every kind of possession, but no car, since we had no loft, we were bursting at the seams. The children seemed happy enough though Joe, having had to go to four schools in two years, was getting terrible school reports for a likeable small boy. I succeeded in getting him into my old school, Eltham College, thanks to the generosity of the Head, but he spent most of his time becoming the 'form fool'. On one occasion I took him out into a local park, talked to him very bluntly, beat him with a walking stick and bought him an ice cream. I had, I hoped, got the point home that we would not waste time and money on his education unless he made some effort to co-operate. Fortunately, the girls caused much less trouble and Rachel won a scholarship to Sydenham High School. Jill and Sue, the twins, bounced about happily.

Our house was on a small private estate and I was elected chairman of the residents' association. The secretary, who lived close by, was a retired New York policeman and he was an officious pain in everyone's neck. He claimed 'to know the law' but grossly misapplied it to everyone's discomfort and I had to defend the members against his constant interference which didn't make for neighbourly relationships with him. Inevitably I won the day but never succeeded in building any friendship with him.

One of the local clergy, Dennis Runcorn, Vicar of Shortlands, asked me to preach a series of advent sermons. I called the three addresses 'Good God', 'Christ Almighty' and 'Hell and Damnation', which certainly captured attention, and good-sized congregations turned up. As I stood in the porch after one of them, a retired military figure, with the look of a brigadier, strode up. 'Jolly good sermon, padre,' he barked. 'Thank you,' I replied, 'I hope it was a help to you.' He stopped in his tracks, looking as if I had shot him with a twelve-bore. 'Eh!' he muttered, then 'Oh,' and marched off. Clearly he was disconcerted to think that a padre was daring to do him some good. Like so many former service officers, he obviously regarded sermons as brief interludes before sherry, to be sipped and assessed. The idea that they were somehow to be regarded as God's word to sinners was quite outside his comprehension.

That same series produced another interesting reaction from another elderly member of the congregation. 'Do you know,' he said, 'I've been coming here for sixty years and that's the first time that a preacher has ever mentioned hell and judgement. Thank you.' Three years later in a large suburban church in Seattle I again, in quite a different sermon, referred to the same theme. An elderly American couple said almost identical words and, like their English counterpart, thanked me for what I had said. It made me wonder whether both the Church of England and its sister American church had failed to deliver what St Paul once called 'the whole counsel of God', assuming that people would reject the idea of judgement and a holy God. If they have, both churches will pay dearly for their cowardice.

Towards the end of 1971 I found myself with five days of leave outstanding. 'I need to be completely alone,' I told Jackie who, unenthusiastically, conceded the point. I tried various travel agents and discovered to my surprise that England was far more expensive than Majorca. Indeed, in early December, they could do me five days full board in a three-star hotel in Magaluf, flight included, for the vast sum of £19. 'Done,' I said, and set off. Almost empty, 'full board' was largely thin-sliced galantine of ham and lettuce in the island's concrete jungle but, at £19, who was grumbling?

I rented a small car and drove up the island's north-west coast road. One of Europe's outstanding mountain-and-sea roads, it was bereft of traffic and I only saw three cars in three hours. It was a totally memorable day and proved that there is much more to Majorca than Arenal and Palmanova, which, together with Magaluf, provided the fish-and-chips quarter of the island. The only hardship during my five days was having to fend off a ferocious farm dog who came at me when I took a short country walk. Fortunately, it didn't actually bite me but at one point it seemed to be touch-and-go. I returned to London refreshed and in one piece.

My time at Church House was drawing to an end and I began to wonder about what might happen next. The Archbishop and Adam Block agreed to my going on the mid-service clergy course at St George's House, Windsor, which was the nearest the Church of England has to a Staff College. The powers that be always strenuously deny this but a large number of Anglicans who receive senior preferment seem to have been on the course at a crucial point in their ministry. I went in January 1972, for the full month, and it was a tremendously stimulating time intellectually as well as offering the fascinating experience of living in Windsor Castle.

I treated it as a challenge through which to cut my teeth, in amicable debate and argument, with a wide range of eminent academics and public figures. I took on all comers, thoroughly enjoying the cut and thrust. To my surprise I found myself constantly defending 'historic catholicity' (rather than Evangelical opinions) and the Church of England. There were about twenty Anglican clergy, plus five Free Church ministers, and four of the former were also in the Evangelical tradition. All four allowed me to be isolated in debate, keeping their heads down throughout. Since my participation did not endear me to Windsor's liberal establishment and its lackeys (who, to my satisfaction, seemed largely unable to counter my arguments) the silent Evangelicals left me, like Uriah the Hittite, betrayed and alone. I took this up with them towards the end of the course and they excused themselves by saying, 'You don't need defending, you make the case so well.' That, while apparently flattering, was, in practice, no more than cowardice or incompetence, leaving them protected at my expense.

One of the encounters that I most vividly remember was with the multi-talented Jonathan Miller. He walked into a room of twenty-five clergy and said, 'Come on, let's all admit it, none of us actually believes in God, do we?' I wasn't going to let him get away with that, so, after he had given his lecture, I quizzed this atheistic Jew in front of everyone. 'You say that nothing has any meaning, that you're a total nihilist, and yet you are one of the most exciting and talented men I've ever met, bubbling with vitality and creativity. How do you manage to combine these two incompatible elements in one personality?' 'I can only do it', he replied, 'by closing my mind to what I believe and living as if that didn't exist.' 'So what you're telling us', I pursued him, 'is that you're a classic schizophrenic who can't face up to reality, that you're living a double life?' 'Yes, that's exactly it,' he replied. 'Well,' I responded, 'I believe in God and that offers me the hope of personal integration while you deny him and end up with personal disintegration! I know which I would rather have.' I could understand only too easily why John Wells calls Jonathan Miller 'the most God-haunted atheist I've ever come across.'

On the final night, Canon Stephen Verney, the most liberal of the Windsor staff, decided to sneer at me publicly. It being 25 January, the 'Conversion of St Paul' in the church's calendar, he made a speech ending with the remark that there was 'still hope for Michael Saward – even St Paul could be converted.' I wasn't putting up with that and replied, 'He could indeed, but then Stephen had to be stoned to death first.' There was a mild guffaw round the room. Stephen Verney did not smile.

On my return I duly reported to Michael Ramsey. 'I think you should know that the orthodoxy taught at St George's House is not historic catholicity but a mixture of liberal and radical theology garnished with a doctrine of corporate management.' I had done my Windsor thesis on 'episcopacy', having interviewed a range of senior diocesan bishops, and the value of it became clear when in the 1980s I was appointed to the General Synod's Dioceses' Commission, and fought hard for the historic doctrine of 'the father-in-God' against the fashionable Windsor-inspired 'bishops as corporate managers'. I also told Ramsey that I thought the Cambridge Regius Professor of Divinity, Geoffrey Lampe, had a heterodox theology of the inspiration of Scripture. To my gratified surprise, Ramsey said, 'I agree.'

One afternoon Adam Block called the senior male staff into his office. 'This', he said, pointing to a large book, 'has been sent to us for review.' There was no indication as to who was to review it, or for which periodical, but it was 'on no account to be shown to any of the female staff'. Our ears pricked up. 'You can take it and read it if you wish, in order of seniority,' concluded Adam. A few days later it reached my desk in a buff envelope. I glanced at it surreptitiously and decided to take it home. 'Look what I've got, darling,' I said, holding it out towards Jackie. She took one look, caught my eye, and backed away rapidly. 'If you think . . .' she whispered.

I did, and, in due course, she did and so we did. At one point we actually fell over, laughing. The book came from Denmark, was called *Forty-Two Ways to* . . . with full photographic supporting evidence. We scored forty-two out of forty-two in a riotous evening's entertainment. The Danes in the photos, were so solemn. We weren't.

A few weeks later, my office telephone rang. 'It's Canon Bryan

Green,' said the voice. He was the Rector of Birmingham's famous St Martin-in-the-Bull-Ring church. What could he want, I wondered. 'You may know', he added, 'that I am the secretary of the Peache trustees. We have an important living vacant in the east Midlands . . .' I interrupted him, 'Oh, you mean Holy Trinity, Leicester.' 'How did you know that?' he went on. 'My good friend Symon Beesley is soon to leave there and mentioned it to me in conversation.' 'Well,' continued Green, 'our trustees believe that you are the best person in England to succeed him. Would you be interested?'

I was stunned. Had he really said those words? Yes, he had. Exactly. 'The best person in England.' And Holy Trinity, Leicester. Symon had done a tremendous job. I had preached there and was due to go again, quite soon. It was exactly what I had hoped for. 'I should be very interested,' I said. 'I hadn't dared to think it possible but it's just the sort of parish I had hoped for.' A city-centre ministry, with many professionals and university students, plus the city prison chaplaincy. 'That's marvellous news,' said Green. 'You're just what we want. I shall, of course, need to take up a couple of references but that's a formality.' I promised him two names and he rang off. I called Jackie and she was as thrilled as I was. 'Who will you get as referees?' she said. 'I'll ask the Archbishop and Norman Anderson,' I replied. 'You couldn't do better,' she concluded.

Both Michael Ramsey and Norman Anderson agreed. Norman was chairman of the General Synod's House of Laity and the senior elected layman in the Church of England. We had known each other for nearly ten years. What a coup! The top cleric and the top layman. Ramsey's reference would, I knew, be supportive. To my surprise, Anderson sent me a copy of his, which was highly embarrassing Archangel Gabriel stuff. I spent Easter on top of cloud nine.

Nothing arrived from Green for a week. I decided to ring him since we hadn't actually settled whose was the next move. 'Oh, my dear chap,' he said, 'I was about to write to say that you're totally unsuitable. No pastoral gifts, I'm sure you will agree.' I was shocked into a momentary silence. Then I said, 'Well, of course, it is your decision and we have nothing in writing but I could not possibly agree that I have no pastoral gifts. I've spent eleven out of the past sixteen years in parish ministry and you're asking me, in effect, to say that I should never have been ordained.' 'Well, there it is,' he replied. 'Good bye.' And he rang off.

What on earth had happened? One week I'm 'the best person in England' and a fortnight later I'm 'totally unsuitable'. It was an awful moment, with no kind of explanation available. I rang Symon Beesley to tell him. He had been keen for me to follow him and was deeply shocked. 'Well, you'll still come and preach at the end of the month?' 'Yes, of course,' I said, 'but it's going to be horribly embarrassing if it gets out.'

In the following few days four phone calls created even more concern. Michael Turnbull, a Peache trustee (now Bishop of Durham) was the first. 'Why on earth have you turned down Leicester?' he enquired. 'You seemed absolutely right for the place.' I told him what had happened. He was shocked and angry. 'I'll see what I can do,' he said. 'Well, remember I've nothing in writing,' I replied, 'but I can promise that those were Green's exact words.' He rang off. Minutes later, a second trustee, Bernard Jacob, was on the phone with a repeat performance. 'You must sort out your own trustees,' I said. 'I can't possibly get involved.' Again the phone rang. The Bishop of Leicester, Ronald Williams. 'Michael, this is an appalling story. Come to the diocese and I'll find you something.' I made appreciative noises but declined. Some village in the hunting shires was hardly my cup of tea. Yet another phone call. 'Archdeacon of Leicester here,' said the voice. 'I want to make a fuss in the General Synod.' 'That's up to you,' I answered. 'Don't count me in, I can prove nothing.'

Ten days later I preached, morning and evening, at Holy Trinity. 'Why can't we have him?' said the churchwardens. In the evening there was a party. 'Michael,' shouted the local radio station manager across the room. 'Why don't you come as rector?' I smiled and said nothing.

Eventually the truth leaked out. Bryan Green had mentioned his offer to an elderly trustee, the retired Archdeacon of Liverpool, Hubert Wilkinson. He and I had crossed swords once in my

Liverpool days and he blackballed me. The trustees had been kept in the dark.

Some weeks later Symon rang me, really angry. 'Green came here to meet the churchwardens and church council. I couldn't believe my ears. He told them a pack of lies!' Slowly as time went by, I began to discover that Green, famous in Britain and America, had treated quite a number of other people as he had treated me. On one occasion, it seems, five different clergy had all been led to believe that he had offered them the same parish at the same time.

To me, Green was no longer credible. In the later 1970s I served on the Archbishops' Council on Evangelism, of which he was also a member, and I watched him stick knives in other people's backs. Gavin Reid was one of these unwitting victims. Green's friends, especially in the States, thought he was the acme of perfection. I knew better, and from bitter personal experience.

But God in his providence had something better for me. It took years for me to realise it but what followed was evidently his plan.

'What about St Matthew's in Fulham?' said one of the trustees of the Church Patronage Society. In no time a formal offer arrived from the secretary, who happened to be the father of Virginia Wade the tennis star. The previous vicar, Michael Botting, was someone Jackie and I had known for years and he and his predecessors had done a tremendous job in this Thames-side parish in west London.

It didn't take too long for us to meet the churchwardens, and come to the conclusion that here was scope for real continuing development. Gratefully we accepted and on the anniversary of Agincourt, 25 October 1972, I was instituted as vicar. With all due humility I chose five of my own hymns, all suitable, for the service and, amid the knowing nudges of my friends, launched on the next stage of my ministry.

Chapter Ten

Pause for Thought (2)

He was just twenty-four when we last met him, a brand-new clergyman and a newly-minted husband. Idealistic, optimistic, a young man with a mission to the world. Now, as we rediscover him, he has just turned forty, has a middle-aged wife and four children and is about to become, for the first time, a fully-fledged parish vicar. How have the world, the church and the years treated him?

Surprisingly, perhaps, he isn't disillusioned. He never was the kind of idealist who hadn't had to face up to reality and from his early years he had little time for the kind of Christians who live in their own pious dream world. He's been hurt, badly bruised, by a succession of clergymen who have managed to behave quite intolerably and yet who think they are highly spiritual characters.

Temperamentally, he remains a risk-taker. That has meant that, depending on your viewpoint, he is either a man of courage who, having calculated the risks, still takes them because he believes that someone has to stand up and be counted and if others won't then he will. Or, he is a fool, always on the lookout for controversy, out to make his name by tackling issues which would be far better left as sleeping dogs. To those who take the latter view, he can be vulgar, predictably outrageous, never missing a chance for self-publicity, above all, not 'safe'.

Whether or not he is 'safe', it is hard to deny that he has ability and talent. He has set himself the goal of being a competent professional and he is well-read, a powerful writer and speaker, an excellent organiser, and a man who can lead and inspire others. In the words of a bishop who knows him well, he 'takes up a lot of space', and that is distinctly threatening to some people who certainly would think twice before taking him on in public. To such people he can be infuriating because, as a well-known theologian once said of him, 'Most of the time he's right,' and that, certainly in England, is a sure way to make yourself unpopular with those who think you're wrong but haven't got big enough guns to go into battle with you. He is, in consequence, not scared of debating with, and disagreeing with, eminent public figures in both church and, even occasionally, State.

In his thirties, he has spent much of his life with archbishops and bishops and knows almost everyone who is anyone in the Church of England.

So how has he developed as a person? His sense of humour remains earthy, if anything more so as he gets older. He loves reading and began in 1959 to keep a complete list of all the books he has consumed which, by 1972, is over a thousand volumes. He reads these in bed at night and rarely puts the light out before 12.30 or 1 a.m. So he not only reads books – he buys them. The majority are biography, history, travel, and accounts of the two world wars. He enjoys poetry, the occasional novel, and has no compunction about detailed study of the history of human sexuality. He's probably read more books in this field than all but a tiny handful of clergy and sees no reason to feel embarrassed about it since the subject is one of perennial concern to human beings and prepares him for much counselling. This, interestingly, was something he hadn't foreseen before his ordination but turned out to be a major area of pastoral concern in parochial life. The appreciation which this knowledge, used in counselling, has produced among unhappy and frustrated people has made it all well worthwhile even if some of the onlookers regard it as somewhat dubious as an area of ministry for a clergyman. He's learnt to live with the nudge-nudge attitudes, not least from the occasional journalist who can only think of sex and vicars with the prurient eyes of tabloid newspapers.

Another area of development has been that of classical music. Starting with a youth which was dominated by Bing Crosby and the Andrews Sisters, he has moved through Gilbert and Sullivan to Beethoven, Schubert, Mozart, and the vast range of music available on records. His collection has grown and grown and he plays them incessantly as background, able by now to identify hundreds of symphonies, concerti, and operas.

More recently he has begun to get to know the world of cinema and, partly through his media job, has seen most of the French, Italian and German films of the 1960s, having come to enjoy Truffaut, Chabrol, Fellini, Antonioni, Pasolini, and so on. This interest, and especially from the French films, has given him a new sensitivity to the complexity of human emotions and relation-ships, and coloured (though rarely altered) his moral views on these.

Outside cinema, he has started to look at the work of sculptors and has a tremendous admiration for the wonderfully fluid cre-ations from the hands of Auguste Rodin. He wanted to use Ro-din's Eternal Idol for a book cover and was incensed when the Christian publishers thought it 'too erotic'. Capturing, as Rodin did, the mutual awe between man and woman, he was angry to find Christians unable to see beyond and through the nakedness to the utter love and worship expressed by the work.

Politically, he has, especially in the 1960s, had to face a world largely unknown before. Coming from solidly Conservative outer suburbia, he has had to come to terms with working-class Lon-don and, even more, with the social disintegration of inner Liver-pool. To Conservatives (e.g. his parents) he seems to be an extreme left-wing Socialist, while to Labour supporters he is dis-missed as a true-blue public-school boy. The truth is that he hasn't much time for most of the politicians he has met but votes, uncon-vinced, for the Conservatives as being the least worst option on offer. He isn't proud of that.

It's at the point where theology and politics meet that he has sensed an inner change. The Calvinist theology of his student days, while still his framework, has come up against the human suffering and grief illustrated in the Gospels. Christian Aid gave him a new insight into the magnitude and horror of war and its consequences and he was deeply moved to find Abraham

Lincoln's phrase that he felt 'sorry for the man who could not feel the lash on the slave's back'. Michael isn't a man who weeps but tears sometimes came to his eyes in 1972 which he would never have felt in the 1950s.

Clergy do not earn much but he and Jackie have deliberately spent a disproportionate amount of their income on holidays, especially in travel. Their conviction is that such travel is much more important than owning furniture and cars. They haven't had their own car since they married and they rent one when they need one.

The travelling has taken them both to Germany, Austria, Italy, Switzerland, France, Belgium, Holland, Luxembourg and in the summer of 1972 to Tenerife. He, additionally, has been to Norway, Denmark and Majorca. They have used buses, cars, vans, cycles, a Lambretta, trains, ships, river steamers, aircraft, and even their own legs. They have camped, stayed in peasant houses, small hotels, pensions, inns, and even a five-star grand hotel. Once they slept, wearing crash helmets, underneath a motorway bridge in Belgium and were trodden on at 2 a.m. by a local drunk. They have ended up penniless on occasions, borrowed money from friends, drunk their first wine, eaten mixed grills with beetroot, sauerkraut, apricots and plums, and been violently sick after a plate of moules marinières went off in the Place du Tertre in Montmartre. They have seen Passion Plays, Puppet Theatres, Palace Concerts, Oompah bands, comic opera soldiers, and scruffy Palace guard soldiers. They have been confronted by helpful policemen, indifferent policemen, and bastard policeman. They have worshipped in cathedrals, formal churches, ugly ecclesiastical huts, and he has even celebrated Holy Communion off the tailboard of a Volkswagen van, with a red plastic plate and cup. They have toured fantasy castles, mediaeval fortresses, dungeons and real 'lived-in' schlossen. Finally, they have talked garbled German to Germans, fractured French to the French, incoherent Italian to Italians, doggerel Dutch to the Dutch, and even a word or two of blemished Flemish to some uncooperative Belgians. The hardest task of all was to get American tourists to grasp English. He recalls with unabashed horror the indescribable old Midwestern crow with the corncrake voice who, faced with one of Austria's most photogenic mountain-and-glacier scenes, croaked out, 'I have been in fourteen countries, I don't know where I am now, and I am bored!' Who says that travel doesn't broaden the backside?

Back home, Michael loves his children but is too busy to spend much time with them. He's always available if they want him (he's said so often enough) but he hasn't yet learnt that that isn't how children want their parents. As a family, the Sawards have always existed happily enough for three generations or more without being in each others' pockets all the time. They generally enjoy being with one another but can manage quite happily for weeks or months at a distance. The new generation may well not find that so satisfying and only time will tell whether that is true or not.

And what of the lovers themselves? As both Michael and Jackie expected, it's been a bumpy ride and the early seventies are as bumpy as ever. Sexually, the marriage has worked very well but both perennially argue and squabble, almost as much in public as in private. It is arguable that by letting off so much steam in small eruptions they avoid really volcanic explosions. Certainly they have watched a growing number of clerical marriage breakdowns following the changed divorce laws and not a few of these seem to have exploded from behind façades of clerical propriety. Michael and Jackie have at least been open and honest about their humanity. She nags him rotten and he turns on her with verbal, if not physical, violence. He controls his temper quite easily with everyone except Jackie but far too often boils over when she pushes him too far. So the marriage has its flaws and they're easy to see from inside and outside. Both smile ruefully about it. 'No,' they declare with firm intention, 'there's no way we could divorce. Murder? Yes, that's a constant possibility.'

Lastly, has their faith survived intact? Yes, but it isn't particularly conventional. When they married, Jackie and Michael said, 'We will always say grace, for meals but we won't attempt family prayers or the like.' They've kept that vow all along. Their beliefs are intact and real and they've never forced them on the children. As a family they go to church, they say grace, and beyond that it's up to the individuals. Some might call it a sparse diet, others might say it's a sensible low-key way of keeping the faith without creating a hot-house. Time will tell.

So there they are. Two forty-year-olds, battling along to keep the faith intact, the family intact, and themselves in touch, if not entirely intact. And now a completely fresh challenge lies ahead. The pale young curate has crossed and recrossed the Mersey, has completed the Lambeth Walk, and now faces the Wandsworth Bridge Road as the 'Dear vicar'. God help him – there are some tough customers down there.

Chapter Eleven

I Am the Vicar

St Matthew's vicarage in Clancarty Road was built in 1824 and was one of the three oldest buildings in the district. Nell Gwynne had been set up in one of the others by Charles II to be both his mistress and that of Sandford Manor. Sands End was the local name for the south-eastern riverside strip of Fulham where St Matthew's Church has stood since 1895, a Blomfield red-brick Victorian-Gothic building of no great distinction. The whole area had been market-garden land for centuries, the soil black and fertile from Thames overflows.

Between the 1860s and 1890s, two-thirds of the area had been turned into a network of small streets, filled with terraced housing, definitely downmarket from Mr Pooter, but nevertheless clearly graded, with the dwellings closest to the river being the poorest of all. The South Fulham peninsular was neatly bisected by the Wandsworth Bridge Road which ran from Eel Brook Common to the bridge itself.

My immediate predecessor as vicar, Michael Botting, had been known to me since the 1950s. He had brought some major changes to St Matthew's, virtually all of which I should want to continue. The three major features introduced in his time had been a lay eldership, a creatively principled policy for infant baptism, and a strong degree of informal Sunday morning worship, liturgical but relaxed in style. A further major change which had begun in the 1960s was the slow but inexorable transformation of Fulham's sociological make-up. What had, for almost three-quarters of a century, been a solidly working-class inner-London suburb was now being altered in two quite different ways. On the one hand, there was the influx of West Indians and, on the other, the gentrification created by young well-to-do couples who could not afford Chelsea and Kensington prices but could, and did, find Fulham's terraced property easily accessible and well worth radical modernisation. St Matthew's, by the mid-1970s, had a mixture of old working class, Old Etonians and blacks, some of whom were high-flyers and some who were not much above the literacy line. This was, socially and politically, a heady cocktail.

St Matthew's was offered to me at the same time as Holy Trinity, Leicester, and the fiasco there pointed me straight at Fulham. I accepted in May 1972, knowing that Michael Botting would be leaving in the late summer and that my Church Information Office contract would run out in October. A major consideration would be the children's education and they would need to start at new schools in September. The twins, Jill and Sue, could move to Peterborough Junior School, a mere two hundred yards from St Matthew's vicarage. Jonathan, a day-boy at Eltham, would become a boarder, while Rachel, our eldest, could move, we hoped, to Putney High School. She had won a scholarship to Sydenham High, a sister school within the Girls Public Day Schools Trust and the transfer was acceptable to them. Then the blow fell. Hammersmith was a Labour authority. They would honour the scholarship if Rachel stayed at Sydenham (an impossible two-hour journey each way) but declined to allow her to take up the Putney place (a twenty-minute journey). If ever I had contemplated voting Labour that settled my mind for good and all. Fortunately, we found her a place at Lady Margaret School, a Church of England grammar school half a mile away, where she became a model pupil.

These changes inevitably required us to move from Beckenham in early September but the vicarage would not be available until mid-October. A flat in Chelsea, the vicarage of an old friend, Michael Ward, fell vacant and we camped out there for six weeks. Our Beckenham house went on the market (and didn't sell for nine months) which, even with the first major inflationary surge, promised us a good profit. This allowed us to pay boarding fees for Jonathan, to buy a Rembrandt etching as an investment, and enabled Jackie and me to have a major holiday on our own in a luxury German hotel in Tenerife. We felt we needed a break from camping holidays to set us up for the new job and the Semiramis in Puerto de la Cruz was exactly the tonic we required. In the midst of this magnificent holiday we discovered Gordon Savage. Gordon had been Bishop of Southwell, had retired early 'due to a hiatus hernia' but was actually living with a delightful young dancer, and their baby, while he acted as an estate agent on the island. A year or so earlier the tabloids had done a typically lurid story soon after his retirement and he told me, with wry amusement, how Michael Ramsey had called him back from Tenerife to give an account of his activities. 'We spent an hour together,' said Gordon. 'There was only one essential question which he needed to ask, namely, "Are you sleeping with the girl?" Michael rambled all over the place but he simply couldn't bring himself to ask me the only question that mattered.' The tabloids had presented the girl as a tarty stripper. She was, in fact, a middle-class ballet dancer. That didn't morally justify the relationship, which had developed out of his unhappy marriage, but they remained together till his death many years later.

A holiday in Tenerife, an educational insurance, but what should we do with the rest of the profit from the Beckenham house sale? I walked into Harrods' fine art department and invested in an etching by Rembrandt. Their expert assured me that it would double in value every year for about five years and, in any case, they would guarantee to repurchase it at the selling price if I had second thoughts at any time. We put it into a bank vault to go on maturing and forgot about it for five years. Then one day I took it to Sothebys for a valuation and got a nasty shock. They priced it at about a quarter of its 1972 price. Really? 'Yes,' they said, with a disparaging remark about Harrods. I took the etching, by taxi, straight to Harrods and demanded an explanation. 'Sothebys are always dismissive, you know,' was the tit-for-tat response. Smouldering, I asked for my money back. 'A great shame' they said, but paid up. Five years appreciation had gone down the drain.

Meanwhile I was looking for a curate. I placed an advert in the *Church of England Newspaper* seeking 'the Perfect Curate' which drew many ribald comments from my fellow-clergy. None of them seemed to realise that my goal was to get the vacancy as widely known as possible and in that I was hugely successful. The final irony was my appointment of Andrew Warburton, who had not seen the advert (being on holiday) but had heard about it from friends. He alone, of all potential curates, had not been aware of the 'perfect curate' description or he probably wouldn't have dared to apply! He came with his Czech wife, Alena, from a not-very-happy first curacy and we were able to build up a good working relationship. Indeed, in my nineteen years as an incumbent, in Fulham and Ealing, I had nine full-time curates and eight part-time or short-term assistants, and only one of the former turned out to be almost impossible to work with. One really unhappy relationship as curate to vicar and one as vicar to curate isn't too bad a record out of a total of twenty-three such combinations in my thirty years of parochial ministry. Between 1956 and 1991 I worked with sixty-eight men and women, lay and ordained, including lay elders, lay workers, and colleagues and, of these, only three produced a basically unhappy relationship and I had a fairly hard time with three others. My relations with the latter group have remained courteous throughout the years while of the former, one is dead and I have no wish to meet the other two if I can help it. Happily, I've only come face to face with each once in the last fifteen years. Since both have acquired reputations which are less than admirable I feel relatively unblameworthy.

I was duly installed as vicar on 25 October, St Crispin's Day. Being the anniversary of Agincourt, I have always since been able to quote, convincingly, 'These scars I had on Crispin's day,' and there were to be a few before I finished in Fulham six years later.

Jackie had put in many hours with a paintbrush and I had laid acres of vinyl and carpet. The house, a Georgian building, was delightful. It had, to us, the disadvantage of four separate gardens plus some broken down brick boundary walls. Gradually we rebuilt the latter and tamed the former, using money from parking space which we let out to locals. The Warburtons lived in a separate wing, with their own small garden, so we were close but not obtrusively so.

One very unusual feature of the new parish was that, in addition to its churchwardens, Terry Reddin, a teacher, and Peter Reeves, an accountant, there was a 'lay eldership' of four men. These had been selected by Michael Botting, and formally commissioned by Ronald Goodchild, the Bishop of Kensington. Peter Reeves was one, and the others were Courtenay Grebby, who was retired, Fred Luke, an ambulance driver of amazing physique and strength, and Gary Piper, another teacher. Later we added Michael Hudson, again a teacher, and Ellen Marlow, a middle-aged mum. Ellen may well have been the first woman elder in the Church of England. I certainly knew of no others at the time. Our team also included two London City Missionaries (one following the other) and a young Oxford graduate, Jonathan Trigg, who was a Coal Board high-flyer and a lay reader. He in due course married Lynn Hannan from our congregation, went as an ordinand to Durham, where he collected a First in Theology, and a Doctorate, and is now Vicar of Highgate, having also been an Area Dean. They were a very fine and varied team, great people to work with and enough to make any vicar proud.

St Matthew's had some marvellous people in the church. The very day I arrived, one, an old warhorse in her eighties, Flossie Jackson, said to me, 'I've seen 'em all come and go, right from the start in the 1890s.' 'Well,' I replied, 'you've seen me come but I bet you won't see me go!' She didn't and I took her funeral just over three years later. Then there was Percy Emmett. He was ninety-one. 'Vicar,' he said, 'I don't much like what you're doing in church but it's getting the young families in and, anyway, I'll be dead soon so you've got my full support. Keep at it.' I hope I'll be like that if I ever reach my nineties.

Right from the start the church was ready for change. It had been well tutored by Michael Botting and the only problem with so many young leaders was that they expected radical change right away. So many suggestions were on the agenda of the staff and elders' team and the Church Council that it took nearly four years to evaluate them and sort the wheat from the chaff. Having young leaders was a blessing, because they were open to new ideas, but, with one churchwarden in his thirties and the other in his twenties, it was certainly unusual. The four elders included one retired man, with the other three younger than me, and I was only forty.

Michael Botting's last remark before he left was both jocular and distinctly disturbing. 'You'll have some fun with Terry and Gary over baptism,' he said. 'Both the wives are about to give birth to their first babies and all four are dead against infant baptism.' Terry, the younger warden, and Gary, the youngest elder, would pose real problems if their children weren't baptised. They would undoubtedly set a precedent and we would find ourselves in the weird situation of non-churchgoers wanting baptisms and the leading Christians rejecting it. Suffice it to say that, after long talks with all four individually and a promise that neither couple would collude with the other in reaching a decision, Terry and Chris said yes, as did Gary and Norma. I was hugely relieved and their leadership meant that the matter never arose again in my time.

One of the attractions which led me to accept St Matthew's was the plan for the West Cross route, a new major road scheme which would relieve cross-Thames traffic and would require a complete rebuilding of the church. This held out a most exciting prospect but it was a party-political football. The plan collapsed in 1973 and we were left with a pair of tired old Victorian buildings, both church and hall, in need of major renovation. These dogged our footsteps throughout my six years but today at last a new building project is well advanced.

Two hundred yards from the vicarage stood Christ Church and its vicarage. Both churches were Evangelical and some kind of merger was obviously needed. Again, twenty years later, it is still unresolved! The vicar there, Philip King, later to be Secretary of the South American Missionary Society and then Secretary of the General Synod Board for Mission, was, and is, a good friend of mine but our relationship, for half a lifetime, has been marked by our ongoing need to score points off each other. It's all in fun but we can hardly conduct a serious conversation without mutual mickey-taking. It does seem slightly ludicrous for two senior clergymen in their sixties to be locked into this odd battle of quick-witted repartee but neither of us knows how to stop it. Our wives, Margaret and Jackie, sigh at the schoolboy folly of their husbands who go on behaving like fourth-formers. Still, at least we laugh at ourselves, which Philip's successor at Christ Church was quite unable to do.

My first change at St Matthew's was to start a 'Carols by Candlelight' service. It was immediately successful, producing a greatly increased congregation for that night. Six years later, exactly the same thing happened at Ealing, where the numbers trebled and remained the largest congregation of the year. In both places I launched a six-year sequence of themes, breaking away from the tired old rut of King's College, Cambridge. King's has superb music but the sequence has been stuck in concrete for over seventy years. Our six themes were 'Christ the King', 'Glory', 'Joy', 'Peace', 'Light' and 'God with us'. Each year we traced the distinct theme through related biblical passages and carols. The only fixed points were the Isaiah 9 and Luke 1–2 passages together with 'O come, all you faithful' and 'Hark! the herald-angels sing'. Year by year, then, we had the same service, yet varied with readings and carols, old and new. In the two churches I went through the cycle three times. It drew about two hundred people at St Matthew's and between five hundred to eight hundred at Ealing.

Having spent five years working for, first the Church Assembly, and then its offspring, the General Synod, you might think I had had enough of Church House, Westminster. Not a bit of it. London diocese had a by-election for a 'proctor' (a clerical member) at the end of 1972 and I decided to stand. I wasn't elected but I did well enough to plan further campaigns and, a year later, came within a whisker in a second by-election. On this later occasion, to my embarrassment a dozen younger clergy complained that they had been disfranchised and asked me to appeal against the result. The Bishop of London, Gerald Ellison, reluctantly allowed the appeal (the first by a clergyman since Norman times!)

and the election was rerun. John Broadhurst (the disallowed winner) vowed, with a grin, that he would run me into the ground. I explained the circumstances in my election address and asked for votes only from those who believed my account to be genuine. John won, but we both increased our vote, and in the main Synod election in 1975 I was duly elected. I was to stay in Synod for twenty years. John Broadhurst a leading Anglo-Catholic, and a good friend, remained for twenty-four years prior to becoming a suffragan bishop.

At the end of January 1973 I spent a most colourful evening debating censorship at the theatre in Harlow New Town. I was taken there in a huge limousine with the actress Miriam Karlin. We met in Soho and giggled about 'bishops and actresses' in a car which would have allowed us all the space needed had we been so minded. The evening's first high point was when I strongly reacted against an atheist feminist who longed for the day when men would cease being excited by a woman's naked body. 'God forbid,' I said. 'I hope I always find a beautiful body sexually stimulating – there's nothing wrong with that and everything wrong if I don't.' The audience, surprised at such words from a cleric in a dog-collar, applauded loudly. Of course I went on to distinguish between that and lust and lack of self-control which was, I said, the crucial distinction for Christians.

The Chairman was Clive Jenkins, the Welsh Trade Union Secretary, who promptly invited us back to his Tudor house nearby for champagne, pâté de foie gras, and other delicacies. I gently suggested to Jenkins that such opulence was a bit over the top for a militant Socialist (who also owned a house in NW1 and a boat on the Thames). He grinned mischievously like a small boy caught in an apple-orchard, admirably bearing out Barbara Castle's remark that he 'never believed good of anybody but himself'.

Back at St Matthew's, we sold off (with full legal authority) a good many of our unwanted pews and re-angled the rest. Our Communion Table was below the Chancel steps and half our choir stalls – the front row – were removed. Stage by stage we made the building fit the congregation, instead of the reverse which so constricts the worshipping life of so many congregations in the Church of England. We remembered Jesus' words about the Sabbath being made for man, not man for the Sabbath. Fortunately, the wardens, elders, Church Council, and almost all the congregation were of one mind with Andrew and me.

A few weeks later I attended an interdenominational gathering of the National Evangelical Assembly. During a not-very-intelligent debate about the Person of Christ, which was tending to forget the reality of Christ's humanity, I reminded the Assembly that for him to be truly human he had presumably regularly urinated and defecated like the rest of us. No serious theologian would have found that theologically objectionable but a small group of Independent ministers were appalled. They demanded that the sponsoring body, the Evangelical Alliance, conduct a heresy trial with me in the dock. The EA had, of course, no kind of jurisdiction over me and the very idea was ridiculous but they vacillated, issuing a statement which rebuked me for using indelicate language (or something similar). No one seemed to have recognised that the disgruntled group were actually coming close to a heresy. If Jesus was fully divine (which I certainly believe) he was also fully human (the classic credal formula) and I had done no more that make the point in unmistakable terms. Inevitably, the matter subsided but I was, from then on, a marked man in those circles where a rigidly closed mind is supposed to be the supreme virtue. The whole ethos of that brand of Evangelicalism has always repelled me and I remain distinctly uneasy about such areas of Fundamentalist sectarian Evangelicalism. I am and always have been unashamed to be an Evangelical Anglican, rejoicing in the degree of freedom which is the great positive glory of the Church of England. I care deeply about biblical theology but haven't much time for the sort propounded by those who knew all life's answers before they were out of nappies.

Since 1967 I had been on the Executive of the Bible Churchmen's Missionary Society and in May 1973 I found myself compere of a major event, Broken World, at the Queen Elizabeth Hall, on London's South Bank. One of my tasks was to interview a Tanzanian clergyman, Alpha Mohamed, about the Christian church in his homeland. The Anglican Church was seeing tremendous growth but it was having to work out a relationship with a powerful Islamic group in a land of few resources, ruled by a strongly Socialist government under its much-admired President, Julius Nyerere. His policy of collective villages, known as *ujamaa*, was still controversial. In the audience that night was the Tanzanian High Commissioner, so when I asked Alpha some heavily loaded questions about the church and politics, he carefully side-stepped and made the 'right' noises.

A day or two later, after repeating Broken World in Liverpool, we said good-bye and he said, 'I will always remember you as the man who is interested in Tanzanian politics.' 'I'm not,' I replied. 'I know very little about it. I'm just worried that so few of you Anglican Tanzanians seem to care about what your leaders are doing. I'm also worried that, unlike your African brothers further south, you Evangelical East Africans seem to regard it as unspiritual to get involved.' Alpha's a lovely man, from a Moslem family, and now he is a Tanzanian bishop. Whenever we meet, we remember our conversation at Broken World. The situation has certainly moved on since those days.

I found myself Chairman, for two years, of the Fulham Council of Churches. It was a 'one-year' job but my predecessor moved away a week or two after accepting office which left me to be Chairman (while actually Vice-Chairman) with a mandatory Chairman's year to follow. My chief task turned out to be that of organising a local pre-General Election meeting. The candidates were Michael Stewart, the Labour Foreign Secretary and sitting member, plus a Conservative, a Liberal and a candidate from the National Front. The committee agonised over the National Front man but decided that democracy meant allowing him his chance, however much we disapproved of his stance.

Fearful of an angry demo, I ran the meeting with a rod of iron. Afterwards all the candidates said it was the best of all the meetings in the constituency and easily the best attended. There was no heckling and all got a fair crack of the whip. I began by telling them of the voter who promised all the candidates in turn to vote for them. Each was delighted. The voter's wife accused him of dishonesty. 'Why?' he said. 'They were all pleased.' 'What's that got to do with it?' 'Well, today', he replied, 'I've pleased all of them. Tomorrow I shall please myself. In that way, everyone will be pleased and that doesn't often happen at a General Election.' Michael Stewart retained his long-held seat but the demography of Fulham was to change all that within a few years as the Yuppie vote swung it to Thatcherism in the late 1970s.

In the summer Rachel decided to go to a Covenanter house-party while the rest of us rented a car and drove to Venice, camping *en route*. We enjoyed Neuschwanstein's weird Wagnerian splendour, inspected early Christian remains at Aquileia, marched all round Salzburg, and shivered at the ossuary at Verdun. Some excellent colour photos have kept the memory alive, together with some movie footage of the canal at Burano in the Venetian lagoon. We even looked at Blindheim (which the British know as 'Blenheim') for the battlefield but there was nothing to see. Nobody, we discovered, wanted sterling. Deutschmarks were in, pounds were definitely out.

It was also a good, if attenuated, cricket season. I returned to the London side with a batting average of 40 and in the final match made 54 out of 62 in thirty balls having opened the innings. My partner only received six balls before I was out. I hit their opening fast bowler for 6 off his first ball, straight back over his head, reaching my 50 with another 6. I was then caught. We were playing a London Theatre Eleven.

In mid-September I had one of my most memorable weeks. For four years a group of us had been working on the Psalms, turning them into metrical verse. Now, *Psalm Praise* was about to be published and the team, plus a scratch choir of young men and women, boarded a large double-decker bus to launch the project at seven centres round the land. We left London after a lunchtime concert in the City, repeated it in Bristol that night, Leeds the next night, then on to Glasgow, Liverpool and Manchester and finally a repeat performance on Saturday afternoon and evening at All Souls, Langham Place, back in London. Anyway, we sang ourselves into the ground and the BBC said that we 'had taken the corsets off the Psalms'. Many churches were hardly aware of our work, which was their loss, because *Psalm Praise* has some magnificent material, capturing the wide range of material in the Psalter. I provided 19 of the 151 pieces in the book. *Psalm Praise* was a great achievement, largely wasted by the churches, who were soon to opt for trivial and banal choruses, capable of endless and mindless repetition.

Autumn of that year was a very prolific time for me. My book *Cracking the God-Code* was published by the Scripture Union but not as I had wanted it. The book was a treatment of the basic Christian beliefs and roughly followed the Creeds in sequence. The publisher arbitrarily changed the title to *Don't Miss the Party*, which made almost no sense, put a lurid clown's face on the cover (equally nonsensical) and finally wrecked a whole chapter by misprinting a highly significant plus sign where a multiplication sign was in the text. The book was given tremendous reviews which the publisher failed to use for promotion purposes and although it has been republished twice, with the proper title and clownless, and has appeared in American, Swedish and Chinese versions, it has never succeeded in gaining the sales which its original reviewers expected.

A second book *And So to Bed?* had for three years been doing the rounds of the religious publishers. One by one they returned it. None said it was a bad book but they clearly didn't want, as Evangelicals, to be associated with a book about sex which got to grips with the subject explicitly. It was turned down by twenty-three publishers in all. Then, John Capon, also editor of *Crusade* magazine, agreed to serialise the bulk of it in six, monthly, articles. The first appeared in October 1973. It created a huge correspondence, the largest in the magazine's history. Exactly a hundred letters were received, of which ninety-two were in favour and eight against. Unfortunately, with hindsight, Capon published sixteen letters, eight for and eight against. This left the Evangelical constituency with the unshakeable conviction that I had created a fifty-fifty division of opinion. In fact, only two or three of the objectors wrote serious letters. Among the ninety-two supporters were theologians, clergy, doctors, teachers, missionaries, authors, social studies tutors, family planning counsellors, husbands, wives, married couples, those engaged, students (male and female) and grandparents. They wrote from Australia, Thailand, India, Switzerland, Oxford, Cambridge, and all over the British Isles. The essential message was 'this must be published as a book'. Many spoke of their anger at the failure of Christian publishers to accept the book. One professional counsellor said, 'The greatest opposition always comes from Christians.'

Eventually, publisher number twenty-four came on the scene. He had a dubious record, with various bankruptcies behind him, but I had little choice. I made sure that the contract was watertight and in due course the book appeared. Scripture Union, who had originally commissioned the book (and three times turned it down), gave it a full window display in their London bookshop, which seemed like hypocrisy to me. Another large Evangelical bookshop chain, the Christian Literature Crusade, refused to sell it (a few were, I suspect, 'under the counter') as did many of the independent so-called Bible Bookshops. They fairly effectively strangled it and though I made some money (from my tightly worded contract) sales were poor. Twenty years later people still enquire after it and I still sell copies from the few I have left.

But worse was to come. The *News of the World* printed a scurrilous article claiming that its publication had caused 'an unholy row' at St Matthew's leading to 'a storm of protest'. One of the elders, Fred Luke, was said to be 'so disgusted' that he was thinking of withdrawing his three children from Sunday School. These allegations were, of course, lies, manufactured (yes, actually manufactured) by a journalist, Bill Davey, and St Matthew's were a hundred per cent behind me. Together we itemised the lies, pinned down the authors (one was another journalist who apologised but said she needed the money) and secured a public retraction from the *News of the World* and a personal apology from the Editor, Peter Stephens, who informed me that Bill Davey had lost the chance of becoming a staff reporter for the paper.

Still, the fact remains that clergy who attempt to deal with sexual matters openly will always be fair game for the media. Say nothing and you're out of touch. Say something unorthodox and you're a hero, maligned by a stuffy church but lauded by the media. Or, as I have done, say something orthodox but cheerfully robust and pastorally relevant and you'll be crucified as 'the Randy Rector', 'the Sexy Vicar' or the 'Kinky Canon'. No wonder most clergy keep their heads well down. But not this cleric. If it needs saying and no-one else will, then I'll stand up and be counted.

Just one more word. A couple wrote to me from South-East London, asking to see me. They had been married for some years and had never had intercourse. Something, they felt, was wrong! They had virtually never touched each other's bodies for seven years from the time they first met and they felt guilty at even the wish to do so. I saw them and spent hours with them both together and alone. I pulled out every counselling stop I knew. They left and I felt defeated. Months later I received a letter telling me that at last they were enjoying a happy relationship. 'It was your articles and your personal counselling that we now see to have produced the real breakthrough for us . . . we are much happier now after what had seemed an insurmountable problem.' It only takes one or two such cases to help you to cope with the vicious wounds inflicted by the utterly unprincipled tabloid newspapers. Sadly, the wounds inflicted to one's reputation by hostile Christians take a lot longer to overcome.

In the midst of all these lurid goings-on, I presented a lengthy paper to the General Committee of the South American Missionary Society, meeting in London, which called for a coherent strategy and structure to be created by the various Anglican Evangelical missionary societies to replace the wasteful reduplication which had existed for over half a century. I quoted the work done over the previous seven years, and the various conference resolutions, all of which were pointing in the same direction. I spoke as the Society's guest but also as one who had wrestled with the matter for almost a decade. Every serious attempt at dealing with this matter had, I suggested, been blocked by one vested interest or another. Hundreds of parochial clergy wanted action but nothing was being done. It is therefore somewhat salutory, twenty years later, to see that almost nothing has been done to further the vision I proclaimed. And the result? Almost all those same societies are today facing financial crisis and retrenchment. Evangelical Christians

The Jubilate Hymn Words' Group preparing 'Hymns for Today's Church', Ealing 1980

Interviewing Edward Health for 'Partners in Mission', the 25th anniversary of Michael's ordination as deacon, May 1981

Introducing 'Hymns for Today's Church' at Westminster Abbey
1982

Receiving the Winston Churchill Fellowship award from James
Callaghan, 1985

Donald and Jean Coggan at Ealing Vicarage, 1988

Chairing the Billy Graham press conference for Mission to
London, with Gavin Reid and Richard Bewes, 1989

Speaking at the 'ordination of women' debate in General Synod, 1988

At Lochnagar mine-crater anniversary on the Somme battlefield, 1990

The Saward family: Rachel, Jackie, Joe, Sue, Jill and Michael, 1991

Being installed as Canon by Bishop Graham Leonard, St Paul's Cathedral, 1991

George and Eileen Carey hosting John Stott's 70th birthday party at Lambeth Palace, 1991

Princess Anne visits Amen Court, with Dean Eric Evans, 1993

The Queen and Prince Philip greet Michael at St Paul's Cathedral,
1995

© Philip Way

Michael and Jackie celebrate their 40th wedding anniversary, 1996

are tremendous enthusiasts for starting, in every generation, unco-ordinated organisations which, half a lifetime later, are floating half-dead in the water. What they seem unable to do is regroup to meet new situations and challenges. At St Matthew's, for example, I found a congregation of about a hundred, offering financial support (mostly of a nominal kind) to thirty-eight mission organi-sations. A few months later the church decided to replan its support and cut out two-thirds of the dead wood. Sadly, withhold-ing money is the only way to persuade the multiplicity of 'tiddler' societies to think again or shut up shop.

A year after my arrival, the leaders of St Matthew's had really begun to get the bit between their teeth. Ideas were pouring out from me, from the elders, and from those who were working to re-shape our Sunday morning worship and as one of the elders said, 'It takes four elders and an elephant gun to stop Michael in full flight.' One of the most creative consequences was the launching of what I christened The Fifty-Minute Family Hour. This in-volved the scrapping of Sunday schools, the creation of children's teams of mixed ages with three or four adult leaders who, follow-ing a carefully planned syllabus, played a major role, under the su-pervision of the clergy in the conduct of the Family Hour, aimed at families, aimed at outsiders, and extremely informal. We used a framework of liturgy but did not wear robes or sit in choir stalls and a large screen for rear-projected pictures from an overhead projector was the dominant feature. Hymns, psalms, prayers, were all on the screen to obviate the need for books since many of our worshippers were not 'bookish' people. We kept a visitors' book and, in the three years following, over four hundred differ-ent 'visitors' attended, of whom about three hundred were from the parish. I often called it Fulham Weekend Television, so keen was I to break the stuffy image of 'church' which dominates Inner London working-class communities. Not perhaps surprisingly, it was the few local 'Old Etonian' residents who found the informal-ity hardest to bear. To them 'church' meant 'school chapel' with all its rigidities. We, incidentally, by using the term 'Family' meant the whole congregation, the Christian family, and not just the 'nuclear' family. These, in any case, were diminishing with the rise of divorce and 'single-parent' families and the significant number of young singles who lived in the area. As to 'worship', I defined it as 'God's people being happy together, upwards.' This included fellowship, joy, awe and the sense of the reality of God's presence within his community.

With the arrival of Series Three, our Holy Communion was generally held in the evening, using robes and sticking closely to the liturgy. Thus the Family Hour was a stepping stone towards eucharistic fellowship. We wanted to be both faithfully Anglican and a bridge to the outside world.

Our parochial public relations were high profile and quite deliberately focused on me. This followed the personalised strategy adopted in the outside world in both advertising, politics, entertainment and the media. People might accuse me of fostering an ego-trip but I knew only too well that highlighting the leader was an essential part of the strategy so long as it never became the goal. Before long St Matthew's and its Vicar were getting more publicity in Fulham than all the other churches put together and one result was that outsiders came to see what was going on. The visitors' book, already mentioned, was clear evidence of this. What they found was not a circus, or a one-man show, but a large, happy, all-age group of Christians enjoying their worship and fellowship.

The youngest of the elders, Gary Piper, was a Fulham boy, born and bred. A very gifted teacher, he had married Norma Stanborough, a nurse who was also a top-level swimmer. By the end of 1973 he had qualified as a reader and, one day, as we talked, he spoke of his frustrated sense of a call to the ministry. But, he added, he was also sure that he was right to remain a teacher. There seemed no way in which the two could be combined. 'What about becoming a non-stipendiary minister?' I replied. He didn't know what that, a new development, was. I explained. He went away and talked it over with Norma. Later, he said, 'Norma and I simply didn't feel that people like us could be acceptable. Then we said, "Well, if Michael and Jackie can, perhaps we can." ' I thanked him for his unflattering view of us and from that time on we four became the closest of friends. He was duly ordained five years later and in due course became Vicar of St Matthew's and Area Dean of Fulham.

As 1974 began I became aware that two of our leaders were misplaced in their church duties. Courtenay Grebby, a retired businessman and a warm pastorally minded reader was the treasurer but I realised that he wasn't very skilled at keeping the books. Utterly honest, he made a real mess of the annual accounts and seemed to have mislaid a lot of money. It was, in fact, a 'paper' error but it made me realise that Peter Reeves, one of our churchwardens, himself an accountant, would be far better at the job. Peter had a massive stutter and was far more suited to dealing with money than with 'up-front' speaking roles. I broached the matter of an exchange with both and to my delight each agreed. Peter didn't feel 'demoted' and Courtenay, as the church's 'father figure', would be a kind churchwarden, balancing well Terry Reddin's much more 'go-getting' style. With their agreement, I informed the Church Council and hoped for their support at the coming Annual Meeting.

Trouble started to brew. Some of the younger members did not want an older warden. They decided to nominate the PCC Secretary, Trevor Grant. Trevor, a local bachelor, was hostile to much that I was doing and made it plain that, if elected, he would give me a hard time. I warned his group that I was not legally bound to declare the election result and would not hesitate to choose my own warden if pressed. They persisted. When the result of the count was passed to me, I announced that I was not bound to accept it and wished to appoint a vicar's warden while they could appoint a people's warden. I then appointed Courtenay Grebby as my warden, knowing that the congregation would elect Terry rather than Trevor which they duly did. This unhappy procedure was entirely legal but inevitably divisive. It led some weeks later to a massive collision between Trevor and me when, privately, we each did some very straight speaking which, thankfully, cleared the air. We became friends and, three years later, he was elected churchwarden. We kept in touch and I was one of the last people to see him in hospital almost a decade later when he died of cancer in his early forties.

Somehow, our verbally violent confrontation had lanced the boil of his class-based bitterness and we prayed together as death approached. Most of my memories of Trevor are now warm and appreciative ones.

Wormwood Scrubs is no place for softies. One evening I was asked to go and lecture in the recreation room about television. A large crowd of men came in. 'There's about a dozen murderers here,' said the warder in charge. It was a very stimulating evening with plenty of thoughtful debate. I little thought that I would be the victim of three future residents of the Scrubs a decade later.

That same week Jackie and I went to see an Athol Fugard play at the Royal Court Theatre. Yvonne Bryceland and Ben Kingsley were post-coitally stark naked on stage as the curtain went up. Increasingly, as the play developed, they were physically covered up as the South African police emotionally stripped them of all dignity. As an attack on the apartheid laws about mixed-race sexual encounters it was incredibly powerful and deeply moved me. We walked the length of the Kings Road from Sloane Square to Fulham in silence. The only other drama that has ever made such an impact on me, years later, was *Miss Saigon*.

In recent years, Holy Trinity, Brompton, has become a church famous for being a Yuppie centre of charismatic worship. John Morris, Vicar in the 1970s, asked me to be the conductor of a weekend house-party at Ashburnham Place in Sussex. 'You'll find they're a real mix,' he said. 'One lot are terribly top-drawer, respectable Kensington churchgoers; the others are all for holy groaning and hand-clapping.'

Somehow we survived and both groups seemed to play fair with each other. I wonder how far, in more recent years, the congregation has managed to contain the first lot. Ex-ambassadors and their ladies don't usually take kindly to the Toronto Blessing and rolling around the floor. Certainly the emotional journey from the Royal Court, HTB and Wormwood Scrubs within a mere ten days can tax even the most relaxed of clergy.

Perhaps I was looking tired when, a few days later, I was on a train from Wandsworth to Waterloo. At an intermediate station I was enjoying my empty compartment when a gaggle of teenage schoolgirls flung open the door, recoiled, and ran to another compartment. 'What was it?' shouted one of them. 'I don't know,' said the first, 'but it moved!' Well, at least I was alive. As the *CEN* put it, a week or two later, 'Michael Saward is never, but never, dull.' That morning I certainly felt my age.

To my surprise, following the Brompton invitation, I was asked to preach at St John the Divine, Kennington. Not far from the Oval cricket ground, St John's was famous for its exotic Anglo-Catholic tradition of Gothic ritual. In such places the sanctuary is usually packed with acolytes, servers, crucifers, thurifers, boatboys and, of course, clergy. St John's didn't fall short in that direction and I certainly felt myself on a different planet from St Matthew's. What did, however, feel very odd was to discover almost more people in the sanctuary than were in the congregation. 'You won't be surprised to know', said the Vicar, David Martin (a member of the General Synod Broadcasting Commission), 'that we've cut out most of the old ritual.' 'You could have fooled me,' I replied. 'What on earth did they get up to before?'

I was working in my study one afternoon when I glanced out of the window and saw an amazing sight. Walking up the drive to my door was none other than Mr Thomas. I grabbed the phone, rang Andrew next door and said, 'I'm sending you someone. Listen. Watch his technique but whatever you do don't give him a penny. I'll explain later.' Then I called Jackie and said, 'Send the chap at the door to Andrew.'

Half an hour later Andrew came in. 'What was that all about?' he asked. 'Did you give him any money?' 'No,' he said, 'but I really think I should have done.' 'Why?' I asked. 'Well,' said Andrew, 'his wife's in hospital in Liverpool, having a hysterectomy and he's short of cash. He seemed very honest. I feel awful.' 'Listen, O gullible one,' I said. 'Mr Thomas came to my curate's house in Edgware in 1960. He was, he said, in spiritual need and we talked for twenty minutes about the state of his soul. He really impressed me and, what decided me was that his shoes were clean. He never mentioned money until he got up to go then he said, almost in passing, that he was short of cash and that his wife was in hospital in Liverpool.' 'Not having a hysterectomy!' gasped

Andrew. 'Exactly,' I said, 'and I fell for it. He promised to repay me and I gave him the train fare. It was a lot of money.' In due course clergy friends in Liverpool told me he was well known there and roared with laughter at my discomfort. Well, you learn as you go along. Andrew got up to go. 'I haven't finished yet,' I said. 'One day in 1964, blow me if Mr Thomas didn't turn up again at my Edgware front door. I can only guess that he assumed that curates move after three years. I pretended not to recognise him and he either did the same or didn't recognise me. I invited him in to my study (I was twice his size) and decided I was going to get my money's worth out of him. Unbelievably we exactly repeated the performance. When finally Mrs Thomas was about to have her second hysterectomy I finally sprang the trap. 'You've made a bad mistake, Mr Thomas,' I said, 'you haven't checked your records. You told me all this nonsense in 1960 and I paid your fare home.' He tried to bluff his way out but was trapped. 'Get out and don't ever dare to show your face in Edgware again or I'll go straight to the police.' 'Andrew,' I concluded, 'I'll never forget that man and I could hardly believe my eyes when he turned up today, all those years later. Being a clergyman has some delightful sides to it. Think yourself lucky you didn't fall for it.' 'I certainly would have done,' admitted Andrew. 'He was really a brilliant con artist.' 'He's not the only one around,' I said.

Early in 1974, the team of hymnwriters, under the chairmanship of Michael Baughen, met to plan for the future. 'We've done two *Youth Praise* books, we've done *Psalm Praise* – what now?' we asked ourselves. The answer wasn't long in coming. The church was moving fast towards a fully 'you-form' liturgy. Modern Bibles were doing the same. *Psalm Praise* had followed suit. Most recent hymns addressed God as 'you'. 'We must take the risk,' we said. 'A new, full-size hymn book with not only modern "you" hymns but a revision of the archaisms in the old hymns.' This was bound to be controversial and it would take many years to complete. Still, we would attempt it.

We broke into two teams, a Music team under David Wilson and a Words team which I would chair. We had to face one major loss. Timothy Dudley-Smith, perhaps the finest modern hymn-writer, did not agree with the policy of modernisation. He would go on writing, and would submit his work to us. He would keep a close link but he wouldn't be in the team. Sadly, we agreed though we greatly missed him. Meanwhile, Michael Baughen would be our titular editor, though he wouldn't be involved in the ongoing work until we reached the final pre-publication stage.

My Words team, augmented to nine members, including six clergy, two Baptist ministers and one woman journalist, set about defining its strategy. Our goal was about six hundred hymns, of which a quarter would be modern, post-1960; a quarter would be newly written for the book; and the remaining three hundred would be selected from traditional hymns revised into 'you' form. We didn't know it then but eight years' work lay ahead of us during which well over fifteen hundred new texts crossed my desk, most of them demonstrating only too well how few people there were who could actually write good hymns. We agreed to assess every hymn on an anonymous basis, with no author's name attached. It was hard for some of our writers but it tested quality ruthlessly. One unknown author submitted fifty texts by the same post and we turned every one down. Another writer on the team, watched in silence as his colleagues rejected almost all of a large batch of his biblical paraphrases. It not only tested our skill, it tested our friendships, and we persevered on that basis. I'll come back to the story later.

Late one night, around midnight, I was getting ready for bed when the doorbell rang. 'Who is it?' 'It's the police.' I opened the door. 'Can you come, Sir? There's a man on a fifth-floor balcony threatening suicide.' I grabbed some clothes and we drove, siren blaring, to North End Road. 'Why me?' I asked. 'It's way outside my parish.' 'We know you,' said the copper, 'and it's too urgent to argue about it.'

A crowd had gathered. The firemen and an ambulance were there. Floodlights picked up the wild-looking solitary figure high up on the ledge. Up I went in the lift. I got to about fifteen feet from the man. 'Don't come closer!' he yelled, 'Or I'll jump.' We looked at each other. He had a thin rope round his neck. 'Are you a priest?' he shouted. 'Yes,' I replied. He said he didn't believe me.

'I'll throw you my driving licence,' I shouted. 'That'll prove it.' I got it out of my wallet and deliberately threw it, seemingly accidentally, to a spot about five feet in front of him. That would get him away from the ledge. 'Don't you move,' he bellowed. He paused. 'I'm going to jump,' he said. 'I really am. If you're a priest, bless me first.'

By this time I reckoned he was probably an Irish Roman Catholic and not a little superstitious. I took a chance. 'Bless you?' I said. 'Not likely! You jump and you'll go straight to hell. I'm not blessing you.' I played on the 'fear of hell' theme for all I was worth. 'You let me come closer. We can talk about it.' Inch by inch I got closer. 'No nearer, I'll jump.' 'And go straight to hell?' I enquired. It took about half an hour but eventually I reached him, put an arm round him, and shouted to the police, 'Don't move! We're coming down quietly.' We did. He went to hospital. Needless to say, I got the 'local hero' treatment all over the local front pages, for getting him off that ledge. Months later, however, he successfully committed suicide. I've never before, or since, tried the 'you're going straight to hell' line but I'm quite sure, that night, that it was that alone which prevented his death.

The local press by then knew me quite well. I sometimes wrote a column for the *Fulham Chronicle* and was often quoted in the *West London Observer*. One journalist came regularly to the vicarage and we got on good terms. She was young, cynical, promiscuous, and claimed to have slept with various politicians in order to get a story. She drank too much and was hard beyond her years. One day she launched a violent attack on me and then suddenly burst into tears. 'You think I'm a whore,' she wailed. 'I've never said any such thing,' I answered. 'Well, I am,' she went on in floods of tears. As time went by she knew what she had to do to save herself from sinking into the slime of total self-disillusionment. Eventually she married and we lost touch. One day, in the mid-1970s the phone rang. 'We're in trouble,' she said desperately. 'The paper goes to bed in half an hour and we haven't got a front-page lead story.' 'I'll call you back,' I said, and, twenty minutes later I dictated a news story over the phone. It just beat the deadline. Some weeks later it happened again. They never paid me a penny for either but I bet there aren't many clergy around who have pulled a newspaper's chestnuts out of the fire like that.

The two Archbishops (Donald Coggan and Stuart Blanch) invited me to serve as one of their Advisers on Evangelism under the Chairmanship of Cuthbert Bardsley, Bishop of Coventry. Cuthbert was a man's man, tall, ruggedly good-looking but a great flatterer. We Advisers sat in a large circle. Canon This spoke strongly. 'I do so agree,' said Cuthbert. Mrs That followed, saying the exact opposite. 'You are so right,' purred Cuthbert.

It went on like this for months. Oodles of treacle but not much action. When, in due course, Cuthbert retired he was followed by a totally spineless bishop who effectively ruined whatever good was left in it. I resigned and the Archbishops had the sense to apply euthanasia after a decent pause. Sadly, it was a perennial talking shop which resisted all attempts to get some 'evangelism professionals' on board. Thus we rambled round and round and got nowhere. Some years later the subject came up on a General Synod debate. I spoke about the need for a gospel which offered forgiveness of sins. David Brown, Bishop of Guildford, replied to the debate and caricatured my speech. I wrote to him objecting strongly to this treatment. He asked me, together with a friend who is now a bishop, to go to his house to talk it over. To our amazement, and embarrassment, he bared his soul and then declared that in all his life he had 'never had any sense of sin'. Not surprisingly, he had no gospel since 'all are saved anyway'. No sin, no gospel, no evangelism. He was a sad, not to say pathetic, man trying to chair a body committed to evangelism, for which he saw no need. A few weeks later he died very suddenly. What can one think in such circumstances? He was just a nice man. And some people thought he was an Evangelical! He was the second much-loved, well-known, allegedly Evangelical bishop who, within a decade had effectively denied, in my presence, some of the classic ingredients of the Christian gospel. No sin, no gospel, no evangelism. Well, that genial pleasantness may get you a bishopric but it won't save a soul, will it?

Early in June, the Bishop of Kensington, Ronald Goodchild, took all the local clergy away to a conference at High Leigh near

Hoddesden in Hertfordshire. I, and two others, organised the whole thing and among our speakers was Fritz Schumacher, famous for his 'small is beautiful' epigram. He was naturally brilliant but, like most Germans of eminence, not happy at being criticised. In discussion I queried his definition. 'Surely,' I enquired, 'it isn't large or small that is beautiful but whatever is appropriate?' That went down like a lead balloon though it seems obvious enough to me. Such epigrams as 'small is beautiful' or 'the medium is the message' (that one was McLuhan's) are no more than fashionable clichés of dubious verity. It amazes me how people fall for them so uncritically.

As the conference ended, we organisers were each given five minutes to speak to an unannounced topic. Mine was 'the fool in the Christian tradition'. My mind raced. I plunged in with Jack Point in the *Yeoman of the Guard* and the jester tradition, then on to *I Pagliacci* and the clown theme, to St Francis of Assisi, and finally to St Paul's 'fool for Christ'. It was something of a *tour de force* off the cuff in five minutes and I was glad that my love of opera and church history had made it possible. One of the local clergy later called me 'a pompous prat who never stopped talking' but since he is more or less clinically mad I haven't taken him too seriously.

A week or so before the High Leigh conference a terrible tragedy hit Sands End. Just outside our parish boundary stood Jepson House, an eighteen-storey council tower block. High up on the sixteenth floor was a flat occupied by Mrs Barbara Todd and her fair-haired, blue-eyed, three-year-old daughter, Simone. One Sunday morning in late May, Simone was playing in the living room and she climbed up onto the window sill. A few seconds later her little body landed on the ground, 150 feet below. I was called, since the next-door parish, Christ Church, was in between vicars. Mrs Todd, her separated husband, and her family and neighbours were distraught. How had it happened? The flat had windows which opened on a horizontal pivot without any safety catches.

I conducted the packed funeral service and, at the end, and with the parents' approval, issued a press release calling for 'just anger to impress upon those in authority that human life must not be wasted in accidents which can easily be prevented by proper planning. To put swivel windows', I added, 'without safety catches, in council tower-block flats and then to allow young mothers with little children to live in them, seems to be incredibly irresponsible. I hope some civil servant is feeling heavy in his conscience.' Inevitably the Borough Housing Chairman, Ian Gray, made the foolish error of issuing a statement saying that he was 'satisfied' with the safety of windows in council flats. In the words of the *Fulham Chronicle*, 'a storm of protest followed'. Gray made the further mistake of trying to rubbish me by a snide remark that 'as a man of God' I must 'have very powerful allies'.

The other local paper, the *West London Observer*, sent a photographer to the flat to measure the validity of another Councillor's claim that the windows would only open to 'six inches'. His photo, with a tape-measure in view, showed a twenty-inch gap. The case against the planners was conclusive. Then, to my utter horror, another leading councillor, who had long been a member of St Matthew's, accused me of trying to score party political points! I was sickened that any Christian man should value the reputation of his party above the life of a child, whose death implicated his party's irresponsibility. He ceased attending St Matthew's and I was, frankly, relieved. Politicians of that ilk are better outside than inside the church.

But there was a long-term benefit. Little Simone was never to know that her death was the trigger that led to the creation, nearly three years later, of a campaigning residents association, which I christened ARISE (Association of Residents in Sands End), of which I was then elected the first chairman. It is still going strong over twenty years later, championing the many concerns of a needy area in relation to those in local authority. Many of the residents were puzzled at my vocal involvement (and that of St Matthew's) in a range of social concerns. Empty housing, lack of parks, road safety, teenage vandalism, racial hatred, lorry routes avoiding 'rat run' streets, direct access to the Thames riverbank. 'What', said one of them, 'has all this got to do with God and religion?' 'Because God loves the world, because he made human beings, and because he wants justice,' I replied. 'It's all part of the gospel of Jesus, which I preach.'

I was thrilled to see St Matthew's people, and their leaders, combining these concerns with their traditional Evangelical desire to 'see souls saved'. The local press got the message and we featured in yet more coverage. The *Fulham Chronicle* summed it up in a leading article a few weeks after Simone's death. Citing our social concerns, they linked Christ's 'compassion at the plight of the deprived' with my public utterances about 'real day-to-day practical problems' and concluded that 'when all clergymen speak in these tones, plain men and women will find the Church's spiritual message the easier to understand'. It was good to get such support, which showed that they understood that I was not on some mega-ego-trip for its own sake.

And so, six days later, to the Hyde Park Hotel on 25 July. The invitation was unexpected and came from the Advertising Association. The chairman of one of its committees, Brian Henry, was also a Director of Southern Television and he and his members were giving lunch to a group of clergy. Would I care to attend? I duly turned up and enjoyed an excellent lunch with a fine view of Hyde Park. The party broke up and I went down the stairs only to come, literally, face to face with John Wayne, who was in the middle of making the film *Brannigan*. He took one look, grinned his craggy grin and said, 'Stick around, Padre, I need all the help I can get.' I smiled back – and failed to ask for his autograph! What I didn't know was that the lunch was a vetting operation and I was being checked out.

A second letter invited me to become a member of AA's Professions Liaison Group. The members were 'an eminent architect, a senior solicitor, a high-flying doctor, a TV bigwig' and me. I was to be 'Mr Church'. And so I became for the next three years. They even published a paper of mine in the AA journal, entitled 'Sell me the old, old story,' which posed a series of social, ethical and moral challenges to both the churches and the ad men. The Director-General, Roger Underhill, spoke of 'the wonderful way in which you have helped us' when I eventually stood down but then top ad men are experts in knowing how to say thank you convincingly. I hope I did some good – I certainly enjoyed the challenge.

She was a very large black lady who had come to get help 'frarm de vicar'. Her husband, it seemed, had paid a witch doctor in Chelsea (I kid you not!) to set a 'duppy' on her. This 'presence' had come through, or under, her locked bedroom door and frightened her excessively. Naturally, I asked her why her husband had taken such an extreme course of action. 'E get ten children by me an' I say, dat enough. E no happy with this so I lark de bedroom door.'

I decided to meet this husband. He was a fascinating rogue, with flashing eyes and a leering smile. 'I like women,' he informed me. 'When I go with a woman, I drarp she when she pregnant. So far, I get ten women pregnant. My wife, she get ten children so I got nineteen children in all. I still want more. When she say "no more", and lark de door, I put de duppy on her.' They didn't teach us how to handle this in my theological college. Men who were proud of their virility and wanted to get women in the sack, them I understood. What I hadn't met were men pulsating with fertility. You don't meet many of these in London. I told him that he was just greedy and that any woman was reasonably entitled to a bit of a break after ten kids. I went into the bedroom and gave my impression of a schoolmaster ticking-off a recalcitrant fourth-form duppy. Weeks later I heard that all was well. She had employed a second Chelsea witch doctor to scare off the first one's duppy. I never heard whether Mr Fertile Fred had succeeded in further impregnating her. It's a funny old world.

I was standing on a platform at Piccadilly Circus underground station when a small child, with a penetrating voice, noticing my clerical collar, squeaked, 'Mummy, what is that man *for*?' After the duppy incident, it seemed a question distinctly below the belt.

As a family, less Rachel, we set off for Paris to take on a locum for the Anglican chaplain. Three quite memorable incidents marked our stay. First, I took a funeral at Vincennes. There were three people present, plus undertakers and coffin. Only one spoke any English but it was agreed that an 'English' interment was the order of the day since the corpse was one of our lot. At the cemetery gate, the undertaker's men grabbed the heavy coffin handles, and trotted off, holding it at thigh height, while I sedately walked towards the vault. They really did trot, so I was soon far behind them. When at last I reached the grave, they were lounging about smoking, with the coffin roughly propped up against a stone. I conducted the minimal liturgy with decent decorum and, at the appropriate point, they grabbed the coffin and threw it (yes, threw it) into the vault. I silently blessed English undertakers and took my (enormous) fee. The total cost was absolutely horrific – at least four times the going rate on the civilised side of the Channel.

Then there was Versailles. I remember it, not so much for its undoubted splendour and a delightful, if exhausting day but because Jill, one of our twins, aged nine, was violently sick in the Hall of Mirrors. Look in any direction and there was Jill noisily vomiting. Not a pretty kaleidoscope of sights.

For the Sawards, the most significant, and sadly disturbing event, concerned the famous Crippen cables. My grandfather, Henry Kendall, having recognised Dr Crippen, the murderer, and his lady-friend, Ethel Le Neve, as passengers on his ship, SS *Montrose*, in 1910, had made the first use of radio in the detection of crime and the so-called cables were to be handed on to me, his only grandson. Not long before his death, he had lent them to a close friend, Sir Norman Vernon, who had, for reasons unknown to all of us, not returned them. Soon after Sir Norman's death, his son, Sir Nigel, offered them for auction to Bonhams the London auctioneers. I heard about this just as I was off to Paris and attempted by letter and phone to claim my right to them. However, understandably, my formal title to them could not be sustained since they were not mentioned in my grandfather's will and my mother's sworn testimonial could not override the actual possession by the Vernon family. So, our Paris trip was overshadowed by the auction in London on 30 July at which they were bought for £1,600 by an unknown bidder and have since vanished completely. My only consolation came thirteen years later when I, in my turn, anonymously purchased at an auction a first-edition copy of Edgar Wallace's *Four Just Men*, which my grandfather had lent to Crippen during the ill-fated voyage. It was identified as such and so inscribed by Grandad and it cost me £128 to get it. It was worth every penny in the circumstances.

Back in Fulham we faced a matter of no small consequence. The newly elected Labour Government had abolished the Direct Grant and Joe, a boarder at Eltham College, was going to cost us considerably increased fees. The Head agreed that we should be wise to seek an Anglican school with some substantial bursaries and we opted for Haileybury. But Eltham did not, understandably, prepare boys for Common Entrance and Joe promptly failed it. Haileybury agreed to hold the place for one term if we sent him to a 'crammer' while Eltham generously kept his place open until he resat the exam. At considerable cost he did a term at the Talbot-Rice agency near Harrods and passed at his second attempt. Nevertheless, Haileybury, even with a bursary, was going to bankrupt us so Jackie got a job and a close friend lent us about £2,000 to tide us over. Jackie became a shelf-stacker at Sainsburys, in the Kings Road, and really enjoyed it. She met, and worked for, or with, an extraordinary collection of people including a marquess, the wife of a Lord Chief Justice, and a Spanish boss, Leo Torné, who remained a good friend until his death in 1996. All in all, she worked for Sainsburys (later in West Ealing) until 1987 by which time we had completed all the educational expenses of bringing up four children.

Having had five years' involvement in the radio and television world but, for bureaucratic reasons, almost no actual broadcasting, the mid-1970s saw me involved in scores of programmes. As the years went by I appeared on virtually all the national radio and TV channels. It was an amusing boast of mine, in due course, that I was one of only a tiny handful of people who had been on Radios 1, 2, 3, 4 and 5. Plenty of folk have appeared on 1, 2 and 4, or 2, 4 and 5 but to get on to 1 and 3 is not given to many. I only know of Richard Baker and Pauline Webb (the Methodist leader) who have done all five. Add to that my first session on the *Jimmy Young Show* and, once more, the streak of humility was under intense pressure. Not a lot of people get fifteen minutes with Jimmy Young.

One evening I was enjoying a pleasant dinner with a would-be publisher in Mon Plaisir, a French bistro in Monmouth Street, when there was an enormous explosion nearby. No immediate danger was evident but it turned out to be one of the earliest mainland attacks by the IRA. The bomb had gone off only four hundred yards away. Quietly the restaurant emptied out. There was no panic, or any need for it, but clearly people could no longer enjoy their meals.

On the cricket field, I was diocesan Vice-Captain and ran up a quick fifty against our neighbours across the Thames, even if Southwark did beat us.

The supreme accolade came, not on the cricket field but almost outside Buckingham Palace. I was sitting on top of a number 11 bus when the driver and conductor got off and left it at the roadside. I, and a family of American tourists, were the only passengers left so I offered to walk them to the palace which was close to my intended route. Father, mother and a child of indeterminate age and sex accompanied me until the latter asked in time-honoured transatlantic style, 'Do you mind if I ask you a personal question?' 'Fire away,' I said. It asked politely, 'How long does it take to get an accent like yours?' I assured the hermaphrodite infant that it was totally authentic and I had made no conscious effort to speak the Queen's English. It looked at me long and hard, entirely unconvinced at such a casual explanation.

While on the subject of language I was delighted by two priceless examples from my Fulham neighbours. One somewhat literalist howler came from a small girl, Linda O'Brien, who informed me with an assured look that 'I know what you do in church. I've seen it on the Telly. You eat God!'

Almost as intriguing was the remark of an old lady at a nearby Free Church who informed me that she had been there 'at the desecration of this church, fifty-five years ago'.

Two further, and gorgeous, malaprops came not long after. 'I don't quite understand this bit in St Matthew, Vicar,' queried the funny old lady. 'It says, in chapter one, that "his mother Mary was exposed to Joseph".' Wow! Some engagement that must have been. The actual word was, of course, 'espoused'.

Then there was the Sunday night when I came back from

church and asked Jackie, who had the TV set on, 'Darling, were you watching Zeffirelli's *Jesus of Nazareth?*' 'No,' replied the pious vicar's wife, 'I've been watching *The Good Life.*'

Life at St Matthew's, despite a few ups and downs, was developing well. It was a good indication that all was reasonably happy when all the leaders took the mickey out of each other at the Harvest Supper and other similar events. Gary Piper had a great gift for spotting my repetitive phraseology. That year he did a brilliant impersonation, sweeping his right hand through his hair and saying, 'You see, my dilemma is this.' Not till then did I realise how often I did both. You need good friends to make such points and to do it in a way that creates gales of laughter from your congregation. I haven't had any 'dilemmas' in the past twenty years though I fear that my hair still needs an expansive gesture now and then.

It was that year that I managed to persuade the St Matthew's Church Council to accept an Overseas' Bursar for a month. These men, mostly from Africa and Asia, were clergymen specially selected for a year's training in an English theological college, punctuated by two vacations spent in parishes.

Our first Bursar was a young Tanzanian, Simon Makundi, who was about five foot three and seemed prone to sleep for about eighteen hours a day. On his first morning at our vicarage, he came down to my study quite late, knocked and entered. What happened next was quite crazy. I can't imagine why I said what I did because it was almost certain to cause grave offence to him and I shouldn't have had a leg to stand on by way of defence or explanation. I simply acted instinctively and took a huge risk. I looked at him and said, in my most military manner, 'Stand to attention, Makundi, and call me "Bwana".' He stopped dead, his eyes narrowed, and he said, with great deliberation, 'Capitalist, Imperialist, Swine.' We have never looked back. What it was that made both of us do it, I'll never know, but we were friends from that moment. Fifteen years later we met in Leicester at the enthronement of Bishop Tom Butler. Simon popped out from behind a large English bishop, himself now a Tanzanian bishop. 'From now on', I said, 'I shall have to stand to attention and call you "Bwana".' I love him dearly and thank God that we both have the same capacity to pull each other's legs. He, and Martha, his wife, have stayed with us on various occasions and we hugely enjoyed watching her confound the English on the London Underground by yanking out a large black breast and clamping her latest child onto it. Not a lot of women did that in the London of twenty years ago.

Early in 1976 I went to Zermatt, expenses paid, as a holiday chaplain. It still cost an arm and a leg, and not by means of any accidents. I discovered that I lack the necessary fluidity of hips to ski or dance (and what else is there to do at a ski resort? Don't answer that!) In short, I never got out of the car-park ski school, leaving permanent signs of my presence on the terrain by my fundamental (and I mean fundamental) capacity to fall over. I enjoyed a free *abonnement* and travelled high up on the slopes by train and down again by footpath or the same train. Famous personalities abounded, of whom I recognised Robin Day and Chris Chataway (once a subaltern when I was a gunner) who seemed to be enjoying the female company.

Back home it soon became clear that Jackie's mother Eileen was seriously ill and she died in Frinton on 19 March. I conducted a not-very-easy cremation service and spent many months as executor for her will.

Jackie used a part of her mother's legacy to buy a colour TV and a freezer, both of which were new experiences for us. We enjoyed our twentieth wedding anniversary with a brief stay at a luxury hotel in Kent. Not long afterwards I had a brief but spectacular cricket season, scoring 140 in two innings, peppered with fours and sixes and missing the chance of a maiden (and only) century by going for a six when on 95 and being bowled in the process. That was at Forest School, against the Chelmsford Diocese, and gave me the pleasurable experience of a season's batting average of one hundred times that of fifteen-year-old Joe's.

Having read scores of books about the First World War, I decided to go for a couple of days to the Somme to drive the length of the battlefield. Thus it was that on the sixtieth anniversary (1 July

1976) at 7.30 a.m. I was standing on the tip of the Lochnagar mine crater at La Boisselle. No-one else was in sight as I watched in my mind's eye the infantry from Tyneside and Lincolnshire being mown down in their hundreds as they walked, with no hope of concealment, across wide-open slopes into the relentless artillery and machine-gun fire. I little thought that for seven years, just over a decade later, I should be chaplain to an annual gathering of up to five hundred people on that very spot at that selfsame time who would come to pay their respects to the twenty thousand who would die on that first day of the battle, and the further forty thousand who would lie wounded alongside them. Lochnagar's enormous crater, silent for half a century, would become a great symbol of sacrifice, drawing British, French, and eventually, Germans, to its vast embrace.

As the school year ended, Rachel duly collected her 'O' levels, Joe was well settled at Haileybury, and the twins left Peterborough School with glowing reports. Jill, it seems, was 'mature, original, and discerning' while Sue was gifted with 'imagination, sensitivity, reliability, and enthusiasm'. Jackie and I pondered these eulogies sceptically. Sue's powers of imagination were, however, somewhat limited. 'Will you go away,' I said. 'I'm trying to kiss Mummy.' Her reply did not indicate much grasp of matrimonial bliss. 'Why?' she grumbled. 'You gave her one yesterday.' Joe, for his part, promptly fractured his wrist on returning to school. An adult friend commiserated with him. 'Yes,' Joe replied, 'it was a nuisance since we hadn't got a gynaecologist on the staff of the school sanatorium.' Jill and Sue joined Rachel at Lady Margaret School in nearby Parsons Green.

My second speech in General Synod was, in due course, to have consequences I couldn't have foreseen. I offered some sympathetic, but highly critical remarks about the Church Commissioners' so-called popular report. I had distributed 125 copies to St Matthew's congregation but 'virtually nobody read them' and most went on believing that 1 Millbank was the home of 'The Big Bad Wolf'. The eminently stylish little report was light years away in presentation from what was normality in Sands End, namely the *Mail*, the *Mirror* and the *Sun*. I could have added that the only figures that our *Sun* readers understood were on page three. As someone later said of the *Sun's* attitudes, 'It's tit tit on page three and tut tut on page four.' Anyway, my point obviously struck home for the popular report was transformed and two years later I was elected a Church Commissioner, which I remained for fifteen years (through six elections).

As 1976 ended, I discovered that my little book *Cracking the God-Code* had been translated into both Swedish and Chinese. Since it also had an American edition, it became my most widely published book. I was not, however, pleased to discover that the Americans had deleted the final chapter, without consultation, since they didn't approve of my having referred to the Oscar-winning film *The Graduate* as a reminder that knowledge had to be applied. So much for American Fundamentalist publishers! They'll never get their hands on my work in future.

It seemed appropriate that 1 April should mark my one and only visit to the Penthouse Club in Mayfair where Thames TV were making a programme entitled *Thou Shalt Not Commit Adultery*. Thames only had space for six of the Ten Commandments and Adultery was obviously a crowd-puller. Scheduled for Peak Period transmission we had thirty minutes in which to do battle, compered by two ITN newscasters, Trevor McDonald and Carol Barnes. I was head to head with the editor of *Forum* arguing the issue in principle, while Jenny Guinness, a former *Vogue* fashion model of stunning beauty (and considerable brain), argued as a Christian against a somewhat mindless blond 'model'. I reckon we Christians won hands down and even the *Forum* man conceded that we made the best Christian case he had ever heard.

The latter years of the 1970s saw me engaged in a long-running battle with the leaders of the Church Pastoral Aid Society. This fine organisation, the most reputable body in the Evangelical Anglican galaxy, was deeply flawed in one respect. For many years it had been run by a self-appointed and elderly oligarchy of clergy, some of whom had served for twenty years or more on its General Council and had never once been up for re-election in any meaningful sense. The so-called election, quite farcical, took about one minute in a public religious meeting in Central London. The President, Norman Anderson, proposed them *en bloc* from the chair, year by year, and woe betide anyone who queried the procedure. Since, as usual, no-one would take the risk, it was left to Yours Truly to put his reputation on the line and call, in 1973, for a revision of the Society's Constitution in order, first, to create a proper membership, and, secondly, to provide for a democratic postal ballot.

As might be expected, I was maligned and traduced by a combination of the oligarchy, their sycophantic friends and the General Secretary. Battle raged in the church press in a series of encounters spread over about five years. I was strongly supported by not a few people but, since, in those days, any Evangelical clergy were largely dependent on CPAS who as major patrons controlled hundreds of parochial appointments, very few clergy would take the risk of having their names linked to mine in the ongoing skirmishes.

One day I was telephoned by a member of the CPAS General Council who said 'in confidence' that my objections were absolutely on target, that the Council was largely a fiction and the whole thing was controlled by the Secretary and a small reactionary cabal. 'Keep fighting outside' was the message 'while some of us work for change within'. But change didn't come, and, utterly depressed, some of the 'insiders' gave up the struggle and resigned. At the point of despair, and badly bruised by the attacks made on me in the press, I felt ready to throw in the towel. Suddenly, to everyone's amazement, the Society announced that it would initiate a major reform and, in no time, almost all I had campaigned for came about. Since I had no axe to grind against the Society as such I warmly welcomed the change and sat back to relax.

But a greater irony was yet to come. When, a few years later, the General Secretary retired, I was urged by the Chairman, Richard Wilkins, a former Edgware YPF man, to let my name go forward as his successor. I laughingly declined absolutely to apply for the post but was, even so, shortlisted and called for interview. Since I was godfather to two of Richard's children, and a close friend of the Vice-Chairman, I felt the situation to be quite ridiculous and campaigned in my interview for Gavin Reid, a longstanding staff member also on the shortlist, to be appointed. In the event, the Council appointed John Moore who did a quite outstanding job. Gavin, in due course, became a bishop, so honour was satisfied.

The final move was to take place in the early nineties when I was elected to the Council, on which I duly served for six years. At my first meeting the new Chairman, Canon Michael Perry, welcomed me as the one whose David-versus-Goliath fight in earlier years had effectively created the revised Constitution and Council which I was now joining. Applause all round!

Returning to St Matthew's, the leaders decided to make 1977 a year of mission and gave it the general title 'All Change' (which I later used as the title for another book). It all began with a barn dance which was, in those days, a very radical way to launch such a year in an Evangelical church. Next came Pasolini's film *The Gospel according to St Matthew*, which avoided all the schmaltz so common in religious films, in favour of a Christ who was tough, urgent, aggressive and willing to die for his gospel. It drew people who would never normally have come to a church service. A week or two later, at the pressing request of the PCC I wrote urging the then Dean of St Paul's to refuse entry to President Idi Amin of Uganda, or any representative of his government, at the forthcoming Queen's Silver Jubilee service in the cathedral. 'I can't believe it right', I added, 'to allow a known butcher of Christians to attend divine worship on such an occasion while clearly seen to be impenitent!' I haven't often allowed myself to try to influence matters of national or international policy but I am glad that I, and St Matthew's, pressed this matter. Having once met Archbishop Janani Luwum, I had a personal axe to grind with Amin. Both the local and the church press carried our plea.

While all this was going on, I was up to my neck in the planning of the Second National Evangelical Anglican Congress to be held at Nottingham University in April. Once more I was Press Officer (as I had been at Keele ten years earlier) and when, on the first night, we had a bomb alert which delayed the opening speech by Stuart Blanch, Archbishop of York, for nearly an hour I was hopeful that we should hit the front pages (a Press Officer's dream). Alas, Fleet Street couldn't care less, only being interested in an actual explosion which even I had no desire to provide!

Not only did I handle media and official Observers but Raymond Johnston and I also wrote much of the draft of the media chapter for the report. Being very restricted for space we concentrated on the 'structural' issues. This provoked a different kind of explosion from the Evangelical media performers who wanted to say lots of positive things about opportunities opening up. They attempted a totally new chapter, omitting all the crucial 'structural' issues. After a head-on collision we persuaded the Report Committee to allow me to incorporate both. Thank God we did. Both elements were vital and I remain impenitent. Had I not stressed my points, no-one would ever have tried to include them in an 'opportunities' chapter. In the end we had our cake and ate it. Raymond Johnston and I were more than vindicated by later events in the media world.

Continuing our 'All Change' year at St Matthew's, we were drawing more than fifty men and women to our midweek Bible Study groups and we were involved in all the local street parties for the Queen's Silver Jubilee in June. Hundreds attended our highly imaginative Jubilee Commemoration Service which incorporated both sound and vision as we covered major events in the Queen's reign. 'Can you appear on Jimmy Savile's *Speak Easy* TV programme next Thursday?' said the BBC TV researcher. 'No, I'm playing cricket out at Snaresbrook.' 'We'll send a car for you.' 'Well, if I'm batting you'll have to wait.'

I wasn't, the car duly arrived, I changed in the back seat, and we got to Lime Grove or (wherever) just in time. Savile, as presenter, virtually ignored me and I got one thirty-second bite in half an hour. 'Don't ever waste my time like that again,' I complained to the BBC's Head of Religious Broadcasting. 'I wasn't needed at all, got no chance to speak, and anyway, it was a lousy programme.' In the years since, the practice of playing God with people has got worse and worse. These days, you're often lucky to get one sentence quoted from a ten-minute recorded interview. More and more, TV producers have decided on their 'angle' in advance and only want a single quote which may radically distort your view when scissored out of context. I speak from much bitter experience.

The climax of the parish 'All Change' mission came in September when Alan Godson came to lead a team of theological students. Alan, a former Cambridge rugby blue, is an extraordinary man and a gifted personal evangelist. He functions like a Tiger Tank and can seriously frighten those of sensitive and nervous disposition. We chose him, knowing that he might just be used by God to get through to some of the fairly down-to-earth men in the area and in that he was very effective. Ex-sportsmen are his meat and drink and one well-known Fulham footballer came to the Christian faith in consequence. Alan and I have long been sporting adversaries on the cricket field and personal friends off it, but we were united in horrified anger when a local vicar declined to allow us to hold an open-air meeting on a pavement ten yards over our parish boundary in a shopping area. Alan was, in less than Christian mood, threatening to go and 'land one' on the unfriendly incumbent for this quite extraordinary stupidity. This apart, 'All Change' was a very successful operation.

Richard Attenborough's film *A Bridge Too Far*, with its powerful presentation of the attempt to break into Germany through Nijmegen and Arnhem in 1944, was the subject of much controversy at this time. I had a letter in *The Times* criticising his 'playing God with men's hard-earned reputations' (he had conflated a living, somewhat eccentric, Airborne officer with a posthumous VC and shown the character dying in a cellar and, then, made things worse by altering the name of another officer to avoid confusion with a general of the same name). Attenborough was offended by my attack (one of many by people who knew the battle well) and wrote an aggrieved letter to me. I pointed out that if the public were likely to be confused by men with the same surname, I hoped that he or his brother David would change their names. He wasn't amused. I, having experienced the manipulative attitudes of film-makers over *Cromwell* ten years earlier, wasn't amused either. The *Sunday Times* incorporated my objection into a major article in October of that year which set out in full detail the wide-spread anger at Attenborough's film. He was, it said, 'badly shaken'. He deserved to be. I was interested, years later, to read Dirk Bogarde's critical views in his autobiography. He had played 'Boy' Browning in the film which was, in his words, 'a disastrously unhappy experience', into which he had 'been jollied'. It had, he said, 'everything about it that was most detestable and unpleasant in the business'. He felt himself to be 'cheap bait'. I, incidentally, received a thank-you letter from Kenya from the 'somewhat eccentric' Major Digby Tatham-Warter who had not been at all amused to see himself die on celluloid. Film producers, in my limited experience, hardly know the meaning of the word truth. They will happily torture and butcher history to make their films. *Cromwell*, when I finally saw it in the 1990s, was a travesty of what had actually happened in the 1640s and 1650s.

In mid-November, Gerald Priestland made a leg-pulling reference to me in his Saturday morning *Yours Faithfully* Radio 4 programme. Obviously, because we were friends, there was no malice in it, but he used the phrase that I was a 'self-confessed dirty-book vicar'. A number of Fulham people were shocked and angered at the implication and suggested that I must call for an apology on air and demand that the phrase be retracted. I wrote a gentle letter to John Lang, Head of Religious Broadcasting, saying that I didn't object to Gerry's leg-pulling but that a large radio audience was not the place for it, not least because I had never described myself in such terms. John Lang's reply was probably the shortest letter I have ever received. 'We agree. Gerald Priestland will act,' was all that he said. The following Saturday Gerry laughingly apologised. 'Last Saturday', he said, 'I called the Reverend Michael Saward a "dirty-book" vicar. Well, he's the cleanest vicar I know.' It was a typical media shrug-off but it was better than nothing. It is, I suppose, some consolation, to have had public apologies from the *News of the World* and from Radio 4. In later years he would have another go at me in a book but I couldn't help liking him.

As 'All Change' drew to its close, I was conscious that I needed a sabbatical leave. I had served for twenty-two years without a major opportunity for relaxed recharging of my batteries and I made plans to go to the United States for nine weeks following Easter in 1978. Various friends helped me with contacts and I concocted an itinerary which began in New York and took in Pittsburgh, Niagara, Denver, Seattle, San Francisco, Los Angeles, the Grand Canyon, Houston, New Orleans and various towns in Florida. Jackie, somewhat reluctantly but gallantly, agreed to hold the fort in Fulham.

In those days, one of the most prestigious invitations was for an Evangelical clergyman to be asked to give a paper at the annual Islington Conference. In January 1978 it was held in All Souls', Langham Place, and the theme was 'Evangelical Identity Today'. The four speakers included three theological college principals (Robin Nixon, Alec Motyer and Jim Packer) and me and I had the notoriously tough 'post-lunch' spot. A little folding of the hands to sleep was often the audience's response to that slot so I had a job on my hands. My task was to spell out the pros and cons of the great changes in Evangelical lifestyle which had occurred with the 1960s and 1970s and I began by describing the old ways and, to the audible sound, through the PA system, of a lavatory flushing, what had happened to them. No-one, before or since, had ever used any sound effect, let alone that one, at an Islington Conference. If I had done nothing else, I kept them all awake that afternoon, with 'Liberty, Licence, and Responsibility', the title of my paper.

Ten days later my election as a Church Commissioner was announced at the General Synod. My first task was to serve on the Redundant Churches' Committee. It was our responsibility to hear appeals against diocesan proposals to find uses for, or to demolish, parish churches no longer in use.

Plans were almost complete for the coming sabbatical when I met an old friend, Eric Vevers, at the London diocesan Synod in Church House, Westminster, on 28 January 1978. We ate our lunchtime sandwiches together in the Bishop Partridge Hall (where my sister Moira had held her wedding reception) and he mentioned, confidentially, that he was shortly due to leave St Mary's, Ealing, where he had been vicar for ten years, and wondered if I could suggest suitable names for a successor. We talked of a dozen or so possibles and he then said, 'What about you?' I didn't know the church but expressed interest and he agreed to propose my name to the Bishop if I would also let the Diocesan secretary know of my interest. Shortly before, Derek Hayward, the Secretary, had explicitly said, 'Don't hesitate to tell me if something suitable falls vacant.' I took him at his word. Things progressed quickly and before long I had seen the Bishop of Willesden, Hewlett Thompson, looked around the parish and vicarage, met the churchwardens and agreed to accept a formal offer if it came. Timing was the problem. Eric was leaving, I couldn't announce it till he'd gone, nor could I tell Fulham with only a few days to go before the sabbatical. The time pressure was so tight that the Bishop of London, Gerald Ellison, rang me and said, 'This is a formal offer. Yes or no, and I'll hold you to your answer?' 'Yes,' I said. St Matthew's was holding its Annual Church Meeting on Palm Sunday afternoon and I ended the meeting by announcing the move. Two weeks later my sabbatical started.

Jack Wolton and Eric Lindsley, the elderly Ealing churchwardens, had had one anxiety about me. Eric Vevers had been defeated when he tried to remove one pew from the church. It had been quite a row. The wardens had heard rumours that I had removed pews in Fulham (I had indeed – nearly twenty – but with general approval). Their first question was, 'Do you believe in moving pews?' I laughed, said 'I don't know – what do they look like – I've never seen a moving pew?' They looked puzzled by the credal levity but somehow reassured. Eighteen months later we removed twelve in Ealing and it hardly caused a raised eyebrow.

The Bishop of Kensington asked to see me before I flew out to New York. 'Michael,' he said, 'I think we should suspend presentation on St Matthew's when you go. What do you think?' Suspending presentation meant not appointing a 'freehold' vicar but keeping reorganisation options open. 'I agree,' I replied. 'We ought to be united with our next-door parish.' 'So what would you say', he went on, 'if I said that I'm considering putting the curate in charge?' I gulped. 'I don't think that is a proper question for you to put about a man's successor,' I answered. 'I want your opinion,' he pressed me. 'I don't want to comment,' I replied. He gave me a hard look. 'I really want to know,' he added. 'I wasn't expecting this,' I said, 'but I do know what I, the churchwardens and elders think, because they've told me.' 'So you tell me,' he insisted. 'On your own head be it,' I began. 'No-one actually wants him to take over. Most are strongly opposed. Two or three can live with it, but there is no enthusiasm.' 'Thank you,' said the Bishop, 'that is actually very helpful information.'

Thus it was, that knowing the general view, the Bishop of Kensington duly appointed my curate to be Priest-in-Charge of St Matthew's, Fulham, on my departure. I sometimes wonder why I am, broadly speaking, in favour of bishops.

America came and went. I recorded the journey on sixteen audio cassettes as I moved from place to place. It was a marvellous experience, the first of many later visits. I made good, lasting friendships, enjoyed wonderful hospitality, preached many times, and vividly remember a series of incidents, including the following.

On my first night I was invited to take part in a Jewish *seder* meal on Long Island. With Auschwitz survivors present, I was asked to read from the Old Testament. It was strange and sad, because I, almost the only Gentile in the room, seemed the only one to treat it with any respect. Next morning, in New York, I asked a cab driver to take me from Penn Station to Broadway. 'Where's Broadway?' he asked. I had to direct him! Three days later, in a small Pennsylvania shop I was congratulated by the owner who told me, 'I just love your Scottish brogue.' I told her I had no Scottish blood and that it was a deadly insult to a true-blue Englishman!

A day or two later I drove out into the Amish area and passed successively the evocatively named villages of Bird-in-hand, Intercourse, and Paradise. Quite a climactic journey! Strangely, what struck me with greater force than anything else in the Eastern States, was the enormous quantity of trees. No-one had ever before mentioned the existence of so many trees, mile upon mile of them stretching for almost a thousand miles from the Canadian border to Florida.

I spent a weekend preaching for the parish weekend house-party of St Stephen's, Sewickley, near Pittsburgh. All men, including one US Senator and an ex-convict convert, we took over a magnificent wooden lodge in nearby Ohio. To my amused delight I discovered that the parish women's group, desperately keen to be 'English', had taken the title 'The Crumpet Club'. Since the rector was an Englishman, I asked whether they were aware of its English significance. He grinned and stayed silent. I gently told my kind host and hostess. He roared with laughter and said, 'Honey, I never knew what you women got up to. Now I understand.'

I flew to Buffalo, drove via Niagara Falls to Elmira near Toronto, then on by plane, stopping briefly at Chicago, until I reached Denver. There I saw my first buffalo herd, and the great snow-clad vista of the eastern wall of the Rockies. In the Anglican Cathedral I attended a weekday evening service in the sanctuary – we all sat on the floor, the Bishop (Bill Frey, the former disc jockey) and his clergy in tee shirts!

The next flight took me to Seattle where I met Henry and Barbara Aydelott. He was a grain-broker and they lived in splendour in The Highlands, the city's classiest area. They gave me a whistle-stop tour of that dramatic city and its fascinating covered market by Pioneer Square. I have never seen, or tasted, such fabulous salmon or crabs and they really feted this unknown Englishman. It seems that some friends of the Sewickley rector had rung the Aydelotts, whom they hardly knew, and landed me on them at a day's notice. We've been friends ever since.

After Seattle came San Francisco where I stayed at Castro Valley on the East Bay with a rabid Fundamentalist 'country boy' who had never been on a train, wouldn't use the superb new BART underground system 'because it goes under the bay and the water might get in', and who, memorably, wouldn't have a copy of Shakespeare in the house because 'that man wrote dirty books'. He was quite convinced that he only had to fly into England and start preaching for the whole nation to return to the Christian faith. My other reason for remembering San Francisco is because, getting out of a helicopter after a brief flight over Alcatraz, my cotton trousers tore round the seam and I spent the rest of the day, in what is probably America's gay capital, trying desperately to keep my nether regions from looking like an open season invitation.

While driving around Los Angeles, I headed for Long Beach and the *Queen Mary* and, believe it or not, as she hove into view my car radio launched into 'Land of Hope and Glory'. I hated Las Vegas so much that I went straight back to the airport at eight in the morning and ordered a Knickerbocker Glory for breakfast in the airport café. The bottle-blond waitress looked stunned, smiled, and responded with 'it's whatever turns yew on, honey'. The Grand Canyon was too vast to comprehend from the South Rim. Years later, it was equally staggering from the North Rim. Not so Oak Creek Canyon, south of Flagstaff, which was beautiful and man-sized. Houston was chiefly remarkable for the storm which hit me on the way to the airport. Water was hub-high in minutes and for the only time in my life I experienced a jet of water inside the car. The rain pressure was so great that it came down the outside of the window, forced its way under the closed glass, up the inside and sprayed all over me on the front seat. I ate my first frogs' legs in New Orleans and then walked down garish Bourbon Street in the late evening tourist crowd. I kept my cassette recorder inside my briefcase while I talked into it, describing the scene. 'My God,' said a passing black man, grinning from ear to ear, 'I never before seen a guy talking to his briefcase. Man, you OK?' I sure as hell was, and it's all on the tape to prove I'm not making it up.

America did cause me one serious shock. As I flew from city to city I preached more and more on Jesus as the 'Suffering Servant'. The churches seemed to be obsessed with 'dollars, bricks and souls' and Robert Schuller's so-called Crystal Cathedral, four feet high when I visited it, was the supreme example of this. The surprise came when, after a 'Servant' sermon, a well-heeled man said to me, 'Is this in the Bible? I've never heard a word about it before.' World Vision, an aid agency, published it in their magazine and years later a man rang me in London. 'Did you write that?' he enquired. 'Yes,' I said quietly. 'Well I want you to know that I've carried that article with me for seven years and I show it to everyone I meet. We've never heard of this Suffering Servant in the States.' He didn't surprise me but he did sadden me.

In Florida my hosts took me all round Disneyworld. They were obviously proud of it. I can only say that, for me, Disney has been all downhill since *Dumbo*. I can't be doing with the sickly sentiment even if the artwork of the cartoonists and skills of the latter-day computer graphics people are outstanding. Just not my scene. That is not a popular view in Florida.

For two weeks I was chaplain at an Episcopal youth camp at St Teresa's Beach on the Gulf Coast near Tallahassee. They were great kids, highly emotional, and could not even begin to grasp it when I said I had laughed all the way through Hollywood's *Love Story*. 'You mean you didn't cry?' they enquired, genuinely upset that I hadn't been in floods of tears. Despite that we all got on well enough. The final communion service taught me one valuable lesson. When we got to The Peace I was submerged by a heaving mob of adolescent bosoms whose owners seemed intent on turning a sacred moment into a non-coital orgy with me the prize. The only prize I got was the boob prize which was, if I'm uncharacteristically honest, a delightful bonus for a 46-year-old dad but hardly a spiritual high. I have many American friends but after ten trips I still don't operate on the same octane of emotional gas.

I was very much taken with one young ordinand and his family and tentatively invited him to come, after his ordination, to join my staff in Ealing. He looked like Michelangelo's *David* and I thought it might be a great start for them and good for Ealing also. How wrong can you be? It was my good fortune that he eventually declined since he left his wife and kids and took up, I think, with a homosexual lover. He is still an Episcopal clergyman in the States. I was, I reckon, extremely lucky to avoid what might, indeed would, have been a major parochial disaster in my first couple of years at Ealing.

There was just one actual disaster at the very end of the sabbatical trip. The plane home was five hours late and it meant that I couldn't get to St Paul's Cathedral for Gary Piper's ordination. I think he's forgiven me but I much regretted it as I looked down while we flew right over the great dome as the service was going on. If I couldn't be there at least I could brood like a dove as I prayed over his head.

Twenty-four hours later Jackie and I went to Lambeth Palace for a Garden Party to mark the thirtieth anniversary of the Church Commissioners. Amazingly, for late June, it was cold and wet and as we walked up the main staircase we were met by Jean Coggan, the Archbishop's wife. 'Gosh! I'm cold,' said Jackie. Jean smiled her warm smile. 'Can I lend you some woolly underwear?' she offered. Not many people have been invited to wear the archiepiscopal wife's thermal knickers but Jackie politely declined. Quite spoilt the story, I thought. Out in the marquee she noticed an older woman whose face seemed faintly familiar. Each smiled but said nothing. A few days later in Sainsburys, Jackie saw her again. 'Sorry, I didn't place you the other day,' she said apologetically. 'Is it you or your husband who's the Church Commissioner?' 'Oh, it's my husband,' came the reply. 'He's the Lord Chief Justice.' It was an amusing commentary on modern life. In an earlier era the idea that Lady Widgery, the wife of the Lord Chief Justice, would meet Jackie Saward, a shop assistant, socially, was unthinkable. But so, for that matter was the thought that a Church Commissioner's lady would be stacking supermarket shelves. *Autres temps* . . .

Our farewell from St Matthew's was on the anniversary of the outbreak of the Second World War. Trevor Grant, now churchwarden, had invited us to get gifts to the value of a fixed sum which had been collected. He would give us the cheque on the night. Jackie and I cycled all over London looking for a small terracotta statuette but could find nothing in the price range. On our return, just outside the parish, we saw some carved wooden figures in the window of a Polish cafe in the New Kings Road.

One was a beautifully carved nude female figure which had superbly captured and used the grain of the wood. 'That's it,' I said, but the shop was shut. I spotted the phone number on the door, cycled home, rang, and a male Polish voice answered. 'How much', I enquired, 'is the wooden nude figure in the window?' 'Nude, nude?' said the voice harshly. 'That's the Wirgin Mary.' I bought it and now claim to own the only nude Wirgin Mary in the world. It has been a memorable figure on my study wall ever since.

Our last evening came and went. I told Frankie Howerd's famous story of 'the vicar's farewell'. Frankie, dressed in cassock, and rolling his eyes to distraction, pleads, 'Do I hear voices crying "No, vicar, no. Don't go, vicar. Stay on in the parish, vicar." Do I hear those voices? Do I Buckfast Abbey!' After more fun and laughter, Trevor presented us with an envelope with the cheque to cover the agreed presents. We opened it, and found it was £100 less than we had been led to expect. It was a strangely ironical way in which to leave Fulham. In due course Rachel explained that she and Trevor must somehow have accidentally misled one another as to the exact amount that had been donated. Whatever the reason, Jackie and I ended up with large pieces of household equipment which we had bought on the strength of the misunderstanding for which we were £100 out of pocket.

Years later I was invited back to preach at the centenary celebrations. They still seem to remember us with affection. Best of all, Gary and Norma Piper, among our dearest friends, are now occupying the vicarage. I smile to recall how I persuaded them to have their first baby baptised and to consider going forward to ordination. How different it all might have been.

Chapter Twelve

Queen of the Suburbs

That, emphatically, is not a self-description of the vicar of Ealing but simply the title which Victorian Ealing bestowed on itself. We Sawards lived there for thirteen very happy years though one incident threatened to destroy that pleasure. Fortunately it didn't succeed.

The Deanery of Ealing East contained some eighteen parishes, of which thirteen were, in varying degrees, Anglo-Catholic in tradition. This was about par for the course in the Diocese of London and I had no particular qualms on that score in moving from Fulham to Ealing. Not that is, until I received a snorter of a letter from one of the Anglo-Catholic vicars telling me that he wouldn't attend my Institution because of my 'arrogance' but that he would pray for me and 'offer Mass' on my behalf.

And what caused this outburst? I had written to the *Church Times* a few weeks earlier defending a group of Evangelical clergy, who called themselves 'The East End Five', from a violent assault from another cleric accusing them of not being Anglicans because they had shown sympathy for members of the Free Churches.

I carefully explained this in a humorous reply to Ian Henderson, my angry opponent, and was delighted to get a warm and penitent letter by return. 'I have instructed the postman', he began, 'to have an olive branch in his mouth when he delivers this.' He called my letter 'charming' and wished me 'every blessing'. We stayed good friends though it didn't stop us conducting leg-pulling correspondence in the local paper. Sadly, some local residents couldn't understand how two clerics could joke about our respective neck-gear (he liked dog-collars and I didn't) and thought our banter was motivated by mutual hatred. Even our Bishop was fearful that we weren't joking. Clergy, it seems, are not supposed to have a public sense of humour.

I was duly installed as Vicar of this parish, made famous by its film studios and comedies, by Hewlett Thompson, Bishop of Willesden, on 7 September 1978, and discovered that he, like me, had once been a subaltern in the Royal West African Frontier Force. We became good friends and stayed so when he became, in due course, Bishop of Exeter.

One week later I was blazoned across the *Ealing Gazette* as a 'sex expert' under the caption 'Sex Book Author is New Vicar of Ealing.' Photographed in an open-necked shirt and coloured silk scarf, I was obviously being 'set-up' to shock the burghers of 'the Queen of the Suburbs'. The author of *And So to Bed?* had arrived. All my instincts said, 'Meet it head-on with a laugh', so I wrote to the paper saying how shocked I was that the new vicar was a 'sex expert' since I, as the new vicar, was 'desperately wondering what I have to do to live up to such a title'. I told them that 'my wife can't stop laughing' and my children kept eyeing me with a 'What, Dad, at forty-six?' kind of look. 'Give me a break,' I pleaded, 'or I'll die of exhaustion.' It was the best possible reaction. Everyone knew that there was a new 'vicar of Ealing' and that he could laugh at himself.

For many people, their first contact with the church is in a vicar's study and I was especially keen to make it as 'un-threatening' as possible. Clergy tend to pack their studies with bookshelves, giving themselves a 'learned' image. I decided to take a very different line. I purchased a large eight-sheet mural poster of a Caribbean bay with surf and palm trees, and used it to cover the whole wall of my study behind my desk. Thus, when people came to see me, they, and I, had an immediate 'non-religious' topic of conversation and it relaxed almost every visitor I had over nearly thirteen years. Journalists, photographers and TV cameramen all chatted about it and often used it. Did this vicar, without a dog-collar in sight, live in a fantasy world of waving palm trees? They soon found that he didn't.

The vicarage was a modern, brickbuilt house of five bedrooms. It was large and comfortable, though its upper floor creaked ferociously with badly laid sheets of compressed woodflake. It replaced a Victorian 'country-house-type vicarage' about four hundred yards away. The new house was built on the site of part of the old graveyard. Occasionally bits of bone surfaced and on one occasion half a lower jawbone appeared on the front lawn. It was in beautiful condition with all its teeth and must have predated sugar since it had no fillings or gaps. I presumed that it was two hundred years old. The garden was on top of a mass of hard-core and about two inches of top soil. Apart from grass, it did not have a single flower or bush. I tried to soften it, fenced off the back area, and planted brightly coloured annuals for summer and daffodils for spring. The whole place was secluded, behind the churchyard.

The six of us moved in. Rachel went straight off to Newcastle University to read Biblical Studies. Joe had a final year to complete at Haileybury. Jill and Sue commuted to Lady Margaret School in Parsons Green by tube from nearby South Ealing station. Jackie continued to work at Sainsburys.

Eric Vevers, my predecessor, and a long-standing friend, had done a good job at St Mary's but the church hadn't made much impact on the town itself. As incumbent of the ancient parish church of Ealing he was entitled to call himself 'Vicar of Ealing' but he never had. 'Why not?' I asked him. 'They wouldn't know which church "Ealing Parish Church" was,' he told me. 'They will by the time I go,' I replied and from then on all our printing, publicity, notice-boards and so on were 'Ealing Parish Church' and I was always 'Vicar of Ealing'. It had little or nothing to do with status and everything to do with impact on the borough, town and community. St Mary's had a tall and widely recognised church tower and I coupled it with myself as the two images which could be recognised all over Ealing. All my training and experience in communications had taught me that such visible imagery was a crucial tool in the church's hands. Twenty years before, and ever since, the Christian public relations world had used this philosophy. 'Hear Billy Graham' was universally recalled. I intended to do just the same at the local level. I have always disliked baked beans but, if the day ever comes that I want some, I shall remember that 'Beanz meanz Heinz'. I worked on exactly that model, confident that if a non-churchgoer needed a church, and knew of none, then 'Ealing Parish Church' and the 'Vicar of Ealing' would surface in their memory.

Thus it was that a few weeks later a bunch of fairly ordinary working-class men turned up at my front door one Sunday afternoon in late November. 'We're the committee of the Burma Star Association,' they said by way of introduction. 'We need a chaplain and from what we can gather you look a likely lad.' Six days later Jackie and I were their guests at their Annual Dinner. That was my way in, later, to the chaplaincy of the Royal British Legion and from then on I was almost always a major participant in the annual Remembrance Day parade at the Ealing War Memorial. Time after time I pulled the chestnuts out of their fire when other clergy messed up the timing for the Two Minutes Silence, on one occasion having to ad lib for nine minutes (having prepared three) when the organisers got the schedules hopelessly wrong. 'Thank God', wrote the Mayor's Secretary 'for Michael Saward. We know we can rely on him.' The officer in charge of the annual parade grinned at me one year. 'When you're doing it we know you'll get it right to within five seconds of eleven o'clock. I can breathe easily seeing you on that platform.' None of my recent predecessors (or, indeed, my successor) ever bothered to be 'Vicar of Ealing', concentrating all their time and effort on the St Mary's congregation and largely ignoring the Mayor, the Borough Council, the community organisations, the local Members of Parliament, and the Deputy Lieutenant. I believe they made a major mistake by failing to take the town seriously. Such a failure did not go unnoticed.

St Mary's, nevertheless, was a magnificent church. The building was highly eccentric, having been jazzed-up by a Victorian architect, S.S. Teulon, who took a Georgian 'Plain Jane' preaching-box and turned it into a cross between a Byzantine temple and the mosque at Cordoba. It was a delicious monstrosity and I used to say that it was like an old wife – 'I've grown accustomed to her face.'

Adjoining the church were two further buildings. In the 1960s a yellow-brick square 'church lounge' had been added and in the 1970s a larger red-brick set of rooms had been slotted in to link up the whole complex, provide teaching rooms, a kitchen, cloak-rooms and a fine lobby which was to become the main route in and out of the church. Eric and I together opened it a few days after my arrival and I christened it 'The Polygon.' Eric had called it 'The Parish Centre' but I argued that the church itself, the heart of our worship, had to be at 'the Centre', so a non-religious, descriptive one-word title was essential. No-one was wildly enthusiastic but the name caught on. Using it as the entrance and exit lobby had one huge advantage. People stayed talking and drinking coffee for a good hour after the morning service and this, plus a bookstall, and lots of notice-board space, made it a tremendous asset. It was just the place for relaxed conversation, with kids running about, seats for the elderly, and monthly after-church lunches.

The wardens and staff were tremendous people. Jack Wolton, in his eighties, and Eric Lindsley, in his seventies, were totally supportive but both made plain their intention to stand down in the 1979 Annual Meeting. 'You need new, younger wardens,' they said and they happily handed over to Michael White and Denis Osgood, thus halving, at a stroke, the age of the leadership. Michael was an accountant, a theologically literate leader, while Denis was a builder, a man who was much more physical than cerebral, and they complemented each other superbly. I had inherited a curate, Neil Weston (and Maureen, his wife), plus a Dutch woman worker, Nelly de Keijzer. The five of us were a happy team.

St Matthew's, Fulham, had generously invited me to change almost everything on my arrival there but it had, in reality, taken years to do what needed doing. At Ealing I didn't want to be landed with similar uncritical generosity and I determined to learn from the Fulham experience, to create, if possible, a strong team, lay and clerical, male and female, which could guide the pace of change.

Unexpected circumstances forced my hand in one significant

area. St Mary's needed, ideally, a lay parish administrator but it couldn't house such an animal. However, as an *ex officio* member of a large Ealing housing charity, the Bowman Trust, I discovered a new estate of 'sheltered' property needing a woman warden and offering a 'tied' flat on the premises. Could the jobs be linked? I contacted my old friends, John and Jean Place (she had been in my Croydon YPF in the 1950s) who jumped at the chance. St Mary's PCC and the Bowman Trust agreed to make the two appointments which gave the Places a small flat and a reasonable joint salary and they arrived in February 1979. John and Jean continued in Ealing till well after my eventual departure and became important figures in their own right in parish, deanery and local sheltered housing projects.

Early 1979 saw the launching of what was to become the most strategically important event in all our years at Ealing. On Saturday, 20 January, we invited the whole adult congregation to attend 'Target Day'. About 120 people came and between 11 a.m. and 4.30 p.m. I outlined, and they discussed, some key proposals for the future. They all completed survey forms about themselves and an 'I wish' card in which, anonymously, they indicated what they wanted to see happening in the church. From Ash Wednesday until Easter, a weeknight 'Time To Grow' course (with an attendance of between fifty and ninety) sorted out a range of matters of importance and in July the Church Council agreed to choose a 'Strategy' Committee to evaluate these and form priorities for their implementation. In due course, in consequence, the church interior was reordered to improve congregational worship, an 'eldership' team was appointed, a new style of Sunday morning worship was introduced, and various other smaller matters were put to, and accepted by, the Church Council. In this way the whole pattern of church life was slowly transformed and it was achieved with maximum goodwill and a high degree of unanimity.

Nelly went off for further training in Bristol (where she soon married); Neil moved to a rural incumbency of ten connected villages, wanting to be 'a pastor' and not, as he put it perceptively to me, 'like you, the managing director of an ecclesiastical corporation'; and I was joined by John Sharpe and Chris Skilton, two outstandingly able curates who played a very full part in the continuing reorganisation of St Mary's. Both worked with me for four years. I enjoyed working with all my Ealing curates but John Place (who saw them all) and I agree that the team of ourselves, John and Chris, was the real vintage period.

It came as something of a surprise when, in the early summer of 1979, Bishop Hewlett invited me to become Area Dean (the London name for 'Rural Dean'). Since I was one of the newest incumbents in the deanery, this wasn't universally welcomed but, at my first deanery Synod as Chairman, a group of vocal opponents treated me so outrageously that many of those who might not have instantly supported me were so incensed that they gave me full and vocal backing from then on. It was a valuable insight into the Anglican attitude to rudeness. Even those who don't agree with you won't tolerate personally directed invective.

Like most clergy, I was faced with a major financial challenge in Ealing. Already a generous congregation, St Mary's took off in my first year. From the 1978 Gift Day total of £800, they leapt to £8,000 in 1979, while the annual income doubled from £20,000 to £40,000. It had topped the £100,000 when I left in 1991. On top of that, they gave over £300,000 in a Restoration Appeal in the space of three months in 1987. Ordinary people of no great wealth or income were giving nearly £10 a week and we abolished collections!

One morning I was sitting next to an old friend, Michael Brown, who had been an archdeacon prior to his retirement. We were both attending a Redundant Churches' Committee in Millbank and he suddenly said, 'Are you interested in a Feibusch painting – there's one going cheaply in a Castelnau gallery?' Hans Feibusch had fled the Nazis in the 1930s and for sixty years was to go on painting religious pictures and murals distinctive for his vivid blues and oranges. I had seen perhaps a dozen of them and liked them a lot. 'This one's a Pieta,' added Michael. 'I'll go and see,' I replied and later that day I purchased it for £60. It was on wood, about four feet square, and I offered it to St Mary's to hang in the Polygon. It portrayed Mary, with the dead body of Jesus, together, unusually, with a second woman. The Church Council's reaction was distinctly negative. 'Much too Roman Catholic in style,' they said. That posed me a problem. It was far too big to hang in the vicarage so I wrapped it up and hid it away in a secluded corner of the church tower. It sat there for ten years until eventually, with a good deal of regret, I sold it at an auction at Phillips in the West End for about £600. Today it's worth about £5,000. You win some, you lose some. With Rembrandt I lost, with Feibusch I won. I've still got my Kokoschka. I've also got a John Bratby nude which I like a lot.

Ealing was going though convulsions that year. The two political parties were locked in battle over the future of the run-down secondary modern school in Acton which had been the subject of a highly critical TV programme. There was considerable local pressure for the Church of England to take it over and run it as a high school. Two or three vocal Anglicans on the deanery Synod, of extreme left-wing views, did everything to stop it but failed. They bombarded the local press, and the *Church Times*, with grossly misleading presentations of the situation which I, as Area Dean, had to counter. The result was that Twyford Church of England High School, as it became, was radically transformed under two successive Heads and is now one of the educational highlights of the Borough. I, up till then, knew almost nothing about church schools but I was so appalled by the plethora of politically inspired lies which flew about that I did all I could to back the school, under its new flag. It was a hugely satisfying experience to see what could be done by two first-class men, both of whom were eventually to become clergy themselves.

We received two unusual invitations. The first was to the Diamond Jubilee of the Ealing United Synagogue. Having learnt some Hebrew at university I was just about able to follow the service which was naturally well-attended and quite a few VIPs were present. However, it was a remark by a very senior Jewish layman at the 'Bunfight' which sticks in my mind. The meal began without any saying of grace, which seemed rather strange, so I gently enquired about it. 'Our "grace" takes forever,' he said, 'so we've made sure that all the food is made of such ingredients as do not require us to give thanks for them.' He seemed not to have any awareness of just how extraordinary such a statement would sound to Christian ears. How to eat without thanking God for the food evoked memories of harsh words which Jesus had delivered to the Pharisees for not dissimilar behaviour. I changed the subject rapidly.

The second invitation was to the presentation of the Freedom of the Royal Borough of Kensington and Chelsea to a certain Margaret Thatcher. I don't know how we got such an invitation since we had no obvious connection with the borough or the lady but it was the first time that we actually saw her, newly-elected as Prime Minister. The second time, seven years later, was to have far more significant consequences for me. At the time I was quite unaware that the mayor, who actually made the presentation, one Christopher Walford, would in the 1990s be virtually our next-door neighbour and that I would be present at St Paul's Cathedral when he was blessed in his new role as Lord Mayor of London.

Joe left Haileybury on his eighteenth birthday and asked that his birthday present should be a trip to Silverstone for the British Grand Prix. It cost me an arm and a leg to hire a Volvo Estate to take him, Jackie, a schoolfriend, and all his luggage to this extremely boring event at which noisy vehicles roared around the countryside for hours on end. Little did I guess that Jackie would become obsessed with Formula One racing or that Joe, after university, would carve out a career as one of the world's leading motor sport journalists, travelling hundreds of thousands of miles to report on the races.

At St Mary's, we were planning to celebrate the church's eight hundred and fiftieth anniversary with a dramatically splendid service. The Bishop of London, Gerald Ellison, was to be our preacher and our drama group set out to highlight some of the great events of our history. One of my mediaeval predecessors, Thomas Bradwardine (who features in Chaucer's *Canterbury Tales*) was the shortest-lived Archbishop of Canterbury. After the Battle of Crecy, he went to Avignon, returned as Archbishop, and died of the Black Death after just one week in office. I warned

Gerald that he would meet an archbishop during the service but even he was visibly startled when 'Bradwardine' bowed solemnly to him. He responded with his own stately inclination of the head. Ten years later, when we celebrated the building's two hundred and fiftieth anniversary in the presence of his successor, Graham Leonard, our drama group were not pleased when Leonard dismissed their participation as mere theatrical behaviour in church. Years later, I learnt that John Place, our administrator, also robed as a 'bishop' on that occasion, had castigated Leonard afterwards for his ill-mannered remark. Ellison, who had in earlier years been not a little pompous, became a very good friend, in whose interment I later shared, while Leonard, whom I had greatly respected in the 1960s, became unbearably and obsessively unpleasant. It gave me a strange pleasure in 1991 to see him off the diocesan premises at his farewell at St Paul's in my first forty-eight hours as Canon-in-Residence.

Bishop Hewlett, with whom a friendship was warmly developing, conducted his Michaelmas Ordination in St Mary's and the church, which seated nearly eight hundred, had people standing. It was the largest single service in my time, though his farewell, also in our church in 1985, was almost as well attended.

The launching of the Alternative Service Book in 1980 and especially Rite A Holy Communion resulted in two major TV presentations from St Mary's. One, by the BBC, contrasted our style of conducting the service with that of a very dry and dull Prayer Book service in a Hertfordshire village, while the other, with London Weekend Television, included delightful encounters with Gladys Hensman and Cliff Johnson both of whom (in their eighties and seventies respectively) warmly supported the new liturgy to the great surprise of the interviewer. The LWT service was, at my insistence, a real service in the church lounge (where we generally conducted Sunday evening worship) and not merely a 'mock-up' for the programme. Once again, the contrast between our worship and that of a starchy one from Hampstead was markedly in our favour.

I found myself in a quite different conflict in the *Ealing Gazette* with another very traditional retired clergyman. He, a very elderly

Anglo-Catholic named Canon Hetherington, regularly expressed horror at my views and actions. When I did not often wear a dog-collar, he urged me to leave the ministry! He cited its value by reminiscing about his having pulled bodies out of blitzed houses during the war. His namesake, Bob Hetherington, later to be Mayor, told me that his father, when bombed, had been trodden on by the aforesaid Canon when half-buried in rubble and had bawled at him, 'Get your bloody foot off my face, vicar!' Dog-collar or no, Canon Hetherington seemed to delight in, metaphorically speaking, treading on me whenever he could. I was tempted to offer him the same reply.

Plans for a reshaping of our style of Sunday morning worship were developing. The Church Council invited Trevor Grant, from Fulham, to describe what had happened there. One of our curates, John Sharpe, and his wife Maggie (who would, years later, herself be ordained) then presented a carefully worked-out package and, after much discussion, this was accepted and was launched in February 1991. John had prepared a year's teaching syllabus and, months later, followed it with a three-year syllabus. His work was of outstanding quality and, together with Chris Skilton and me, we used it to great advantage for our Sunday services, children's groups and midweek home groups. It gave the church a coherence which is rarely found and, coupled with a meticulously planned and unanimously supported eldership team, set the whole church on a corporately led pattern of life which lasted for much of my time. This in turn gave rise to a request from the Church Council that I should take time out to write the full story which I did in October 1981 in a very well-received book entitled *All Change*. This was serialised in both the *Church Times* and *Church of England Newspaper* and favourably reviewed by George Carey who called it 'a pleasure to read' and a 'splendid handbook' which he commended 'with the greatest enthusiasm' since it 'could do nothing but good' and might 'revolutionise your church life'. It was later included as one of the 'Books of the Year' by the *Church Times*. In a second review, Carey called it 'gutsy and invigorating . . . vintage Saward.' Such compliments may not be good for the soul but they certainly keep one's morale bubbling along quite merrily.

Jackie and I had by now passed our Silver Wedding anniversary which we celebrated in opulent style at the sybaritic Maison Talbooth at Dedham, in Constable country. We have always believed in the legitimacy of being overlavish at anniversaries. Clergy have little enough by way of money and many feel that they must, as Christians, be frugal. Jackie and I much prefer the biblical contrast between fasting and feasting, eating and living fairly simply for much of the year and really going to town for the big occasions like birthdays and so on. That way you blend the ordinary and the memorable into your marriage. We certainly have no regrets about the stimulating contrast that results.

Being a 'high profile' kind of clergyman, known widely as colourful, dynamic, and so on, leaves one open to jealousy and criticism from one's brethren. A brilliant parody newspaper, *Not the Church Times*, was published by a group of clever, but somewhat bitchy, London clergy who enjoyed themselves at the expense of quite a number of us. It was cruel, funny and faintly redolent of the *Private Eye* kind of journalism, to which I was, before long, to fall victim.

The relevant bit was a five-line Small Ad. I read it, laughed, read it again, winced, and finally decided that I could live with it however unpleasant its implications. I also guessed pretty quickly who the perpetrators were. All it said was

WANTED: Bishopric required, urgently and in any condition. Diocesan preferred but will accept suffragan. Distance no object. Advertiser will collect in person. Apply Ealing Vicarage, London.

Did people believe it? I really don't know but I dare say that some clergy view 'promotion' as life's be-all and end-all. My own view, for as long as I can remember, has been that Christian ministry is all about serving God wherever he wants you. I had been very fulfilled in my various responsibilities and all I wanted was to use my experience and skills to the full. I was also aware that, to change the metaphor, the playing field wasn't flat and that, in those days, Evangelicals were generally at a disadvantage.

Rachel, having graduated from Newcastle, married Chris

Hudson just a few days after Prince Charles and Diana Spencer tied their own granny knot. It was a glorious occasion and I genuinely felt that I had gained a son, cliché or no cliché. Their children are Jenny and Matthew. Rachel has made her own very significant impact on the Christian world in the eighties and nineties. Joe, in the meantime, was heavily involved in producing student plays by Sartre and Colin Welland at Bedford College, in Regents Park, and in editing the college magazine. He even found himself stage-managing at the Edinburgh Festival fringe. Jill and Sue were sixth-formers, the former on the church youth group committee and reading lessons in church while the latter was at a local catering college and had covered herself with orange paint and glory repainting the Polygon. She reported, with marginal modesty, that a man had called her 'cute'.

The climax to my cricketing career came just two days before Rachel's wedding when I got a vital, towering catch, in the *Church Times* final, which we won. The batsman happened to be Alan Godson and London comprehensively beat Liverpool in a game won almost single-handedly by Andrew Wingfield-Digby. I did, I believe, set up a record by being the only cleric to play two finals with a 23-year interval between them. A year later we re-played and this time Liverpool won. I caught their hard-hitting opening bat in exactly the same spot as I'd got Godson but, as it came to me, like a rocket, head high, I realised that I was wearing bifocals and could see two balls, at two heights, and two speeds. I caught it, but badly tore a muscle doing so and that put paid, at fifty, to my cricketing career. I'd made over a thousand runs for London, taking plenty of wickets as well, and ended up with a batting average of twenty-five which, since I got only four or five games a year, seemed satisfactory. Not exactly your Ian Botham but OK for clergy cricket.

At forty-nine, I thought it was time to inject a bit of gravitas into the swashbuckling Saward visage so I grew a beard while away writing a book. It became dark and luxuriant and clearly melted a few female hearts in the General Synod ('glamorous' said the middle-aged nun; 'gorgeous' gasped the retired woman banker; 'handsome' chimed in the elderly former head mistress). It didn't please

Private Eye ('vulpine and maniacal') but Jackie liked it and *The Times* published my letter defending the hirsute style.

One Sunday morning I was standing in the Polygon saying goodbye when Mrs Nina Goldsmid, mother of our lay reader, swept out like a galleon in full sail. She wore a fox fur and carried a silver-topped cane. Her hats were legendary. In short, she was a *grande dame* of the old school. 'Vicah,' she said, imperiously. 'Yes, Mrs Goldsmid.' 'Do you get your beard twimmed at Hawwods?' The thought of my going on a daily visit to Knightsbridge, and its legendary store, for a beard trim was quite ludicrous. 'I'm afraid I don't,' I replied bashfully, 'but I do go there for a haircut.' She beamed. 'That will do vewwy nicely,' she proclaimed, as she sailed past. It's a funny old world, as another imperious lady was heard to say some years later.

Four years later, I cut the beard off in a hotel inside the walls of Carcassonne, deeming a memorable setting to be essential for so traumatic a piece of barbering. I even got Jackie to take three photos (full set, half-off and clean-shaven) as proof. 'What nonsense!' she complained, at the half-cut look. 'It's the only moment in a lifetime at which to get such a picture,' I chortled. 'Press the button!' She did and we have the print to prove it.

For over ten years our friendship with Bob Libby, my American Episcopal counterpart, had gently developed. Joe had stayed with him and his artist wife, Lynne, in Jacksonville and I had seen them on my 1978 sabbatical. In the 1980s our links began to grow much stronger and he and family came to stay in Ealing in February 1982. Together we saw *Evita* and *Amadeus*, they being theatregoers of a fanatical kind. Jackie was so impressed with the latter that she saw it a second time a few weeks later and then, again, as a film. Since that time the Saward–Libby contact has blossomed and we've crossed and recrossed the Atlantic, between us, over a dozen times since. We value not only the friendship but also the various pastels which Lynne has given to us and which decorate our walls.

'Come and preach in Jersey,' said the letter from Dennis Gurney and off I went, flying from Shoreham in a light aircraft. Not, of course, as pilot, but as one of half a dozen passengers. The sensation of flying so low is totally different from that of a large aircraft and I wouldn't have missed it. I rented a car and drove all over the island in between sermons. It added colour to the *Bergerac* TV programmes to be able to recognise so many, even obscure, settings all over the coast and interior. I still have a delightful close-up photo of an orang-utan taken in Gerald Durrell's zoo. His many books had caused me great pleasure and much laughter since I read, in the 1950s, *The Bafut Beagles* and literally rolled about the floor in stitches at his superb recapturing of the Pidgin English I had spoken so fluently as a young subaltern in the Gold Coast in those long-gone days of empire.

To my great surprise the Ealing group of CND – the Campaign for Nuclear Disarmament – asked me to chair a public debate in the Town Hall between Mgr. Bruce Kent and Sir George Young, our local MP. I was, they believed 'non-aligned' and I didn't disillusion them. I hope I chaired it fairly and dispassionately but I knew very well which side I was on and, as an avid reader of military history, it certainly wasn't theirs.

Joe, meanwhile, was winning some fame squiring Elizabeth Taylor around one evening, during which he also kept Richard Burton well plied with vodka. To his chagrin, he could never discover a single photo of himself with either and his friends have had to take his word for it. He was runner-up in a Motor Sport journalism competition (shades of things to come) and twice in one day was nearly blown up by IRA bombs in Regents Park and Knightsbridge. Since many were killed, he was a fortunate young man.

The year ended with one of those 'howlers' you never forget. The church choir decided to give a small present to the lady organist, a retired headmistress. They bought her a pack of perfumed draw-liners for her bureau. She thanked them with a grateful letter placed on the choir vestry notice-board. 'I am sure', she wrote, 'to get much pleasure from using my nicely scented drawers.' How the choir reacted I do not know, but my curate colleagues and I fell about laughing. Each, unknown to the others, had photocopied the letter. Whenever I met her, from then on, I had great difficulty in keeping a straight face.

Clergy do sometimes face agonising situations. Not of grief (though obviously they occur), but of 'laugh at this if you dare'. There was, I remember, the Irish labourer who said sadly that his mother-in-law had just had a 'hysterectomy of the heart'. *The Times* published that, but deleted the word 'Irish' for fear of a charge of racism. Then there was the black girl on the phone who wanted to arrange a marriage. She was not an Anglican 'but we're much the same – we're Rastafarians'.

Talking of weddings, on another occasion we were in the vestry, signing the registers, bride, groom, parents, and so on. As the photos ended the buxom blonde bride let out a shrill yell. 'Oohh,' she squealed, 'I've just lost me knickers!' If you want to be a vicar you have to keep a straight face and on such occasions it can be absolute agony.

It was around that time that Neil Kinnock, who lived two hundred yards from our church, was involved in a motorway accident. He promptly ascribed his escape to Someone up There who loved him. Kinnock was, and is, a likeable person and usually acknowledged himself to be an atheist. Certainly he wouldn't enter St Mary's church, even for a concert by a Welsh male-voice choir which was secular enough. As his vicar (well, he lived in our parish) I wrote him a friendly note saying that I was 'glad that he had emerged unscathed' from his 'stark reminder of mortality'. I added that I had on that very day been 'reading the *Anglo-Saxon Chronicle*' (not my usual diet) and had found out that King William Rufus in 1093 'became so ill that . . . in his sickness he made God many promises to lead his life aright . . . which he soon took back when he was healed'. I couldn't resist advising Kinnock 'to take care' since Rufus 'ended up transfixed by an arrow'. It wasn't to be our last contact.

As the eighties developed, the ignorance of local children concerning Christianity became more obvious. One morning I was standing close to, but outside, the rear churchyard gate, in a soft collar. A small boy, about ten years old, looked up at the church across the graveyard then turned to me and said, 'Oi, Mister, wazzat big building for?' In such a way it dawned on me that we had spawned the first generation for thirteen hundred years who had no idea what a church was. Not long after, the headteacher of the local State junior school advised me not to select 'Hark! the herald-angels sing' for their carol service, 'since hardly any of the children will know it'. Naturally, they were completely familiar with donkeys, stars and Rudolf the red-nosed reindeer, the phenomena accompanying the true focus of the season – Father Christmas.

Life at St Mary's was undergoing slow but thorough change. With the advent of the eldership team of clergy and laity (about which enormous preparatory care had been taken) it had become vital to ensure that thoroughly creative and non-confrontational links were established both with the Church Council and the Standing Committee. Fortunately, one of the elders was usually also a churchwarden, not always the same person, and this kept the possibility of polarisation between the 'pastoral' and the 'administrative' leaders from happening. We were extremely fortunate in having elders whose long links with the church made them almost universally respected while the Council was kept fluid by a constant stream of fresh faces being elected from year to year. In my thirteen years at Ealing 108 people served on the Council, of whom 9 were clergy, 49 women, and 50 men. Two of these died, 39 moved away, and since the Council usually had about 24 members, the variety was considerable. Indeed, apart from me, only one person (both a warden and an elder) served throughout without a break. One awkward problem of this fluidity was the number of people who kept trying 'to re-invent the wheel'. Even so, our policies, once worked out, remained, in essence, stable, though not without much peripheral reshaping.

In all this, I had two boasts. First, that in thirteen years (covered by 640 typed pages of minutes) we only had one occasion in which a member lost his temper and that, at a time of great personal stress, shortly before the break-up of his marriage. We had lots of good-humoured cut and thrust including one memorable occasion when two churchwardens went hammer and tongs at each other's opinions but never even faintly looked like bruising their well-known friendship.

The 1980s were a time of tremendous reform, with dozens of changes but I do not recall a single occasion when we had a 'vicar-versus-the-rest' situation. Every change, except one, went through by consent, following open voting, and on that occasion I had to exercise a casting-vote from the chair. On three similar occasions I had voted against change (we were obviously not ready for it) but on this one evening everyone knew my conscientious commitment and all honoured my casting-vote for reform. The issue (I can't even remember it!) was simply taken on board and accepted. Ealing was, in short, a church committed to holding together and change was by vote (or even occasionally congregational referendum) paced to carry, not divide, Council and congregation. As far as possible I employed the same principles as Area Dean, with regard to the deanery Synod. My conviction has always been to lead by persuasion and corporate decision-making and not by autocratic bullying.

One highly effective way of doing this was through a network of subcommittees regularly reporting to the Church Council. This meant that much of the nitty-gritty discussion was handled in these groups and the Council accepted, rejected or deferred, their proposals. That way the Council covered vast areas of work. It certainly made for a highly structured church, which some people don't like, wanting spontaneity, but in my experience the first method unites, and the second divides, congregations. Sadly, as so often happens, one's successor often up-ends everything and creates chaos out of order.

So how did John Sharpe and Chris Skilton react to all this? Years later, at my invitation, they recalled their curacies. John, who came in 1979, after an earlier curacy, greatly enjoyed his four years in Ealing but wondered whether we (and he probably meant me) 'tended to accentuate the mind and did not really explore the full range of our human emotions'. We were weak on 'the exercise of bereavement care, marriage preparation and general pastoral care'. He went on to wonder whether we 'always took full account of people's emotional responses and reactions to change'. He fully supported the changes which were 'thought out in detail', both in terms of 'presenting a way forward, the decisions involved, and communicating them with enthusiasm'. He also valued the freedom which I gave all my staff, recalling 'one occasion when the three of us ordained colleagues took quite different standpoints' in a Church Council meeting. I was, said John, 'a professional who always challenged us to rigorous thinking and the discipline of critical evaluation and this professionalism ran through everything'. Both he and his wife Maggie remain our good friends, calling me 'Big M' whom they regard as a 'flamboyant evangelical'.

Chris Skilton, who joined us in 1980 straight from theological college, and of quite a different temperament from John's and mine, was, apparently, warned by a part-time member of his college's teaching staff 'of what a dangerous situation he was entering' by coming to be my curate. I can easily guess who tried to frighten him off! He, too, was, however, 'profoundly grateful' for his years in Ealing, not least for being allowed to oppose my wishes at the Church Council at which, on one memorable evening, he led 'a revolt against the provision of a staff car' when I was, as I always was, not well enough off to own my own vehicle. He was amazed at how trusting I was 'of a raw young curate' in contrast to the many horror stories of the experiences of his peers with their oppressive, overbearing vicars. Nonetheless, Chris, whose essential loyalty I have never questioned, was by no means uncritical. 'Michael was very traditional in outlook, at home with things as they had always been done' and some events 'lacked life and originality. I found', he added, 'the Sunday worship hardest to cope with. It was well ordered and well organised' but there was no sense of 'risk and openness in worship; it was shut down and controlled – in the end a disappointment to me'. Nevertheless, he saw me, as he put it, as someone who 'sparkled' in front of large audiences and could 'keep a congregation spellbound for over thirty minutes'. He did, however, detect that I 'seemed shy, awkward, and difficult to know', with whom he 'never engaged on a personal level'. In that Skilton saw what few do, that I have a distinctly shy side, not being gregarious by nature. Chris went on in 1984 to work with a vicar who 'couldn't have turned out to be more different to Michael', but, he says, 'the experience of both was invaluable'. We remain in affectionate touch with Chris and his wife, Barbara.

Both John and Chris offer fair comments, though I suspect many lay people would find the idea that I was 'very traditional' and that our worship and church life was lacking in 'originality' extremely surprising. In the sense that we didn't take up most of the extremes of charismatic style and music I would certainly agree but, in comparison with most Anglican worship we were remarkably relaxed. Still, Chris has a fair point.

At home the twins were making their mark in the world. Now just twenty, Sue was asked by a 'breast-feeding' counsellor to make an appropriate cake for her local organisation. Sue was a dab hand at 'novelty cakes' and came up with a specimen which was obviously indebted to Dolly Parton. I have a delightful colour photo to prove it and, if poverty strikes, I shall offer it to the *Sun* or *Playboy* magazine. It's a different world from the vicarages of Jane Austen and Trollope. We, you remember, have Susan Howatch as a friend! Jill kept the more Trollopian flag flying, having been elected to the Church Council, the deanery Synod, and the Willesden Area Synod. That, at twenty, was quite an achievement.

And so to my gall-bladder operation. I hadn't spent a night in hospital since 1938 but the surgeon, Michael Henry, took one look and mouthed the medical equivalent of 'out, out, damned spot'. He extracted a one-inch gallstone and left me with a nine-inch scar, which I am willing to show, at a price, to any interested and nubile young ladies. I riposted with an advertisement in *The Times* Personal Column saying that 'Prebendary Saward has been safely delivered of a 1 inch gallstone. Both doing well.' Alas, no-one seemed to notice and Jackie, I suspect, has long since mislaid, or sold the jewel itself.

A few days prior to the operation I was in conversation with the local school caretaker and mentioned it. He, a brow-furrowed Irish Roman Catholic, suddenly stopped looking puzzled as light dawned. With his background he could conceive of only one source for clerical illness. 'Aahh,' he said cheerfully, 'dat'll be de drink.'

I enjoyed a few days convalescence in St Luke's, the clergy hospital in central London, and then, after a few days in Brighton, went alone to the South of France for a week. Two or three nights in Nice, two more in Cannes, interspersed with a night each in Menton and Villefranche were wonderfully relaxing. I enjoyed a quiet dinner in a small restaurant in the underground gallery in Villefranche and emerged, to my horror, realising (for the first and only time in my life) that I was drunk. To have reached the age of fifty-two, a model of sobriety, and then to find oneself hardly able to walk a straight line was enough to make me guilt-stricken. I very much enjoy wine, good wine, but cannot understand why anyone should want to get drunk and, least of all (recognising the Bible's strictures about inebriation) if they are Christians. I got back to my hotel, went straight to bed and woke up in the morning feeling fine. I had, in reality, not drunk much wine (only about half a bottle) which would not usually have caused any problem. So, it was the post-illness weakness that had left me so vulnerable. I still drink wine, more if anything, but certainly never enough to go over my level. It all reminded me of William Wilberforce, who two hundred years previously, a virtuous Evangelical, had defined his goal in these matters as 'Simplicity. In quantity moderate. Never more than six glasses of wine.' Good advice, in my book, especially when coupled with Archbishop Desmond Tutu's 'We are meant to enjoy good food, glorious music, beautiful girls and lovely men, attractive scenery, noble literature, refreshing recreation. They are all part of what life is about . . . Jesus celebrated life.' All these, joined to the powerful epitaph which I found in the Menton hillside cemetery, to 'J.R. Green, historian of the English people. He died learning.' I came home, mildly chastened, but greatly refreshed. Why did those Edwardian English go there to die? It really lifted me and gave me new vitality. Would I could afford to retire to Provence or the Côte d'Azur.

At the end of November, David Bubbers, the General Secretary of the Church Pastoral-Aid Society, and a friend of thirty years' standing, wrote a delightful, tongue-in-cheek letter about me to the *CEN*, whose readers know me well. He, a trombone-playing ex-Salvationist, referred to me as 'The Man from Ealing, who seems to pop up everywhere, who always (or nearly always) says something worth listening to.'

Right, I thought. It's time for some facetious fun. I wrote a letter to the editor, in the following terms:

That scoundrel Bubbers has got to be stopped! How can one exercise a normal paternalistic and properly authoritarian incumbency among the local peasantry if they are going to be told that their spiritual paterfamilias is not absolutely fire-proof on all subjects on which he pontificates?

The Rascally Bubbers – smilingly devious as always – says of me that I 'always (or nearly always) say something worth listening to'. How diabolically he undermines my absolute impeccability of judgment when delivering my weekly *ex cathedra* utterances! How will my usually submissive peasants be kept from open revolution if they discover that I am only 'nearly always' right? How long will my impressionable young curates continue to genuflect before me if they cannot place absolute confidence in my utter infallibility? I fear even now that one of them believes himself to be similarly endowed while yet a lowly assistant.

My solicitor will be seeking adequate compensation to enable our church building to be completely restored next week. Half a million damages should just about do it! A CPAS cheque signed by the egregious Bubbers will prevent legal action. I shall watch tomorrow's post expectantly.

I'm glad to say the editor published it. How important it is for Christians to have some public fun. Those who only read the national press could well be forgiven for thinking we do nothing except complain about other people's misbehaviour and, somewhat too frequently, get up to no good ourselves. I'm all for some unsolemn leg-pulling by the clergy so long as it is matched by deadly serious words when needed.

My words were, indeed, deadly serious when I wrote, via our Member of Parliament, Sir George Young, to the Home Secretary in January 1986 urging that a member of our congregation, Joseph Lagu, former Vice-President of the Sudan, and his family, be given political asylum. He, once described as 'the Montgomery of the Sudan', had for years fought a Civil War against the Muslim majority, was a man of great courage and Christian leadership. To my great joy he was granted asylum and still lives in Ealing.

Then, on Thursday 6 March 1986 we hit the Big Time in the most unpleasant way possible. A fund-raising consultant came to see me at eleven o'clock, left soon after noon, at which point the second post arrived, delivering me two bottles of champagne, a gift for introducing Joe to membership of the Diners Club. Five minutes later the doorbell rang, I answered it, and found a large sharpened kitchen knife an inch from my stomach. The story of what happened next was told by every newspaper and media outlet in the land and is still a regular candidate for feature story treatment. One of the very first news accounts in the *Daily Star* contained fourteen factual errors in 600 words. That is simply incredible. Virtually every assertion was wrong in some way and, consequentially, since the media feed off each other's copy incestuously, countless articles have repeated two particularly stupid pieces of invention. First, it was alleged that David Kerr and I had had a fight with the villains and, secondly, that we had been forced to watch what was done to Jill. Both statements were totally untrue.

So what happened? Jill has given her account in her book, *Rape: My Story*. What follows is the event as I recall it, in essence, though I shan't attempt to cover all the peripheral details.

Robert Horscroft, leader of the trio, was the man with the knife. He pushed me backwards into my study, followed by Martin McCall and Christopher Byrne. All were quite unknown to me. Horscroft began by screaming, 'Where's the f—ing safe?' which he repeated again and again. I explained quietly that there was no safe, but only some loose money in a desk drawer which I indicated. Silently I was irritated at the thought of losing my bottles of champagne, which were highly visible. Amazingly, they never touched them.

One of the others left the room and returned with Jill and David, who was a very recent boyfriend, from the sitting-room next door. The three of us were made to sit down in a corner of the room with the knife against Jill's face. David stiffened, as if to fight, and I held his wrist firm. 'Sit still,' I said. We had no chance against three thugs with knives and my brain was racing as I wrestled with a way to keep us alive. Passivity was absolutely vital. More threats and effing. We had no money. 'Vicarages aren't places where church money is kept,' I said.

Jill was taken off, by one man, to 'find the jewellery'. 'My wife has nothing of value,' I said but, obviously, seeing a large modern house, Horscroft and co. assumed that we were well-heeled. A few minutes passed. 'You two come upstairs!' shouted Horscroft and forced David and me to drop our trousers to our ankles and shuffle along. Upstairs we entered the second bedroom, at the south front, to see Jill's naked back. She was quickly hustled out, after we had been ordered to lie face downwards on the floor. Only at that moment did the idea of a sexual attack enter my head but we saw nothing, beyond her back, before she was lost to view.

Face down, unable to see anything but the carpet, the blow was quite unexpected. There was a crash, I saw stars, and thought I had been shot. Just conscious, I was still alert enough to think 'sham dead' and I did just that. In any case, I passed out almost at once. Not till days later did I learn that David, also struck, had rolled around and the villains beat him up badly, damaging, probably permanently, his hearing.

Unconscious, I heard a loud crash and recognised it, somehow, as the front door being roughly closed. My brain said, 'Don't move – it may be a trick,' and I remained still. Time meant nothing but I heard the room door open. Still I lay silent. Jill came to me and said, 'Are you all right?' 'Have they gone?' I whispered. 'Yes,' she said. 'Did they . . . ?' I said not knowing how to frame the verb. 'What do you think?' she replied and I lapsed back into unconsciousness. I heard a distant siren, and woke again to find myself being carried in an ambulance chair down the stairs. Out cold again, I became aware through the ambulance window of a car park and recognised it as Ealing General Hospital. When I next came round, I saw a bishop's pectoral cross and a purple shirt two feet away. It was Tom Butler, Hewlett's recent successor, just three months into his new job as Bishop of Willesden, and a good friend. And that was all I recall of 6 March. No fights, no visible or audible sign of rape, just Jill's back and her 'What do you think?'

What followed was horrific enough. Jill had been raped and sexually assaulted by what she called Man One and Man Two. Man Three (Horscroft) had said to Byrne and McCall, 'We didn't come for this,' and, 'Remember, I didn't do it,' to Jill. Between them they had buggered her also and used a knife handle to penetrate her.

The media went berserk. Massive coverage of the 'vicarage virgin' who had been raped. She couldn't be explicitly identified but, collectively, they all knew who it was and so did the general public. The Vicar of Ealing was far too well known and since she was an identical twin there was no legal reason why Sue couldn't be photographed. In the event, the *Sun* published a full-length photo of Jill, with just her eyes masked. The tabloids invented lots of details and made the story ten times as horrific as it already was. The *News of the World* produced a cartoon of a girl, with half-open blouse, being threatened, while men fought in the background.

Day by day the story grew more lurid. Eventually, some days later, I was interviewed in my hospital bed, first by BBC-TV news and then by ITN. I looked wan and was sporting a huge black eye. I had a hairline fracture of my skull from the blow (apparently by my cricket bat). 'If I had to be bashed with a cricket bat I'm glad it was a "Don Bradman" which was imprinted on my skull,' I joked. By then, I could just about joke.

Having made hundreds of broadcasts, I naturally expected both BBC and ITN interviews to be heavily edited down to perhaps a minute or two. To my amazement BBC ran two on the six o'clock and nine o'clock news of something like six minutes and four minutes, while ITN did four minutes on *News at Ten*. As a semi-pro, I knew that these were unique and broadcasters later confirmed that, to the best of their knowledge, no-one had ever got such solo, 'straight to camera', interviews of that length. I didn't waste my chances and Gavin Reid, weeks later, said with a grin, 'Well, Michael, if any of my friends had to get what happened, I'd rather it was you than anyone else – at least you would know how to do such interviews.' We both smiled.

At home, they told me, it was like the Chelsea Flower Show. Fourteen hundred letters and cards poured in, from as far off as New Zealand. Some, from churches, contained scores of unknown signatures. The Prime Minister wrote, the Leader of the Opposition, the Speaker of the House of Commons, the Archbishop of Canterbury and dozens of other eminent persons. The Archbishop of York, John Habgood, informed Jackie, in a seven-line letter, that his diocesan Synod had asked him to write. Graham Leonard, Bishop of London, wrote Jackie a kind and thoughtful letter from the airport as he was about to fly but he spoiled it by never again asking even one question about Jill's well-being. Meanwhile, we were borne up by the prayers of millions of people and it made a great difference to us all.

The men were caught, we gazed at them (carefully disguised, to our surprise) at various identification parades and the police did a marvellous job which we as a family will never forget.

Jill had been absolutely magnificent. She had kept calm, noted identifying marks, gave detailed descriptions, and 'lay back and thought of England', consciously detaching her inner self from the brutal violation to which she was being subjected. We were all naive about it, congratulating her on having 'come through' it all. Little did we know how much emotional trauma she would suffer in the four years ahead before she 'killed it dead', wrote a book about it, made some superb television programmes and now lectures to police forces across the land about how to handle rape victims.

On the TV News I called her 'the jewel in my crown' and knew at once that it was over the top as a phrase. She hated it and I regretted it but it just came out, connected in my mind with a much-praised film recently in the cinemas. It was utterly out of keeping with my style but she has, I think, forgiven me.

The attack provoked much discussion about the question of forgiveness and punishment and I had articles in the *Sunday Telegraph* and the *Daily Mail* seeking to clarify the issue. Then, in his Easter sermon in Canterbury Cathedral, Archbishop Runcie spoke about forgiveness and said that 'we've seen a fine and impressive example of this quiet Easter faith shining through personal tragedy in a Christian congregation in Ealing. Such heroic healing power', he added, 'could hardly fail to move the most determined cynic.' I was glad that he set it in the context of our church and had not just focused on us as a family since St Mary's had been such a tremendous strength to us. He kindly sent me an advance copy of the text and I wrote, in the congregation's name, to thank him and mentioned it in a tape played over the church's public address system on Easter morning since I couldn't be present.

Media coverage, which never ends, has produced over eight hundred stories, some very factual, some supportive, but two stood out in the first ten days as thoroughly unpleasant. Both appeared on Sunday 16 March, one by Marcia Falkender in the *Mail on Sunday* and the other by Christopher Booker in *Today*.

Falkender had watched my TV news broadcast and called it 'smooth and professionally unengaged'. How could I, she enquired, 'be quite so cool and professional in front of the camera?' I was, she acknowledged, 'a superb media performer' because, she maintained, there had been 'few trendy causes' which had not had me 'at their head'. This ridiculous and snide remark was supported by the allegation that my book *And So to Bed?* had 'caused an enormous row in the church'. How any of this was supposed to cauterise my feeling about the violent rape of a much-loved daughter she didn't explain. Presumably I was supposed to forget all the experience of hundreds of broadcasts and provide a 'bumbling vicar' TV interview. She dropped miles in my estimation after that.

She was bad enough with her 'trendy way to turn the other cheek' piece but Christopher Booker was worse. I had enjoyed his book *The Neophiliacs* in the early 1970s, but he obviously had decided that I was one of them. He began with a stunning lie. 'Mr Saward had . . . at his own request [had] the TV cameras . . . brought to his bedside.' Anyone who has any knowledge of the broadcasters will laugh at such a ridiculous idea. Both BBC and ITN urged me to allow them to film me in hospital (I have it in writing) and I only agreed when the police and medical advisers raised no objections.

Following the lie, to present me as publicity-hungry (the old

Private Eye canard), Booker attacked me as 'unctuous' about 'Christian forgiveness' demonstrating 'Pharisaism'. I was, it seems, 'putting over a certain line, without real conviction'. By relating justice and forgiveness I was showing my 'own state of spiritual muddle'.

What was Booker's motive in all this? He told us. I was, it seems, 'a leading progressive churchman'. I had played 'a key part in promoting new forms of liturgy' and had (Lie Number Two) dismissed 'supporters of the Old Prayer Book as asinine and infantile'. Needless to say, I had once used that phrase but I had used it of some ignorant journalists! I certainly had never used it of Prayer Book supporters. Strange. To speak on TV to over ten million people about justice, forgiveness, and love of one's daughter, in the aftermath of a horrific rape, and to do it both competently and caringly, and to be attacked as 'a trendy progressive' by two media gurus was a puzzling experience.

The charge of 'spiritual muddle' concerning the relationship between justice and forgiveness, while explicit in Booker's piece, was a general mark of the reports and comments in the secular press. Most journalists seemed incapable of grappling with the issue. Revenge was OK. Forgiveness was for wet wimps like vicars. Not until the *Sunday Telegraph*, a year later, offered me space to put the Christian case did a newspaper print anything other than such polarisation. 'Why', they captioned my article, 'I Can Forgive the Men Who Did Such Evil.' In it I roundly rejected the idea that I was a 'trendy progressive' and set out the biblical case of, on the one hand, 'an eye for an eye' as the basis for retributive justice (the duty of society faced with crime) and, on the other, Christ's command to the individual victim to 'forgive those who sin against us'. Years later I was to make the same case in the General Synod when it debated justice and punishment.

One valuable result, many months after the rape, was an interview with the family in which all six of us met Levana Marshall, a psychologist, and Felicity de Zulueta, a psychotherapist. They deliberately set it up as part of a course of therapy for Jill (and Sue, who had been emotionally badly hurt by her twin's horror). It allowed the whole lot of us to open up and dispense with a lot of inner anger and unhappiness and it greatly improved all our relationships. They hadn't been bad, as far as I was aware, but clearly all four children had hurts – real or imagined – which would not otherwise have been brought to the light of day. So, much good eventually came from the horror, and, for all but one of us, faith in a loving God was strengthened.

I was encouraged to recover with about three months of convalescence and light duty. My colleagues, by now Eric Culbertson and Ian Tarrant, together with John Place, did a tremendous job sustaining and upholding the church which had itself been badly shocked by the attack. They, and the elders and churchwardens kept the ship firmly on course and took all the pressure off me. Jackie and I went off on a tour of our honeymoon hotels for our thirtieth anniversary, before which I had spent a week hibernating near Colchester at Layer Marney Tower, the Tudor mansion of Gerald and Jane Charrington, good Synod and Church Commissioner friends. I spent much of it sorting out scores of press cuttings which eventually ran to nine volumes. The latest count has brought the total to seven hundred cuttings.

On 22 April the new YMCA, just two hundred yards from the church, was officially opened by Princess Anne. I was invited to be one of four on the platform, to conduct the brief prayers. The Secretary had got himself at loggerheads with our church, had sacked Jill from his staff, and did not include me among those invited to meet the Princess, which was, to put it mildly, an extraordinary way to behave. After the formal opening I kept well away from the royal area until the national president, Lord Someone-or-Other, said, 'Have you met Her Royal Highness yet?' 'I'm not on the list,' I replied. 'Nonsense,' he said and put me at the end of the line, just two away from the lady. The ironical consequence was that, after meeting thirty or forty people for the obligatory ten seconds, Princess Anne and I had a conversation lasting over eight minutes, in which, once the ice was broken, we chatted away merrily about everything under the sun, including the recent attack and rape.

I was about to excuse myself after two or three minutes but realised that one can't walk out on a member of the Royal Family, not least when it would leave them alone. The *Daily Express*, always alert, ran a front-page lead story, with a photo of the Princess, inspecting my cuff links. 'How did you get those?' she asked. I explained that the royal cypher on them was that of the Duke of Connaught, Queen Victoria's favourite son. 'I recognise that,' she added, 'but how did you get them?' I told her that my Kendall grandfather had brought them back across the Atlantic during the First World War, when the Duke was Governor-General of Canada. He, the Duke, offered Grandad a commemorative gift. 'I'd like a pair of your cuff links,' said the Captain. 'I'll get my tailor to send you some,' responded the Duke. 'No, Sir,' said Grandad, 'I want the ones you're wearing now.' And he got them and now they're mine. I only wear them on royal occasions. The Princess smiled and made an Anne-ish remark. Whenever we've met since we seem to have hit it off very well. I think she's a tremendous asset to the House of Windsor.

Two weeks later I duly presented myself at the front door of 10 Downing Street. It was Friday 9 May and Margaret Thatcher had just had a terrible night, losing hundreds of seats in local elections. I expected my visit to be extremely short and the lady to be occupied with a salvage operation. It wasn't like that at all. I was there because, following the rape, she had written a wonderfully kind and sympathetic letter and I had, without much hope, replied that I should like to thank her personally on behalf of the whole family. To my amazement, she told me to call in and see her.

Thus it was that I arrived, to be shown upstairs to a comfortable small drawing room where she greeted me most affably, offered me coffee, and sat me down together with Michael Alison, her Parliamentary Private Secretary (whom I had known for years as a fellow-Evangelical member of General Synod) and Robin Catford, her Secretary for Appointments. This was virtually an interviewing panel and I wasn't slow to realise it. What was she up to, I wondered? Well, I wasn't going to play the part of a sycophantic, place-seeking vicar, so we all talked amicably until I told her that I had a theory about the distinction between Tories and Socialists. 'Do tell me,' she cooed, seductively. 'Socialists believe in the perfectibility of man and are then conned by the actual reality.' 'Oh, I do so agree,' she clucked. 'And what about the Tories?' 'Well,' I said, taking my life in my hands, 'they believe in original sin and capitalise on it.' She came out of her chair, like a cat with claws extended. A frightening transformation had occurred in the well-coiffeured *grande dame*! No wonder Tory MPs were scared of her. Anyway, we parted cheerfully enough after half an hour. I reckoned I had blown all possibility of preferment by my witticism but, since I hadn't gone there with that in mind and was genuinely surprised to find Catford in the room, I felt content that I had made no pretence of place seeking. Three years later Robin was to tell me that 'the Crown was well- disposed towards you' so although for five years nothing appeared to come of it, ultimately, it all came right in the end. In the meantime I sent her a couple of my books which she said she would read.

I was not exactly short of work in Ealing but the vicar of our next-door parish, St Paul's, died and the Bishop asked me to take on the extra responsibility of being Priest-in-Charge. He would, he added, let me have a curate (since he was about to remove one of those on my St Mary's staff it was hardly a bonus!). Following the rape it could hardly have come at a more difficult time but St Paul's was at a very low ebb after a twenty-year incumbency by a kind but stuck-in-the-mud vicar who had himself told me, to my amazement, that he saw his job as being to hand on the parish to his successor 'exactly as he had received it'. It was sadly reminiscent of the parable about 'burying talents'. The consequence was that St Paul's had hardly been touched by any of the developments common to most urban parishes in the 1970s and 1980s.

I accepted the extra post, amused to learn that the Church Council had expressed anxiety about the appointment of a 'well known Radical' like me! To join me, came Michael Hawken, a dynamic curate from Harrow, and his wife Caroline. I chaired the key meetings and preached while Michael did all the day-to-day pastoral work. He and I agreed that I would 'be the surgeon' (to cut off the dead wood) while he would 'be the physician' (to put ointment on the injured) and by this means he could have the credit as 'a lovely man' while I would take the brickbats as 'a hard master'. Since it was clear from the start that a lot of surgery was going to be needed and that he would, before long, become vicar, this seemed the obvious way forward. I had a broad back and he needed to gain maximum support for the future. In the event, it was never as starkly contrasted as that but in my three-year stint we reset the ship's course and when I handed over he was well on his way to a really successful incumbency. Before he later left, he had transformed the church and today it has grown and become a major church in Ealing. Sadly, not long after his move, he fell ill and died, leaving his wife with three youngsters. St Paul's is his monument to a ministry much blessed by God.

I actually enjoyed my short time at St Paul's. Only one person seemed incapable of accepting the changes that were vital and he became increasingly out of touch with what most of the church's leaders were welcoming. One of the key figures was Bob Hetherington, who had been Mayor of Ealing and Chairman of the local Health Authority. As treasurer of the church he fully supported me as did Richard Webb, the Campaigner leader, later to be ordained, and John James, a churchwarden who was also Secretary of the Lawn Tennis Association. Years later he invited Jackie and me to Wimbledon for lunch and Centre Court seats for the Women's Final.

Meanwhile, a heated row had broken out in the town over the proposal by Councillor Hilary Benn (Tony Benn's son) to 'promote sex equality' in the borough's schools. Since Labour's election victory in May, Benn, as education chairman, had prepared a new policy document, ostensibly aimed at removing discrimination on the grounds of gender. This laudable goal had, however, been confused with a clause which sought to foster 'acceptance of homosexual lifestyles as being equally valid to heterosexual ones'. The town's Tories were in uproar. So too was a Parents Action Group. As Vicar of Ealing, I called together a group of Anglican clergy of varying traditions urging them to issue an 'open letter' calling for the controversial clause to be deleted. I prepared a draft which, after discussion, was modified slightly, and issued over the signatures of six of us, Catholics, Evangelicals and Central churchmen. We welcomed the Borough's desire to remove gender discrimination but, we added, 'in seeking to uphold the importance of family life, we find ourselves unable to accord "equal validity" to other heterosexual and homosexual lifestyles'. We said we welcomed toleration but we could not possibly equally validate homosexual unions with those of heterosexual families. In the light of the furore and the widespread hostility created, the Borough reluctantly modified their plans.

Clergy, even if not expecting violent attacks when they open their vicarage front door, are used to a strange mix of would-be customers. Many of them are Irish, who come begging because Roman Catholic priests won't, or don't, give them money. I also recall a family from, shall we say, west of the Irish Sea who turned up. Mother and a straggle of small kids, a real bunch of tinkers. Could we spare them some food, they were hungry? Jackie gave them tea, sandwiches and some tins. Two weeks later the kids reappeared. 'Mother says can we have more food?' said the eldest, about ten years old. Once more Jackie ransacked the kitchen and brought out a pile of tins and packets. The urchin inspected the loot. 'No, we don't like those. Or those.' 'Clear off and don't come back,' said the heartless vicar. 'If you're hungry, take what you're given or buzz off.' They departed and didn't reappear. Doubtless we were castigated as being 'bloody mean Protestants'.

Then there was John. John was one of society's sad inadequates. He had been inside, not clever enough to carry off petty crime successfully. A Brummie, he came to the vicarage trying to wheedle money out of me. Now, sad as it may seem, in forty years of ministry, John is the only man who has come begging at my door that I found I could trust. They came, promising to repay loans, and no-one ever has. Not one. Until John. Why did I take the risk with him? Because, as I recall, he owned up right at the start and said he had been inside. He also offered to work. Lastly he mentioned a vicar in Swindon who would vouch for him. I rang the vicar and to my surprise he supported John's story. John had dealt honestly with him. So, ready to be convinced, I lent John a few pounds. A few weeks later, he repaid me. Amazing! It's nearly ten years since I first lent John money. I still do. He does his fairly pathetic best to repay me though he's almost always behind on a long-running debt. Sometimes I wipe the slate clean. Once he even admitted to having cheated me with an overimaginative hard-luck story. John, I fear, will never be able to control his minimal finances. He's inept, pathetic, and yet somehow he needs my help and, while he isn't absolutely honest, he isn't a rogue. Sometimes I'm tough and deny him help and sometimes I lend him another tenner. He does at least try to gain some self-respect. John has been part of my life for over ten years now and will doubtless keep trying, failing, feeling pathetic and slightly guilty. He's almost part of the family.

The first major event of 1987 was the trial at the Old Bailey of the men who had created the *Ealing Vicarage Rape Case*. Soon after the attack I had warned the whole family that, like it or not, we were going to be part of a *cause célèbre* for the rest of our lives. 'Grandad was the Crippen Case skipper for over fifty years,' I reminded them. 'The press will treat us the same.'

The police were magnificent. They prepared us, supported us, and assured us that the men were undoubtedly going to receive very stiff sentences, possibly even 'life'. On the day, 2 February 1987, all three pleaded 'guilty' and we heaved huge sighs of relief. Now for the sentencing and we would start to forget it all. Little did we realise.

The judge listened carefully to the usual 'do-gooders' doing their best to exonerate them from blame. It was nauseating to hear the attempts of psychologists to minimise the responsibility of these three thugs. Jill sat in Court Number-One (the same Court as had witnessed the Crippen trial seventy-seven years earlier) quite impassively, as the defence did its best to get their clients light sentences. Then came the ultimate shock and the, unintended, but cruel decision of the judge, Sir John Leonard. McCall, the most vicious of the three, 'five years for rape and five years for aggravated burglary – ten years in all'. Byrne, 'three years for rape and five years for aggravated burglary – eight years in all.' Both men greeted the sentences with smiles. With normal remission they would be out in six and four years from the date of the trial. A doddle compared with the expected life sentences. No wonder they left for the cells with smirks all over their faces. As for Horscroft, the leader, who hadn't shared in the rape (but hadn't tried to stop it) and who had a hundred or more vicious burglaries to his name, Sir John gave him fourteen years. He left the court screaming 'what about the effing rape?'

Then the vultures of Fleet Street descended. I was appalled at the sentencing but even more at the journalists. I marched from the Old Bailey to St Paul's Cathedral Chapter House, surrounded by scores of journalists. There, I gave a Press Conference and various television and radio interviews. I never smiled once. To the media's evident surprise, I didn't attack the length of the sentences. Having been inside three or four maximum security prisons, I knew they were no easy or pleasant rest cures. No, what angered me was the way in which the judge had treated crime against the person and crime against property as being on a par. That seemed to me to be outrageous and I said so in no uncertain terms. Then I turned my attention to the callous statement which Sir John had made about Jill. She had, he announced, suffered 'no great trauma'. It was an unbelievably foolish remark, off the cuff, and he paid a terrible personal and professional price for it. My mind went straight to Gilbert and Sullivan's *Trial by Jury*, in which female tears, hypocritically induced, had seduced a judge. Had Jill sobbed and screamed in court, it seemed as though the judge would have passed tougher sentences. The fact that she was controlled and dispassionate was misread. The consequence was that she found it much harder to forgive the judge than the rapists. He at least was supposed to behave in a responsible manner and, in her eyes, he betrayed both her and civilised society.

The media went for him. Screaming headlines, vicious cartoons, they set out to disembowel him with maximum hostility. In a strange way they behaved as violently as the three criminals. I was sickened. They seemed to think that they were defending us. They had bayed for the thugs' blood. Now they were baying for the judge's entrails.

I wrote to Sir John, dissociating myself from the campaign of hate. I said quite plainly that I thought he had badly miscued in the framing of the sentences and then he had been desperately unfair and insulting to Jill in his 'no great trauma' remark. To my absolute amazement he wrote back. Judges simply don't do that! His letter was, understandably, marked 'Confidential' and it would be improper for me to betray his confidence. Suffice to say, that he admitted (and later did so publicly) that he had made a serious error and deeply regretted the 'no great trauma' remark.

The long-term consequences of the *Ealing Vicarage Rape Case* have been, as I foretold, that Jill has been a national media figure ever since. Four years later she (with a friend Wendy Green) wrote a book. She, believing that God had been the source of strength who alone had got her through the four-year agony, wanted to call it, *Rape – a Love Story*. The publishers failed totally to comprehend how the two ideas could be connected and insisted that the much less powerful *Rape – My Story* be substituted.

Later she, and I, attempted to set up a Trust to help rape victims. We called it HURT (an acronym for 'Help Untwist Rape Trauma'). It gained huge publicity, and, backed by the Archbishop, George Carey, was launched at Lambeth Palace. The very first cheque came from Sir John Leonard! Sadly, half the Trustees didn't attend the first main meeting which launched it, nor did they attend the second which closed it down. Jill was desolated by the lack of active support from Trustees and general public and felt yet again betrayed. Fortunately, the vast majority of the initial donors agreed to let her keep the money raised, which was administered by two sympathetic former Trust members. She, for her part, has built up a clientele of police forces across the country where she regularly lectures on care of rape victims. To her surprise, she found herself unacceptable to some of the other rape counselling groups since she likes men and isn't willing to support an aggressively anti-male feminist philosophy. One such group refused even to interview her for a counselling job which was openly advertised.

Ten years on, Jill and the whole family have learnt to regard the attack and its immediate consequences as 'water under the bridge'. It is family history alongside the Crippen Case, there, but not intrusively. Even so, anything which Jill or I do is usually linked to it. Newspaper captions are almost predictably, 'Rape victim/vicar . . .' This autobiography will probably provide similar captions for subeditors. We can, fortunately, live with that.

One more utterly unpredictable consequence of the rape emerged in the mid-1990s. One day a girl rang up to ask if she could come and see me. Her name meant nothing and she duly arrived with a small, and beautiful, baby girl. At some length she told me her story. She had met, lived with, and duly married, a man by whom she had produced this child. When she gave birth, a nurse had quietly said, 'Do you know who your husband is?' She gave his name. The nurse said, 'Well, that's not his real name,' and revealed that he was one of the two men who had raped Jill. The young mother was so horrified and knowing how much he had brutalised her, as he had Jill, years before, left him and hid, changing her name. Thus it was that I found myself dandling this beautiful baby girl on my lap and seeing his face in this infant. Even the most illustrious of novelists would never have considered trying to get away with such a far-fetched story. Jackie and I tried to help them, bought the baby some clothes, but they have vanished out of our lives as suddenly as they entered. It was a great shock, a year or so ago, to hear that she had committed suicide. How tragic!

The first anniversary of the attack, Friday 6 March 1987, was marked by a major tragedy. Outside the Belgian port of Zeebrugge, the Townsend ferry *Herald of Free Enterprise* capsized with a horrific death toll of passengers. I heard the news late that night and at once set out to rewrite a sermon for a BBC Radio 4 morning service which I was due to broadcast from Torquay on the Sunday. Jackie and I went to Paddington to catch the train, to be met with a public address announcement calling us to the station master's office. The BBC producer was on the phone. 'You'll have to re-write the sermon,' he urged. 'All done,' I said. 'You're a pro,' he responded. 'You said it,' I replied. It was a strange coincidence. Not only was I broadcasting because of the attack's anniversary but also the ferry tragedy opened up the *Empress of Ireland* episode seventy-three years earlier when Grandad's ship had been sunk with terrible loss of life, far greater than the Zeebrugge disaster. Call these occasions coincidences if you will, but for me God was at work in it somehow, giving someone with the right experience the moment to speak to thousands, or even millions, through radio and television. The post-broadcast mail-bag was evidence that the sermon had touched the right chord for many.

Two weeks later, Sue got married in St Paul's Cathedral crypt chapel. She, Jill's identical twin, had been much affected by Jill's rape and it exacerbated her natural premarital hesitations. She wanted a 'splendid' wedding, which it certainly was, but, sadly, the marriage was only to last three years. Her husband took off, owing me a substantial sum which he declined to pay. She later married again but that, too, ended in divorce and she returned to Liverpool to read for a degree. She remains very much involved in her local church.

This was a convenient point for Jackie to give up her part-time job with Sainsburys. She had taken it on very reluctantly at Fulham in 1974, had come to enjoy it a great deal, made some new friends right outside the circle of home and church, and earned enough to help us see all the children through their teens and well into their twenties. It was a new experience for her to become, at fifty-five, a lady of leisure and she took to it like a duck to water. In due course, she was to become a devotee of the public galleries at the Old Bailey, engrossed by trials, lawyers, judges, police and a whole range of highly unpleasant criminals. She even organised Old Bailey tours for St Paul's Cathedral staff and Cathedral tours for Bailey staff. To these activities she added three hobbies. Throughout the years she has built up a huge collection of sugar papers from all over the world. A fan of soap operas, she avidly absorbs the various doings of *Eastenders*, *Brookside*, *Neighbours*, *Emmerdale* and *Coronation Street*, plus the inhabitants of *Ambridge*. She combines these with Jane Austen and scores of less-demanding novels. Most recent of the hobbies has been grandmothering which looks likely to develop in the coming years.

Dominating much of my life in Ealing throughout the middle and late 1980s was the need to do a major restoration job on the church building. My first hope had been to reorder the interior, removing most of the pews to allow much greater flexibility for worship and other activities. We took advice from all the obvious people but, before long, realised that a major reroofing had to take priority or all the proposals for the interior would be swamped by heavy rainstorms. The Church Council called a special meeting of the congregation, after a short Sunday morning service, on 8 December 1985, in order to put a proposal that the whole task should be undertaken as a single entity likely to cost in the region of £500,000 at current estimates. This the congregation endorsed almost unanimously, and the work of raising the necessary money began. A year's study by a working party and a pilot project led to a decision by the Church Council in December 1986 to employ an Australian firm of fundraisers, Everald Compton Associates, who assessed our giving capacity at a figure of £400,000 or more. Some members of the Council were (very understandably) hesitant to launch into an appeal for so huge a sum, which Comptons suggested could be raised within a period of eight weeks! At that critical point I called on the Council to launch out in faith, adding, 'I have spent seven years bringing us to tonight's decision. If we do not go ahead it will be the end of the restoration plans for me. We must go ahead in faith or I must leave it to the next incumbent.' More anxious discussion followed with the decision seemingly hanging in the balance. Finally, after almost two hours of debate, the Council paused for extended prayer and then voted twenty-five in favour, none against, and two abstentions, to go ahead. It was probably the single most important moment in my thirteen years as their vicar and the atmosphere was, first, electric, and then euphoric. Two weeks later a contract with Comptons was signed and their consultant began the pre-appeal groundwork on 16 February. The formal launch was on 10 April and was inaugurated by the switching on of a new floodlighting scheme for the church tower by one of the descendants of S.S. Teulon, the Victorian architect who had rebuilt the church in the 1860s. Jackie and I gave the floodlighting as our own personal contribution to the restoration.

The appeal was staggering. £300,000 was raised within the projected eight weeks and the full £400,000 would have been achieved had not English Heritage failed to honour their regularly declared intentions to give around £80,000. It was cynical. They got everything they demanded of us (at considerable extra expense) having encouraged us to expect their donation. Then, quite suddenly, they told us that we had done so well that we obviously didn't need their grant. I have rarely been so angered by such outrageous behaviour and English Heritage has never featured high on my list of trustworthy organisations since that day. They did offer a small grant to the PCC on the usual condition that they would get a decisive say in the later phase of internal reordering. Needless to say, the Council turned down such a cheeky request with scorn. The Council's letter was polite but its mood was certainly not.

The commencement of the external reordering (new roof, major stonework, and full cleaning) was dedicated by Lord and Lady Coggan on 28 February 1988. Donald Coggan had been Archbishop of Canterbury and there was a great local clan-gathering for the event. It was completed by the end of the year and the Church turned to consider Phase Two, the interior and the creation of new offices and vestries. This was going to need a further half-a-million pounds and although we completed the imaginative plans, the financial task was not launched until after my departure. Sadly, my successor failed to invite me back to see the opening of the new offices and vestries and the interior work remains to be completed. To my surprise, some of the architect-designed new liturgical furniture, given as memorials to past members between 1989 and 1990, has since been removed, with what legal authority I do not know.

The vision of a reordered church, both outside and inside, is something I shall always treasure. To see ordinary people, with no great financial resources, ready and willing to give weekly at an average of nearly £10 a head and then to add a sum of £300,000 to it, in two months, was humbling. Compton's consultant expected to raise the money from the rich and the general community. He was amazed to find it coming from Christians living in small terraced houses and flats. It is a memory I shall always cherish.

One unusual event connected with the restoration appeal was a concert in the church given by the Ealing Symphony Orchestra on 18 July. The orchestra frequently used the church for its concerts but this particular one had a unique element embedded within its programme. Wedged in between Roger Quilter's *Children's* Overture and Percy Grainger's *Country Gardens* at the beginning and, later, Dvorak's *Slavonic Dances*, Bizet's *Carmen Suite* and Leopold Mozart's *Toy* Symphony, was that old and delightful orchestral standby, Prokofiev's *Peter and the Wolf*. Nothing unexpected about that, were it not for the fact that the narrator was not Richard Baker, Peter Ustinov, Terry Wogan, or even Sting. It was me. Not a lot of parsons have, I suspect, narrated 'Peter' in their church with full orchestral backing and I immensely enjoyed the experience. I even have a cassette recording to prove it and I only missed one cue by about half a bar!

St Mary's was a great theatre of a church and every now and then I would go in there on my own, after dark, and, with only a single light on, would declaim chunks of Shakespeare or some piece of epic verse to the empty void.

Such secret rehearsals produced unexpected results a couple of years later when, after preaching the Advent Carol Service sermon at the Mercers' Company Chapel in the City, an elderly retired actress, of Edith Evans manner, informed me, in the fruitiest of tones, that 'Young man, you are a very great loss to the Royal Shakespeare Company.' I was fifty-seven at the time which gave added satisfaction to the compliment. Old ladies seem to be remarkably susceptible to confusing my age. Soon after, another, after a sermon in Bolton, said to me at the church door, 'As I was sitting listening I said to myself, "How sad that that young man must die." ' Yet another, a regular attender at Ealing, once stopped me in a local park. She was almost totally blind. 'Vicar,' she murmured, 'I have a confession to make. I don't come to church for the services. It's your voice. I just love to listen to it.' Now there are three seductive threats to one's humility. Perhaps an even greater challenge came from a fellow-cleric who said, 'Have you had professional voice-training? I just wish I had a voice like yours.' Even *The Times* once praised my voice as 'clear and forceful' and, to crown it all, an American cleric once wrote that his wife 'says that you have the finest speaking voice she has ever heard'. Later, just to cut me down to size, I once heard a bishop's wife say to her husband, not knowing me, 'Darling, there's a very posh voice on the phone.' You can't please them all. The only response I can offer is to thank those old ladies at Petts Wood Preparatory School, who, in the early 1940s, gave me such a love for spoken words and made me learn and recite publicly those reams of poetry.

Both my colleagues left that year. Ian Tarrant (caftan-clad) and his wife Sally (who insisted on being known as 'Dr Sally Barton', to most people's amusement) joined the Church Missionary Society and left to work in the new Anglican Church in Zaire. Later Eric Culbertson, soon to gain his doctorate, and Kay, his wife, also joined a missionary society, BCMS, now known as Crosslinks, where he became their Northern Area secretary, based in Bolton. Eric had been unique among all my curates. Apparently, when he came for interview and stayed overnight he was 'very impressed' because, it seems, I 'argued copiously about Clement of Alexandria over breakfast'. He came to view me, in due course, as having 'an almost Churchillian energy and determination', and who had been 'one of the main creators of the modern evangelical movement in the Church of England'. A very erudite Scotsman, with a preaching style of florid oratory more in keeping with Victorian times than today, he had enjoyed working with me, 'a very fair and helpful boss', and had handled the rape episode extremely well despite his highly emotional personality. Being authoritarian by temperament and conviction he wasn't to everyone's taste in the congregation or among the staff and elders' team. He once went so far as to suggest that he was 'no longer in communion' with me but I didn't take that threat too seriously and we parted, and remain, often in theological conflict but affectionately fond of each other. I especially admired Kay for the way she quietly but firmly kept her talented but abrasive husband on the path of sanity!

They were succeeded by David Francis, the oldest and most judicious of all my assistants. A man with a rich and broad experience in the field of educational administration, David is shrewd and a solid pastor of great worth. His delightful and sparkling wife, Jenny, suffered great pain from pancreatitis and wrote a moving book of her trials and the way in which her Christian faith had undergirded her in her misfortunes. No glib solutions from Jenny. They are a splendid pair. Among those who had written kindly, the year before, at the time of the rape, was our near-neighbour, Neil Kinnock. I wrote back thanking him and inviting him, and his wife, Glenys, for a meal, or drinks, or whatever they could manage in their busy schedule. No reply. Fifteen months later, in June 1987, I wrote, following a General Election, to renew the invitation, this time for August, when the House would not be sitting. Once more, silence. Weeks later, Jackie and I returned from a 'day off' at about six o'clock. The phone rang. 'This is Neil Kinnock's secretary,' announced a female voice. 'They're on their way and should be with you in under the hour.' 'What!' I said vehemently, 'It's the first we've heard about it.' 'Oh,' said the voice, 'didn't we reply to the invitation?' and rang off. Two Sawards rushed around like mad things, tidying up, nipping out to the nearest off-licence and wondering whether they expected a meal, or just drinks.

We were, to put it mildly, irritated. Two unanswered invitations in nearly eighteen months and now the Leader of the Opposition, and his Commander-in-Chief, were landing on us at less than an hour's notice. All (hypocritical) smiles, we greeted them, discreetly discovered that they only had time for a couple of drinks (what a relief!), and spent a pleasant enough hour, avoiding all political hot potatoes. From then onwards our occasional meetings (usually outside his house, as we passed on foot) were very much in the 'allo Boyo' tradition. Jackie and I often wondered how Neil, at the time of the rape, had managed to get himself quoted in the media, saying of us (whom at that stage he had never met) 'lovely family, do a lot of good in the neighbourhood'. Typical rugby-playing, pint-swilling, Welsh politician, we thought. As for Glenys, she could well have been another Margaret Thatcher. A tough cookie, that one.

That autumn Southern England was ravaged by the 'Great Storm'. I spent the night of 15 October in Bristol at a two-day meeting of the Church of England Evangelical Council, on which I served for seventeen years. It was quite windy but next morning the news broke of a tremendous hurricane that had torn across the country from the New Forest to East Anglia, destroying thousands, perhaps millions, of trees. I rang Jackie to see if all was well at home. She had been woken by the wind, but it wasn't until the morning that she had discovered a large branch ripped off a black lime tree. Fifteen feet of branch had just missed the bedroom window.

I and two friends drove back preferring to risk coming by car than to get stuck on the train. Not till we got back did we realise from the TV news just how dramatically destructive the storm had been. In Ealing scores of trees were down. Cars had been crushed and the catastrophe was really evident on Ealing Common where huge forest trees were lying uprooted all over the place. It was a terrible and memorable vista.

Even so, a dead tree can be given a powerful significance. Year by year, Good Friday had been remembered in Ealing in a very distinctive way. Although it was beginning to become unfashionable, I had introduced a Three-Hour Service the year after my arrival and, year by year, it was well attended. It was utterly different from every other service, the church being stripped down to a stark emptiness in the middle of which stood a rough, wooden cross, the upright of which was an eight-foot high birch tree. This, one of a dozen in the vicarage back garden, had died and I had made a virtue of its demise by putting it into a corner of the church, ready for its annual appearance on Good Friday. Each year I conducted the Three-Hour Service in a style so stark and uncompromising that it stood out in all the year's events. 'I wouldn't have believed you could have done something so lacking in bounce and cheerfulness,' said one old lady, and she meant it as an appreciative compliment. 'There's nothing bouncy or cheerful about Good Friday,' I retorted. 'It's a day on its own, a day about pain, grief, suffering, and a man in agony on a cross.' A day of ultimate triumph, of a man who ended it with a ringing 'It is completed!' but not before he had carried the world's sin to that terrible cross on that lonely hill, surrounded by a jeering mob.

In the late 1980s, the town's main churches processed silently from north, south, east and west to the centre for a short open-air service. I, and my colleagues, carried our rough birch-tree cross, followed by scores of worshippers from our part of town. Then back we came for our own Three-Hour Service. My one sadness was that our neighbours, a large charismatic Anglican church, politely declined to join in. They, of course, were pioneers, later, of a noisy, 'tell the world' confrontational 'March for Jesus', out to exorcise all the demons in the High Street.

The March for Jesus has, in recent years, become a worldwide event drawing millions of people on to the streets. I have no objection to such a demonstration of Christian presence but in the late 1980s the English March for Jesus made the foolish mistake of linking itself to a particular, and extremist, attitude to what was called 'corporate exorcism'. Huge crowds in procession were urged to assault the Devil's bastions, the banks, government offices, and so on, with verbal shouts and songs seeking to 'reclaim them for God' and to expel the demons.

The leaders of Ealing Parish Church studied the matter carefully and then, unanimously, declared that, as Anglican Christians, our historic relationship to the State was not, and should not be, one of aggressive confrontation with society. Obviously we did not always agree with society's institutions or their decisions but we were not, in principle, hostile since St Paul had taught that 'the powers that be are ordained by God'.

Our stand was widely reported and drew both support and criticism. The latter came almost always from charismatics and often from those 'House Church' leaders whose charismatic convictions had been the inspiration behind the development of the March for Jesus. Inevitably the press picked up the story. A major feature in the *Independent on Sunday* quoted me freely and inaccurately occasionally putting words into my mouth especially one phrase criticising an American, John Wimber, which I certainly never used.

Radio 4 hosted a short debate between Clive Calver of the Evangelical Alliance and me. We discussed amicably the issues but, off-air, Clive asked me why I had 'gone public' with our criticisms. Surely, he said, the Bible tells us that 'if your brother sins against you you should talk to him privately'. It was an interesting point and illustrated the difference between the ethos of the Church of England and the House Churches. 'But,' I said, 'my brother didn't sin against me. We simply disagreed.' Belonging as I do to the Church of England I was quite used to the idea that holding different opinions was a legitimate stance. If the leaders of the March for Jesus planned an activity with much publicity without consulting me then I was perfectly entitled to disagree with them with equal publicity. Clearly, one of the reasons why other Christian groups so often break up is because they have been created in such a way that the leaders expect to be obeyed by others whose choices are limited to doing what they are told or having to leave and start up their own groups. It isn't, thank God, like that in the Church of England. Clive and I remain good friends but the difference of ethos had been well illustrated.

The year was almost through when Jill got herself married. The young man had been kind and considerate to her at a Christian beach mission and may even, unknowingly, have saved her life, when, at her lowest ebb of post-rape depression, she was contemplating suicide. However, the whole Saward family was appalled at her choice, fearing that her eyes would open a decade later. Relief when he eventually walked out on her was a strange feeling for Christians who believe in the permanence of marriage. Twin daughters, both divorced. Jill's second marriage, to Gavin Drake, produced Myles, Rory and Fergus. Coupled with her recovery from the rape and its consequences, this was a joy in which we all shared.

Joe eventually married in 1992. He and Amy, his American wife, live in France and we have a Saward grandson, William, to keep the line going.

For over thirty years of marriage we had managed without a car of our own. When we needed cars, as I have already mentioned, we rented them. It wasn't ideal but, living in London, we were able to survive on public transport. My mother and father had been driving a Mini, in Devon, throughout the 1980s and, needing a new one, they gave me theirs in 1988. It was a bit of a rattletrap but we were glad to have it and when my mother, her eyesight almost gone, was finally forced off the roads by her doctor (to our great satisfaction since she was, by then, lethal behind a wheel) she handed on the second, newer, Mini and the old one passed on to my niece, Fiona.

Early in 1989 we purchased a timeshare flat in Calahonda on the Costa del Sol not far from Malaga. It was excellent value for money though it started off a saga which is not yet over and which was in due course going to involve a massive court case for fraud. Not our fraud, you understand.

The first half of the year was dominated by Billy Graham's 'Mission '89' to London. I had had considerable hesitations about the whole idea and when it did, finally, get launched I was more than surprised to be, first, chairman of the Ealing Borough committee for local Mission '89 preparations and, then, second, chairman of the media committee for the whole Mission '89 and a member of the executive committee. Thus it was that I found myself introducing Billy Graham to the nation's media at the Queen Elizabeth Conference Centre (opposite the Houses of Parliament) at the national launch. There remains something ludicrous about the idea that Billy Graham needed to be introduced to anyone! On the platform were Billy and me together with Gavin Reid (one of my closest friends for over thirty years) and Richard Bewes, Rector of All Souls, Langham Place, and one of my 'Words' team for *Hymns for Today's Church*, almost a decade earlier.

Mission '89 began at West Ham football stadium, moved to Crystal Palace athletic track, and then to Earls Court. Enormous crowds attended, despite a major transport strike across London, and everything reached a climax at Wembley Stadium, when, in a torrential downpour, a thunderbolt hit the place as Gavin Reid was appealing for money! Jackie and I had afternoon tea with Ruth Graham, Billy's wife, and we were especially delighted when, in reply to my off-the-cuff comment that Billy was a Baptist, Ruth declared firmly, 'He is not. He is a lapsed Presbyterian!'

After the initial Press Conference I invited Billy to lunch with me at the Athenaeum, to which I had just been elected. He graciously declined saying, 'I'm afraid I have to go to meet President George Bush, at his request.' There was no way of arguing with that. At least I can honestly claim to have been upstaged by the President of the United States.

For many years I had been a member of the Diners Club and when they ran a competition in which members had to hook up appropriate wines to the courses planned by Michel Roux for a special dinner at his restaurant The Waterside Inn at Bray on the River Thames in Berkshire, I entered and to my great joy won a prize, namely two free dinners. The final competition tie-breaker was a sentence explaining why I should like to go to The Waterside Inn. 'Because', I wrote, 'it's the only way I can possibly afford to go there.' Forty winning couples dined there, overlooking the river, with free vintage champagne and one of Roux's books, duly autographed, as a memento. I calculated, roughly, that the dinner had cost the Diners Club at least £10,000 which was something like £250 for each couple.

It was also a good year for both cinema and theatre. We both thought Kenneth Branagh's *Henry V* better than Olivier's, and David Lean's augmented *Lawrence of Arabia* a real improvement. We immensely enjoyed Covent Garden's *Die Fledermaus*. Bob and Lynne Libby spent two weeks with us in Ealing and we saw the tremendously moving *Miss Saigon* together. With them we then joined in the Silver Wedding celebrations for John and Jean Place, making it quite a week.

Joe, by now the International Race Editor for Autosport magazine, published a magnificent volume, the *World Atlas of Motor Racing* (Hamlyn) with a first run of 40,000 copies. His articles were beginning to get worldwide coverage and he travelled the Grand Prix circuit from Silverstone to Montreal, and Brazil to Japan.

One evening in October, Jackie and I went to Bristol where I was due to speak. We stayed the night with Chris and Nelly Davis (she had been on my team in Ealing before her marriage, at which I had spoken a few words of Dutch for the benefit of her family). At tea her mischievous five-year-old, Ruth, was misbehaving. 'You'd better behave,' I said, putting on a mock shocked attitude, 'because I'm the vicar.' She looked me up and down, with a twinkle in her eye. 'You're not a vicar,' she riposted scathingly. 'You're too naughty to be a vicar.' Like mother, like daughter. It may be that she was right, of course.

An important annual element in the life of St Mary's for many years was the Civic Service. Each year the Mayor, the Deputy Lieutenant, the Members of Parliament, and many of the Councillors attended a special Sunday morning service. Every other year I preached and on the alternate year I invited an eminent visitor. Early in my time one Mayor, Lady Henniker Heaton, decided not to allow us to hold such a service. Why she declined was never adequately explained but I and the churchwardens, while expressing our sadness, were fortunate in being able to arrange an eight hundred and fiftieth anniversary service with Gerald Ellison, Bishop of London, as already mentioned. The dignitaries attended this, so to some extent honour was satisfied.

In the late 1980s we had a much more highly publicised run-in with another Mayor. By this time I was well-known to the Town Hall and the decision came as a distinct shock. It all came about when Neil Richardson, Rector of Greenford, who was also a militant Socialist Councillor, invited the Mayor, Fred Dunckley, to a Civic Service in his own church. Neil was hardly unaware that he was inviting the Mayor to break a sixty-year old tradition and the Mayor was, I suspect, lulled into accepting without realising how long-standing the tradition had been. When in due course I sent my annual invitation the Mayor was put on the spot. As a Socialist, he had already accepted Richardson's invitation and attempted to defend his action by suggesting that it was only fair to hold the service 'in another area of the Borough'.

My churchwardens and I wrote expressing our disquiet. It was of course his privilege but to break such a tradition without consultation and at short notice was bound to be widely misunderstood and the decision to go instead to Greenford would exacerbate the misunderstanding 'for reasons too obvious to have to elaborate'. Richardson's opposition to almost everything that St Mary's stood for was well known. St Mary's had, moreover, a special mayoral pew and a ceremonial processional cross provided by an earlier Mayor. Would the Mayor reconsider? No, he would not, came the reply from the Town Hall. In order to avoid any further misunderstanding, I wrote to the Deputy Lieutenant and the Members of Parliament explaining briefly our regret at the Mayor's decision to break the tradition without any consultation and his intention to go to Greenford instead. I did not ask them to take any action, merely to be aware of the decision.

The Deputy Lieutenant, quite properly, acknowledged the situation without comment. Both MPs expressed considerable regret and one wrote criticising the decision to the Mayor himself. Opposition members also objected though I had not mentioned the matter to any of them. One told the Mayor he would certainly not attend at Greenford and the leader of the Opposition discussed it at his party meeting. To make matters worse the Mayor circulated the correspondence between us without telling me and someone, not me, leaked it to the local press. Things were getting out of hand and the Mayor and I agreed to a compromise by which he and the usual people attended our morning service shortly before Christmas. Sanity was restored and his successors returned to the usual Civic Service in the years which followed.

Finally, surprise, surprise, the *Ealing Gazette* published a malicious piece in Christmas week misrepresenting the whole situation a month after the matter had been finally resolved. Fred Dunckley and I remained friends throughout, both of us the victim of a regrettable example of politicking, the architect of which gained no credit from the event.

My one and only regret about more than a decade of generally good relations with the Borough Council was the refusal by most of the local Socialist Councillors ever to attend Civic Services. Their absence was in stark contrast to the regular attendance of the Tories. It was certainly never my wish that such a service should be a matter for party politics. At least two Labour Mayors expressed regret that their party was becoming dominated by Marxists and the Civic Service absences were evidence of this.

During their years in office Labour declined to give anything to the St Mary's Restoration Appeal to do work which was entirely beneficial to the town's conservation area. It would have been understandable had they objected to internal work on the church but to play no part in the restoration of the town's historic parish church's exterior and churchyard was plain evidence of their general hostility as a party towards the Church of England.

The seventh and last of my Ealing curates came in the early summer of 1990. David Francis had, at the Bishop's suggestion, been made vicar of St John's, Wembley, and in his place came James Roskelly. James had suffered a desperately unhappy first curacy in rural Somerset and his Bishop urged me to give him a chance to regain his confidence in a strong and secure team like ours where, as one of ten people, lay and clerical, male and female, he could settle down. We took him on, knowing that he, while a gentle, joyful, caring pastor, was also, due to a combination of childhood cerebral meningitis, coupled with dyslexia, scared stiff of administration and organisation. An eligible young bachelor, enthusiastic about cars and speedboats, James was almost a caricature of a West End Hooray Henry. Though a less than adequate preacher, he was and is a lovely man who would later find a happy niche in a brigade of Guards.

By this time our lay eldership team had grown to eight. The original four were Michael White, already mentioned as churchwarden; Ian Goldsmid, an ecclesiastical architect and lay reader, with an interesting pedigree of Jewish and Japanese blood; Joan Porter, a down-to-earth social worker and administrator; and Rene Reeve, the verger's wife, who ran the largest, most imaginative, and spiritually mature older women's group I have ever met. To these we had added Angela Barnfather, a highly competent deputy headteacher at a local church school; Tim Cheung, a Hong Kong Chinese shopkeeper from Soho's Chinatown who lived nearby; Lisa Coleridge, former fashion journalist, mum, and wife of a QC-to-be; and, finally, John Place, our parish administrator, who had served on the team before becoming, in his own right, a fully-fledged elder. His wife, Jean, was by now secretary of the deanery Synod and I was godfather to their younger daughter, Lucy.

My years at Ealing were drawing to an end and Jackie and I took our last summer holiday. We had never seen much of Scotland and we rented a car in Glasgow and drove all over the country. Taking the car on the ferry we drove from east to west across Skye and then from south to north of Lewis itself. Far out in the wild west of Lewis we went to the Church of Scotland on the Sunday where a lay preacher gave us a forty-eight-minute sermon. After thirty-five minutes he announced, 'That was a brief exposition of the doctrine of the Holy Spirit.' He then 'applied' it for almost a further quarter of an hour. He had earlier preached a ten-minute sermon directly at the only child present, who squirmed uncomfortably throughout. It was a *tour de force* which few lay members of the Church of England would have attempted or, for that matter, have much appreciated, sitting on those hard benches.

Back on the mainland we drove to the far north and stayed one night in a small guest-house on the shores of Loch Eriboll. Four couples, including ourselves, were there for dinner and, unbelievably, one of the three others was a vicar and his wife from London diocese. These priests get everywhere!

One idea that the Scottish trip put into my mind was created by seeing a car on the quay at Stornaway harbour. It bore the number plate MJS, my initials, and was the first I had ever seen, since that registration is for cars in those distant parts. When I got home I contacted a garage on the shores of the Atlantic and within a few weeks I was the proud owner of MJS 750S, which has since graced my more recent cars. Unlike the prices advertised in the weekend newspapers I got MJS for a very reasonable sum. A year or two ago I saw that 1 MJS was being auctioned. It went for over £13,000, nearly three times the predicted price and more than thirty times the amount I had paid. Finally, I once saw MS1 on a car. It was a superb Rolls Royce, near Bristol, and I felt that such a plate was entirely appropriate on such a magnificent vehicle.

Thirteen wonderful years at Ealing brought to an end my thirty years of parish ministry. They had, for the most part, been tremendously fulfilling. Nearly thirty men and women were in full-time ministry themselves as, in some way, a consequence of our own ministry over those three decades. We had worshipped, prayed, laughed, taught and slogged away at being in the Anglican parochial ministry. We had been blessed with fine teams of leaders, administrators, secretaries and friends. We had tried to lead them throughout those years and they had stood by us when we needed them. Of course we had failed in many ways. Everyone in Christian ministry does. There is no known instance of a man or woman who can say, 'I never put a foot wrong.' We didn't do this. We didn't do that. We were too busy in this department and should have spent more time in that. That's the nature of ministry. As Jesus said, 'When you have done everything you must still say, "We were unprofitable servants." '

Time to move on. But how that happened must wait to the end of the next part of the story. Suffice to say that both at Fulham and Ealing I was succeeded by much younger men, both of whom rapidly obliterated almost all trace of my work and my presence. It's strange how insecure some clergy seem to be. In both places I greatly valued the inheritance of my predecessors. By Michael Botting and Eric Vevers I had been bequeathed going concerns. I, in my turn, handed on happy and united churches, well organised, and with high-quality local leadership teams.

Chapter Thirteen

The Wild Wood

Life was overwhelmingly busy outside as well as inside the parish. In my first year at Ealing I was not only Vicar and Area Dean, but a Church Commissioner, a member of General Synod, chairman of the new hymn book Words' committee, a member of the Holy Communion Rite A revision committee, and on the Church of England Evangelical Council. I helped to create a new diocese in Europe and served on the National Partners in Mission committee.

It was many years since I had heard any real news of one of my closest friends from Bristol days, who had spent all his ministry in the North. For reasons that I never discovered, he had gradually cut himself off from all his Tyndale friends and, even though I always called in to see him whenever I was in Cumbria (which wasn't often), he seemed less and less to welcome my arrival. By the mid-1970s we had almost lost touch and after he moved from the Scottish border, first to the Lancashire border, and then to the Lakes, we were virtually out of touch. Then, suddenly, news began to trickle through from people in his Diocese that there were serious marital difficulties. Yet another friend spoke of his having gone into hibernation with a local husband and wife, virtually incommunicado.

Was there, I wondered, anything that I could do? I wrote to the husband, pleading that he would pass on an enclosed letter. He was kind enough to do so. My letter spoke of past happy memories of a deeply satisfying friendship. I had, I wrote, no intention of trying to be do-gooding, no judgements, no pitying looks, no helpful platitudes. I simply offered my home, my friend-ship and anything else he wanted – a short open-ended offer of help.

He replied. He was quite capable of handling his own affairs. He was very well. He couldn't understand my 'sudden, tremen-dous concern after so many years'. And that was that. I have never had another word from him. His marriage did break up soon after and what he has done since I do not know. Some les-sons are hard to learn and painful to undergo. I don't think the scars left on me will ever completely heal and the most hurtful thing of all seemed to be his complete unawareness of the situa-tion. Yet I was not the only one to get such treatment. Other college friends felt similarly ostracised. Whenever any of us meet we all ask for news of him and none of us ever has any. So we share our sense of bereavement and continue to recall him with affection and much sadness.

The final creation of the new Alternative Service Book by the General Synod involved me in three ways. I helped to prepare the new Communion Service and can still remember the sense of ex-citement as we achieved an agreed text (which had not been thought possible for over half a century). Prior to that I made an extraordinary mistake in a General Synod debate. Caught up in conversation, I voted, by accident, the wrong way and (in, as I sus-pect, the providence of God) thus unintentionally permitted the inclusion, by a fraction of a vote, of what is now called 'Rite B', into the Alternative Service Book.

My third action was to make a fighting speech in a Synod de-bate on 7 November 1979. Some days beforehand a group of fa-mous personalities had launched a broadside at modern liturgy and Bibles in a booklet called *PN13* (with a bright red cover). It received considerable press and media coverage and I thought the time had come to fire a salvo of torpedoes. I soon got into my stride, calling it a 'red flag of reaction' and scornfully rejecting their charge that we were 'barbarians and vandals'. I would, I added, 'be glad that I was on the revision committee to my dying day,' and thanked God that the Bible and our gospel had been 'in the *koine* of the marketplace' which our new Bibles and liturgies had restored, putting God 'back where he belongs' not in 'a book designed to be read as literature' but in 'heart of word and sacrament in the midst of his believing people'. 'We have for far too long', I concluded, 'been spiritually castrated by the intellectual arrogance of the cultural establishment . . . I hope we shall keep our heads and ignore their advice.'

I don't ever recall any speech of mine receiving such tumultuous applause. It was exactly right for the moment, stinging in its scorn for the sneering minority of unbelieving arty characters who had attempted to teach the Church of England its liturgical business. Some of them had, months before, laughed at the Evangelicals and Anglo-Catholics who were appointed to the revision committee, calling us 'fourteen scorpions in a bottle'. The time had come for one of the scorpions to sting those who foolishly trod on them. I loved every minute of that speech and never, for one moment, have I ever regretted making it. Incidentally, of the eleven clergy on that committee, eight became bishops, one an archdeacon and I went on to a St Paul's Cathedral canonry. Sadly, the eleventh, Brian Brindley, left the Church of England under a large nimbus cloud. None of us were, I think, novices, either then or since.

Probably the most influential was Colin Buchanan who was, without question, the most knowledgeable of all the Evangelicals on liturgical matters. As a student he had scored a hundred per cent in his liturgy exams which had, as far as I know, never been achieved before (or since!). Later to become Bishop of Aston and, even later, Bishop of Woolwich, Colin combines the content of a library with the action and sound of a Kalashnikov and there are very few people who would willingly take him on in debate. I did once beat him on such an occasion and I also made sure that one or two of my books gave accounts of events (like Keele) at which I had been present and he had not, which had not deterred him from writing magisterially about them. The Church of England owes him an enormous debt which not all its leaders have been willing to concede.

Soon after this Donald Coggan retired and there was much speculation about the vacancy at Canterbury. I wrote to the

Crown Appointments Commission urging the appointment of Stuart Blanch and warning them against one candidate who 'follows the winds too obviously'. There was little doubt from the replies I received that the reference was understood. Time was to prove how right I was.

This is perhaps a good point at which to add a little more about my Synod career which lasted twenty years. I was forty-three when elected and, including questions and other interventions, I made, in all, 126 speeches. Thirty-five of these were full-length (ten minutes long) and I also asked 41 formal questions. My chief area of concern was in the field of doctrine and liturgy (29 interventions) including 2 on the virgin birth, and 1 each on the Bible, the resurrection, the so-called *filioque* clause, which relates to the Holy Trinity, and subjects like baptism, priesthood, and matters of interfaith worship. One long-running battle concerned the need for more principled scales of representation in Synods, and I spoke 14 times on it before finally achieving my goal. I was 9 times called to speak about sex, marriage and divorce and made 13 comments on issues relating to baptism (on which I also wrote an appendix to a Synod report). It would not be immodest to say that I was a well-known Synod figure and, on many occasions, a major exponent of the view of the Evangelical movement in the Church of England. I certainly represented its widespread concern on baptism more fully than any other Synod member of the era.

Over the years my exposition of the doctrine of the virgin birth both in Synod and in sermons drew much favourable comment. The chaplain of a large independent school said that he was amazed at how effective it had been especially among naturally sceptical sixth formers. The President of an American university wrote, on a later occasion, that 'as a professing Christian for fifty-six years' he had never before heard 'a more persuasive sermon on the subject' which I had presented 'in such a profound and convincing fashion'.

To be generally well received was not, in the ethos of the Synod, necessarily to be agreed with but that body has an excellent reputation for civilised courtesy. Very occasionally my opponents seemed deliberately to diminish my points by misrepresenting them in the ongoing debate.

Archbishop Habgood did this after a speech on baptism in which I had grounded the sacrament in God's covenant with Abraham, a position expounded by St Paul and St Augustine among others. Habgood appeared to be quite ignorant of this, saying how strange it was that when I was 'talking about the theology of baptism it was all about covenants and nothing to do with salvation'. 'Surely if baptism is about anything', he continued, 'it is about our theology of salvation . . . and the theology of the church.' It takes your breath away to hear an archiepiscopal theologian fail to grasp that the divine covenant with Abraham is the very foundation of salvation, of the doctrine of the church, and of the sacramental symbol of justification, namely baptism.

I only recall one instance of blatant rudeness and boorish behaviour in Synod and again, sadly, it was perpetrated by Habgood who, immediately following a much-applauded speech of mine on the virgin birth, walked up to me and said bluntly, 'That was a load of rubbish.' I was, and still remain, shocked at a brand of rudeness which I found utterly unacceptable. Only once, years after his retirement, did he ever conduct a civilised conversation with me. In this he was quite unlike his fellow-Liberal, Robert Runcie, who never ceased to be charming and gracious. Habgood has a tremendous brain, and did many important things for the Church of England, not least in the wake of the decision to ordain women but I thank God that he was kept out of St Augustine's chair. I have never ceased to respect his ability but try as I might, and I made at least four attempts to offer him friendship, I could never get anything from him but an icy and disdainful response. When I made the journey to Bishopthorpe to offer him a copy of my well-received pre-Lambeth Conference book *Evangelicals on the Move* he never even stooped to acknowledge the gift. Twice I obeyed the advice of his lay assistant to 'Try to write him a friendly and appreciative letter if you can,' but on both occasions his response was no more than a few lines of a duplicated sheet. Others may take quite a different view but he is to me the reincarnation of that other frigid Etonian, of whom it was written, 'My name is George Nathanael Curzon, I am a most superior person.'

Habgood aside, I have known and liked all the Archbishops of Canterbury and York since my ordination in the 1950s. The five at Lambeth – Fisher, Ramsey, Coggan, Runcie and Carey – have all felt like good friends, as have Stuart Blanch and David Hope at Bishopthorpe. I suppose it was inevitable that just as I found it impossible to work amicably with one of my five vicars and one of my thirteen curates, so too I had to suffer from one Archbishop out of eight.

Among the growing number of speaking invitations I was receiving was one from the Petts Wood Crusader class, where I had grown up and been nurtured in my adolescent faith, and they asked me to be the speaker at their Golden Jubilee celebrations. Without their early influence I might not even be a Christian today so I felt greatly honoured.

Henry and Barbara Aydelott, friends in Seattle, paid all my expenses for a visit to that beautiful city in order that I might address the eight hundred members of the Seattle and Tacoma Rotary Club. I flew to Calgary and then went, via the Rockies, to Jasper and on by train to Vancouver. The journey down the Fraser River canyon was stunningly beautiful. When I began my Rotary talk I was virtually ignored so I took the bull by the horns and told them that as a Church Commissioner I was one of those responsible for assets totalling six thousand million dollars. Complete hush. That taught me a lot about American businessmen. In my address I happened to tell a joke about Churchill and Clemenceau in which the punchline was in simple French. Not a smile. A week later, Henry showed me the current Rotary leaflet. In a glowing report of my address I read, 'Saward gave a scholarly talk.' 'What was scholarly about it, Henry?' I enquired. 'Michael, you told a joke in French,' he answered. 'Nobody understood it, but in Seattle, that's scholarship.' I was, incidentally, flattered to learn that the speaker previous to me had been the President of General Motors.

On my way home I stayed one night with Jim and Kit Packer in Vancouver. He was a professor of theology there and next morning we left together for the airport. He was due to give a series of lectures in Oklahoma, forgot to bring his briefcase with all his lectures in it, and waved me off saying, 'I'll have to knock up a new set on the plane.' We clergy do sometimes have to live dangerously. The Baptist preacher Spurgeon once said to a woman who wondered how long it had taken him to prepare 'that wonderful sermon' that it had taken 'thirty years' hard work and half-an-hour's sweat'. You can't ignore the background careful work but you sometimes have to manage on the 'half-an-hour's sweat' when the going gets tough. There is a plaque on the wall at Ealing which describes John Bowman, a rector who died in 1629, as 'a paynful preacher of God's word'. It doesn't mean he caused 'payn' but that he took 'payns' over his sermons. I hope I have earned a similar epitaph.

At that point, the Church of England decided it had another job for me. All across the Anglican Communion, provinces and dioceses were holding Partners in Mission consultations and it was the turn of England to invite shrewd observers from different parts of the world to assess us. I was charged with introducing them to England by means of a slide show. Richard Bewes, then Vicar of Emmanuel, Northwood, and I were sent out to conduct interviews with three public figures whose comments might add colour to our commentary. First was Bernard Levin, a Jewish journalist on *The Times*, whose flat in Marylebone High Street was groaning with the weight of his books. He delivered himself of some shrewd, if waspish, insights. The second was Len Murray, Secretary of the Trades Union Congress, a well-respected Methodist, who held the kind of power that has not been seen since Margaret Thatcher destroyed it in the early 1980s. What he said on tape was interesting. What he said after we stopped the tape was riveting. I especially recall some damning comments about a particular union boss whom he didn't identify but which seemed likely to refer to Clive Jenkins.

Finally we arrived at Wilton Street and the home of Edward Heath, former Tory Prime Minister. Richard and I were shocked at his state of health and assumed that he was dying, but time has obviously proved us wrong. He had just returned from a convalescence in the south of France and we obviously caught him at a bad time. I was embarrassed at trying to interview him in such a state but he coped better than we had feared. Richard taped and photographed all three interviews which I conducted. A month later, in June, I launched PIM with the programme at High Leigh, in Hertfordshire, and warned the overseas visitors to remember that, whatever any provincial figures might say, London was the seat of power and influence. The Archbishop of York, Stuart Blanch, a dear friend of mine, promptly got up and played the provincial card with a big grin but I think both he and everyone else knew only too well the realities of English life. I may be a Londoner and thoroughly metropolitan in outlook but the fact that power is focused on London seems so obvious as not to merit serious argument.

Pope John Paul II duly descended upon us and I found myself oddly described as 'a leading English prelate', joining with the Jesuit, Edward Yarnold, on a live TV transmission to New York at about three o'clock in the morning. The television company put us up in a London hotel, in a twin room, which allowed me to dine out on the delicious fact that 'I've slept with a Jesuit priest.' All too soon we were on the train to Canterbury where, on a blazing hot day, I found myself in a long queue of clergy outside the east walls, waiting to get in. To my amazement, I saw Michael and Joan Ramsey well back in the queue. I went straight to the policeman on the gate. 'There's an eighty-year-old retired archbishop back there,' I pleaded. 'Surely he can come in?' The bobby at once agreed and I was cheered by my brother clergy as I piloted the Ramseys past the crowd, through the postern gate, and into the Close. Not being naive, I went with them and got a front seat in the nave. Thus the Pope passed me at arms length!

Overnight Jackie and I set off to Port Grimaud, near St Tropez, where we rented a small studio right on the Mediterranean. We certainly needed, and enjoyed, the sunshine and rest of a virtually private beach. Port Grimaud is a pastiche French fisherman's village, created by the architect Spoerry from an empty marshland. It isn't cheap but it's unique and we've enjoyed three summer holidays there over the years. We came back to Paris on one of the new TGVs. They really are magnificent trains and reached 160 m.p.h. on the journey. More recent TGV Atlantiques to Bordeaux do nearly 200, as we have experienced. All they lack is the ability to serve a snack meal in less than half-an-hour's pushing and shoving at a bar. It's funny to contrast their superb hi-tech splendour with the dreary *croque-monsieur* cuisine.

A month later I was back at Canterbury for a special service in the crypt conducted by Bishop John Hughes (already retired), for the group of us who were celebrating the Silver Jubilee of our ordination. He was, and still is, a lovely man and we smile together over his 'faint streak of humility' jibe about me all those years earlier.

Only six days after this, Jackie and I went to York Minster for the consecration of Michael Baughen as Bishop of Chester. He and Myrtle have been among our closest friends since the 1950s when our ordinations were on the same day and our marriages only ten days apart. It was a memorable occasion even though Jackie and I had driven though a police cordon *en route*. 'What's up?' we asked, and discovered that we were in the middle of a massive murder hunt right across the Vale of York.

The backdrop to all this was the Falklands War and on Sunday 1 August 1982 my journalist friend John Capon announced in the *Sunday Telegraph* that a group had just written an alternative National Anthem in which the words 'Send her victorious' had been replaced. This startling revelation came only days after a row had blown up over the thanksgiving service at St Paul's Cathedral at which Archbishop Runcie and Dean Alan Webster had soft-pedalled triumphalism in favour of penitence for war. The *Mail on Sunday* and the *Sunday Mirror* launched an attack on Michael Baughen and the Jubilate team and by the Monday the media were in full cry, baying for our blood. By the end of August I had acquired twenty-six A3-size pages of press cuttings, most of which were classic examples of 'silly season' journalism. Some of the many cartoons were hilariously funny and there were some brilliant parodies.

So what had we done? We had offered a set of words for

consideration to those who found commands to the Almighty to 'scatter our enemies', to 'frustrate their knavish tricks' and to 'confound their politics', just a little bit archaic. Others had done it before in early hymn books, even in Westminster Abbey of all places. Our fate was to have done so in the calm of 1977, not knowing that by the summer of 1982 we should be at war with Argentina. In that jingoistic climate we were damned out of hand. As the Words editor, I was, according to various far-right Tory MPs, 'a leftist, trendy, unpatriotic, liberal, pacifist' who was 'ashamed to be English'. The fact that I was demonstrably none of those things (except for the undefined 'trendy', which, having a beard, I was presumed to be) seemed not to matter. To write about liberty, unity, peace and guarding our Queen was, apparently, wimpish showing me to be no 'brandy-and-soda Tory' but 'Perrier-water' in political orientation. The irony of it all was the fact that as my team reminded me, I had said to them, when we agreed to include the text back in 1977, 'Well, you lot can carry the can for this, because I'm blowed if I'm going to!' I hadn't written a single word of it.

Thus it was, as the storm burst over our heads on Monday 2 August, that I found myself (on my day-off) racing around radio and TV studios all over London. I did fourteen broadcasts in two days, defending our text, not as a substitute for the National Anthem on public occasions but as a reasonable version for singing in churches. I remember the *Jimmy Young Show* when, wearing a dark suit and sober tie, I pleaded, 'Do I look like a trendy?' and was rewarded by Young saying, 'Yes, you do, a little.' I should have remembered Michael Caine's first film *Gambit* back in 1966, when he fell for the same answer. 'Do I look like a crook?' he enquired of Shirley Maclaine. 'Yes, you do, a little,' she replied. Young, being on radio, left his audience assuming that I was looking outrageous and I had no visible defence.

The most enjoyable event was when I was rung by French Television. 'Ve 'ear zat you 'ave shannged ze Nash'nal arntem,' said the voice. 'Give me five minutes', I answered, 'and I'll knock you up a new "Marseillaise".' I heard the roars of Gallic laughter in the background. Next day they sent a camera crew to Ealing where I sang the first two lines in French, 'Allons enfants de la Patrie, le jour de gloire est arrivé,' in our churchyard.

There was, in fact, a lot of church support for our 'Anthem', but the media had gone crazy and anyone sensible kept his head in the trench. Runcie distanced himself from us but wrote me a friendly and supportive postcard since, after the St Paul's service, we were 'comrades in adversity'. Lots of the journalists spoke well, to me, of our words but slammed us in print to keep their editors happy. On TV, radio and in print, I and my Jubilate colleagues mounted a sturdy and rational defence but we were trampled on by the Gadarene Swine who were pig-ignorant bigots for the most part. Hardly an intelligent letter or article was published by the anti lobby, mostly Tories, which concerned me since I am, and have always voted, Conservative. Peers, knights, MPs, and even a former Cabinet secretary, leapt on to the abuse bandwagon, pulled by Quintin Hogg, the Lord Chancellor, himself. It was an amazing experience to realise that so many of those who governed us were so foolish.

So what had we actually done to provoke such an uproar? The Jubilate words, offered as an alternative, not as a substitute, were:

> God save our gracious Queen,
> God bless and guard our Queen,
> long live the Queen;
> guard us in liberty,
> bless us with unity,
> save us from tyranny;
> God save the Queen.
>
> Lord, be our nation's light,
> guide us in truth and right,
> in you we stand;
> give us your faithfulness,
> keep us from selfishness,
> raise us to godliness;
> God save our land.

Spirit of love and life,
healing our nation's strife,
on you we call;
teach us your better way,
grant us your peace today,
God bless our Queen, we pray,
God save us all.

These words, said Christopher Idle, one of the Jubilate team, were 'more democratic, more Christian, and no less respectful to the Queen'. Bearing in mind, as the tabloids discovered, that most people didn't even know the second and third verses of the official National Anthem, our words seemed hardly treasonable. How amazing, then, that no less than the Lord Chancellor should have got his ermine knickers in such a twist over them. Fortunately, John Bickersteth, the Bishop of Bath and Wells and 'Clerk to the Closet' (the head of the Queen's Ecclesiastical Household), kept his sense of sanity unimpaired and declared that the Queen would not see the words as a 'betrayal' but he, along with the rest of us, was lucky not to have his head stuck on a pole on London Bridge by the idiotic backwoodsmen of the Tory party in the name of patriotism!

Three months later, in the middle of the November General Synod, *Hymns for Today's Church* was launched in St Margaret's Church, Westminster, in the shadow of Westminster Abbey. The book had taken almost ten years of my life and, as the chairman of the Words team, I had, with Michael Perry and Christopher Idle, carried most of the responsibility. The book contained about three hundred new, and post-war, hymns and another three hundred well-known traditional hymns. The former caused little stir, most of them being excellent texts which had emerged from over two thousand 'possibles' (which we had assessed 'anonymously', that is to say, as texts without the authors' names attached). We evolved a sophisticated marking system and no hymn got into the final list unless it had acquired a high rating from the Words team of nine members.

Furious controversy broke out about the older three hundred.

We had dared to revise them, removing not only the 'thees' and 'thous' and the 'ests' and 'eths' but, treasonably in the eyes of the woodenly (and usually ignorant) traditionalists, we had actually altered archaic ideas and words. Needless to say, the tabloid newspapers howled execration at these wicked clerics who had changed 'our hymns' or omitted well-known hymns (which were usually about 'rich men in castles' which had not appeared in any hymn book for over half a century). In piled the usual ruck of Tory MPs and literary experts, few of whom knew anything about the day-to-day life of churches but were well able to scare the pants off 'Disgusted of Tunbridge Wells' who believed that the *Telegraph*, *Mail* and *Express* were the final arbiters of taste and orthodoxy.

Churches and clergy with any imagination, who were keen to use intelligent modern liturgy, Bibles and hymns, gave the book a cautious welcome and many large churches began to use it, with a warmly positive response. Today, over fifteen years later, it still contains a better selection of wide-ranging hymns than any other book on the market but, sadly, it fell between the Scylla of blind tradition and the Charybdis of charismatic clap-happy repetitive choruses.

Why was the traditional reaction so hostile? Certainly ignorant prejudice was a major factor. Most people were quite unaware of how many of their old favourites had in early days been heavily edited. 'Hark! the herald-angels sing' had first appeared as, 'Hark! how all the welkin rings'. 'Eternal Father, strong to save' had been radically altered long ago. 'Lo, he comes on clouds descending/Once for favoured sinners slain' had originally been 'descending, see the Saviour's bloody sign'. To such critics 'what I like' is 'right', even if it was far from the earliest known text.

One excellent example of intelligent editing appeared in the final verse of 'Once in royal David's city', the Christmas hymn. The version usually sung ends 'Where like stars his children crowned all in white shall wait around'. Such a conclusion is a terrible, banal anticlimax in which heaven offers a vision of kids in nightshirts standing about doing absolutely nothing! *Waiting around* for what? Godot?

My team transformed those dreary words to 'There his children gather round, white like stars with glory crowned'. That gave meaning and biblical significance to the hope of heaven. It lifted the final words to a new and lofty level. Sadly, the prejudiced traditionalists wanted meaningless nighties. With time, we may still win. A coming generation may have brains in place of porridge!

I owe a considerable debt not only to both the Words and Music teams but also to John Barnard, one of the latter, for writing a magnificent new tune, 'Guiting Power', to my best-known hymn 'Christ Triumphant'. From 1966 to 1982 it was chiefly sung to Michael Baughen's tune, 'Christ Triumphant', and is still widely set to it, especially in non-Anglican circles. However, once 'Guiting Power' came on the scene, its sheer majesty opened up many doors in cathedrals and on television and today the hymn continues to perform well under two quite separate guises. John Barnard's tune-writing skills are now widely recognised.

And so we come to the *Private Eye* saga. It began in 1980 when I wrote a letter defending Bishop John Trillo whom they had styled as 'the silly old Bishop of Chelmsford'. He was, I said, 'one of the most genuine pastoral bishops we Anglicans have got' coming near to being 'top of the pops on my list of episcopal goodies'. I wasn't, I added, 'an episcopal ring-licker'. Little did I know that one day his daughter-in-law would be my secretary and would type this book. Richard Ingrams, the *Eye* Editor, bided his time. Then, two years later he struck venomously. His anonymous columnist 'The Devil' charged me, as Words editor of 'the appalling new hymn book' with having 'single-handedly destroyed the work of poets like Milton'. As a 'powerful member of the Liturgical Commission' (which I wasn't) I had attempted to 'destroy the Book of Common Prayer' (which I hadn't), describing its supporters as 'asinine and infantile' (which I didn't). Further, I had 'dismayed local residents by suddenly and unexpectedly entering their sitting-rooms and exhorting them to switch off their television sets and turn to God'. (Never!) There was more of the same kind of rubbish.

So what does one do? My reaction was, and is, to send up such journalists rotten. I replied saying that 'The Devil' was, in the New Testament, 'the father of lies' and was, therefore, running true to form. I cited seven lies, all factual, and ended by joking that my 'wild staring eyes and vulpine grin' had provoked my family into buying me some 'vampire teeth for Christmas' so that the *Eye* could call me 'the monstrous vicar of Ealing'. Battle was joined. Ingrams, or his hack, produced two more lies which, again, I shot down and, in response to his claim that I was 'burning with ambition', I promised an 'inter-galactic "Saward for Pope" rally at Nuremberg on April 1st' for which 'God and Mrs Thatcher were clearing their diaries'. With such burning ambition as mine, one 'shouldn't be too reticent'.

Round Three damned me for 'craving publicity' and went on to offer 'a fiver for further details' of my 'intimate and mysterious connection with the infamous murderer, Dr Crippen'. I, at once, claimed the fiver, explaining my grandfather's role in catching Crippen. 'We can't go on meeting like this,' I concluded. 'But isn't it time you took me out to lunch at the Savoy? I adore grilled gnome.' 'Gnome' was, of course, one of Ingrams' pseudonyms. Back came the *Eye* with five more lies, this time attacking our modern churchyard notice-board, about which no-one had complained since its erection three years earlier. ' 'Ello, 'ello, 'ello, at it again, I see,' I bantered. I couldn't resist pointing out that Ingrams hadn't come up with the promised Crippen fiver which I was 'patiently awaiting'. Perhaps, I suggested, his promise to pay was 'on a par with your many other terminological inexactitudes?'

Soon after this I was invited to take part, at a fee of £150, in a TV programme in which Janet Street-Porter was the hostess. She had, as a girl, been a pupil at Lady Margaret School where my three daughters had also been (though not in her time) but she stood for almost everything that I most disliked in the media and I firmly declined. A not dissimilar character, Robert Kilroy-Silk, frequently tried to get me on his programme *Kilroy* in later years and again I wouldn't play ball. Such programme formats are always in danger of providing a great deal of heat and hardly any light on the subjects they handle and I loathe that kind of punch-up television.

Turning to the national press, I was commissioned in the following years to write articles or obituaries in *The Times*, the *Guardian*, the *Independent*, the *Daily Mail*, the *Daily Express* and the *Sunday Telegraph*. Sadly, the *Daily Telegraph* became increasingly hostile to the Church of England and I never managed to get a foot in their door.

In 1984 David Jenkins was appointed Bishop of Durham. I thought at the time that it was an imaginative, if unexpected, move but he at once attacked the General Synod (which he had never attended). I wrote to the *Church Times* saying that if a newly-appointed vicar attacked his Church Council before he arrived then he deserved all he got! A week or so later, Jenkins began his crusade against the bodily resurrection of Christ and, later, the virgin conception. A kind and caring man, he has nevertheless gone down in history as a wild Radical. I took him on, under Brian Redhead's chairmanship, on television, and also spent an hour or two with him at his home, Auckland Castle. His motives were, I'm sure, honourable, and he was traduced by some parts of the press, but he was carried away by his Celtic verbosity and ultimately did much more harm than good, at least to the public image of the Church. Funnily enough, I was in York the night that the thunderbolt hit the Minster and woke up at that very moment, not knowing what had caused me to stir until the morning.

General Synod, which I dearly loved for twenty years, was nevertheless seduced by him. Twice they gave him standing ovations even when at least half of them disagreed profoundly with his opinions. Both occasions were, I suspect, orchestrated by Liberals who applauded him loudly, stood up, and the synodical sheep followed tamely. I almost always applauded good speeches, from whatever source, but, with press and cameras present, there was no way that I was going to stand and clap, loud and long, speeches by David, however emotional (and they were emotional – he was almost in tears) which dismissed the church's historic understanding of the incarnation and resurrection as no more than 'divine laser-beam miracles'. Jenkins had a lot in common with Lloyd-George, the Welsh wizard, and both of them cost church and state dearly. He, like me, had once been a Crusader (in Bromley, I think), and the movement, having no firm church links, was to prove very vulnerable to converts like him who rejected Evangelical theology.

Meanwhile, an unfortunate row was going on between the Evangelical mainstream and the Church Society. The latter had been effectively taken over by a coup conducted by a group of extremist Protestants and it appointed as Secretary one of the most untypical men in the whole Evangelical movement who would, in later years, secede from the Church of England and become 'bishop' of a tiny sect. He and his hardliners sacked the Editor, Peter Williams, of the *Churchman* magazine for being too liberal in outlook and policy. Since Peter was a much-respected theologian on the staff of Trinity College, in Bristol, the charge was trumped-up, but sacked he was. I and a group of 'mainstreamers' met to decide on a response and we created a replacement magazine, to be called *ANVIL*, for which I designed the initial front cover. I have, since then, been a regular book reviewer for it.

To my surprise, I was invited to give a lecture at St Stephen's House in Oxford, generally regarded as the most extreme Anglo-Catholic theological college. The theme, which I had developed in my book *All Change*, was that of effective parish communication. The morning was an eye-opener. It was clear that many of the ordinands were simply not interested, seeing their ministry almost solely in terms of 'priesthood', which meant saying Mass daily, hearing confessions, and sick-visiting. The idea that a parish needed to be well-organised and the clergy communicators of a gospel to the neighbourhood seemed to have quite passed them by. I mentioned, in passing, my 'clergy filing system' but there was no interest. Since the Church of England has, as far as I know, no other comparable system it has been interesting to see that out of the two thousand systems I have sold to clergy and ordinands only two have been purchased by St Stephen's ordinands. This compares with well over a hundred to one college, and over fifty to three or four others. All in all, I have sold nearly five hundred to ordinands.

Meanwhile, the biggest and most publicised debate in the General Synod at that time was concerned with 'the Church and the Bomb'. As someone who had spent years reading military history I was keen to take part but the only reasonable way to guarantee getting 'called' by the chairman (Bishop David Sheppard) was to put down a formal amendment. The night before the debate I rang him and explained the situation and offered him a deal. I would withdraw my amendment if he guaranteed to call me for a ten-minute speech in the main debate. He, quite properly, declined but, knowing my military interest, said, cryptically, 'I hear you.' That was the only time in twenty years of Synod membership that I ever tried to lean on a chairman. Next day, he did call me for a ten-minute speech which I gave in the full glare of international TV coverage. It was a speech which avoided pacifism on the one hand and aggressive militarism on the other but it called for the retention of nuclear weapons on the grounds that dictators understood and respected force and nothing else. I cited many instances and authorities in support of that position.

One unexpected consequence was an invitation to a free trip to Brussels and Mons to discover something of the way NATO and SHAPE functioned. The group was led by Emma Nicholson, then a Tory Member of Parliament, and my most powerful memory is that of a brigadier on the SHAPE staff maintaining that NATO land and air forces could not expect to hold Warsaw Pact armies, with their huge tank element, for more than two weeks. They would, he predicted, reach the Atlantic coast of France soon after that breakthrough. It all sounded like a rerun of 1940 but with far greater forces engaged.

When I got home I reread my Synod speech. I have read it again recently with the benefit of the hindsight of thirteen years, the Berlin Wall demolition, the collapse of Communism in Eastern Europe, and the realisation that it was the West's unceasing pressure and the financial investment needed to keep the arms development in balance that finally cracked the Soviet system. I wouldn't want to remove a line from that speech. It was one of the most important that I ever made in the General Synod. It stood firm against the influential liberal argument which for so many years attempted to commit the Church of England to a wimpish doctrine of appeasement to the forces of world Marxism. I steered far short of the extreme hawkism of the American right wing.

Months passed. I was awarded a Winston Churchill award for a study on churchyards in the USA. The *Eye* rushed in again. Ealing's 'ominous vicar' would be going abroad, 'publicity crazed' as usual. 'Regular readers will remember' Saward's 'huge and offensive churchyard notice-board'. Two days later a group of young adults was seen to come out of a local pub and smash the notice-board irreparably. My last communication with the *Eye* was angrily to complain about this 'act of criminal damage' which even the police regarded as likely to have been perpetrated by 'Sid Yobboe-ish *Eye* readers'. Since the board had received all the proper legal authorisations of borough and diocese, it seemed not unreasonable to suppose that the *Eye* approved and was 'doubtless rejoicing that someone had struck a blow for liberty'. The *Eye*, needless to add, had nothing further to say. They left me alone after that. One of the local newspapers, however, congratulated me. 'Well done, Michael Saward,' said their editorial. 'When the *Eye* tried slinging mud at him . . . it refused to stick to the vicar. In fact, he was quite adept at slinging it back. That's the spirit, Michael.'

Suddenly, the truth came out. *Options* magazine did a 'face to face' piece with Ingrams. In it he admitted that 'I rather like taking some person that no-one's heard of and elevating him into a national figure, like the Reverend Michael Saward. That's one of the great joys of *Private Eye*.' So there it was, in black and white. I, the supposedly 'publicity crazed' clergyman 'burning with ambition' had merely been an Ingrams' victim. He was merely trying to play God with my reputation, blowing me up to ridiculous proportions with something like fifteen lies. Fortunately, I was not totally unknown and had learnt a trick or two about how to respond to dishonest journalists. The episode was discreditable to him, damaging to me in some eyes, but the result was certainly at least a draw. I, for one, had learnt a good deal about how much trust and integrity the self-righteous churchgoing and organ-playing Ingrams could command. Incidentally, he never did pay up that fiver.

He was not the only journalist to have a go at me that year. A so-called Canon Russell Russell (no such animal existed in reality) coupled me in the *Tatler* with David Jenkins, John Habgood, Don Cupitt, Donald Reeves and Paul Oestreicher as one of the 'modernists' who believed in 'Series 3, disabled toilets, deaconesses, and coffee-morning matins'. He even chucked in Michael Green for good measure. What a mixed bunch. Green and I were, by no normal definition, 'modernists', but neither the *Tatler* nor the *Eye* had readers who were likely to be skilled in such sophistries. So who was the *Eye*'s 'Devil' and the *Tatler*'s 'Russell Russell?' For my money it was the same man but my reaction as to his identity was well summed up in Rhett Butler's famous walk-out line at the end of *Gone with the Wind*, 'Frankly, my Dear, I don't give a damn!'

The Churchill Travelling Fellowship was something of a surprise. I discovered from the application form, in August 1983, that there were no appropriate themes suitable for the 1984 year. A more careful reading suggested that I might be able to tailor a project under the category 'Care, maintenance, and appearance of the countryside'. It would certainly be a long shot, even perhaps cheeky, to attempt a study of old churchyards in the south-eastern USA as a prelude to trying to get the local authorities to take greater responsibility for Ealing's churchyard. All they had done was to cut the grass, while allowing old tombs to decay and collapse. To my surprise I was short-listed. I suspect that having two local Members of Parliament, Sir George Young (a future Cabinet minister) and Harry Greenway, as my referees may have helped. I was duly interviewed by three trustees – the Duke of Marlborough (whose family had once owned nearby Ealing land), Sir Peter Scott and Christopher Pratt – and I obviously said the right things. The odds were thirty to one against, but I was successful and I set off to combine the project with a church exchange, lasting in all seven weeks. Jackie joined me and we swapped with Bob and Lynne Libby taking over their church in

Orange Park, just south of Jacksonville in North Florida, while they very successfully substituted for us in St Mary's.

Bob's church, Good Samaritan, was a lively and informal family, not at all like the somewhat stuffy image which the Episcopal church has often fostered. We enjoyed our time with them but our most vivid memory was of a meal with one elderly man, a member of their 'Vestry' (the Church Council), together with two old blue-rinsed ladies. The subject of gun-control came up. 'I have a small revolver,' said one of the ladies, in a deep Southern voice, 'but I would only use it to wound an intruder.' 'You're a stupid woman,' said the old redneck. 'Gotta shoot to kill. If you don't they'll take you through the courts and win every dollar you got.' My eyes opened wide. Just imagine a member of a Parochial Church Council in England talking like that. Clearly the old frontier attitude was alive and well a mere ten miles from the centre of a major American city. Incidentally, he meant it. No doubt about that.

My Churchill award was worth over £4,000 and I bought a camera and cassette recorder, completed a fifty-page report, with some fifty-seven photos, five maps, nine radio, TV and press cuttings and transcripts, and my comments on fifteen churches. James Callaghan, sometime Prime Minister, presented me with my award medallion. I greatly enjoyed the project, which was quite unlike anything I had ever done, or would ever do, but, despite all my advocacy, the Ealing Borough Council responded in a quite minimal way. The majority party in power at that time was Labour and they refused to do anything which could be seen to support 'the church' even though I pointed out that restoration of a historic graveyard was hardly a party political matter and that the church building was not itself in any way involved in the plan. They did eventually clear acres of ivy off one section of the churchyard but ignored all the major work which I had suggested. They did have a statutory responsibility but interpreted it in the cheapest way possible. In a related issue, concerning children and road safety, it took the Borough Council almost ten years to agree to a cheap, but vital, widening of a few feet of road by the churchyard. That issue involved both Labour and Conservative administrations. Since we had far closer links with the Council than any other church in Ealing, and were asking for 'non-religious' help, I couldn't help wondering what one had to do to get things done.

Harry Greenway arranged for me to be invited to a fringe meeting of the annual Conservative party conference, at Brighton, in October 1984, where I spoke to a large gathering on 'Christianity and Conservatism'. It gave me a good opportunity to defend myself against all the extreme Tory idiocies which had followed the 'National Anthem' business and to assure people that it was perfectly possible to be a party member (which I have never been) and give full support to intelligent revision of the liturgy, to modern hymns and Bibles, and the creative reorganisation of Anglican parish life. To my great pleasure I found a good measure of sympathy and support for the kind of Christian reform which I was propounding.

Security had been quite stringent so it was a shock and a surprise to wake up next morning, back in Ealing, to the news of the IRA bomb attack which killed and maimed some senior Tories.

It was around that time that I was made a trustee of Hartlebury Castle in Worcestershire, home of the Bishop of Worcester. I was appointed as a representative Church Commissioner. It was something of a sinecure, involving a couple of visits a year, and I had rather hoped to get the Wells trusteeship, vacant at the same time. After all, to be trustee of a palace (home of the Bishop of Bath and Wells) did seem slightly more of a 'desirable residence' than a mere castle. Bishop Philip Goodrich and his wife were most hospitable though Hartlebury certainly wasn't a house that I envied them.

The early 1980s saw the creation and development of the annual Anglican Evangelical Assembly, of which the Church of England Evangelical Council became the standing committee. I served on the latter for seventeen years and, when AEA was founded, I called for it to include a new Basis of Faith to replace the very minimal and inadequate statement which was otherwise available. A small group of four, I among them, were charged with producing a document. I wrote the first draft, creating a totally new framework for a theological Basis, grounded in the concept of divine grace. The draft was considerably amended, mostly in detail, but the essential framework was retained and was accepted by the AEA and various other related Evangelical organisations, who have since incorporated it into their own constitutions. I was not very pleased when, a few years later, the comparable international body, the Evangelical Fellowship in the Anglican Communion (EFAC), whose minimal Basis we had dismissed as hopelessly inadequate, took over the AEA Basis, and spoiled its shape and balance, without consulting us, at the behest of one Australian member who had an axe to grind over a single word which he managed to get added. The result is that today the Basis, in its AEA form, is widely used by many bodies, while EFAC sails blithely on, with a pointless extra phrase which contributes nothing to the statement.

Around that time a small but influential group came into being calling its members 'The Young Fogies'. These were almost all youthful Thatcherite Tories, generally from Oxford, of whom Charles Moore and A.N. Wilson were to achieve some fame as authors, journalists and editors. Moore invited me to have tea with him at the Savoy which was a somewhat stilted occasion. Not surprisingly, I attempted to present a view of the Anglican church, and its Evangelical element, which ran counter to his extraordinarily closed-minded unwillingness to consider that anything good could come out of either body. He seemed wedded to the idea that the English were constitutionally Christians and were entitled to be given every privilege which accrued while rejecting the related responsibilities. It was a position which, in essence, the Elizabethan Settlement of 1559 had sought to create and it had never worked effectively from the rise of Puritanism onwards. Moore and his friends wrote copiously, attempting to link their Bunthorne-like aestheticism with a long-dead Erastian theory of church and state. The ongoing life of the *Daily Telegraph* is evidence that they were not entirely unsuccessful though A.N. Wilson jettisoned Christianity *en route*. I wrote a fairly critical review of Moore's first symposium which appeared soon after entitled (inevitably) 'The Church in Crisis'. What a foolish title! The church has always been 'in crisis'.

St Paul's Cathedral is endowed with thirty Prebendal stalls and

Hewlett proposed my name for 'Caddington Major', to which I
was duly installed on 19 January 1985. Being a Prebendary is entirely an honorific office, involving one midweek sermon a year
and attendance at a small handful of cathedral events. Thus I became for six years 'Prebendary Saward'. One small, but real, pleasure was that of holding the same stall as my old rector, Gordon
Harman. He had been succeeded by Fred Secombe, Harry's clerical brother, whom I had known well as a fellow Area Dean. I, in
turn, was duly followed by Ron Swan, now Master of the Royal
Foundation of St Katharine, who had also succeeded me as Area
Dean of Ealing East and Chairman of the Willesden Area House
of Clergy. Thus does continuity express itself in the Church of
England over thirty years.

Three weeks later I won another hymn competition. BBC
TV's *Songs of Praise* presented me, and seven others, with a
handbell at the televised final at St James's church in Piccadilly.
The hymn was a version of the Beatitudes, from the Sermon on
the Mount, entitled 'Happy are those who acknowledge their
need' and set to the tune of the old drinking song 'Here's to the
maiden of bashful fifteen'. Since the Greek word, more traditionally translated 'Blessed', means 'happiness', I wanted a cheerful,
bucolic, tune. I submitted the text under the pseudonym 'John
Kendall' (my second Christian name and my mother's maiden
surname) since the judges all knew me and I didn't want to be assessed as 'it's old so-and-so'. Even so, I reckoned that its style
would commend it to Sydney Carter (one judge) though not to
Cyril Taylor (another). The church press gave it good coverage,
with the *Church Times* appropriately stressing that 'happy days
are here again' for the Vicar of Ealing. Sally Magnusson duly
broke my cover in interviewing 'John Kendall'. It was a fun
event.

It was during the mid-1980s that I was invited to the BBC, to
do, in all, about thirty 'Thought for the Day' scripts on the *Today*
programme. I greatly enjoyed them and got on excellent terms
with Brian Redhead, John Timpson, Peter Hobday and others.

When, eventually, I was dropped from the 'Thought' team it
was, I was led to understand, because of a change of policy. The

tradition had been for speakers to do a trio (Tuesday to Thursday) of connected talks which were often, if not actually biblical, at least coherently Christian. One morning I happened to notice on a BBC notice-board that the *Today* producer wanted the theme to become, in effect, a 'thought about today's news'. I regarded this, and still do, with considerable suspicion. It is no secret that the BBC would love to ditch 'Thought' (though publicly, they strenuously deny this) and they can afford to take a very long horizon. Gradually they have cut its length – it's not much over half of what it once was – and 'thoughts' about today's news force the speaker towards politics and ethics and away from the Christian faith. Eventually, or so I suspect, the time will come when 'Thought' is dropped because it has become too 'political and controversial' and has drifted away from being 'religious'. That is not to say that some of the 'Thought' speakers are not excellent but others are so wimpishly bland that they do no more than offer light entertainment. My final Thought was disliked by the producer because it was too 'religious'. Even so, to my surprised amusement, whenever I met Brian Redhead, right up to his death, he always greeted me, or introduced me, as one of our 'Thought for Today' team. 'Not since 1988,' I reminded him, but he always forgot. He was a delightful man and we worked together about twenty times in one way or another.

As time went by I found myself being interviewed on radio or television by almost all the major newsreaders and media journalists. In no particular order of significance or time these included Sue MacGregor, Michael Buerck, Carol Barnes, Trevor McDonald, Sue Lawley, Jennie Bond, Jenny Murray, Valerie Singleton, Joan Thirkettle, Mike Smart and Nick Higham. I also made programmes with Jimmy Young, Ludovic Kennedy, Anne Robinson, Kenneth Robinson and David Frost and also met Kate Adie. There were probably others but these are the ones I remember.

In the summer of 1986, the Willesden Area clergy elected me unopposed to be their chairman and this was encouraging since eighty per cent of them were Anglo-Catholic and I was an Evangelical. The election was almost embarrassing. I was the only candidate and the Archdeacon, Eddie Shirras, a fellow Evangelical and my predecessor as chairman, spent almost ten minutes trying to get someone to stand against me before eventually declaring me elected. It was totally improper for him to do such a thing and left people wondering what it was he had against me. He told me later that he didn't want it to look like a 'party set-up' (which it wasn't) but he certainly made me look a fool. I don't hold it against him personally but he undoubtedly behaved in a manner quite contrary to Standing Orders.

I was also appointed to be a member of the Board of Governors of the Church Commissioners. This is, in effect, the board of directors and it had taken me eight years from my election as a Commissioner, far longer than for anyone else since the formation of the Board in 1948. I was gravely suspicious that I had been 'frozen out' for much of that time, and others on the Board made it plain that something of the kind had gone on. I was at the point of resigning in disgust when the appointment was finally agreed. I don't have much doubt in my mind as to who had wielded the knife in my back but death absolves (or at least softens) the responsibility. I eventually served for seven years on the Board.

The Americans, meanwhile, had invited me to provide a regular column, 'Our Man in London', for the *Diocesan*, the newspaper of the Episcopal Diocese of Florida. I did it for some six years, in the course of which I won a so-called Polly Bond Award. 'Who was Polly Bond?' I asked Bob Libby, the editor. Bob, in cheerfully abrasive style, recalled that 'Polly Bond was a lady with very large breasts. I took her out to lunch once', he added, 'and we had a very good time'. 'I'm sure you did,' I smiled gently. Anyway, I have a certificate to mark the award, though when I asked for it to be a relief map of the lady's features they all looked duly coy.

Joe by now was rushing around the world from Grand Prix to Grand Prix. 'Gerhard Berger drove me across France' was followed by 'Niki Lauda used to be my taxi driver'. Jackie has various signed photos and posters inscribed to 'Joe's mum' by some of the world's most famous Formula One drivers. She is, or would be, given the chance, a groupie in Damon Hill's entourage. Joe's talents also extended to radio and television commentating and, on occasion, providing Murray Walker with hot facts when the latter was not actually at the track across the world but covering the race from a London monitor. Not a lot of people know that.

In October I was invited to preach the annual Lawyers Christian Fellowship sermon in the Temple church. I took as my subject 'True Law' and to my surprise they duly published it. I set out to show that, for Christians, God himself is the foundation of true law. 'You shall be holy because I, the Lord your God, am holy.' I went on to grapple with the relationship between law and morality and the ultimate question of a society answering to a just Judge who is also a loving Saviour.

A few days later I spent many hours in a West End cinema watching the film *Shoah*. A treatment of the Holocaust, it unveiled not only the callousness and mass-production methods of Nazi killing of the Jews but also the indifference and hostility of many of those Polish villagers among whom many Jewish communities were intermixed. I mentioned this in a BBC 'Thought for the Day' and was bombarded with hostile letters from Poles claiming total innocence for their nation. The documentation offered by Martin Gilbert in his books seemed to be conclusive evidence of some hostility.

Richard Holloway, Bishop of Edinburgh in the Episcopal Church of Scotland, invited me to meet him at the National Liberal Club on 12 December to discuss a new series of books of which he was editor. 'Would you', he asked, 'be willing to write a preparatory book, for the 1988 Lambeth Conference of Anglican bishops, with the title "Evangelicals on the March"?' 'Not with that title,' I replied. 'Give me something less militant. What about "Those Evangelicals?" ' We compromised with 'Evangelicals on the Move' and I agreed to play my part in the series – one Evangelical, one Central, one Anglo-Catholic, one overview, and so on. It would be a pleasure to try to give both a personal and an objective treatment, though I had no illusions that anyone as committed as I could be genuinely objective. I began to gather material for a book that would be part historical and part contemporary with a fair flavour of autobiography since I had been up to my neck in the movement for nearly thirty years.

One of my tasks as a Church Commissioner was to serve on

the committee which kept a weather eye on bishops' houses. Not many of these are the kind of 'homes' that any normal family would choose to live in and, in that respect, most bishops' families are quite normal. We Commissioners agonised about what to do with them. Who would want to buy them if we tried to sell the really large ones and, anyway, we should be violently assaulted by the Heritage lobbies if we did anything as sensible as attempting to dispose of them. And what was the alternative? A bishop, for perfectly valid reasons, needs space for offices and social gatherings so we should have to replace the castles and palaces with 'executive' homes. These would excite even more hostility, as did indeed happen when Oxford Diocese bought a house for one of their bishops which included a swimming pool. I didn't, and still don't, know the right answer. The problem was well summed up by one delightful and low-key bishop who told me that the most threatening thing he ever did in his very conservative diocese was to drive a Morris Minor. He was, some of his 'county' lay people told him bluntly, letting down the Church by not using the chauffeur-driven Daimler! You can't win.

Lochnagar is not a name that means much to most people, though some may associate it with a Scottish mountain or a whimsical children's book by Prince Charles. To me, however, Lochnagar will always be a large hole in the ground. On 1 July 1916, immediately before the British Army launched into its bloodiest day, resulting in nearly twenty thousand deaths and a total of fifty-seven thousand casualties, Lochnagar was no more than a French field on the chalk uplands above the River Somme. Then, at 7.28 a.m. the earth erupted hundreds of feet into the sky as a vast explosion tore it apart and minutes later a mine crater, ninety feet deep and three hundred feet across, was all that remained of that part of the German front line six hundred yards to the south of the village of La Boisselle. Half an hour later, hundreds of British bodies, dead and grievously wounded, scattered the nearby landscape. The Battle of the Somme had begun.

Sixty years later to the very minute, totally alone, I stood on the lip of that great chalk hole and tried to call to mind what had happened. I felt in that great silence that somehow I spoke for England in thanksgiving to that dead generation. I wouldn't have known about it had not a Lincolnshire farmer, Martin Middlebrook, written a book of survivors' memories entitled *The First Day on the Somme* in the early 1970s.

Ten years later, in July 1986, there was a correspondence in *The Times* about the rightness, or otherwise, of commemorating such terrible, but long-past, events. I wrote, describing my own deeply moving experience of ten years earlier. Some days later a letter arrived. The writer, Richard Dunning, a businessman who lived near Guildford, explained that he had bought the crater from a French farmer in the late 1970s and that an annual 'pilgrimage' of veterans and others gathered there each year on the anniversary. Would I be willing to go, all expenses paid, to be their chaplain, and add a Christian element to their annual commemoration? So it was that from July 1987, for seven years, I found myself meeting a collection of British, French and, eventually, German men and women to whom Lochnagar was a symbol of courage, terror, sacrifice and, above all, ordinary humanity facing war in its most personal and bloody pain.

The Times published a second letter from me, to mark the eightieth anniversary, which brought the story up to date. By then, some nine hundred people were at the crater for the annual commemoration.

The first year, there was one survivor who had actually been there that very morning in 1916. Harry Fellowes's experiences had turned him into a bitter atheist and he wrote a lot of verse to express his cynicism, especially of the generals who had led the army. Strangely, in the hour or two of our only meeting on that day, we had hit it off well and when, less than three months later, he finally died, in his nineties, it was me that his son, Mick, asked to conduct the cremation service in Nottingham, where they owned a pub. Imagine my surprise when I discovered a packed crematorium, with press and TV cameras. I hadn't realised that Harry's verse was well known in the area and that he had become a feature of the region's television. 'Mick,' I said to his son, 'would he really want a Christian funeral?' 'Do your best and don't worry. Just be honest,' said Mick. 'He trusted you.' I didn't duck the problem, said what had to be said and tried, head on, to tackle the issue of why people blame God for human evil. From then on the Lochnagar men and women took me to their heart. They knew I was well-up on military history and accepted my desire to use the Lord's Prayer in English, French and German at the July ceremony. The French found it harder than the English, because they had twice lived under German military rule and one or two had been tortured by the Gestapo. Then, in my sixth Lochnagar ceremony, a voice joined me in the German *das Vaterunser* (the Lord's Prayer). He was a young German journalist, whose grandfather had died in the battle and was buried nearby. He published an account of our doings in Germany and returned a year later. By then over five hundred people were gathering in the early morning on that July day. Why did they come? Seemingly because it lacked any military or 'official' presence – just ordinary people by a large wooden cross on the edge of a vast mine crater. Memories, verse, wreathlaying, a sermon and prayers and absolutely no regimentation. One year Leonard Cheshire, VC, and his wife Sue Ryder were there. So too were Lyn Macdonald and Martin Middlebrook, historians of the battle. The only jarring note in seven years was when I said something about the battle, which angered Middlebrook. It was a legitimate opinion, backed by eminent historians, but Middlebrook marched off, never to reappear again. Having greatly admired his many books, I was sad that a difference of opinion, three-quarters of a century after the event, should cause such anger. Years later, when I offered him a special seat at the national VE service in St Paul's Cathedral, he declined to accept it.

Lochnagar, in its commemorative form, owes everything to Richard Dunning who, for years, largely financed it. If ever a man deserved an honour from the British Crown it is Richard, whose quiet, reticent, undemonstrative generosity has restored a long-past sacrifice to future generations. I hope his actions will not go unrewarded, though he would probably be highly embarrassed if they were so recognised. He and I got on right from the start. He expressed his own feelings at the end of my seven-year stint by remarking that I had captured 'the mood and thoughts of us all and had led us gently and at times dramatically into new areas of understanding'. I was, he said, someone 'who consistently acts the way he talks and someone who talks the way he believes'. I wish it were true! Michael Ramsey once said to the clergy that it should be their goal that people might say of them 'not necessarily that you talked about God cleverly but that you made God real to people'. You can only do that, added Ramsey, if you have humility.

My next book *Evangelicals on the Move* was generally well received and seemed to be regarded as the most significant of the pre-Lambeth conference series. It was accorded the privilege of an extended two-page treatment by the Secretary-General of the Synod, Derek Pattinson, in the preface to the 1988 Church of England yearbook. As the first item in the preface it was welcomed as 'timely' and 'a fascinating guide'. As with my earlier *All Change* George Carey reviewed it warmly but not uncritically, as also did Donald Coggan in *Theology*. Like *All Change* it was one of the *Church Times*'s 'Books of the Year', which was very gratifying. It was not, however, palatable to the Evangelical 'hard right'. Two of their reviews in *Churchman* were distinctly hostile, giving advance warning of the reaction against my generation's attitudes which was to emerge in the mid-1990s from a revived fundamentalism and isolationism associated with the so-called Reform group. Members of this group were quite willing, even before its formal inauguration, to say publicly in print that I was no longer 'an Evangelical Anglican'. The only sensible response to such an idiotic charge was to laugh it out of court. In the *Church of England Newspaper* I responded to one of these critics, Dr Gerald Bray, by announcing that I 'trembled before his judgement seat' but that it was 'the tremble of laughter and not guilty fear'. In general, virtually all those who counted in the Church of England knew very well where I stood and what I had defended through thick and thin for almost forty years. One really should not cringe before the assaults of the ghetto-minded and I never have. My only worry is that such attitudes, once in decline, are nowadays growing as religious fundamentalism of every kind sweeps across the world.

Before the year was out, a tragic event was to cause much heartsearching within the Church of England. For generations *Crockford's*, the clergy directory, had contained an anonymous preface, assessing the previous year or two's progress. In the 1980s it was generally thought to have been the work of David Edwards, Provost of Southwark, one of the church's most prolific and gifted writers and a man whom I regarded as a friend over many years. Himself a Liberal, but, latterly, firmly an Establishment man he had in the 1960s published the highly controversial *Honest to God*, by John Robinson, and more recently had published twenty or more books of his own, including the magisterial, three-volume *Christian England*, a history of the faith since Roman times. Edwards had, it was reckoned, produced a judicious series of *Crockford* prefaces, somewhat liberal in slant but generally fair. Now, in the last weeks of 1987 a new preface burst upon the world, making headlines in even the national press. Clearly Edwards hadn't written these blistering paragraphs lambasting Robert Runcie, the Archbishop of Canterbury, for nepotistic appointments, so who had? Journalists rang any likely candidate, me included, knowing that the author, traditionally bound to secrecy, was hardly likely to come clean. I was intrigued at the half-a-dozen calls I received, knowing, first, that I certainly hadn't written it and, secondly, that they seemed unable to spot the author's trademarks, which were unmistakably academic and Anglo-Catholic. I guessed pretty quickly at two possible authors and was spot on target. One had consulted the other and the actual writer was Dr Gareth Bennett, an Oxford don.

Bennett, according to John Grigg in *The Times* magazine, had claimed that there was a 'supposed liberal conspiracy, which, under Runcie and Habgood, was allegedly denying preferment to conservative church men'. Runcie remained silent but Habgood produced a foolish attack on the unknown author as 'a disappointed cleric'. When, a few days later, Bennett, indisputably the author, was found dead in his gas-filled car, Habgood, in Grigg's words, 'was widely accused of having driven him to his death'. This, as Grigg added, was 'absurd' but Habgood had done himself great harm and, said Grigg, 'his imputation of a personal motive "seemed" unworthy of him'. It probably cost him the Archbishopric of Canterbury when that fell vacant and few readers could have had much doubt who was in my mind when, during the press speculation about suitable candidates for Canterbury, *The Times* published a letter from me asking for a poll of those whom the church *least* wanted to see occupying Augustine's chair.

At the height of the row, George Austin and I, as fellow Church Commissioners, were talking together in the Millbank offices of the Commissioners about the Bennett charge of nepotism against Runcie. Austin, one of Bennett's closest associates, revealed that he had recently prepared a 'genealogy of Runcie clones'. 'Amazing,' I said. 'I've done exactly the same'. The family tree of Runcie appointments ran back throughout his career and it was indisputable that he had been closely involved in filling many senior jobs with his associates. In that, Bennett was absolutely on target.

Almost a decade later, in a radio interview, Runcie openly admitted that 'If you wanted to make a case against me on the grounds of croneyism and liberal attitudes then you could and, as for liberal attitudes, I frankly admit I have a liberal catholic agenda . . . a liberal elite was part of my agenda.'

George Austin, later to be appointed Archdeacon of York by Habgood, agreed with me that day in Millbank, that Bennett's great mistake was to ascribe a nepotistic motive to Runcie. Archbishops, like politicians, always have tended to appoint men they know and trust. There was nothing intrinsically wrong with that, though the results were often too obviously connected for the good of the church. Had Bennett merely printed 'the genealogy' the point would have been devastatingly obvious. No comment would have been needed.

Perhaps the supreme irony was Habgood's appointment of Austin some years later. If it was intended to muzzle Austin it certainly failed, as he became more vociferous (and extreme) in his public comments. Brave, or foolish, depending on your standpoint, Austin became, with Tony Higton – an Evangelical charismatic vicar from Essex – the instant media pundits of the 1990s. I suspect the media approached me almost as frequently as the two of them but I was careful not to take up such outlandish positions as either of them and wasn't, in consequence, quoted anything like as often. I simply provided background off-the-record material which was unattributed.

During this period, for almost ten years, I was writing my column for the Florida *Diocesan* under Bob Libby's editorship. I provided a piece on the Bennett affair, at Libby's request, in which I set out the facts, without any personal opinion. To my surprise, and Libby's irritation, Ed Browning, the Presiding Bishop of the American Episcopal Church, viciously attacked me publicly on a visit to Florida. Libby, who was present, defended the article as legitimate factual journalism. Browning ignored him. Merely to present information which might be detrimental to the Archbishop of Canterbury was unacceptable to him. He, Browning, the archetypal Liberal, had no wish to permit American episcopalians to gain any insight into the long-standing criticisms of Liberals which had been a part of the English scene throughout the 1980s. He, and the Episcopal Church, have paid a terrible price in consequence of such an attitude. As everyone knows, there is no-one so illiberal as a threatened Liberal and the American Episcopalian Liberals are among the most illiberal of all. In England the Runcie–Habgood era is long gone and Browning's days are, thankfully, ended.

Not long before the Bennett furore, Jackie and I invited Gerald Priestland, the BBC's Religious Affairs Correspondent, and his wife to dinner at our vicarage. Gerry was a delightful, huge man, a Quaker, who regarded Evangelicals with smiling disdain. He had, on air, as I have already mentioned, called me 'a self-confessed Dirty Book vicar' and then wittily retracted it. We had stayed friends despite that and now, ten years later, and not long before his sad death, we shared dinner with Ron and Celia Swan. Ron had succeeded me as Area Dean and would later repeat the succession as chairman of our Synod's House of Clergy and as a Prebendary of St Paul's. Celia, his cheerful, rotund and highly articulate wife, was a faculty member at the London School of Economics. It was, in consequence, a most enjoyable dinner. Gerry, like many journalists, never bothered to send Jackie a thank-you letter and, in his published diary, later referred to

Dinner at Ealing vicarage with Michael Saward, a not-too-triumphal evangelical. I bow before the rushing might of the born again and shelter in the palpable holiness of a fellow guest, the Rev. Ron Swan, who is going to be vicar of Harrow-on-the-Hill. Being an Anglican priest is a bit like being a bank manager: some are generous, some are narrow, all are dreaming of transfer to a bigger and better branch by the sea or in the country. How many times have I heard the wistful murmur, 'All I want now is a nice little residential canonry somewhere in the West Country . . .' though not from these two, I hasten to add.

One other 1987 'first' sticks in the memory. Since 1956 I had built up a huge collection of classical records, then cassettes, and finally compact discs. I had heard Elizabeth Schwarzkopf in *Così fan tutte* at Salzburg and one or two other operas, mostly in English. Now for the first time, Jackie and I queued for seats in the 'gods' at Covent Garden. To sit, halfway to heaven, in cramped seats and almost suffocated by the rising heat, only marginally distracted us from two superb performances of *La Bohème* and the *Marriage of Figaro*. Years later, I asked Sir Georg Solti, at an Athenaeum dinner at which I sat next to Lady Solti, if he could only have three opera houses, which he would choose. He paused, then said, 'Covent Garden, La Scala and Rome'. He was, perhaps, biased, having been musical director at Covent Garden throughout the 1960s, but I know what he meant and why.

Talking of music, my output of hymns was now up in the fifties, with my best-known 'Christ Triumphant' starting to get known around the world. Only in America has it never caught on. What it did achieve, apart from eventually being sung in St Paul's Cathedral, Westminster Abbey, Canterbury and various other cathedrals and regular outings on BBC Television's *Songs of Praise*, was a quite unexpected appearance as background 'audible wallpaper' on BBC1's *Eastenders* soap opera. There, as the Fowler family went about their Sunday morning, entirely secular activities, the radio in their kitchen had a morning service on and, lo and behold, up popped a verse or two of 'Christ Triumphant' half hidden behind the family's voice-over comments. To have made

St Paul's, Canterbury and Westminster is one thing but, to have been background noise on a hugely successful TV soap opera, that's really something else.

Westminster Abbey is an unusual place in which to preach and not least because the congregation is hard to see, being in front, behind, and to both left and right of the pulpit. While occupying the pulpit on Ash Wednesday was an interesting experience, it left me with little doubt that I would far rather preach in St Paul's Cathedral where, as a Prebendary, I was required to provide an annual sermon at a weekday evensong. There, despite the huge space of dome, nave and transepts, you can at least maintain eye contact with most of the congregation, which is so important for a preacher.

Another stimulating experience is lecturing to ordinands and, over the years, I have lectured or preached at theological colleges in Oxford, Durham, Bristol, Lincoln and London. These have covered all the three Anglican traditions – Anglo-Catholic, Evangelical and Central, and allowed me an interesting insight into the very different styles adopted by the various traditions. I was quite ignorant of the fact, until quite recently, that I had once lectured on 'parish communications' at the London College of Divinity (long since transformed into St John's, Nottingham) and provoked a sharp dispute with a young ordinand whose name didn't register at the time. He was, so his wife, Eileen, tells me, none other than George Carey, now Archbishop of Canterbury.

In March 1988 I was giving a similar lecture, this time on the use in church of overhead projectors, entitled 'Ealing Weekend Television', and, among scores of illustrative acetates, I included a series comparing and contrasting the four Gospels. These I had used on four successive Sunday mornings at Ealing. They had been very well received and many of the adult congregation had asked for photocopied sets from the acetates. Imagine, then, my surprise (and impish delight) when almost the whole student body at Oak Hill theological college asked for sets since, as one said, 'They're far more intelligible than some of our New Testament lectures.' I certainly wish I had had something similar when I was a theological student. The compliment was, however, unintentionally two-handed. While I was glad that I was making sense to ordinands I was also worried that some of them clearly belonged to a sound-bite TV generation which couldn't easily cope with the need for some real scholarly thinking. Not all clergy need to have academic skills and certainly few will make much of preaching to ordinary people if they adopt a pedagogic style. Even so, the church can't afford to fill its parishes with clergy who can't grapple with the kind of questions which stretch the brain. There are many clergy in the Evangelical tradition who have excellent minds but also far too many who try to forget what they learnt at college and whose preaching can become banal. Simple answers to complicated questions has always been the curse of the Evangelical preacher and some very famous names have made reputations on just such lightweight patter in the pulpit.

Almost all Evangelical graduate clergy have been, in their time, members of University Christian Unions, affiliated to what was the Inter-Varsity Fellowship (IVF) and later became the Universities and Colleges Christian Fellowship (UCCF). I was a member as a student at Bristol and remained a paid-up member for the next thirty years. I was also a speaker at twenty-one of the University CUs (virtually all of the pre-1960 foundations), sometimes on three or four occasions over twenty years. Then, in 1981, UCCF changed parts of its theological basis of faith. My daughter Rachel, reading Biblical Studies, was vaguely aware of the proposed alterations but most members were, I suspect, not informed about it and I certainly didn't grasp the implications until 1985. The crucial clause was about Jesus and, while most of it was entirely acceptable, the final words spoke of 'his present reign in heaven and on earth'. This was demonstrably false, in historic credal terms, and even contradicted the Lord's Prayer ('thy kingdom come . . . on earth as it is in heaven'). The change stemmed from a triumphalist mood gaining ground in the movement and it was, I believed, sufficiently serious to be described as 'heretical'.

After a three-year discussion and correspondence with the Secretary, Robin Wells, I finally resigned my membership. UCCF made various attempts to explain the clause but would not go back to their earlier, uncontroversial form of the words. I was sad at their lack of theological awareness of the consequences of such a change of meaning and particularly sad to leave them after thirty-six years of membership and many years on their team of speakers. It was oddly amusing to find myself being criticised by some more fundamentalist Evangelicals as being 'no longer an Evangelical' when I was accusing UCCF, a true-blue Evangelical flagship, of false theology!

UCCF, for all its many virtues, fails to grapple with the great issues of church, ministry and sacraments, and as these are vital areas for any Evangelical Anglican and just as divisive as they were in the 1660s, sooner or later, I fear, the UCCF edifice will find its foundations are unable to sustain it. Evangelical Anglicans, recovering their own doctrine of the church, will find it harder and harder to let their students spend all their university years in a body that is unwilling to give them space to debate and discuss such vital areas of belief. The huge growth of pietistic hand-clapping religion is at least in part due to the lack of understanding of the inheritance which Evangelicals have in the Church of England. My last few speaking visits to university CUs in the 1980s absolutely horrified me with the infantile content of the main meetings. They bore no relationship to the high-quality teaching which we received in the 1950s. Sadly, those who grew up in that period have little realisation of what has been going on in recent decades.

I was surprised to receive an invitation to be one of that year's speakers at 'Spring Harvest', the huge gatherings in three holiday centres to which up to sixty thousand people go year by year in the Easter period. Year by year it has a focal theme and the major speakers are assured of audiences of five hundred up to perhaps three or four thousand. The music is almost uniformly noisy, belted out by Christian pop bands and the quality of the addresses varies greatly. For the first time in my life I received, as a speaker, a full brief of what I was to say, which contained not only a few factual errors but also omitted much material which I thought essential and which I would never have felt happy to leave out. Thus I found myself providing the engine-room section of what was otherwise more obviously cruise liner theatre.

Then, at short notice, I was asked to give a separate talk on a highly controversial aspect of personal heterosexual friendship. I warned the organisers that I should take a line which, while biblical and thoroughly defensible, would not please some of their more rigorist clientele. Needless to say, some of the latter were enraged and tried to get the tapes expunged! I was not invited back.

Then, in the summer holiday period, I was a speaker at 'Greenbelt', the huge Christian pop festival in Northamptonshire. I greatly enjoyed doing a series of Bible lectures on the theme-word 'image'. Whether I gave them what the organisers wanted, I don't know, but I do know that it was one of the best things of its kind that I have ever done, firmly rooted in all the related ideas in the Bible and offering a critique of the fashionable idea of self-image which has so swept the Western world. The committee also offered me a second spot and, knowing Greenbelt to be wide-ranging and sometimes highly esoteric, I did two lectures about genealogy. In the first, I described my own family's history, with illustrative material, while in the second I extended the idea to the genealogy of church history. To ignore either, I suggested, was to fail to care about continuity, putting, instead, all one's eggs into the basket of spontaneity, the fashionable existential philosophy, which was, I claimed, destructive of Christianity. I was not invited back.

As a lifelong Evangelical, I occasionally get depressed at the small- and fixed-mindedness which seems to dominate so much of the Evangelical world, especially of those outside the Church of England. Whenever I go to the really big events organised by 'interdenominational' Evangelicals I wonder why I go on identifying myself with the Evangelical movement since I feel so ill at ease with the rowdy *bonhomie* which is supposed to pass for 'worship and fellowship'. Were it not for the long tradition of sane, biblical, orthodox Evangelicals, particularly (but not only) in the Anglican Church who care about Scripture, tradition and reason and who go on standing for solid, thoughtful, mind-stretching faith, I should, I suspect have long since parted company with the happy-clappy, ten-miracles-before-breakfast circus which is currently seeking to sweep all before it. I am, I suppose, a man who stands unashamedly in the Cranmer, Jewel, Hooker, Simeon, Griffith-Thomas, Stott succession.

Talking of John Stott, the man who has probably, more than any other, influenced my life and ministry, brings me to Caister, the scene of the so called NEAC-3 conference in Norfolk in April 1988. Third in the succession of National Evangelical Anglican events, following Keele in 1967 and Nottingham in 1977, it demonstrated very clearly the direction which the movement was taking. Keele had restored to Evangelical Anglicans a real consciousness of, and their commitment to, the Church of England. Nottingham had built on that and attempted a Statement touching on a wide range of concerns relating the faith to individuals, the church and the wider world.

Much good work was done at Caister. I remained press officer for the third NEAC and shared in some of the internal television interviewing but, without question, Caister, although three times the size of Keele in attendance, was little more than a jolly jamboree. Unlike the Statements, thrashed out at Keele and Nottingham, Caister charged John Stott with producing a brief concluding paper. He did so, as always, judiciously, but with little clay or straw with which to build his bricks. I recall much of what Keele and Nottingham said but hardly a word from Caister. The only crucial challenge at NEAC-3 came from Robert Runcie, a visiting speaker, as Primate, who called on Evangelical Anglicans, as the coming force in the Church of England, to get to grips with their doctrine of the church. I, and others, had been making similar pleas in the Church of England Evangelical Council and the Anglican Evangelical Assembly throughout the previous decade (and would do so into the 1990s) but the mood had shifted. Evangelicals wanted to relax and enjoy their faith, not have to think about its implications which were, after all, so time-consuming. Noisy, undemanding 'worship' and small-group 'sharing' were so much more pleasant ways of being Christians. Caister provided us with rhythmic peanut-and-popcorn chewing and pointed the way ahead, to what would come to seduce one large segment of the movement in the 1990s and be countered by an aggressive and hostile recrudescence of the old-style, hardline ghetto kind of Evangelicalism. The mainstream of the movement stood against both extremes and was blamed by both wings for its sane, open-minded moderation. Needless to add, most of those who were to lead the Church of England, and who came from the movement, were from its mainstream making them inevitably vulnerable to the old extremist charge of having sold out.

Jackie and I flew off for our summer holidays to Denver, Colorado, where we rented a small Japanese car and began a 4,000-mile journey around the American West. We followed the old Oregon Trail across Wyoming, cut north through the Grand Tetons and Yellowstone and drove nearly a thousand miles across Montana, Idaho and Washington on interstate roads at a sedate (and desperately dull) 55 m.p.h. Henry and Barbara Aydelott gave us a room in their new skyscraper apartment in Seattle, with a panoramic view of the Puget Sound and the northern end of the city.

From Seattle we drove down the coast of Oregon, taking in a primaeval cave of sea lions, deep in the cliffs of that superb barrier where continent and ocean collide in great and serried ranks of surf. The sound, smell and sight of that cave, seen from a man-made gallery cut high within the living rock and reached by a lift from the land above, is one of the memories of America's splendour that will remain while we have any of our faculties left to us.

On again via Crater Lake, Golden Gate, Big Sur, Hearst Castle, Solvang (a Danish village), to Pasadena, where we stayed in the beautiful house of David and Sandra Schultheis, friends since the 1970s. Then, across the deserts, to Las Vegas (hell on earth!), the Grand Canyon, Monument Valley, and into the Rockies. Special memories include a French restaurant in Durango (where, said the proprietor, the French wine was cheaper than that from California since Americans prefer to believe that higher prices must mean better wine. He made a lot of money that way and we drank superb French vintages at prices below those in France). We passed through Montrose (the name of Grandad's famous ship) where we saw, yes, honestly, the Crippen Funeral Parlour!

No-one there had ever realised the connection. Finally, high in the Rockies, I ate, first, fresh shark (flown in apparently), and, then, fresh elk. As regards the former, I couldn't help quipping that Saward had come face to face with Jaws and guess who had had the bigger mouth?

Back home, I was photographed speaking in the General Synod debate on the ordination of women, followed by the great Lambeth Conference service in St Paul's Cathedral and the Buckingham Palace garden party where, quite illegally, John Miles, the Archbishop's chief press officer, took a photo of Jackie and me. Cameras are strictly forbidden so it was quite a souvenir.

I had greatly enjoyed Ealing but was very clear in my mind that for their sake and mine I ought after a decade to be moving on. I had discussed it quite openly with our Bishop, Tom Butler, and, a little later, with my staff and elders team and the churchwardens. I had been under consideration for over a dozen posts, some of which were very senior. None had materialised. I was given a very clear indication that Graham Leonard, Bishop of London, was not going to do anything to ease my path towards any major preferment, indeed, members of his own staff suggested that quite the opposite was likely.

By early September I reached the decision to write to the Archbishop, asking for his advice. I had always found Robert Runcie friendly and charming (and quite unlike his wife, Lindy, who never smiled or said a civil word to me that I can recall in almost a decade of dinners and receptions at Lambeth Palace. Nor has she done since). I did not really trust Runcie or have much confidence in him as Archbishop but his wit and urbanity and unfailing courtesy made him a very different prospect from his northern counterpart. He would, I felt sure, offer me a sympathetic ear if nothing else. So, I wrote, spelling out my happiness and fulfilment at Ealing but mentioning also my frustration at the almost total lack of opportunities on offer and my concern that, at fifty-six, I was rapidly approaching my sell-by date.

His reply was a model of gracious concern. He had read my letter 'with interest and great sympathy'. He made no promises, except 'to keep my eyes and ears open over the next month or so'. I was, he said, 'a product of Canterbury diocese' which meant that he had some responsibility 'for seeing that your talents are used and that you do not get lost!' If I heard no more, would I please speak to him at the November General Synod? In closing, having noted that books by Runcie and Saward were next to each other in Church House bookshop, he hoped 'that your sales do not suffer by proximity to such liberal thought'. It all sounded friendly enough and certainly wasn't discouraging. Typical Bob Runcie stuff.

By November's Synod nothing had happened. I asked to see him and he invited me to his room in Church House, Westminster. I walked in and he gave it to me, straight between the eyes. 'You aren't going to be a bishop,' he said bluntly. By this time I had few illusions on that score and said so. It certainly wasn't the end of the world. Then, to my considerable surprise, he told me why. 'There are three reasons. You are too autocratic. You are too divisive. You are unacceptable to the Evangelicals.' 'May I respond to that?' I asked. He nodded. 'I can', I said, 'think of various good and fair reasons why I shouldn't be made a bishop but those three amaze me. First, I have worked in teams all my ministry and no-one has ever before charged me with being autocratic. Certainly I could be, but I never have been and I've done everything I can to counter such a possibility.' I added, 'I believe that that reason is completely wide of the mark.'

'Secondly,' I said, 'you say I am too divisive. In two parishes for twenty years I have hardly ever been involved in any action that caused division. I've consistently carried people through periods of radical reform. Outside the parish, I was an Area Dean for five years. No division, that I knew of, in the deanery. I was then elected, unopposed, in a largely Anglo-Catholic constituency as Chairman of Willesden Area House of Clergy. No divisions caused that I know of. Occasional disagreements, of course. Your second reason won't stand up. Only in General Synod where I have had to speak plainly, often countering your own line, have I been divisive. A synod dealing with highly controversial issues is bound to produce disagreement. Half of your bench of bishops take up views which cause division. That doesn't stop them being bishops.'

'Thirdly,' I continued, 'you say that I am unacceptable to the Evangelicals. I was under the impression that bishops were not chosen to be party men. I have always been known as an Evangelical but I have never been a "my-party-right-or-wrong" man. I reckon I'm much more acceptable to most Evangelicals than a large number of existing bishops.'

I had one more comment to offer. 'Archbishop,' I said, 'I assume that these are the notes in my file at Lambeth. I don't know who put them there but I want your permission to allow me to write a letter for inclusion in that file defending myself from those damning remarks.' Runcie agreed. A few days later I sent my *apologia pro vita sua*. His reply was brief but, again, courteous. 'I take all that you say in good part and it is good to have it put down so clearly on paper . . . I do not need convincing of your record in this matter and your integrity in reporting on your experience.'

I could now do no more than wait. The waiting lasted for a full two years. If he did anything then I have no evidence of it. My impression is that his successor did more in five minutes on my behalf than he did in ten years.

So who put those notes into that Lambeth file? Unlike the services, where officers see their annual reports, we clergy have no idea, or power to challenge, what is being recorded about us. I am perfectly prepared to accept fair criticism and don't believe myself to be above it. What I do strenuously object to is being damned by some unknown who, for all I know, has it in for me and has a golden chance to destroy any possibility of preferment.

Back in the early 1970s I had written some (not even the majority) of the Synod's *Broadcasting, Society, and the Church* report. It was heavily critical of the BBC who did all they could to ignore it and snuff it out. Later some former BBC executives were then appointed to major positions by the church and I took longer to become a member of the Board of Governors than any other Church Commissioner since its foundation in 1948 and my Lambeth personal report was heavily loaded by someone with access to the files. I cannot imagine that there could be any connection. It is too far fetched and sinister even to consider.

Robert Runcie may not have organised any new job for me but he did invite me to become a trustee of the Church Urban Fund and a member of its grants committee. CUF (as it's usually called) was chaired by Sir Richard O'Brien whom I came quickly to respect and like. He had once, as a young man, won two Military Crosses and served on Monty's personal staff. His dynamic leadership and that of his fellow trustees had, with the support of most of diocesan bishops, helped the trust to raise, ultimately, over £20 million which was used to support creative and imaginative projects in some of the most deprived urban areas of Britain. Among the trustees were two very old friends: Jill Dann, Vice-Chairman of the General Synod's House of Laity, and John Stanley, Vicar of Huyton and a college friend and fellow-cricketer from Bristol days. John was later to become Prolocutor of the York Convocation (the senior clergyman) and a Queen's Chaplain. The Stanleys and the Danns had both stayed with us and we with them and our convictions were very similar. Indeed, at that time half the Church Commissioners' elected members and CUF trustees were Evangelicals.

One evening, out of the blue, came a phone call from a distant relation of my one-time secretary, Rosanne Dill. 'Would you', said Mr Dill, 'allow your name to go forward in the election for the new Bishop of Bermuda?' That certainly wasn't an approach which I had ever had any reason to expect. 'Tell me more,' I replied. 'I know nothing about it.'

Bermuda, it seems, has about a dozen parishes, 16 clergy and a cathedral. No islander had ever been Bishop and some of the men who had, had come to fairly sticky conclusions. It had various internal squabbles, some of them racial, some anti-clerical, and a strange mixture of British and American influences. The Bishop is also the Dean of the Cathedral and the Archdeacon, the kingmaker, had been in office for many years. Altogether a hiding-to-nothing sort of place full of cruise ships and wealthy landowners.

I reached a firm conclusion and wrote to the Archdeacon, Thomas Dyson, on 1 April, which seemed an appropriate day. I had not, and would not, 'apply' for the post, nor would I canvass any of the electors, since 'I do not believe that the episcopal office is a "senior rank" to be coveted so much as an honoured trust to which Christ and the church call a man.' I could only promise that were the Synod to elect me . . . and were I to accept it, 'I would give myself heart and soul to the task of being a Father-in-God to the best of my ability.'

Not one of the electors having ever met me or spoken to me, the whole operation seemed a strange farce to me. On 22 April, out of about half-a-dozen candidates I came top of the poll in the House of Laity and bottom in the House of Clergy. The leading candidate ended up with twenty-three votes while I got nineteen. Neither of us having got two-thirds in both Houses the election was void.

They repeated the ridiculous process in late May with much the same result. Deadlock. The matter was then handed to Robert Runcie for a decision. He picked someone else, also from England. I did not exactly end up with egg on my face but I can hardly imagine a more frustratingly pointless way to try to provide a small island with a bishop. I continued patiently to see what God had up his sleeve for me. When it did finally arrive, Bermuda faded rapidly into the long list of might-have-beens, its only claim on my memory being that it was the nearest I ever came to being a bishop.

It was around that time that I was elected to the Athenaeum and also found myself included for the first time in *Who's Who?* The Athenaeum has for years been a cartoonist's dream of stuffydom but as with so many caricatures the reality is not a little different. Only a handful of bishops are members these days, the food is excellent, and the company generally very congenial. Nevertheless, the first time I was conscious that I had really 'arrived' in the club was the day when, after a pleasant lunch, I woke up in one of the leather armchairs after a postprandial doze. Somehow, that seemed to typify the essential cartoonist's Athenaeum and it gave me a good laugh.

I wasn't so amused over the Spong affair. Bishop Spong is the Episcopal Church's carbon copy of David Jenkins, then Bishop of Durham. He was the vocal leader of many a way-out liberal cause and he was in London to promote his latest book *Living in Sin*. TV-AM invited me to take him on in a breakfast-time programme and I gladly accepted the challenge. I read the not-yet-published book and was fully prepared when, late the night before, TV-AM pulled the plug on me. In my place they got a well-known huff-and-puff extremist Anglo-Catholic who made a real fool of himself. Spong emerged victorious. I knew I could have done far better and suspected that TV-AM had set things up to enhance Spong's credibility. Then, to add injury to insult, they declined to pay me the promised fee. Since I had done all the work and had been explicitly assured that I would get it by the highly embarrassed broadcaster who had commissioned me, my only consolation was that they lost the breakfast contract not long after. Spong and I tangled years later when he published a virtual denial of the Creed. I attacked it in St Paul's Cathedral and on the BBC *Sunday* programme. I told the Church to ignore him and urged him to resign his bishopric. I was widely supported.

Much more enjoyable was a sixth-formers' course of lectures which I gave at the London Institute of Contemporary Christianity on Darwin, Marx and Freud. This was quite a challenge but it made me read areas of their work with which I was not familiar and offered me the chance to present a critique of three men whose thinking had done more to shape the mind of the twentieth century than anyone else.

The third edition of my paperback *Cracking the God-Code* was published and produced an unexpected sequel. Glancing at the magazine section in a W.H. Smith branch my eye saw a caption on the front page of *Cosmopolitan*, the women's glossy. There it was. *Cracking the Guy-Code*. Someone, I don't know who, had obviously seen, or read, *God-Code* and decided to do a bit of cannibalising. I can't think why I felt flattered at such shameless pilfering but, in reality, one has to recognise that plagiarism has a long history, with some very eminent exponents of the art. I dare say I've probably done it myself.

The job situation remained static. I was short-listed for Bath Abbey but not appointed. One of the churchwardens told me that if I were to be accepted, with eight years before my retirement, he 'would strenuously counsel me not to make any changes for the first seven years'. That, in a church desperately stuck-in-the-mud and described by its then bishop as 'an outpost for clapped-out businessmen' was simply not worth accepting had I been invited to take it on.

I turned down the excellent team rector's post at Morden in Surrey because, first, I was twenty years older than most of my predecessors had been, and, secondly, because I should have had to drop out of the General Synod, the Church Commissioners, and so on, if I were to leave London Diocese. It gave me a certain adolescent pleasure to say no since I had, thirty years earlier, been turned down for a curacy in that parish! On the grapevine I had heard that I had been considered for various cathedral deaneries and that, had my friend Brandon Jackson not been made Dean of Lincoln, I should have been offered the post. Thank God I wasn't. If ever there was a poisoned chalice the Deanery of Lincoln was it. An impossible situation in which the Dean was on a hiding to nothing however good he was. The only way a Dean of Lincoln can live peacefully is to lie back and think of England. Brandon was far too able a man to have done that (especially when the Prime Minister had sent him to sort out the appalling mess) and I certainly wouldn't have gone there for a rest cure either.

Early in 1990 the Dean and Chapter of Canterbury offered me a 'plurality' in the City of London. They were keen to have me there, so (I was led to believe) was the Bishop of London and his Archdeacon, George Cassidy. All I had to do was to satisfy the two 'parish reps' of the adjacent and connected parishes. I was, however, warned that while one of these was an excellent and godly man, the other was likely to prove difficult. The interview went pleasantly, Mr 'Awkward' trying to trap me and failing to produce any problems. I left, went straight to a phone and rang Michael Till, the Archdeacon of Canterbury. 'Michael,' I said, 'I would never normally do this but since both you and George warned me, let me tell you that our friend didn't find anything, or object to anything.' Till was appreciative and glad to have my assurance. Mr Awkward, nevertheless, without consulting the other 'parish rep', turned me down flat. It was generally assumed that he wanted another candidate (whom the patrons didn't want) and was ready to block until he got his way. Thus it was that one man, representing a minute Church Council of less than a dozen and a congregation not much larger, was able to blackball a candidate who had satisfied the Dean and Chapter of Canterbury, the Bishop and Archdeacon of London, and the other interested parish. Nothing, it seemed, could be done. He got his way in not having me. He didn't get the man he wanted. Eventually the matter ground its way to the Archbishop of York (Canterbury being vacant) who sent it back to the Bishop of London who eventually appointed someone from within the diocese. I happened to know and like the successful candidate but the process added to my own discomfort and frustration.

On 14 March the Queen gave a reception at St James's Palace for the trustees and supporters of the Church Urban Fund. I found myself in the 'top' room, third in the line after a duke and a viscount. I was presented to Her Majesty by Robert Runcie with the extraordinary words 'He's a writer of modern hymns.' The Queen then said, unsmilingly, 'I don't think I've sung any of them,' which reduced me to total, stunned, silence. Very few people have ever done that. She passed on to Jill Dann, leaving me to face Prince Philip, who, it was soon evident, was in a distinctly curt mood. 'What is a pre-*ben*-dary?' he barked at me. Prince or no prince, I'd had enough. 'Well, for a start,' I replied, 'he's a *preb*-endary.' The Prince snarled and moved on to be rude to Jill.

This was the first time I had met either the Sovereign or her Consort and it wasn't an auspicious beginning. Fortunately on all subsequent occasions the Queen has been warm and charming and didn't seem too disquieted when, at a great memorial service, I said how much I liked her royal purple coat and hat. 'Not too garish, you think?' she enquired. Should one congratulate monarchs on their clothes? I thought it was courteous though I don't suppose most people would dare to do such a thing. Ah well, I've always been a risk-taker, not only with her but with the Duke, Prince Charles and Princess Anne. They haven't sent me to the Tower yet though the Duke's manner can vary from occasion to occasion. You never know whether it will be a snort, a snub or a merry laugh. 'Your Canons,' he once said to Eric Evans, then the Dean of St Paul's, 'why, they're the best barber-shop quartet in London.' As the bass, I had once or twice had him well within range when I was in full flow.

After the CUF reception, I sent the Queen a bound set of twenty of my best hymns. Since then, she's certainly sung 'Christ Triumphant' in Westminster Abbey at the opening of the latest General Synod.

But why, I wonder, did Bob Runcie introduce me in so eccentric a way? I'm not, and never had been, 'a writer of modern hymns'. I simply write hymns. Stravinsky once told a journalist that 'I don't write modern music, I only write good music.' Amen to that. Did anyone introduce Mozart as a writer of 'modern music' or Charles Wesley as a writer of 'modern hymns?' I can't imagine it. In the nature of things, all writers write 'modern' words or music. One day I must try to introduce Runcie as 'a modern Baron'. Maybe he'd get the point.

Musicians, of course, can give great pleasure. A few days after the CUF reception I was waiting to pay for some CDs in Tower Records, the huge shop at Piccadilly. Standing next to me was Bernard Haitink, the Dutch conductor. 'Thank you for giving people so much pleasure,' I said to him. He seemed quite taken aback to be so accosted in a shop. Still, I'm glad I did thank him.

Some weeks later I found myself requesting, and being given, an interview with Cardinal Basil Hume, the Roman Catholic Archbishop of Westminster. No, I wasn't considering a transfer to his club, but had found myself uncomfortably embroiled in a matter within his jurisdiction. I was quite appalled at a situation which had been brought to me by a Roman Catholic. He had tried every means at his disposal, had been disgracefully fobbed off, and had finally come to me. I was extremely embarrassed and sought the Cardinal's help to get the matter dealt with. Basil Hume could not have been more gracious, more sympathetic and ultimately, I suspect, more effective. I was to meet him again on a number of quite unconnected occasions and have always found him to be a man of great warmth and integrity. It was a great pleasure to find this, as also I did later with George Stack, Westminster Cathedral's

Administrator who, once, on a very public occasion, knelt down and, with a huge grin, kissed my non-existent episcopal ring! It is quite a rare surprise for someone like me, an orthodox Evangelical, who has distinctly critical views of the Roman Catholic system, to have been made so welcome and, indeed, on two occasions to have pronounced the final blessing at a service in Westminster Cathedral. Not a lot of people know that.

Following a Synod debate in 1989, Canon Martin Reardon was commissioned to write a report on the subject of baptism. I was closely involved in this and together with Gordon Kuhrt (Archdeacon of Lewisham and later Chief Secretary of the Advisory Board for Ministry) wrote two appendices on baptismal theology. Gordon, who lived at the time next door to my father's boyhood home in Mottingham, had been a good friend for years. He carried much of the burden for the newly created Evangelical Anglican Leaders' Conference which had taken shape in our home and at my suggestion.

In the midst of all these occasions my parents celebrated their Diamond Wedding anniversary in early July 1990. They were, as far as I know, the first couple in our family's history ever to reach that landmark and were excited to receive the Queen's telegram on the achievement. Eighteen months later, both died, within two weeks of each other, an appropriate climax to a long life of ordinary, unsung marriage. They began courting in 1922, were married in 1930, and so were as friends, engaged and married, together for sixty-nine years.

I've had plenty of media coverage over the years but even I was flattered to be the subject of a Valerie Grove interview in the *Sunday Times*. An excellent large photograph accompanied the piece in which she partly sent me up but, in journalistic terms, presented a pretty fair picture of her subject. I had told her I was 'fairly cold' but she countered by talking of my 'chubby face, cheerful amiable manner and an evident liking for good food and fine wine'. I was, she supposed, 'a large expansive man' even if rather 'self-congratulatory'. There is, she went on, 'something touching, even innocent, about his breathtaking self-absorption'. That was, it seems, because I had shown her a collection of documents about my childhood and youth, and fished out various statistics which I had kept. She ended with a side-swipe, coupling what she called my holiness and my lack of 'real affection' for Jill, my daughter. That was utterly untrue and a real shock. Jill certainly felt estranged after the rape but that was understandable since I couldn't protect her. It soon passed and our old love and affection was rekindled. Isn't it strange the way journalists feel themselves free to invent supposed bad relationships? Despite this alleged coldness, I was, said the subeditor's caption to the story, a 'blithe spirit'. The article was published on 16 September, just seventeen days before The Letter arrived.

Jackie walked in on Wednesday, 3 October, with the morning post saying, 'Here's one from the Inland Revenue.' I glanced at the buff OHMS envelope. 'Funny,' I said, 'I've never before had a letter from the tax people marked "Personal". I wonder what it is?' I opened it and two white envelopes fell out. One glimpse was enough. 'I don't know *what* it is,' I said quickly, 'but I do know what it *is*'. The first letter was from Margaret Thatcher asking whether I would be agreeable to her putting my name forward to the Queen for the vacant St Paul's Cathedral canonry. The second was from Robin Catford, her appointments secretary, offering any help that I might need.

The canonry had been vacant for many months, as I was well aware. It had even been briefly touched on in a short conversation with Eric Evans, the Dean, who had expressed concern that I hadn't gone to any of the previously vacant deaneries. He was quite surprised to think that I might even be interested in the canonry but the months passed, and I heard no more. Then, out of the blue, here was the Crown's offer. What lay behind it?

Many months earlier I had been sitting on a garden bench, at a conference, with George Carey, then Bishop of Bath and Wells. We discussed my long wait and I expressed my sense of frustration. I was very happy at Ealing but it would be good for everyone for me to move on. He was sympathetic but had nothing, realistically, to suggest. Then, out of the blue, he was, to everyone's amazement, appointed Archbishop of Canterbury. Not long after, before he took up his new role, he was in correspondence with Eric Evans.

According to Eric, George added a brief postscript expressing his hope that I might be given the vacant canonry. Eric passed the message to Downing Street and the rest, as they say, is history.

I'm not a man who likes nepotism, but having been the victim of a good deal of reverse nepotism I wasn't going to turn down such an opportunity and I wrote promptly to the Prime Minister saying that I was 'honoured and not a little humbled' to receive the invitation when I recalled some of those who had been my predecessors. Two archbishops, one Bishop of London, and a whole galaxy of eminent clergy within the twentieth century – to follow such men was indeed a tremendous privilege. I concluded that I hoped I would 'be able to fulfil in some measure your confidence' in me. The announcement was made public on 19 October and drew a whole range of kind and supportive letters including one from Robert Runcie who obviously knew in advance. The one man who clearly didn't know initially was Graham Leonard, Bishop of London, who, for some reason best known to Downing Street, was not immediately informed and who, in consequence, was distinctly slow in sending me his good wishes. What was good was to receive congratulatory letters from Alan Webster, the previous Dean, David Edwards, Provost of Southwark, and John Stott, Rector Emeritus of All Souls, Langham Place, all (from quite different traditions) good friends. Both Ealing Members of Parliament, the Deputy Lieutenant, and the Mayor, all wrote most kindly. It was a very encouraging week.

One amusing consequence was to learn that the St Paul's statutes spelt out the normal procedure by which a canon residentiary would become a *Greater Person*. It wasn't surprising to hear the family's raucous and robust reaction to discover that Dad was to become such an object of derision. There are three such offices in the Cathedral – the Chancellor, the Precentor, and the Treasurer – and I was to be the holder of the last of those three offices. It has nothing to do with the money or the accounts but concerns 'the treasures', which are chiefly made up of the plate and the robes.

The Dean and Chapter are a corporate entity. While the Dean has the primacy of honour, he needs to work in close harness with his four colleagues, the last of whom, the Archdeacon of London, is the only one not appointed by the Crown. While holding a canonry, he is chosen by the Bishop of London and spends much of his time in the administration of the diocese and, especially, within the City of London.

My appointment was greeted by the *Evening Standard*, London's daily newspaper, which described the job as 'in business terms, the equivalent of becoming a director on the board of a major company'. That was certainly not a role envisaged by me when I became a clergyman.

My colleagues were to be the Dean, Eric Evans (a friend for almost forty years), George Cassidy, the Archdeacon of London, Christopher Hill, the Precentor, John Halliburton, the Chancellor, and our lay Registrar, Brigadier Bob Acworth. Together with their wives, Linda, Jane, Hilary, Jenny and Liz, we would become a united team – the first such, so I was later told, for most of the twentieth century. The mixture – three Anglo-Catholic and two Evangelical clerics, plus a typical C. of E. soldier – was almost unique in the Cathedral's history. W.R. Matthews, an earlier Dean, had declared that 'great things can be done in a Cathedral when the Dean and Chapter are united in brotherly union and concord' but it had rarely happened at St Paul's. Indeed, in the mid-nineteenth century, Bishop Blomfield of London, driving up Ludgate Hill, had said to Bishop Wilberforce of Oxford, 'I wonder what that great building has ever done for the cause of Jesus Christ.'

Aware of this awesome episcopal judgement, I took the opportunity, on the very day of my arrival, to quote as my inspiration words of the historian S.C. Carpenter about one of my predecessors, Canon H.P. Liddon. 'That voice', said Carpenter, 'rang on, like a trumpet, telling of righteousness and temperance and judgement, preaching ever and always with personal passion of belief, of Jesus Christ, and him crucified.' I might not share Liddon's Tractarian sympathies but I certainly wanted to honour and emulate his preaching goals and skills. He had one great advantage. In his day sermons were an hour long. In mine they would be not more than a quarter of that. That would be a frustration to me, believing as I do, with Donald Coggan, that 'sermonettes make Christianettes' but I should have to learn to be more concise.

One of my first surprises was to learn that there was no canon's house immediately available. Number 6 Amen Court was riddled with dry rot and was going to need about £200,000 spent on it to put it in order. Houses like those in Amen Court cannot be repaired 'on the cheap' even if the Cathedral were keen to keep prices down. No second-rate materials would be permitted by the conservation authorities. I instantly realised the danger. Just let a tabloid newspaper learn that a trustee of the Church Urban Fund was going to live in a house on which £200,000 was to be spent, and they would produce a horrific caricature blaming me, the church and the Church Urban Fund. The Fund's work would be irreparably damaged through no fault of ours. I made a sudden decision, four days after the announcement. I would resign my trusteeship. I wrote to the Vice-Chairman and to the Archbishop, giving two reasons. On the one hand, I suggested that I wasn't able to 'provide the level of ability that the fund needed'. Secondly, my new appointment offered a reasonable pretext with its 'new set of responsibilities'.

Both Sir Richard O'Brien (the Vice-Chairman) and the Archbishop strenuously rejected my first reason but could hardly counter the second and the resignation was accepted. I was hugely relieved. CUF would not be damaged and I had no need to reveal my real reason until now, years later, when the issue no longer of any importance. It was agreed that for our first four months we should live in a small flat above the Chapter House, right next to the Cathedral, while the bulk of our furniture would go into storage. Not ideal but we could live with it. It would be the fourth time that we had had to make a double move so we knew just how inconvenient it would be.

Life in the Cathedral would offer a totally new challenge. Very little of my previous wide-ranging experience would be directly relevant. Congregations would be largely made up of 'one-off' visitors, frequently more than a thousand strong, offering a tremendous scope for preaching, which I should greatly value. Indeed *The Times* would offer a photo of me preaching and cite me as 'an inspiring preacher', praised for my 'clear forceful voice, excellent eye-to-eye contact, and obvious sincerity'. On rare occasions I would find myself preaching to over two thousand five hundred people, the largest Anglican congregation in England, and on another to the Queen Mother.

Another unusual experience would be the chance of meeting a galaxy of internationally famous people. On VE Day I would be shaking hands with the whole Royal Family and over fifty Heads of State from all over the world, including King Hussein and dozens of presidents. There would be scores of ambassadors, high commissioners, and, from England, Lord Chancellors, Lord Mayors, Prime Ministers, and leading politicians. I would talk to John Major about cricket, Paddy Ashdown about life in St Paul's and, from the world of the arts, would meet Andrew Lloyd Webber, Judi Dench, Anthony Hopkins, Edward Fox, Susan Howatch, Thomas Allen, Robert Tear, David Willcocks, and many many more. I would provide seats for Martin Gilbert and Nigel Hamilton in my own 'box' at the VE service. St Paul's was certainly a great place for name-dropping, indeed, one could hardly avoid it.

There would be fun times as well. I especially recall two sparkling episodes during a Lloyd Webber concert spectacular. Our vestry was to be used by three young actresses but I needed to change out of my robes after a preliminary service. 'You can't come in,' they chorused. When eventually I was permitted to enter I said, with a smile, 'What do you think I could have seen that I haven't seen before?' One very pretty girl responded instantly, 'Well, you haven't seen ours!' Moments later, grinning, I asked the make-up girl, 'Do you think I need some make-up?' 'No,' she answered, 'but I could touch you up a bit.' Howls of laughter all round. 'Oops,' she said, going a delicate shade of pink. What would John Donne, our famous Dean, and erotic poet, have said?

During our final week at Ealing vicarage, Jackie discovered a cardboard cylinder in the loft. It had been given to us by Gladys Hensman, who had long since gone to an old people's home in Weston-super-Mare, and is now dead. We had never opened it, aware only that it was some kind of picture which Gladys had wanted us to have. 'Shall we throw Gladys's picture away?' enquired Jackie. 'I think we ought at least to see what it is,' I answered. So she opened it up to discover a print of Frank Salisbury's famous panoramic picture of King George V's Silver Jubilee service in St Paul's Cathedral in 1935. 'How extraordinary,' I said. She had no idea that I would one day be appointed to serve there, nor could she have guessed that I should find myself wearing one of the very copes worn on that occasion by the Dean and Chapter. Salisbury had painted in scores of faces including those of the Queen Mother and our present Queen when the former was Duchess of York and the latter a child of nine. Winston Churchill, then in the political dog-house, was hidden away in the background. Needless to say, we had the magnificent print framed and it quickly occupied a place of honour in our entrance hall in Amen Court.

All too soon the day came for us to say farewell to Ealing. On the Saturday night, 9 February 1991, a bleak Siberian evening, there was a large congregational party in the church lounge. It was a riotous affair, full of fun, nostalgia, and the bitter-sweet experience of parting. Jonathan Place, John and Jean's son, did a marvellous impression of me with all the correct clothes, glasses, mannerisms, and hairstyle. It wasn't far short of Mike Yarwood for accuracy. Then, next morning there was a moving farewell service of Holy Communion, presentations and final goodbyes.

The moment I shall never forget was probably the most irreverent and improper of all. James Roskelly, my final curate, told the assembled host that in time past canons of St Paul's had owned yachts in the Mediterranean and had run a couple of mistresses whereas now all they could afford was a rowing boat on the Serpentine. 'Don't I even get one mistress?' I enquired disconsolately. 'No way,' said James with a glint in his eye, 'all you get is a couple of oars.' The party gasped, then burst into roars of bawdy laughter. Ealing was a great church, deeply spiritual, but with just the right capacity to know when to pull the vicar's leg. It was a magical moment.

I was installed at St Paul's Cathedral on 10 March 1991, where this story ends. It was to mean, among other things: buying a clerical frock coat (for over £700); regularly attending banquets and royal Garden Parties; becoming a Freeman of the City of London; a liveryman of the Gardeners' Company; and even, on three or four occasions, squiring the Queen Mother during Cathedral events.

So why end the story in 1991? It's quite simple, really. St Luke took his hero, St Paul, to Rome and left him there right in the heart of the world's greatest city of ancient times. I thought that, somehow, there was a parallel there for me. He, a Roman citizen, was to end his work in Rome. I, a Freeman of London, was to preach the gospel in his Cathedral in the world's greatest city of modern times.

I cannot resist ending by recalling one last glorious *faux pas* which took place just three weeks before my installation as a canon. The letter came from 10 Downing Street and it was addressed to me. Signed by the Prime Minister's secretary for appointments, it announced, in just five lines, some quite remarkable news: 'I am writing to let you know that the Queen has been pleased to approve that the Right Reverend David Hope, Bishop of Wakefield, be nominated to succeed you as Bishop of London.' Maybe I was never going to be a bishop but at least I have it on Downing Street notepaper that I was once Bishop of London. You will not be surprised to learn that I have the original framed and hanging on my study wall.

> O THOU who camest from above,
>   The pure celestial fire to impart,
> Kindle a flame of sacred love
>   On the mean altar of my heart.
>
> 2 There let it for thy glory burn
>   With inextinguishable blaze,
> And trembling to its source return
>   In humble prayer, and fervent praise.
>
> 3 Jesus, confirm my heart's desire
>   To work, and speak, and think for thee;
> Still let me guard the holy fire,
>   And still stir up thy gift in me.
>
> 4 Ready for all thy perfect will,
>   My acts of faith and love repeat,
> Till death thy endless mercies seal,
>   And make my sacrifice complete.
>
>   Charles Wesley